D1575432

MANHOOD
AT
HARVARD

MANHOOD AT HARVARD

William James and Others

KIM TOWNSEND

W · W · NORTON & COMPANY

NEW YORK · LONDON

FRONTISPIECE PHOTO: Harvard Yard, December 1869. *Harvard University Archives*
CONTENTS PAGE PHOTO: Harvard Square, 1890. *D. W. Butterfield*

FIRST EDITION

The text of this book is composed in Galliard with the display set in Caslon Shaded and Galliard. Composition and manufacturing by the Maple Vail Book Manufacturing Group. Book design by Marjorie J. Flock.

Library of Congress Cataloging-in-Publication Data

Townsend, Kim.
    Manhood at Harvard: William James and others / by Kim Townsend.
        p.   cm.
    Includes bibliographical references (p.) and index.
    ISBN 0-393-03939-0
    1. James, William, 1842–1910—Contributions to concept of
manliness.   2. James, William, 1842–1910—Friends and associates.
3. Masculinity (Psychology)—United States—History.   4. Sex role—
United States—History.   5. United States—Civilization—19th
century.   6. Harvard University—Students.   7. United States—
Civilization—20th century.   I. Title.
B945.J24T68   1996
305.3'0973—dc20   95-50101

W. W. Norton & Company, Inc., 500 Fifth Avenue, New York, N.Y. 10110
http://web.wwnorton.com

W. W. Norton & Company Ltd., 10 Coptic Street, London WC1A 1PU

1 2 3 4 5 6 7 8 9 0

To George Kateb

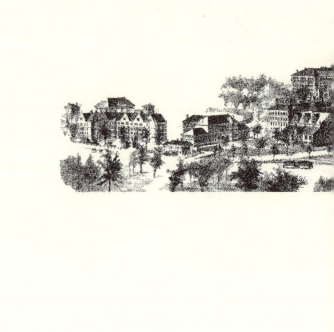

Contents

Illustrations follow pages 64 *and* 160

Whatever patriotism of American manhood comes to the fore, Harvard memory, Harvard ideals, instinctively rise, because Harvard is not merely Massachusetts, Harvard is not merely New England, Harvard is the ideal of America.

Governor Curtis Guild
at the Harvard commencement, June 24, 1908

Preface

Manhood at Harvard: William James and Others is about an ideal that came into being in the decades following the Civil War and about a select group of men who were influential in its creation or—as in a few significant cases—who called it into question. Some of them are well known— Henry Adams, W. E. B. Du Bois, Charles William Eliot, Oliver Wendell Holmes Jr., Theodore Roosevelt, George Santayana—while others, other Harvard students and faculty members of this era, may not be. All of them were either colleagues (however fleetingly) or students (however inattentively) of William James, the man whom I have singled out for special attention.

During this period the country at large obviously did not think of Harvard every time a manly ideal was invoked and honored, but during it Harvard talked and wrote incessantly about what was called "patriotic American manhood," and given the influence of Harvard and of such Harvard men as I have named, Harvard was undeniably instrumental in making the ideal a commonplace. It is still a commonplace; manhood remains a subject of vital interest and importance to many people. From whatever perspective we now address issues of sex and gender, class and race, and whatever our vision of the future, we still have to contend with the typical man who prevails in these pages— even if we try to imagine his absence.

In my efforts to describe this man and account for his existence, I have tried to resist the unearned and unwarranted pleasures of feeling superior to those who have gone before. I have tried especially hard to do justice to those men who defined manhood in terms that were not limited by received ideas. All of these men—however unenlightened some of them may now seem from our perspective—were exceptional in that they thought of manhood not merely as an advantage in the struggle for survival but rather as an opportunity and a responsibility to foster and spread what they thought of as civilized life.

In the pages that follow, I allude to an essay by George Herbert Palmer titled "Trades and Professions." Palmer wrote it in 1914, after having been a member of the Harvard Philosophy Department for forty-one years. To Palmer, academic life represented an ideal "type toward which all organized society moves" because it allowed for "personal expression" while at the same time encouraging a teacher to study "the needs of his neighbor as inseparable from his own." He referred to the teaching profession as "a consecrated brotherhood."

No one talks like that anymore. But after all the obvious and appropriate qualifications have been made, most present-day teachers and scholars can happily acknowledge the essential validity of Palmer's claim.

Among the colleagues and friends who have provided me with information, suggestions, and encouragement are Elizabeth Aries, David Blight, Bob Gooding-Williams, Jay Grossman, Allen Guttmann, Donald Hall, Robert May, Susan Mizruchi, Walter Nicholson, Barry O'Connell, Dale Peterson, Gerry Platt, Cathy Portuges, Bill Pritchard, Christian Rogowski, Andrea Rushing, Mary Jo Salter, Marni Sandweiss, Catharine Stimpson, and Jocelyn Wise.

Walker, Roger, Haig, and Mary, and my wife, Marty, have always been supportive. Julie Howland provided invaluable assistance from the start; Tamara Hartl did the same towards the end. My agent, Denise Shannon, answered many calls other than those of duty. At Norton, Cecil Lyon and Otto Sonntag were especially helpful. I was most fortunate in having as my editor Donald Lamm—a wise and learned man.

The staffs of the Robert Frost Library at Amherst College, and of the Houghton Library and the University Archives at Harvard, were unfailingly helpful. I also received timely assistance from the Arthur and Elizabeth Schlesinger Library at Radcliffe and the W. E. B. Du Bois Library at the University of Massachusetts at Amherst. I have used unpublished material from the papers of William James by permission of the Houghton Library and the James family. My research was supported in part by grants from the Amherst College Faculty Research Award Program.

I am especially grateful to Sacvan Bercovitch, Jack Cameron, Brad Leithauser, and Bill McFeely for their exacting and generous responses to my ideas—and to Brad for his careful reading of my manuscript as well. I owe a special debt to Hugh Hawkins, not only for his helpful reading of *Manhood at Harvard* but also for his *Between Harvard and America: The Educational Leadership of Charles W. Eliot,* which helped me navigate through many foggy patches. George Kateb's readings—of my manuscript, but also of Emerson, James, and others—were a chief source of inspiration. My dedication also gestures way beyond, to our friendship.

MANHOOD
AT
HARVARD

Introduction

EDNESDAY, JUNE 24, 1908, was an unusually hot and humid day, but nothing dampened the spirits of those who had gathered for Harvard's Two Hundred and Sixty-sixth Commencement.[1] Certainly not the weather. One minor adjustment seemed advisable. The conferring of degrees in Massachusetts Hall began at 10:30 instead of 10:00, thus shortening the time between it and the forming of the procession that would march through the Yard and across Cambridge Street to Memorial Hall for the afternoon ceremonies. During those ceremonies, the weather was only a source of amusement: noting "the savage heat," one honorary degree recipient, the governor of Kentucky, Augustus E. Willson (class of 1869), recommended his own state as a "summer resort"; Edward Kent (class of 1883), the chief justice of the Supreme Court of Arizona—a territory that would become the forty-eighth state four years later—was introduced as not caring whether it was hot or not. If Kent did care, being the last speaker, he cared just as much about the lateness of the hour. Comparing himself to the dying sinner who had asked his doctor to pray with him, he said he would be "brief and fervent."

Justice Kent's urgent message was that it was harder for the Harvard man in the West than for the one in the East to represent Harvard's ideals, and that it was incumbent upon Harvard to support the Western man in his efforts. "The farther away we get from Harvard, the more is expected of the Harvard man in spreading the faith," he said. The Harvard men of Arizona needed help; their alma mater had to send out men bearing libations "from the fountainhead of our inspiration." He beseeched the president—Charles William Eliot—to come himself. Dean Briggs' visit the year before had done wonders, but now "Mahomet must come to the mountain." It would hasten the day "when Harvard will be the Harvard of our whole country, our national university." Kent was more than half serious about faith and inspiration and Mahomet. The Harvard he had in mind had the potential of saving the country's soul.

According to the governor of Massachusetts, Curtis Guild (class of 1881), the day when Harvard would enlighten the entire nation had already arrived. Being the second speaker (after President Eliot), Governor Guild was not brief at all, but his concluding words were every bit as fervent as Justice Kent's: "Whatever patriotism of American manhood comes to the fore, Harvard memory, Harvard ideals, instinctively rise, because Harvard is not merely Massachusetts, Harvard is not merely New England, Harvard is the ideal of America." Harvard men were always imbued with America's ideals, he claimed; after they graduated, they were continually embodying those ideals in their service to their country. Wherever one turned—Guild turned to Kansas and Florida, and even beyond, to the Philippines, for his examples—one came upon the inspiriting words of Harvard men. "How far does the influence of Harvard extend?" he asked. "How far does it not extend? Imagine any crisis or any determining event in any young man's life that you will," he replied, and "see how naturally the Harvard idea comes to the fore." He called that idea the "patriotism of American manhood."

Previous generations of Americans had been more concerned with generic man's relationship to his God. Although they made clear gender distinctions in their attempts to understand and strengthen that relationship, and also the family relationships that they created with God's blessings, they did not linger over the question of what constituted their earthly existences *as men*. Or if they did—as had been the case for so long as anyone could remember— they took manhood to be simply a quality possessed by courageous and honorable individuals. In the nineteenth century, according to the *Century Dictionary* (an American equivalent to the *Oxford English Dictionary*), the word "manly" denoted "the highest conception of what is noble in man and worthy of his manhood." According to one of Harvard's most eminent graduates, Ralph Waldo Emerson, even a woman could, at least by implication, possess such manhood. A modern reader of "Self-Reliance" might assume that when Emerson said, "Society everywhere is in conspiracy against the manhood of every one of its members," he was speaking only of men, but we are obsessed by gender. Emerson was not. His vision was broad and embracing. "We want men and women who shall renovate life and our social state," he said in the same essay. There was no more powerful educational presence in the young Emerson's life than in that of his aunt, Mary Moody Emerson; his wife Lidian's advocacy of women's rights (and of abolition) predated and influenced his own; his friendship with Margaret Fuller was one of intellectual equals. He knew, finally, that "superior women are rare anywhere, as are superior men . . . and every country, in its roll of honor, has as many women as men."[2]

But the Civil War brought about a marked narrowing of the common definition of manhood. The exemplary man who had once been closest to God, or who had been most valiant in his pursuit of intellectual or moral betterment, was supplanted by a figure who had distinguished himself on the battlefield—still an honorable man, but now a stronger, a tougher, a less thoughtful man. After the Civil War, men were more concerned about character traits, attitudes, and appearances than about deeds. They felt pressure to be masculine. The word itself took on new meaning, and the word "masculinity" made its way into the language. By the end of the century, "masculine"—once used simply to differentiate traits distinguishing men from women ("masculine clothing" or "masculine occupations," for example)—had become useful to men looking for ways to describe and explain the authority they sought to establish. By 1890 the noun "masculinity" was in the *Century Dictionary*.[3] During this period, men approached all the issues that men face—physical, educational, domestic, and social issues—with a new sense of having to present themselves as manly, and a clear sense of how womanly they would be considered if they did not measure up.

James Russell Lowell reflected the change at ceremonies commemorating the end of the war. "Yea, Manhood hath a wider span / And larger privilege of life than man," he wrote in his "Ode Recited at the Harvard Commemoration, July 21, 1865." What separated the manly from mere men was their willingness to fight and, if necessary, to die for the "Truth." Lowell acknowledged that Harvard men might take other routes to "Truth":

> Life may be given in many ways,
> And loyalty to Truth be sealed
> As bravely in the closet as the field,
> So bountiful is Fate,

but the closeted or the scholarly life was clearly inferior. "Many loved Truth, and lavished life's best oil / Amid the dust of books to find her," Lowell said. A few lines later, though, the phrase "ashes of the burnt-out mind" makes clear how unproductive, and finally unheroic, Lowell considered the man who spent or used up "life's best oil" in his study. And it followed—in lines that look forward to talk of racial superiority at the end of the century—that warriors made infinitely better breeders:

> That is best blood that hath most iron in't
> To edge resolve with, pouring without stint
> For what makes manhood dear.

Of the Harvard men being honored on that July day in 1865 Lowell said, "These hold great futures in their lusty reins / And certify to earth a new imperial race."

When Governor Guild spoke about the "patriotism of American manhood" forty-three years later, he evoked memories of the Civil War and of the Union forged in 1865. He also indicated just how far America's influence had extended in the intervening years. In his consideration of its citizenry as "a new imperial race," he had much more to draw on than James Russell Lowell did. By 1908, America was—to the satisfaction of most of its citizens—fulfilling the "manifest destiny" that had been first defined for it when Texas was annexed in 1845. Having expanded beyond its continental boundaries to possess Hawaii, the Philippines, Puerto Rico, Guam, and the Panama Canal Zone in the years just before and after the turn of the century, the country seemed well on its way to becoming the redeemer and civilizer of the world.

Guild gave evidence of Harvard men spreading the word throughout America's growing domain. He cited a sergeant reading *A Man without a Country,* by Edward Everett Hale (class of 1839)—"And for your country, boy, and for that flag, never dream a dream but of serving her as she bids you, though the service carry you, through a thousand hells"—to boost the morale of the "ragged soldiers" under his command in the Philippines; he told of the time during the Spanish-American War when he heard a Northern band play "Dixie," a Southern band play "Yankee Doodle," and then both bands spontaneously strike up with "My Country 'Tis of Thee," the words of which had been written by "S. F. Smith of Harvard." But of course everyone in Guild's audience had in mind a much more impressive example of Harvard's preeminence as a producer of men who could reshape the world in America's image. They were thinking of the man who had just completed his second term as president of the United States—"just now voluntarily retired from that great office which in his hands had become the greatest seat of power in the world," as the next speaker put it. Though he was not present on this occasion, at the very mention of his name—"Roosevelt of the Class of 1880"—"a hearty greeting" went up in the form of a "Harvard cheer."

But as Guild made clear, proof of the "patriotism of American manhood" was not limited to scenes of civil strife or international conquest. In his speech he called for "a little more earnest everyday patriotism among the educated classes." An educated man could prove his devotion to his country by demanding respect for the law, by working for civil service reform, and by curbing his own desire for mere wealth. He could prove his patriotic manhood by doing battle with dishonor, corruption, and greed. America being a democracy, he said not *noblesse* but *sagesse oblige.*

In these contexts, Harvard's example was also pervasive and compelling. Harvard was not a martial institution. It was, however, an increasingly powerful institution, possessed of tremendous wealth and privilege, and in its day-to-day operation it demonstrated how wealth and privilege could be used efficiently. Harvard was coming into its own as a great educational institution at the same time that America was beginning to emerge as the richest and most powerful nation on earth. It was becoming—arguably—"our national university," not just because it tapped that wealth, but because it devised ways to control and direct it. And it set itself the task of teaching its students how to develop their considerable financial, physical, and intellectual resources as well, to put them to responsible use. It created an educational and social environment in which—ideally, at least—young men learned to become professional and business leaders, an environment in which—again ideally—they learned to be responsive to the forces and energies of the age while at the same time contriving ways to improve or reform them. In doing so, they would join the men who served their country in uniform as exemplars of patriotic American manhood.

Their new theater of operations changed radically in the decades following the Civil War. Between 1870 and 1900, the country's population almost doubled (from just over 38 million to almost 76 million); in another ten years it was 92 million. Immigrants accounted for almost a third of the increase, even as between a fourth and a third of them eventually returned to their native lands. Accounting for about a third of the industrial work force as well, immigrants joined the hundreds of thousands who left their farms and rural homesteads; together they converted the country into an urban industrial empire.

The story of this decidedly material (rather than religious) conversion is a familiar one. The country's seemingly unlimited natural resources—coal and oil, copper and iron, gold and silver, lumber and animal life—were discovered and exploited so fast that by the end of the century there was no longer any wilderness to tame. Or so the story went—most famously—in the lecture called "The Significance of the Frontier in American History," which Frederick Jackson Turner delivered at the Columbian Exposition in 1893. So the story went from the perspective of those who were "destined" to seize this unprecedented historical moment. From the perspective of those whose lands were seized—the *native* Americans—the story reads differently. After the Civil War, settlers moving west overcame Indian resistance and, in 1887, received government approval in the form of the Dawes Act, which endorsed the breakup of communally owned reservation land and established rights of way for telegraph and railroad companies. Indian resistance effectively ended at Wounded Knee in 1890; by 1900, Indian holdings were about half of what they had been in 1887.[4]

In a matter of a few decades, the country had the ability to communicate with itself—by telegraph (Western Union having established itself as America's first monopoly by 1866), by rail (the first transcontinental track was completed in 1869), by telephone (Bell's invention in 1876), by automobile (Selden's in 1877, Ford's in 1892), and thanks to the typewriter (1868), the mimeograph (1876), and the Linotype machine (1885). Countless other inventions and innovations—the Bessemer steel plant (1864), the oil pipe line (the first going from Pithole, Pennsylvania, to a railroad connection five miles away in 1866), the refrigerated railroad car (1868), the silo (1870), barbed wire (1876), a store lighted by electric lamps (Wanamaker's in 1878) and streets by arc lights (Cleveland in 1879), the hydroelectric plant (1879), and the steel-framed skyscraper (1884), to name a few—made it possible for men to transform the country's natural resources into goods and services, and then to transport and to sell them.[5]

Out of the competition and struggle for riches, "trusts"—companies and business alliances controlling the oil, steel, lumber, meat-packing, railroad, and other industries—came into being. It was the Gilded Age. Politicians' pockets received new linings, especially during the administration of Ulysses S. Grant (1869–77). Legendary fortunes were made, and the men who made them—Diamond Jim Brady, Jim Fisk, Mark Hopkins, Collis Huntington, Cornelius Vanderbilt—built monuments to themselves and lived lives that might have shamed even the "barons" to whom they are routinely compared. The first, largest, and most exemplary trust was that of John D. Rockefeller, whose Standard Oil Company of Ohio, incorporated in 1870, controlled about 90 percent of the industry within a decade. "The growth of a large business," he said, "is merely a survival of the fittest, the working out of a law of nature and a law of God."[6] It was his homely expression of Social Darwinism, the philosophy—developed by Herbert Spencer in England, and disseminated most effectively in America by John Fiske (an occasional lecturer at Harvard between 1869 and 1871) and William Graham Sumner (a permanent and highly influential fixture on the Yale faculty beginning in 1872)—that argued that social evolution was a slow and cruel but ultimately beneficent process, and that any tinkering with it, any effort to improve social conditions, could only make the process more painful. No matter that by 1890 some 1 percent of families owned 51 percent of the country's wealth, and that the lower 44 percent owned just over 1 percent of it, with an estimated 23 to 30 percent of the work force being unemployed part of every year during this era. No matter that 5,000 businesses failed in 1873, 10,000 in 1878, and 15,000 in 1893, or that between 1881 and 1905 almost 37,000 strikes were recorded, some of them (at the Coeur d'Alene mines, in Idaho, at Homestead, Pennsylvania, at Pullman, Illinois) involving pitched battles and loss of life. Nor could much be said about race riots and lynchings against Chinese in Los Angeles (in 1871) or Seattle (in 1886), against Negroes in Vicksburg (1874, 75 killed) and Italians in New Orleans (1891, 11 killed). Evolution was taking its course;

there were some peoples who were apparently not destined to survive.[7]

Rockefeller also defended his business practices by explaining that some-one had to "bring some order out of what was rapidly becoming a state of chaos," and in fact—whatever the incalculable costs—American economic and social life became more orderly by the end of the century. Symptomatically, in 1882, Frederick W. Taylor, a gang boss for the Midvale Steel Corporation, introduced a system of "scientific management" that would be applied to industrial operations nationwide; the next year standard time was established, with the railroads dividing the country into four time zones; the captains of industry were replaced by financiers (J. P. Morgan leading the attack) who merged and controlled their trusts; and the number of professional associa-tions and societies ballooned around the turn of the century.

At the commencement of 1908, there was ample evidence that Harvard had grown and prospered in the decades since the Civil War—that it had progressed right along with the nation. It had benefited from the country's successes in obvious ways. Although the number of graduating seniors (only 445, as against 530 the year before) might have been cause for concern, the only reference to enrollments was to their increase over the years, and more than enough gifts received were mentioned to allay any fears for Harvard's future. More to the point, there were specific indications that Harvard had been consciously addressing the question of how men could become successful in whatever business or professional field they entered, and that it had itself evolved into a model of administrative efficiency. Of the several "parts" deliv-ered after the prayer that opened the ceremonies in Memorial Hall—"Com-mencement Day," "Literature and Life," "Harvard Hymnody"—one was titled "The Responsibilities of the Business Man of the Future." President Eliot talked almost exclusively about how Harvard was being managed, about the practical relevance of a Harvard man's education, and about what manly qualities a Harvard man would have to possess if he expected to succeed.

In the address that he gave when he took office in the fall of 1869, President Eliot had said specifically, "The principle of divided and subordinate responsibilities, which rules in government bureaus, in manufactories, and all great companies, which makes a modern army a possibility, must be applied in the University."[8] In 1908, almost forty years later, at what would be his last commencement as president of Harvard, he said that "the best issue" of the preceding year was that "we have accomplished something considerable . . . toward the better organization of Harvard University." First, what had been three undergraduate departments—Harvard College, the Lawrence Scientific School, and the Bussey Institution (devoted to agriculture and horticulture)—had been rolled into one. Harvard College now granted the bachelor's degree in arts and sciences. Secondly, the Bussey Institution had itself become a graduate school, and another, an entirely new one—"a novel experiment in our country"—had come into existence: the Graduate School of Business Administration. (The signals were clear: the nation was no longer a predominantly rural republic; students of business administration and agriculture were passing in the night, the former to become more and more prominent, the latter fated to be absorbed—in the early 1930s—by the Biological Institute at Harvard.) And finally, with one exception (the Dental School), the undergraduate department had become "the gate to all the professional schools of the University." The Department of Dentistry was not yet a graduate school. When that happened, Eliot said, "then will Harvard have accomplished first and alone in our country the true organization of a University—a single undergraduate department and all the professional schools on top of that department, all of them requiring a degree in arts, letters, or science for admission." The requirements of the University as Eliot had defined them in 1869 were all but met.

In his remarks, Eliot devoted an equal amount of time to making the point that there was a direct correlation between "success in college scholarship and success in after-life." He told of a study by Professor of Government Abbott Lawrence Lowell (who the following June would stand—as the next president of Harvard—right where Eliot stood), a study showing that one out of five of the first four scholars in the last twenty-seven classes appeared in *Who's Who*, whereas only one out of 13.3 of the "average" graduates had achieved that honor. Eliot said that he himself could not "arrive at statistical demonstrations." He agreed with Lowell wholeheartedly, but his support was not that of a social scientist. He spoke, instead, as the man who had presided over the moral and physical education of young Harvard men since just after the Civil War.

In language that had become commonplace thanks to "Roosevelt of the Class of 1880," Eliot appealed to the Harvard man's manhood: "It is in college that men begin to prepare for the strenuous competitions of the world, and win the mental power, the nervous power to succeed in them." He acknowledged that many families considered social or athletic distinction truer indications of future success. Indeed, during the preceding decades, many undergraduates—most, some argued—paid much more attention to Harvard's clubs and Harvard's athletic teams than to Harvard's professors. But "social distinction or athletic distinction" were not "the main object of college life." Eliot maintained, "The real road to success is through scholarship, and the acquisition of the power to work hard, and to endure fatigue and have a steady nerve under intellectual and moral stress."

Clearly a young man's coming of age as a man in post–Civil War America would not be easy. The toll on his nerves would be especially heavy. George

Beard explained why in 1881, in his book *American Nervousness: Its Causes and Consequences*. The cause was "modern civilization," which, he said, was characterized by "steam-power, the periodical press, the telegraph, the sciences, and the mental activity of women." From these ills that modern man was heir to, secondary and tertiary causes fanned out, including climate—inexplicably, Beard instanced New England's dry air—institutions of every sort, and personal habits, including "indulgence of appetites and passions."[9] President Eliot's words describing what the ambitious student faced echo Beard's diagnosis: the strenuousness, the drive to succeed, might result in no more than fatigue; the otherwise steady nervous system might collapse under the stress. But nevertheless, the Harvard undergraduate would strive to represent patriotic American manhood—manhood that was distinctly American, the manhood of men who typified America.

Lowell's contemporaries and students would speak another language, but the older men—most of the men—at the 1908 commencement referred often and variously to an ideal manhood that had been developed and represented—even taught—at Harvard since Eliot had become president in 1869. The new ideal of manliness had been realized during the Civil War. Lowell testified to that fact in his commemoration ode. When T. W. Higginson—famous for having commanded a Negro regiment during the war—gathered and published ninety-five memorials to Harvard men who had lost their lives in the conflict, he suggested in his preface that patriotic manhood was to be expected of men who had been "highly educated": "If there is one inference to be fairly drawn from these memoirs, as a whole, it is this: that there is no class of men in this republic from whom the response of patriotism comes more promptly and surely than from its most highly educated class."[10] Harvard education had to have been working in order to produce such martyrs.

In the decades after the war, Harvard would continue to foster manliness. It could not provide a war, but it could provide the next-best thing—combat on playing rather than battle fields. And provide it did, as it developed first a physical education program and then an intercollegiate athletic program that rivaled and (after great effort) often surpassed that of Yale. The men who possessed the qualities of a good athlete—competitiveness, perseverance, strength, endurance—would be rewarded by ending up at the top of their classes. And they would go on to succeed in life—life, at any rate, as most of the speakers imagined it, the active life of business and the professions.

At one point in the commencement proceedings, Governor Willson of Kentucky listed the raw materials out of which Harvard would fashion this man. He described the American man, who, he claimed, was the same the country over, in his own state as well as in Massachusetts, in Texas or South Carolina:

He is the real thing, all wool and a yard wide. He is in earnest; he has courage; he is sometimes a little hardheaded, and it takes a little more than moral suasion to veer him around in the course if he gets set wrong; but he is a man all the time, wherever he is, and a real man who intends to do things.

He was itemizing the same "stuff" that Frederick Jackson Turner had said characterized the frontier man—"coarseness and strength combined with acuteness and acquisitiveness; that practical, inventive turn of mind, quick to find expedients; that masterful grasp of material things . . . that dominant individualism."[11] The Harvard man who was being honored on this hot and humid June afternoon hour was "a real man," an earnest and courageous, acute and practical, individual, but he was neither coarse nor hardheaded, and moral suasion had been enough to enable him to stay the course. In a word, he had had the benefit of a Harvard education.

In his preface to his *Memorial Biographies,* Higginson had defined the "most highly educated class" as an aristocracy "with only an admixture, such as aristocracies now show, of what are called self-made men." The self-made man of which he spoke had become an inspiring household word with the publication of Horatio Alger's (Harvard, class of 1852) *Raggedy Dick* in 1867. As he evolved into the fittest man in the industrial jungle, it was apparent that he needed to be educated in honor, fair play, and social responsibility. Or rather, for the aristocracy to remain in place, it would have to make sure that America's self-made man—or wooly, or frontier, man—shared its values.

Very little was said about his origins. Governor Guild alluded to a recent speech in which President Eliot had advised "citizens of a certain race and creed" to join the Massachusetts Volunteer Militia. In his evasiveness he seemed to suggest—it seemed to go *almost* without saying all afternoon—that the man about whom everybody was speaking was an "Anglo-Saxon." In fact, Harvard did not turn its back on the thousands of recent immigrants; men of surprisingly diverse backgrounds had recently attended Harvard. A man commenting on the *Harvard Quinquennial Catalogue* in the fall of 1908 said, "During the past 25 or 30 years the numbers of foreign names have increased, and the nationalities represented would reach at least a score." He listed "Scandinavians, Poles, Russians, Italians, Hungarians, Armenians, Greeks, Icelanders, Bulgarians, Chinese, and Japanese."[12] But wherever the student came from, whoever he was, he would feel the pressure to fit himself into the mold of the Harvard gentleman, a figure who was more than likely to be relatively wealthy and to have a name that one would not think of as "foreign." Whatever his beginnings or social situation, he obviously had the potential of embodying manhood as Harvard conceived of it.

The same could not be said of a woman. Radcliffe had celebrated its twenty-fifth commencement the day before, but on this occasion her only appearance was in her traditional supporting role as described by Governor Willson: "the character of the American man" was "fortified and ennobled by the influence of the American woman," he said. By 1908, in the country at large, the number of women entering colleges, and then the professions rather than into the holy state of matrimony, and the amount of political and social activity involving women in the sixty years since Lucretia Mott and Elizabeth Cady Stanton convened the first woman's rights convention in Seneca Falls, New York, made it increasingly difficult to assume that her place was in the home. But though Harvard kept up with—or instructed—the culture on every other front, it purposely and determinedly did not do so when faced with questions about women's worth and their appointed destinies. Put simply, Harvard could not do that while insisting on the value of manhood as much as it did.

Before the war it had been possible to imagine women possessing manly qualities and to admire them for it. After the war, the thought of strong women—autonomous, independent-minded, educated women, for example—forced a man to try to become that much more manly. Or to reverse the logic, if a man felt he was about as manly as he could be—or his efforts about as intense as his constitution could bear—he could relax them so long as he could be sure that women remained relatively womanly. As we will see in the pages that follow, that was the logic that dictated Harvard's response to the evolution of Radcliffe College from its beginnings in 1879.

Governor Willson's hopes for Harvard, Governor Guild's assumptions about the institution, President Eliot's boasts, their way of speaking (or not speaking) about the "admixture" of students, and their exclusion of women— the commencement exercises as a whole—are all typical of a period of about forty years in which Harvard developed its ideal of manhood. The ideal both reflected ideas about manhood that prevailed after the Civil War and—as these men preferred to claim—expressed those ideas in their original and most inspiring form. It is still at work in the culture.

———

Manhood at Harvard: William James and Others is about that ideal and about the men who created or questioned it. My subtitle recalls the title of an auto-biographical work by James' brother Henry: *A Small Boy and Others.* Like Henry James, William was one among many others—not a family as in Henry's volume, but a group of extraordinarily distinguished colleagues and, in time, students. In retrospect he may be somewhat diminished by that very fact, but he is still the one who is—like his brother Henry—the most interesting figure in his group. And inasmuch as Harvard strove to become the most influential educational institution in the country during the years that James taught there, all the while that higher education itself was becoming the means by which young men made their way in society, there is ample justification for imagining William James at the center of a much larger circle.

In *The Confident Years, 1885–1915,* Van Wyck Brooks (Harvard, class of 1907), a foremost student of American culture, called James "a type of the epoch," along with Theodore Roosevelt, on the basis of their common commitment to a "philosophy of 'toil and risk.'"[13] It is a characterization that is all the more interesting for my purposes because Roosevelt was a student of James' and a man with whom James debated educational, national, and international issues. They talked the same language, so to speak. James was an extraordinary man in his own right; he was also—for all the important differences—very much a man among men like Roosevelt. He was a man who put his stamp on his community and on his society; he was also a part of that society.

John Jay Chapman, a student and friend of James'—and, in his day, another prominent social critic—called it "a secret society." "Every generation is a secret society," he said, "and has incommunicable enthusiasms, tastes and interests which are a mystery both to its predecessors and to posterity."[14] There is nothing unusual about a generation's being something of a closed society, or about a man's withholding secrets, but Chapman's figure is especially apt for this group of privileged men, who bonded in clubs and societies in elite educational institutions during this particular era. It also echoes one of James' own modest—and startling—accounts of himself, one in which he appears *less* rather than more distinguishable in the shrouded atmosphere in which the men of his generation lived. He was, he said, like a dark planet, "believed to be greater than all the shining ones, because of the many correspondences with the illustrious, all treating him with deference," but in fact saying nothing all the while—"having the wit to suppress his answers." He shone, he confessed, because he so successfully reflected others' light.[15] Positioning him there at the cultural center, among his colleagues and his students, we may also see the world as it was illuminated by them. "There is a Zeitgeist," Chapman went on to say, "about all hero-worship." To a degree, the spirit of an age determines who will turn out to be its heroes. James' greatness lay not only in the way he brought out the spirit of his age but also in the way his own dark spirit reflected it.

In a lecture called "Great Men and Their Environment," delivered before the Harvard Natural History Society in 1880, James expressed his own views on the relationship between distinguished individuals and the era in which they lived.[16] He framed his discussion in the context of a debate with Herbert Spencer and his disciples, the Social Darwinists who so misread their Darwin as to argue that change was due primarily to environmental influences, to mere circumstance, to physical geography, to ancestry, to anything but what James considered vital—namely, "the accumulated influences of individuals." James acknowledged that the environment acted upon a great man just the way it did on what Darwin called "the accidental variations" with which an animal was born, but his primary interest was in "the vital importance of individual initiative." By the same token, whereas many of his opponents thought only of groups, or tribes, or races, and the differences among them, James said he was interested in "the small difference between the genius and his tribe." In a short follow-up essay—titled unambiguously "The Importance of Individuals"—he summed up his argument with a proposition that he claimed he learned from an uneducated carpenter: "There is very little difference between one man and another," the carpenter had said, "but what little there is, *is very important.*"[17]

Even as he spoke, James himself was beginning to play a key role in altering the structure and tone of Harvard University. In the opening minutes of his lecture, he had asked what it was that made "communities change from generation to generation," and he had used the fact that "the Harvard College of today [was] so different from that of thirty years ago" as one of his examples. Though the question as to what made the difference was left open, the obvious answer in 1880 was Harvard's president, Charles William Eliot. But it would not be long before William James would be a correct answer too. From a Spencerian perspective, he was only one member of the faculty that Eliot had brought to Harvard in the last quarter of the nineteenth century. But from the perspective that James encourages us to take in "Great Men and Their Environment," he was distinctive, the "greatest" among that group of men.

James stood out from his colleagues, and from students of the stature of Du Bois and Santayana, on the basis of his monumental *The Principles of Psychology* (1890), *The Will to Believe* (1897), *The Varieties of Religious Experience* (1902), or *Pragmatism* (1907), but equally important was something in his tone, something about his presence. It was discernible in the man himself, and it was what was remarkable about his thinking. "Let me repeat once more," James said in "The Types of Philosophic Thinking" (1908),

that a man's vision is the great fact about him. Who cares for Carlyle's reasons, or Schopenhauer's, or Spencer's? A philosophy is the expression of a man's intimate character, and all definitions of the universe are but the deliberately adopted reactions of human characters upon it.[18]

What made James great was the "vision" that was both his response to life and the philosophical reflection of his "intimate character."

The year before he died, James took the time to read a draft of a Ph.D. thesis in which, he noted, "utterances of mine written at different dates, for different audiences belonging to different universes of discourse," were strung together to form a "philosophy," and then pronounced incoherent. He reacted "with admiration and abhorrence." The thesis deserved a degree summa cum laude, he thought—certainly he would have seen to it that Harvard gave it highest honors—but by the same token, it represented everything he disliked about what he had memorably called "The Ph.D. Octopus." Had the author been a man, he would have left it at that. "Being a woman," however, he said chivalrously, "there may be yet a gleam of hope!" He urged "Miss S——" to devote her talents "to the study of reality in its concreteness," to be constructive and substitute an alternative to his "humanism," to supersede him. But first she had to appreciate his "vision." "The whole Ph.D. industry of building up an author's meaning out of separate texts leads nowhere," he wrote, "unless you have first grasped his centre of vision, by an act of imagination."[19]

This book attempts to approach what I think lies at the center of his vision, and at the center of his contemporaries' vision as well. As I try to show in my first chapter, James' own personal perspective was very much a man's perspective, a masculine or manly one. In two subsequent chapters, I bring out how much it befit the times—how Harvard responded to the pressures of the era and, in turn, how perfectly James represented Harvard's response. In a fourth, I consider how the "highly educated" men of this era responded to women, to African-Americans, to anyone who did not mirror their conceptions of themselves as men. In a fifth, I focus on the simplest and most enduring construction of manhood that emerged during this period: the Westerner, as he was imagined by Owen Wister, Harvard '82, and as he was represented by Theodore Roosevelt, Harvard '80.

"The truth is," Van Wyck Brooks reported in his last year at Harvard, "we deliberately acquire our ungraceful ways in an effort to be manly," and he exclaimed, "How morbid we are on the subject of manliness!"[20] His was a nice choice of words. Most of the men in this book limited, even damaged, their lives trying to be "manly." In the process they were often literally ungraceful. Imagining their bodies as so many forces to be controlled, they reined them in, fought and subdued them. And they often thought of themselves as graceless in the sense of being without Grace, their lives as lonely struggles unto death. One could add that they were also lacking in graciousness, because these manly men tended to be wary of and to exclude anyone who undermined their assumptions about what it was to be a man.

Many years later, Brooks refused to make an exception of James. "He was unable to create values because he had never transcended his environment," Brooks said in 1932.[21] But when he was an undergraduate he would have thought it sacrilegious to speak about James like that. He was "a great man"— "Our greatest teacher," he called him upon his retirement, "one of the great serene figures of Time, above all little disagreements, large, sane, clear, simple, universal."[22] The discrepancy, reflective of the difference between James the dark planet and James the illuminating star, only reconfirms the fact of his central and fascinating presence.

It also throws us back upon ourselves. "The preferences of sentient creatures are what *create* the importance of topics," James wrote at the end of his article "The Importance of Individuals."[23] What are we to make of him? What are we to make of the manhood that he and his colleagues and students represent? What are our preferences?

The subject of manhood was indisputably important to James and his contemporaries. What James made of himself (and they of him) was always influenced by their understanding of what was required of them as men. That much is clear. But it is hard to gauge the effect of their case on others, especially in the past. In the pages that follow, we will hear many claims like Brooks', and like those of the men who spoke at the Harvard commencement of 1908, about the representativeness of individual Harvard men's views and of Harvard's influence, but these are, after all, the claims of Harvard men.

Nevertheless, by the end of the nineteenth century, Harvard was preeminent among educational institutions. Speaking of President Eliot, Yale's historian was prepared to say that "by 1900 it was generally conceded that he had made Harvard into America's strongest and most celebrated university."[24] When one considers Eliot's, and Harvard's, determination to know and to teach the ways of a newly industrialized and secularized world, and to allow the young men in their charge to find out for themselves—in their free election of courses—what was most important to them individually, then Harvard turns out to be preeminent by these more specific criteria too. To extend the obvious comparison with Yale: Yale's first lay president took office in 1899, Harvard's in 1829; Harvard abolished required chapel in 1886, Yale in 1926; Harvard dropped Greek as an entrance requirement in 1884, Yale in 1903; Yale never did allow so free an elective system as Harvard; Harvard was far wealthier, its funds having grown to thirteen million by 1900, Yale's to only five.

For many people such preeminence would be synonymous with more rapid decline (not to mention the fact that to untold millions such distinctions matter not at all). Or, to make the comparison with Yale once again, it could signal deplorable compromises with the world as it is—at one extreme, inattention to students' religious faith; at the other, only halfhearted efforts to generate school or team spirit. More generally, it could mean the loss of a prized sense of community and of tradition. Be that as it may, Harvard's rise to prominence both helped cause and accompanied the emergence of a particular kind of manly individual a century ago, and insofar as we are at present concerned about who and what is a man—and thus, ineluctably, who and what is a woman—we have much to learn from the men in this book. They were an extraordinarily distinguished group of writers and thinkers; they were also the first to raise these questions in their modern form.

1

William James

"Is Life Worth Living?"

IN APRIL 1895, as a sophomore at Radcliffe College, Gertrude Stein went to hear Professor William James give a lecture to the Young Men's Christian Association at Harvard on the question "Is Life Worth Living?" There was no greater authority on the subject in Cambridge—in fact no greater authority, period. After over twenty years as a professor of physiology and comparative anatomy, of psychology, and then of philosophy, James was a revered teacher at Harvard and at Radcliffe. Everybody also knew him as the author of the monumental, two-volume *The Principles of Psychology,* which had been ten years in the making and finally published in 1890; many had been assigned the abridged version (not James but "Jimmie," they called it) in their courses. James' name was well known abroad too. He had studied and attended conferences there; he had published in British and French journals. Just two years before—as if to signal the breadth of his knowledge and the reach of his authority—he had become both the president of the American Association of Psychologists and the honorary president of the English Society for Psychical Research.

Obviously stirred by his presence at the meeting of the Young Men's Christian Association, Stein made the occasion the subject of her next daily theme for English 22, the composition course that she was taking at the time. "Is life worth living?" she began by asking, to which she replied, "Yes, a thousand times yes when the world still holds such spirits as Prof. James." In the paragraphs that followed, she made it abundantly clear that in his lecture William James had proven—or what was more, *was* proof—that life was indeed worth living.[1]

Stein noted that James embodied all that was "strongest and worthiest in the scientific spirit," and all that was meant by philosophy as well, for though he was a skilled logician, he was "too great to worship logic as his God, and narrow himself to a belief merely in the reason of man." But to her he represented even more than the best in the scientific and philosophical thinking of his day. She took Shakespeare's description of "the noblest Roman of them all" for her paper's epigraph—"His life is gentle and the elements / So mix'd in him, that Nature might stand up / And say to all the world, 'this is a man' "—and then from *Hamlet* another famously serviceable line—"He is a man take him for all in all"—for her last words, to suggest that he was for her the new Representative Man. The way Stein put it (in the kind of sentence that would earn her lasting fame but a C in English 22), James was a man "who has lived sympathetically not alone all thought but all life."

In 1895, the question "Is Life Worth Living?" was an especially appropriate one to be asking. The 1890 census had shown an alarming increase in the number of suicides in America. Although Emile Durkheim's famous study of suicide would not be available in translation for a few years, others had already made his point that it was one of the costs of social progress. Powerful societal forces were at work. The strongest men would adapt and survive. Those who failed miserably might take their own lives, but they were not to be held responsible.[2] The characteristics of "modern civilization" that George Beard had cited as putting unprecedented pressure on Americans—technological and scientific advances, the media, "the mental activity of women"—were just too much for some. Over the years, James examined many of the supposed causes of "modern nervousness," and in the pages that follow we will attend to them closely. On the occasion of this particular lecture, however, he looked at only one: on the reflective life that he and his audience led. At the outset, we need appreciate only how his very presence at Harvard showed that such a life could be made worthwhile.

The number of people in James' circle of relatives and friends who suffered from what was generally labeled neurasthenia—literally a weakening of the nerves, otherwise everything from gastric problems to impotence to listlessness to pathological depression—is legion. Men's hold on their lives seemed tenuous, the line between sanity and insanity far from clear, especially among the highly educated. James took his psychology seminars to insane asylums and told his students that very little separated the inmates they saw from their own President Eliot.[3] The year after his lecture "Is Life Worth Living?" he wrote offhandedly, "I take it that no man is educated who has never dallied with the thought of suicide."[4] By 1901, the *Harvard Graduates' Magazine* reported that though the undergraduates were healthy, there had never been a time when so many faculty members were sick. In fact, James' name headed the list he gave. "The pace set—less by teaching than by the general rush and movement of academic life—is a little too fast," the report said. Perhaps "some service needs to be organized for the health of the teaching body."[5]

Many of James' colleagues and associates contemplated suicide. Indeed, *not* having considered taking one's own life might be a sign that one was not qualified for academic life. "I wonder if anybody ever reached thirty-five in New England without wanting to kill himself," wrote Barrett Wendell, James' colleague in the English Department, reflecting on a friend's suicide. "Really, it rather surprises me to see how few do so."[6] In 1891, James told another colleague about a doctor's prescription for longevity—"To be entirely broken-down in health before one is thirty-five" (which applied, James said, "more to nervous than to other diseases")—and then concluded, "*I* was entirely broken-down before I was thirty."[7] When Josiah Royce, his closest friend in the Philosophy Department, was recovering from *his* nervous breakdown and wrote James that he feared a recurrence, James would have none of it: "if you ever *do* relapse," he wittily replied, "it will be the sorriest shame and suicide that ever disgraced humanity. You mustn't, you can't, with your gifts. If you do I'll strangle you with my own hands."[8]

The Jameses themselves were especially attuned to the threat and the potential of suicidal thoughts. Having broken down for the second time, in 1878 William's sister, Alice, conferred with their father about the possible sinfulness of her wanting to put an end to her misery. Reporting on the occasion to his son Bob—who was himself perilously close to the edge—Henry James Sr. said that he had told Alice that when a person's suffering was the result of "diabolic influx into the human mind from the spiritual world" (*her* case, in his estimation) or of "some loathsome form of disease," there was no problem, and he cleverly gave her his "full permission to end her life whenever she pleased"—adding, "only I hoped that if ever she felt like doing that sort of justice to her circumstances, she would do it in a perfectly gentle way in order not to distress her friends." And he proudly concluded, "Now [that] she could perceive it to be her *right* to dispose of her own body when life had become intolerable, she could never do it."[9] Eleven years later, having heard that William's fellow psychic researcher Edmund Gurney had committed suicide, in an exceptionally wry diary entry Alice included both her father's warnings about taking others' feelings into account and what would be her brother's notion about the particular authority of the educated in these matters:

They say that there is little doubt that Mr. Edmund Gurney committed suicide. What a pity to hide it, every educated person who kills himself does something towards lessening the superstition. It's bad that it is so untidy, there is no denying that, for one bespatters one's friends morally as well as physically, taking them so much more into one's secret than they want to be taken. But how heroic to be able to suppress one's vanity to the extent of confessing that the game is too hard.[10]

That Bob could not bring himself to withdraw from the game of life only went to show William how *un*heroic his brother was. Driven to despair by alcohol,

Bob raged at the brother who put him to shame, William told Alice, while asking to be committed to an institution. But Bob wasn't "technically insane," William wrote to his brother Henry. At one point, William wished Bob would simply drink himself to death, for he was incapable of doing what he *ought* to do: "The only manly and moral thing for a man in his plight is to kill himself; but Bob will ne'er do that."[11]

In his lecture "Is Life Worth Living?" James expressed the family's belief that there was nothing inherently sinful about suicide and drew on the family's experience when he said that this belief alone acted as a deterrent.[12] It was a comfort to know "you *may* step out of life whenever you please"; in the meantime, "you can always stand it for twenty-four hours longer, if only to see what to-morrow's newspaper will contain, or what the next postman will bring." In our own time, someone questioning the worth of it all might be more likely to take his cue from Beckett. "I can't go on this way," says Estragon. "That's what you think," says Vladimir. But James was addressing the Young Men's Christian Association, so he was bound to provide more than an argument that Vladimir could have borrowed from him (waiting for the paper, waiting for the mail), and bound *not* to say anything about those who in taking their own lives had done "the manly and moral thing." His purpose was to make the case for life. "To come immediately to the heart of my theme," he wrote, "what I propose is to imagine ourselves reasoning with a fellow-mortal who is on such terms with life that the only comfort left him is to brood on the assurance 'you may end it when you will.' " And then perhaps thinking of Alice, he added, "What reasons can we plead that may render such a brother (or sister) willing to take up the burden again?"

He began by focusing his audience's attention on itself. He asked them to "search the lonely depths for an hour" with him, to attend to "the profounder bass-note of life," and thereby to acknowledge their affinity with "the whole army of suicides . . . for we are of one substance with these suicides, and their life is the life we share." Appropriately enough, what he offered as a remedy against doubt and despair was faith, "nothing more recondite than religious faith," but the faith he recommended was no monistic or natural faith, no belief in any religion limited or corrupted by any theology or any "stall-fed officials of an established faith." No Christian religion. The belief he spoke of was a man's own belief, and a belief in himself; it would be one of his own defining and with his own meanings (just as, for example, "stall-fed" would take on new meaning, punning as it does on the place where both communicants and animals congregate). He would have faith in the fact that life was worth living, and accordingly, he would live on. "Believe that life *is* worth living," he said, "and your belief will help create the fact."

The only proof he offered was the undeniable effects of his faith. It worked. In the Gifford Lectures he gave seven years later and published as *The Varieties of Religious Experience,* he recounted how a "thirst for God," a craving that came from the heart, provided Tolstoy with an answer to his version of the question "Is Life Worth Living?" and thus put an end to his contemplations of "manly suicide." James made it sound simple: "Believe in the infinite as common people do, and life grows possible again." But Tolstoy had in fact turned his back on what James called "the life of the upper, intellectual, artistic classes, the life which he had personally always led, the cerebral life, the life of conventionality, artificiality, and personal ambition," and Professor James was not about to do *that*. Tolstoy had gone against "the movements of [his] ideas and observations"; James would characteristically lead his audience along with his, converting all the obstacles he encountered into challenges.[13]

Thus from James' perspective, the hardships and sufferings that might have weakened the resolve of the potential suicide only gave that man "a keener zest" for life. They gave him something to live for. The potential suicide could be expected "to wait and see *his* part of the battle out," he said in his lecture, to do so not in supine, cowering resignation but, "on the contrary, a resignation based on manliness and pride." Citing the Jews in Babylonian captivity, Germany "when she lay trampled beneath the hooves of Bonaparte's troops," the Waldenses whom Pope Innocent VIII wanted exterminated, James said history was "one long commentary on the cheerfulness that comes with fighting ills." To make the risk and the struggle seem the more worthwhile, James could not point directly to Christ's example (post-Darwinian criticism of the Bible had seen to that), so he reached back to his days as a medical student and came up with another martyred figure:

Consider a poor dog whom they are vivisecting in a laboratory. He lies strapped on a board and shrieking at his executioners, and to his own dark consciousness is literally in a sort of hell. He cannot see a single redeeming ray in the whole business; and yet all these diabolical-seeming events are often controlled by human intentions with which, if his poor benighted mind could only be made to catch a glimpse of them, all that is heroic in him would religiously acquiesce. Healing truth, relief to future sufferings of beast and man, are to be bought by them. It may be genuinely a process of redemption.

Humanity is present here neither as a scientist nor as the beneficiary of scientific experiments, but rather as a bestial soul happily in agony. Were he not suffering, not suffering at least to the extent of being in doubt as to his purpose in life, a man would be less than human.

It followed that were a man not in doubt, he would not be in a position to create his own certainties. Not just in doubt, but in doubt "from one hour to another": "It is only by risking our persons from one hour to another that we live at all." And not in just any situation, but a perilous situation, one in which a man really had to save his own life. In one of his favorite examples, a man climbing a mountain finds himself in a position from which his only escape is a "terrible leap." If he thinks he can make it, he is prepared to succeed; if he hesitates, if he mistrusts himself, he will launch himself "in a moment of despair" and inevitably plunge "in the abyss." Ever mindful of the darkness below or within, even imagining *himself* to be the dark planet, James not only had to believe he could take the leaps necessary to stay alive, but he made a leap of faith to what he called in the Gifford Lectures his "over-belief"—a belief in the existence of an unseen world, a source of higher energies, a higher order that supports and lends significance to all our efforts.

Tolstoy did not to have to go to such lengths, but James' faith required it. So too, as it turned out, did James' God. In closing, he made the point that if we believe in God's unseen world and believe that there is meaning in our struggles, then He is the more likely to exist, and our efforts are the more likely to be purposeful. The very last words of the Gifford Lectures were: "Who knows whether the faithfulness of individuals here below to their own poor over-beliefs may not actually help God in turn to be more effectively faithful to his own greater tasks?"[14] At the Harvard meeting, he restated the argument for the efficacy of faith, bringing it home to his undergraduate audience with a comparison to their own athletic / theatrical experiences:

God himself, in short, may draw vital strength and increase of very being from our fidelity. For my own part, I do not know what the sweat and blood and tragedy of this life mean, if they mean anything short of this. If this life be not a real fight, in which something is eternally gained for the universe by success, it is no better than a game of private theatricals from which one may withdraw at will. But it *feels* like a real fight.

And he left them with Henry IV's words to one who had missed out on a victorious military campaign: "Hang yourself, brave Crillon! We fought at Arques, and you were not there."

Like the "noblest Roman," William James was a man of many "elements," as Sarah Whitman understood. An artist (she did James' portrait), as well as a woman who figured prominently in the social life of Cambridge and in the founding of Radcliffe, she gave thanks to James for inspiring her generation to persevere in an age when God, if not dead, was in need of help. She commended his talk to friends as one "wherein he constructs courage anew for those who must stand upon the little foothold of the naked human Will, and 'yearn upward' according to the conditions of that Will's higher necessities. An eager and noble cry from such a brave and tender heart."[15] But what Stein and other students thrilled to at the Harvard YMCA meeting was something more focused and singular, something more like manliness than ideal humanity. "He stands firmly, nobly for the dignity of man," Stein said of him,

His faith is not that of a cringing coward before an all-powerful master, but of a strong man willing to fight, to suffer and endure. He has not accepted faith because it is easy and pleasing. He has thought and lived many years and at last says with a voice of authority, if life does not mean this, I don't know what it means.

What can one say more? He is a strong sane noble personality reacting truly on all experience that life has given him.

In the presence of William James, hearing Marcus Aurelius or Wordsworth's "Happy Warrior" speak through him, she felt no room for play in her response. "Sincere tone" was all her instructor, William Vaughan Moody, wrote on her paper.

Nor, when the lecture appeared as a booklet the following year, did the reviewer for the *Harvard Advocate* have any interest in James' complex being. He simply credited James with possessing the pugnacious spirit that he said made life worth living, and then expressed the hope that his spirit would represent Harvard in the eyes of the world. He wrote that "Is Life Worth Living?" "arouses a man's fighting spirit, and his contempt for the half-hearted questioner. A few more such words from the University would give the world a new idea of our Harvard Spirit."[16] It was the manliness of the lecturer, and the manliness alone, that he held up as exemplary of the Harvard Man.

Although they did not go to such lengths, many of James' contemporaries also pointed to this aspect of his character. The future musician and composer Daniel Gregory Mason found Josiah Royce, James' colleague in the Philosophy Department, "deeper and more poetic," but he had to admit that when James "moved restlessly about the platform chatting with us rather than lecturing us, his frank manliness and friendliness were irresistible."[17] What his student (and later professor of philosophy at Columbia) D. S. Miller thought most distinctive about James was his "fellow-manliness," and he added that "the sporting men in college always felt a certain affinity to themselves on one side in the freshness and manhood that distinguished him in mind, appearance, and diction."[18] Set apart at Harvard by his Spanish background, his Catholicism, and his sexual preference—disliked but swallowed, as he put it in his memoirs—another member of the department, George Santayana, was even less likely to fall under James' spell, but he was clear about its power. He appreciated James' being "characteristically masculine and empirical" in his opposition to the "scandalous vagueness" of Herbert Spencer's ideas about the relation between man and his environment; he admired James' "masculine directness, his impressionistic perceptions, and his picturesque words"; he knew, finally, that "the normal practical masculine American . . . had a friend in William James."[19]

James was a man; he was manly, but not in any simple way. You knew it when you saw him striding—not walking—shoulders back, between the College and his home on Irving Street, or bicycling in the evening. You could tell by what he wore, especially the Norfolk jacket—a very fashionable combination of elegance and sportiness—that was his signature and that at least one student, Maxwell Perkins, wore in emulation of him.[20] His brow was large—noble, it was said—and he had a full beard, but he was not physically imposing. He was of only medium height (a little over five feet eight), his frame was slight, and if anything he became leaner with the passing of years. His voice was low, but not deep, and he often hesitated as he spoke. His look in pictures is invariably intense, but his eyes were said to change color with his moods—now tawny, now what Sarah Whitman called "irascible blue." He had what one observer called "an informal sort of dignity."[21]

James was an arresting and impressive figure of a man. In the environs of the Harvard of his day, this meant he was also and always a gentleman. Barrett Wendell told him, "Alone among my instructors, you respected the laws of tailoring."[22] It was the impression he sought to give. It was one of those practices he talked about in his widely circulated essay on the general subject of "habit" (1887), a *personal* one in this case, the kind that a student would be wise to cultivate before he was twenty. The way he talked was one such practice. "A youth transferred to the society of his betters," James declared, would have trouble unlearning "the nasality and other vices of speech bred in him by the associations of his growing years." (Twenty-five years later, he thought Americans' *"vocalization"* had become "ignobly awful . . . simply *incredibly* loathsome.")[23] His dress was even more of a problem: "Hardly ever, indeed, no matter how much money there be in his pocket, can he even learn to *dress* like a gentleman-born."[24]

Perhaps playacting a bit for the ladies, James once complained to Sarah Whitman about a student gathering he had to attend—"not a *gentleman* among them I fear, so rare are these birds in Cambridge"[25]—and in the same spirit told his wife about two reformers he met in his travels. Their courage, their disinterestedness, their idealism were all very well but, he said, "I verily believe that the condition of being a man of the world, a gentleman, etc., carries something with it, an atmosphere, an outlook, a play, that all these things together fail to carry, and that is worth them all." He called them "wildcat reformers," whose "spiritual gossip," by his own admission, made him splenetic. Still, his dismissal makes it clear that the cultivation of manhood at Harvard was, among other things, prominently a matter of class.[26] In "The Energies of Men" (1907), he said, "The idea of one's 'honour,' for example, unlocks energy only in those who have had the education of a gentleman, so called."[27]

Manhood involved class. It was also, then, a matter of what one did with one's life—an exceptionally trying matter in James' case.[28] He took an unusually long time settling on a career—first art, then science (at the Lawrence Scientific School at Harvard, among other places), then medicine (at

Harvard's Medical School), then philosophy, and finally—in 1873, at the age of thirty-one—teaching anatomy and physiology at Harvard. When he did settle upon a career, he added the determination that he said a man must display in his life as a whole. "When the moment of solution comes it is often Carlyle that provides the solvent," Ralph Barton Perry said;[29] with indecision and doubt about his career behind him, James embraced the Victorian sage. "What was the most important thing he said to us?" James asked in "The Dilemma of Determinism" (1884). "He said: 'Hang your sensibilities! Stop your snivelling complaints, and your equally snivelling raptures! Leave off your general emotional tomfoolery, and get to WORK like men!' "[30] Once James got to work, he inspired the kind of tribute that comes to seem all but routine in descriptions of the man. Here is James Jackson Putnam, his friend and fellow pioneer in the field of medical psychology: "William James was a manly and a radiant being. Loving and loved, he made all men think, and helped many a doubting soul to feel a man's glow of hope and courage, each for his own work. This was a noble task."[31]

Though James was the oldest, by this conventional standard all three of his brothers beat him to manhood by about ten years. He wanted to serve in the Civil War, but his father interfered, saying that no government was worth the endangerment of his son's life. Meanwhile his two youngest brothers, Wilky and Bob, proved themselves valiantly during the Civil War by fighting—and in Wilky's case, being wounded—while serving in Negro regiments. They then tried to realize their ideals by setting up a farm and hiring freedmen in Florida, but racism and incompetence defeated them, after which failure followed failure. Bob sunk so low as to have to take a job as a railroad clerk in Iowa, but he was at least working. Not mentioning whatever shame he felt over not having fought in the war, William wrote to say that he felt "rather ashamed at my age to stand in the presence of you and Wilky without having earned a cent."[32] Henry settled into the life of a professional writer without a struggle. The steady flow of his publications began in 1864, when he was twenty-one.

A man needed fulfilling work, but to James this did not mean work to get ahead, or to achieve material gain or success. He had no interest in being just another competitor for the spoils of the Gilded Age. A gentleman did not stoop so low. Indeed, it was James who coined the phrase with which one could efficiently distance oneself from the money grubbing that seemed the most common and recognizable characteristic of the era. No longer anything about Mammon; the false idol was now a woman—"the bitch-goddess Success," he called it. It went without saying: no respectable man worshiped her.[33]

Nevertheless, money remained a troublesome issue. A man aspired to complete ennobling tasks, but he was also expected to support a family, and be the man of the family. It was a duty a woman did not have to undertake, he wrote to his cousin Katherine Prince: "Your sex, which has, or should have, its bread brought to it, instead of having to go in search of it, has no idea of the awful responsibility of such a choice."[34] Ostensibly James had little cause to worry. The Jameses were monied. Having emigrated from Ireland at the age of seventeen, his grandfather, the first William James, amassed a fortune in business and real estate holdings that made him the second-richest man in the country, after John Jacob Astor. The father, Henry James Sr., never had to work. The family (the whole entourage) traveled frequently and extensively; the children were well tutored. But James came to his career late—and even as he became successful, he never felt secure. His salary, its supplements in the form of lecturing fees and royalties, and his properties were considerable. Money may have ceased to be a real issue, but to paraphrase him on life as a fight, it always *felt* like a real issue. When William did finally begin teaching at Harvard, and then when he considered assuming his proper role as a husband and provider, he did so with his father's assurances of financial support. Though he came around, he initially protested when his childless siblings proposed giving up a portion of their inheritance in order to give Wilky the equal share their father's will denied him (because of advances made on the farming investment). Jokingly he told Putnam that when he met someone he first asked him his age and then his income, to which Putnam added that "this was almost literally true."[35]

True or not, what James' contemporaries admired in him was his principled response to the age's priorities and the valiant manner in which he prevailed against ignorance and doubt. Life *was* worth living, and it had to be lived responsibly. In answering another momentous question, in "What Makes a Life Significant" (1898), he paid no attention to the likes of Andrew Carnegie and Henry Clay Frick, who together dominated America's steel industry; instead, he pointed out, "Poverty has been reckoned the crowning beauty of many a heroic career." No life devoted to the pursuit of wealth was "significant." Nor was a life driven by a desire for position or power. Accordingly, he was inclined to honor the country's vast laboring class for its courage and endurance, until he found the "usual laborer's life" wanting "ideal inner springs."[36]

By 1895, in the eyes of others, James had come to stand for balance and strength, for significant life, for manhood achieved. Seven years later, from atop the swirling activity of the marketplace, the athletic and the battle fields, James skimmed off his own image of ideal manhood—in a lecture that was appropriately titled "The Value of Saintliness." He was speaking of poverty once again:

We have lost the power even of imagining what the ancient idealization of poverty could have meant: the liberation from material attachments, the unbribed soul, the manlier indifference, the paying our way by what we are or do and not by what we have, the right to fling away our life at any moment irresponsibly,—the more athletic trim, in short, the moral fighting shape.[37]

The figure he evoked clearly reflected the values of the culture—more specifically, the elitist culture of the institution that James typified—but it was also and at the same time an image of William James himself. The arena and the stance within it are familiar. The man is physically fit, not subject to neurasthenic spells. In spirit he is what everyone at the time recognized as quintessential Harvard: he is "indifferent." He is not unduly competitive; he does not really care if his team wins or not. In fact, he himself can quit at any time. It comes as something of a surprise to hear that a man could do so "irresponsibly," especially when the gesture—the irresponsible, suicidal gesture—is performed by a man at the peak of his form, after so much training. But it all goes to show how precarious is the life of the secular saint: the life worth living, by James' account and example, is a breathtaking performance, given on the edge of the abyss.

We know that this performance, this life, attracted an appreciative audience. We know too how much James *was* an appreciative audience—so appreciative, indeed, as to frustrate his colleagues and his friends. His departmental colleague George Herbert Palmer, who was not inclined to speak ill of anybody, thought that James was too lenient with students, and thought, more generally, "His judgment of men was not good; it was corrupted by kindness."[38] John Jay Chapman said he had "too high an opinion of everything. The last book he had read was always 'a great book'; the last person he had talked with, a wonderful being."[39] Santayana was harsher. He said that philosophy for James had a Polish constitution: one vote against any proposition would prevent its going through. According to James the radical empiricist, or "radical agnostic," as Santayana called him, if his "worthy aunt" believed, as she tended her garden, that the earth was flat, she had as much authority as the navigator who circled the earth and believed it was round; "the quarrel becomes unmeaning when we remember that the earth is *both* flat and round, if it is experienced as being both." As for James' religion, it was religion watered down to almost nothing: "He did not really believe," Santayana said; "he merely believed in the right of believing that you might be right if you believed."[40]

His sister, Alice, adored him. He could "lend life and charm to a treadmill," she said. But by the same token, she compared him to "a blob of mercury"—"you can't put a mental finger upon him." She and Henry laughed about the resemblance to their father and agreed that, in William's case, the difficulty stemmed from his "entire inability or indifference 'to stick to a thing for the sake of sticking.' " She said he was like his house at Chocorua, in the White Mountains of New Hampshire, with its fourteen doors, except for the fact that his brain wasn't limited to that number—"perhaps unfortunately," she added.[41]

The doors were literally open in his social life as well. John Reed recalled how the very first time he met James, in his freshman year, at a bookstore, James informed him, "I'm all alone tonight," and invited him home to dinner. On the way to Irving Street, the two talked of "what makes Harvard." Reed's was an eager freshman's Harvard of "great football games . . . big men in your class . . . 'parties in town' "—a far cry from the institution James had defined a few years before in his senior dinner talk called "The True Harvard" (1903), in which he had praised "our undisciplinables" and "independent and lonely thinkers."[42] But James humored Reed, produced cigars, compared notes with him about comic operas, and advised him on how to become popular. It was not until midnight, as he was leaving (Reed claimed), that they told each other who they were.[43] There were other nights when James seemed to have had his fill of students and visitors, when he would complain of never having time alone with his wife, Alice. "I will see that whoever calls to-night is told that you are strictly engaged," she would say, but when the doorbell rang and she would go to see that her instructions were obeyed, he would be right behind her exclaiming, " 'Come in! Come right in!' "[44] One night, Josiah Royce, his neighbor and friend, held a seminar at home. A number of the participants were adults. At around ten, James told his wife, "I'll ask them in as they come by." When she pointed out that nobody would want to stop by at so late an hour, he said, "I'll leave the door open anyhow."[45]

His student D. S. Miller, who related the incident, happily seized upon the metaphor—door left open for new ideas, for fresh perceptions—and we may assume that James, having answered the question as to life's worth, was forever interested in how others answered it. But what we have here is more than just another tribute to James' capaciousness. It is not hard to imagine James' need to fill some void, not hard to imagine the relief that came with taking an interest in others, with being drawn *away* from whatever threatened to drag him down. One hears, in other words, what John Jay Chapman heard: a melancholy note. "There was, in spite of his playfulness, a deep sadness about James," Chapman wrote. "You felt that he had just stepped out of this sadness in order to meet you, and was to go back into it the moment you left him." Chapman went on to cite James' desire to be of use to others, to become an agent "in the spread of truth and happiness," as the cause. He found the same to be true of other great men, such as Lincoln and Tolstoy, who devoted their lives to humanity.[46] But without denying James' humaneness, we can say that the darkness on which he looked out—and which he contained—was more profound than that. Protecting himself with his manliness, he lived with it. He bore up heroically. But he could never completely dispel the darkness with his "manlier indifference."

Late in life, he compared notes with a Polish patriot and scholar about the virtues of Yoga. Typically, he heard the man out about the practice as a means of tapping the "reservoirs of life," but he knew that Yoga was not for him. He characterized himself as a man who balked at "formal and prescriptive methods." He was "a dry and bony *individual*, repelling fusion." In sum, he said, "My deeper levels seem very hard to find."[47]

Chained to a Dead Man

Anyone interested in trying to plumb those depths must go back to the crisis years of the late 1860s, when James, approaching thirty, was all but broken physically and emotionally. In 1865, after stints at the Lawrence Scientific and Medical Schools at Harvard, he had gone with his friend Thomas Ward and a handful of other young men to Brazil to help Louis Agassiz gather specimens for his Museum of Zoology and Comparative Anatomy. While there, he contracted a variety of smallpox that temporarily jaundiced and blinded him, and at some point he developed his form of what he thought was the family's congenital back trouble. Upon his return in February 1866, he resumed his medical studies, but by the end of the year he was mired in depression. By the following winter, he was, as he put it to Ward, on "the continual verge of suicide."[1] At some point, he had himself admitted into McLean's Asylum in Somerville, Massachusetts.* James feared that the root cause of his depression was physiological, which only deepened it and added insomnia and digestive problems to the list of his physical ailments. In the spring of 1867, he went abroad, studying and frequenting watering places in Europe, but he found no relief. Nor would he be buoyed by his eventual completion of the requirements of a medical degree in 1869, for he knew that

---

* Alfred Kazin writes that Henry A. Murray verified this fact for him. Robert J. Richards had it confirmed for him by an archivist at the asylum. The most interesting evidence is the following. In the spring of 1870, James was paid a visit from the prophet of the self-made man, Horatio Alger himself, who had also undergone a severe personal crisis. A few years before, having been charged with—and admitting to—molesting young boys, he had been relieved of his duties as a Unitarian minister. Writing was his second career. Henry James Sr. wrote his son Henry about the meeting, "Alger talks freely about his own late insanity—which he in fact appears to enjoy as a subject of conversation and in which I believe he has somewhat interested William, who has talked with him a good deal about his experience at the Somerville Asylum." See Alfred Kazin, "William James: To Be Born Again," *Princeton University Chronicle*, LIV (Winter–Spring 1993), 248; Robert J. Richards, "The Personal Equation in Science: William James's Psychological and Moral Uses of Darwinian Theory," *Harvard Library Bulletin*, XXX (October 1982), 392; and Gary Scharnhorst and Jack Bales, *The Lost Life of Horatio Alger, Jr.* (Bloomington: Indiana University Press, 1985), pp. 66–70.

he never wanted to practice. He acknowledged that surgery might benefit people, but he thought that otherwise a doctor served only as a supportive presence—that, and "[h]e also extracts money."[2]

Looking back many years later, he spoke of his condition as "this state of philosophic pessimism and general depression of spirits about my prospects."[3] The crisis James underwent during this five- or six-year period was a "philosophic" one, but not in the sense that he was stymied by one or another philosophic problem. It was precisely because he could not and never would just "do" philosophy, precisely because his voracious reading embroiled him in questionings about the course and purpose of his own life, and in turn intensified those questionings, that he was so disheartened. The problem of career bedeviled him, as we have seen. But there could be no social solution for his sickness, nor—in the years to come—would rising in the world's esteem ever cure him. In one respect, his sufferings were aggravated by his fame: he felt the more pressure to keep up appearances. "The fact is that my nervous system is utter trash, and always was so," he wrote his brother Henry on New Year's Day, 1901. "It has been a hard burden to bear all these years, the more so as I have seemed to others perfectly well."[4] He would never again be so miserable as in the years shortly before and after his thirtieth birthday, but he would struggle all his life against anxiety and lassitude, ill health and imagined failings. In 1904, at the age of sixty-two, in answering a questionnaire, he said his belief in personal immortality was getting stronger because he was "just getting fit to live."[5]

As he told Ward, the problem was "not one of being, but of method," not what he should do in life but how he could carry on.[6] The two men were in many ways alike ("both persons of rather wide sympathies, not particularly logical in the processes of our minds, and of mobile temperament," James told Ward), but Ward was the more impatient, the more impetuous of the two of them, and hence the more likely to be discouraged. He could expect "twenty times as much anguish as other people need to get along with," James said. The "unduly *noisy* and demonstrative" form Ward's despair took made James think that he himself looked like "the man of calm and clockwork feelings." He was far from it, but unlike Ward, he could name the measures he was taking to improve his condition—which he did in a long letter, written in January 1868.[7]

James began by stressing the need to create character—or what he called, in "Habit," "a completely fashioned will."[8] At the same time, he spoke of how he had *become* a character, one who could walk out onstage and act heroically. The first thing Ward had to do was distance himself from difficult situations so as to be able to control his responses. It was almost like preparing for a theatrical entrance: look on your feelings as "something as external to you as possible, like the curl of your hair." Then Ward might think back on mornings in Brazil, "the sun is whanging down, and the waves dancing, and the gulls skimming down at the mouth of the Amazon," and "by merely thinking of these matters of fact, limit the power of one's evil moods over one's way of looking at the Kosmos." This was James thinking positively, preaching "the gospel of cheer." It was not a prescription that was likely to calm wracked nerves for long, but he himself had taken a page from it. He had relished the particularity, the tangibility of each specimen that he had gathered on their voyage. Each was observably, categorizably, and then undeniably what it was. The debates stirred up by Darwin might rage on, but certain facts of natural history were facts. Thirty years later, in a memorial essay, James would thank Agassiz for teaching him "the difference between all possible abstractionists and all livers in the light of the world's concrete fulness."[9] On the expedition, he began to lay the foundations of his later "radical empiricism." He also experienced a method for avoiding radical distraction.

He next told Ward that he might read Browning, specifically his "A Grammarian's Funeral." It too was about doing the work at hand and not worrying about the future. ("What's time? leave Now for dogs and apes! / Man has Forever," were the lines he quoted.) "It always strengthens my backbone to read it," James said. He may even have believed what he was saying. It was not at all clear what was causing his neurasthenia, or what might make him better. In time, he would undergo "faradization" treatments for his back, inject himself with a compound that included an extract from bulls' testicles, hoping that "courage and aggressiveness [would] replace pusillanimity,"[10] and use a rented battery to shock his nerves—remedies far stranger than reading Browning. But one notion outlasted all others: "the thought of my having a will, and of my belonging to a brotherhood of men possessed of a capacity for pleasure and pain of different kinds." James went on to imagine how Ward might do something for that brotherhood, "add to the welfare of the race," and how he himself might do the same, how "I might make my *nick*." Whatever he ended up doing, he would do so without sniveling. Echoing the conclusion of Carlyle's "Characteristics," he wrote, "The stoic feeling of being a sentinel obeying orders without knowing the general's plans is a noble one." Not having fought in the war, he was careful to imagine himself as a sentinel, or a sentry, not as a combatant, but his life was to be a battle, nevertheless, one waged to preserve the unity of his own being.

The entries in the Diary he kept between the years 1868 and 1873 are records of intense self-analysis.[11] They are relatively few in number, but as he proceeded from one to the next, he registered how he was gaining control over himself. In them he constructed a character along very sharply defined and severely limited lines. Here he is, to begin with, in May of 1868, in

Dresden, listening to a Miss H. accompany "the Dr. and the Italian lady" on the piano. His "feelings came to a sort of crisis":

The intuition of something here in a measure absolute gave me such an unspeakable disgust for the dead drifting of my own life for some time past. I can revive the feeling perhaps hereafter by thinking of men of genius. It ought to have a practical effect on my own will—a horror of waste life since life can be *such*—and oh God! an end to the idle, idiotic sinking into *Vorstellungen* [imaginings] disproportionate to the object. Every good experience ought to be interpreted in practice.

The music itself would have been problematic for James, especially the music of the period. As he would point out in his essay "Habit," music had its dangers: it created feelings one might be unable to control. Accordingly, he recommended that concertgoers not allow themselves to have any emotion that could not be expressed in action. "Let the expression be the least thing in the world—speaking genially to one's grandmother," for example, "or giving up one's seat in a horse-car, if nothing more heroic offers—but let it not fail to take place."[12] (The injunction was absolute, and it echoed down through the years. After listening to Beethoven's serenades, his wife cited his "good theory of music becoming harmful." The feelings they stirred up were dark enough without her adding to them: she told him that she had resolved never to offend him again by wearing black clothes.)[13] But at the Dresden concert the musicians were disturbing not because of the sounds they made but because they were models of effectiveness. They had wasted no effort. They were geniuses not because they were consummate artists but because they had followed their genius, their guiding spirit. Two years before, James had told Ward he felt he had no right to express himself on any subject, no right even to open his mouth until he knew "some *one* thing as thoroughly as it can be known, no matter how insignificant it may be." Miss H., the doctor, and the Italian lady were geniuses because they knew how to do one thing well.

In his entry for February 1, 1870, it was his back and not just his idleness that he took to be proof of his ineffectiveness. He felt spineless. He experienced "a great dorsal collapse . . . carrying with it a moral one," and he "about touched bottom." By his understanding, it was all a question of will, and his was not yet strong enough. His efforts were still intermittent, he was forever getting distracted. He was not immoral, but easily demoralized, weak—not yet wholly a man. But having asked himself whether he should "throw the moral business overboard, as one unsuited to any innate aptitudes," or "follow it, making everything else merely stuff for it," he determined to "develop the moral interest," by which he meant learn how to take command of his life, to have his feelings under control or sufficiently effective, and to be doing one thing so well that he would have no thought of doing anything else.

Three months later, at the end of April, he was confirmed in his decision to lead a moral life by his reading of an essay by the French philosopher Charles Renouvier. Having come upon Renouvier's definition of free will as "the sustaining of a thought *because I choose to* when I might have other thoughts," James declared, "My first act of free will shall be to believe in free will." For the rest of the year, he vowed to "abstain from mere speculation and contemplative Grübelei [musings] in which my nature takes most delight, and voluntarily cultivate the feeling of moral freedom." In the new year, his "callow skin being somewhat fledged," or being no longer literally (and metaphorically) jaundiced, he might return to metaphysical study, but until then he would read only what contributed to the feeling of moral freedom as he had defined it. Until then, he would remember:

> Care little for speculation
> Much for the *form* of my action
> Recollect that only when habits of order are formed can we advance to really interesting fields of action.

It seemed another "crisis" in his life, like the one that had occurred two years before, while he was listening to music, a moment when he was closer to knowing how to live. He had taken "the exceptionally passionate initiative" that the British psychologist Alexander Bain had said was "needful for the acquisition of habits." On the torn edge of the page, James wrote that when "hitherto" he had felt like taking any initiative, "like daring to act originally," suicide seemed "the most daring form to put my daring to." Now he had discovered a new form, a new method. He would exercise his will, he would act determinably. Above all and in the first place, he would believe that he had the power to do so. He would "posit life," he would act as if his experience was real, and in his act assume the role of a fighter. "My belief to be sure *can't* be optimistic—but I will posit life, (the real, the good) in the self governing *resistance* of the ego to the world." The "world" had threatened to overwhelm him, but he was pushing it back. He would do so in part by channeling all his energy into some one activity. "Every actually existing consciousness seems to itself at any rate to be a *fighter for ends*," he would say in *The Principles of Psychology*.[14]

Three years later, in 1873, their father reported to Henry that William had come into the room exclaiming about the world of difference that now existed between his old, hypochondriacal self and his present self, "so cleared up and restored to sanity." William had called it "the difference between death and life." The father told his "darling Harry" how William had cited Wordsworth and Renouvier, "specially his vindication of the will," and how he had "given up the notion that all mental disorder required to have a physical basis."[15] William had come to believe that he was not doomed to defeat by his body. He had gotten hold of himself and was in control. Echoing Henry James

Sr., Ralph Barton Perry quotes the son's declaration about his "first act of free will," and concludes, "Thus James felt his old doubts to be dispelled by a new and revolutionary insight." Until recently, readers have found this narrative convincing and inspiring.[16] For decades, it was a stirring (and conveniently simple) example of masculine self-control and determination.

What James had done was decide "to stick to biology" and then, in May of 1872, accept President Eliot's offer to teach anatomy and physiology at Harvard. He noted his decision in his Diary and then went on to say that philosophy (by which he meant speculations, questionings, imaginings) was his "vocation," but "as a *business*" it was not normal for most men, certainly not for him. His "deepest interest" would always be in "the most general problems," but what he needed at the time was "some stable reality to lean upon." So he had decided to stick with "the concrete facts in which a biologist's responsibilities lie," and thus avoid "the abyss of horrors" that "would spite of everything grasp my imagination and imperil my reason." It was a sound resolution, one that allowed the family to stop worrying, but it was not sound enough to reassure him indefinitely. The abyss would always be there, and specters would again emerge out of the darkness.

After he had been teaching at Harvard for three years, James wrote a letter to Ward that evoked the potential horror of his situation with a more gruesome figure. "Each of us," he said, "walks 'round with a dead man chained to him, which the world don't recognize."[17] We might recall the image Emerson uses in "Self-Reliance" for the weight of one's past. "But why should you keep your head over your shoulder?" Emerson asks. "Why drag about this corpse of your memory?" Or another that Emerson employs for the same purpose in the same essay: "my giant," the "sad self, unrelenting, identical," that I flee in my travels but that "goes with me wherever I go." In Emerson, "each of us" is any one when he is weighted down by thoughts of his past, especially any one who is concerned about things he has once said that he is afraid to contradict. We fear "the unintelligent brute force that lies at the bottom of society," Emerson writes, "and the other terror that scares us from self-trust is our consistency."

But the corpse James speaks of is a more vibrant presence. Examining Ward's life, James located the dead man in the "actualities" of Ward's situation (his frustrations working in his father's bank, his emotional dishevelment), which prevent his realizing his "potentialities (of intellectual work too)." In James' own life, the corpse is all that depresses him. James does not like his colleagues at Harvard. They are "dry and shop-board like." The naturalist Nathaniel Shaler seems to be the only one with "any breadth of human nature in him . . . but Shaler is a charlatan." And whether a cause or a symptom of his disgruntlement, his health is giving way again. He is "in rather a dilapidated condition": he has dysentery, his energy is gone by ten in the morning, he hesitates to speak of the future "for fear of breaking down before the end of the year." Finally, his relationship with the woman he wants to marry seems *already* to have collapsed. The "delirious affair of last summer is at an end. She cares no more for me than for a dead leaf, nor ever will"—and it is just as well, he says, given his health.

The challenge was still and would always be to find a way to live with the man to whom he was chained. One could join him at any time, lie down with him and quit. But a man could prove himself a hero if he continued to live. Thus James went on to ask Ward, "Is it recognized and credited to him anyhow or anywhere? That is the question to which an affirmative answer would make heroes of us all." If one were strong and determined enough, if one's perseverence were seen for what it was, to involve what it involved, one could be assured of a kind of greatness. One would have gained self-respect, and one's performance would be appreciated.

James was not transformed during this or any other "crisis." His famous declaration about his "first act of free will" is less an affirmation of free will than a flight *from* free will.[18] It is a celebration not of his power to choose whatever course he wanted but rather of his determination to prevent anything spontaneous, uncalculated, unpredictable from ever throwing him off the one course he happened, finally, to choose. "Man needs a rule for his will, and will invent one if one be not given him," James would write in his first great essay, "The Sentiment of Rationality" (1879).[19] Especially during this period, especially among men of James' acquaintance and class, doing as one wanted (in Matthew Arnold's formulation of the issue) was anarchic. The culture called for and created disciplined men. One might spurn material success, but given the accelerated pace of life, just to survive required determination and perseverance and focus.

In a moving reflection on a life that was in many ways the antithesis of James'—marked by poverty, domestic scandal, brilliance unrecognized professionally—his sometime colleague Charles Peirce once defined the ideal to which he wished he had aspired when he was younger:

> If I had a son, I should instill into him this view of morality, (that is, that Ethics is the science of the method of bringing Self-Control to bear to gain satisfaction) and force him to see that there is but one thing that raises one individual animal above another,—Self-Mastery; and should teach him that the Will is Free only in the sense that, by employing the proper appliances, he can make himself behave in the way he really desires to behave. . . . Thus, the Freedom of the Will, such as it is, is a one sided affair.[20]

It is precisely the position James established for himself.

It was also the position he tried to maintain as he contended with the most obvious forces and energies a man must face—forces and energies as yet unnamed. We have come this far without mentioning sex—the one thing, James' and Peirce's contemporaries would say, "that raises one animal above another," the instinct a man must master, lest he be just another animal. Inevitably, ineradicably, it was written into all of James' thinking about his life at this time. Assuming that James had successfully marshaled the power of his will, and fashioned himself anew, most readers of James have been only too happy to ignore what James' father called "the physical basis" of his neurasthenia. But in 1876, his conception of his own body and his conception of women and of his relation to them was integral to his idea of the kind of man he wanted to become—even as he feared he was not physically sound enough to win the hand of the woman he loved.

To go back a few years, in December 1869 James seemed reconciled to a severely limited life. "I may not study, make, or enjoy—but I can still will," he wrote in his Diary. "I can find some real life in the mere respect for other forms of life as they pass." On the assumption that he was incapable of any human engagement, he would be content to watch from a distance: "Nature and life have unfitted me for any affectionate relations with other individuals." While he was abroad, he had tried to reach out, or at least toyed with the idea of trying. Several of the women to whom he had been drawn were literally framed in windows. On one occasion, his communings took place through a telescope; on another, he got as far as the florist's down below, but he was so bashful about buying a bouquet, and then so afraid the "robust beauty" would not accept it, that he "beat a humiliating retreat back to [his] room."[21] He sent home a picture of an actress he professed to be thinking of marrying, but although he managed to worry his mother, his report was heavy-handed enough to preclude anyone else's taking him seriously. He was more nearly touched by the pianist, "Miss H," an American woman named Kate Haven, who was living abroad at the time. There was nothing threatening about her. She was herself in fragile health, "a prey to her nerves and . . . in a sort of hysterical, hypochondriac state," he told Ward. With a well-chosen metaphor, he told him that she had stirred "chords in this desiccated heart which I long thought had turned to dust." She symbolized a kind of genius, and he was moved by her, but there would be little courting. The plans they made to meet in America fell through, and their short correspondence came to an end.[22]

James' contemplations of women intensified his desire for self-control. Women were like music, capable of stirring up feelings a man might not be able to relieve in action. When Ward spoke to him about a woman he was thinking of marrying, James warned him that a woman's imperfections could make life unbearable. If he had any doubts about the woman, if he saw any faults, "any macula *whatever*," he should withdraw. "Damn it, Tom," he wrote in January of 1868, "a little fleck hardly visible to the naked eye at first in the being of a girl we are attracted to, ends by growing, when we are bound to her in any way, bigger than the whole world, so that it mixes with everything and nauseates it for our enjoyment."[23] In his Diary, he pursued his thoughts about imaginings that were "disproportionate to the object." The night he heard Kate Havens accompany the singers, he had reviled himself for his lack of purpose in life. "Every good experience ought to be interpreted in practice," he had concluded. But five days later, it was feelings stirred up by Kate Havens herself that troubled him. They were the feelings—the fears—a man might have of not being able to possess a loved one, "emotions," he called them, "of a loving kind indulged in where one cannot expect to gain exclusive possession of the loved person." He went on to develop the idea: in love, as against friendship, "the interest is deepened and concentrated on the mere possibility in the object of being possessed—without so much regard to those qualities that make it worth possessing." The wise man is one who has no expectation of a lovable quality's being "produced for our benefit as often as we will it."[24] He had brought himself under control, and imagined how a man might do that "wisely" in the long run. For the moment, what he had been able to do was monitor and rein in whatever feelings, erotic or otherwise, he had for Kate Havens. He had peeled back one of the thickest layers surrounding or constituting manhood as he was developing it during these years of crisis, and what he discovered was a man's desire to possess under perfect conditions, to have ideal womanhood at his beck and call. Insofar as he was such a man, he knew that he was indeed still unfitted for any affectionate relations.

His feelings toward women sufficiently deadened, and determined to know some one thing, he could look forward to his body's falling in line as well. He could expect the pains in his back to subside, his skin to clear up, and his eyesight to improve (though his eyes would tire easily for the rest of his life). But though he had withdrawn from women, he was still left with the challenge of his own sexuality. Here he was apparently not so successful. In vowing to make everything "stuff" for "the moral business," he looked back on the way he had been "more or less humbugging himself" up to that point. "Hitherto I have tried to fire myself with the moral interest, as an aid in the accomplishing of certain utilitarian ends of attaining certain difficult but salutary habits," he wrote in his Diary. He said he had tried "to associate the feeling of moral degradation with failure," and that in this he was "cultivating the moral only as a means" and thus "humbugging" himself.[25] It is not hard to imagine what form of degradation he was addressing, or what salutary habits he was trying to attain, with his undeveloped, uninspired will. He was in this, as in so many respects, representative—which is to say, extraordinary in the way he brought out what was typical of men of his time.

The most penetrating exploration James ever made into what precisely he was contending with during these years is to be found in the culminating example that he gives in "The Sick Soul," in *The Varieties of Religious Experience* (1902). He presents it to us thirty years after the event, in an example, he says, of "the worst kind of melancholy," that which takes the form of "panic fear." It will be helpful to have at least the heart of the famous passage before us:

Whilst in this state of philosophic pessimism and general depression of spirits about my prospects, I went one evening into a dressing-room in the twilight to procure some article that was there; when suddenly there fell upon me without any warning, just as if it came out of the darkness, a horrible fear of my own existence. Simultaneously there arose in my mind the image of an epileptic patient whom I had seen in the asylum, a black-haired youth with greenish skin, entirely idiotic, who used to sit all day on one of the benches, or rather shelves against the wall, with his knees drawn up against his chin, and the coarse gray undershirt, which was his only garment, drawn over them inclosing his entire figure. He sat there like a sort of sculptured Egyptian cat or Peruvian mummy, moving nothing but his black eyes and looking absolutely non-human. This image and my fear entered into a species of combination with each other. *That shape am I,* I felt, potentially. Nothing that I possess can defend me against that fate, if the hour for it should strike for me as it struck for him. There was such a horror of him, and such a perception of my own merely momentary discrepancy from him, that it was as if something hitherto solid within my breast gave way entirely, and I became a mass of quivering fear. After this the universe was changed for me altogether. I awoke morning after morning with a horrible dread at the pit of my stomach, and with a sense of the insecurity of life that I never knew before, and that I have never felt since.[26]

James was anything but eager to have his audience get to the bottom of this. There are many layers here, layers that he himself applied. When he finally did relate the event, he did so by fabricating that it was drawn from a letter from a French correspondent, which he is translating "freely." Were it not for a casual remark to a friend, who recorded it after James' death, we would not even know that James was making an example of himself.

James has given us his horrific vision of the aimlessness and drift of his life—his breakdown, we would now say—and no one, not even James himself, can name just what caused it. When a man fears or experiences the dissolution of his financial and professional and public life, it would not be surprising if his private or intimate or sexual life seemed to lack all purpose or definition as well. How specifically James was applying the diagnosis to himself we cannot say, but into his darkest imaginings there seems to have come the figure— perhaps the very figure a nineteenth-century medical student might have had in mind—of a man driven insane by masturbation.

In his book *Disease and Representation,* Sander Gilman cites a text that would seem explicitly to inform James' vision of madness. It is in fact in French, and it contains an illustration of an idiot, in a coarse undershirt, his hair black, his eyes wild, and "his knees drawn against his chin." The text is Jean Etienne Dominique Esquirol's monumental and standard treatise on mental illness, published in 1838. The illustrative image is of one Aba, a man who has no memory, who can do nothing other than feed himself, and whose only utterances are the sounds "ba ba ba"—all the result of his being "a mastur-bator," Esquirol says.*

But James would not have needed Esquirol's text. If the image haunting him sprang out of his visits to the state insane asylums in Northampton or Worcester, it might well have been an image of a masturbator, for according to an influential report on idiocy presented to the Massachusetts state legisla-ture by the superintendent at Worcester, 32 percent of the population in his institution was there because of "self-pollution."[27] (Presumably the report's authors were so dismayed by seeing madmen masturbate, they assumed that their self-indulgence had driven them mad.)

Gilman provides no gloss on Aba, but the name may lead us back to James as well. It is the name of the Father in Hebrew; and on one dramatic occasion James seems to have made the connection between this babbling idiot and one or another all-powerful father. John Jay Chapman recorded (but did not date) the moment in his "Retrospections." He tells of how he once tried "to express to James the consciousness which a simple-minded person might have of the presence of God as the *causa causans* of his own anatomy." " 'Can you not imagine,' " Chapman ended, " 'that such a creature under such emotional conditions should cry out, Abba, Father!' " At which, Chapman says, "James started like—not a guilty—but angry thing surprised, and a trap door opened under the interview."[28] It is a long way back to James' "panic fear" in 1872. The idea of James being reduced to idiotic answerings to his maker for his unhealthy habits may seem unlikely, but when he was a boy he was told about the dire consequences of "that horrible pollution" by his own father—and when the appropriate time came, he duly passed on his father's warnings to one of his sons. "If any boys try to make you *do* anything dirty," he told him when he went off to boarding school, "either to your own person, or to their

---

Disease and Representation: Images of Illness from Madness to AIDS (Ithaca: Cornell University Press, 1988), pp. 74–78. Cushing Strout speculates that as a medical student James would have been familiar with William Acton's *The Functions and Disorders of the Reproductive Organs* and been struck by Acton's warning that the habit of introspection could lead not just to "the suicidal view of life" but to masturbation and madness as well. See "William James and the Twice-Born Sick Soul," *Daedalus*, XCVII (1968), 1066–67. In his Diary, James notes he is reading Henry Mauds-ley, another "authority" on the relationship between masturbation and the morbid brooding of those who are unable to chart a straight course through life.

persons . . . you must both preach and smite them. For that leads to an awful habit, and a terrible disease when one is older."[29]

Whether or not masturbation figured in James' thinking about his physical state, with or without his father's "help," his father played a decisive role in his efforts to assume his proper role as a married and a family man. In what he knew would be his last words to him, William wrote his father in December 1882:

> In that mysterious gulf of the past into which the present soon will fall and go back and back, yours is still for me the central figure. All my intellectual life I derive from you; and though we have often seemed at odds in the expression thereof, I'm sure there's a harmony somewhere, and that our strivings will combine. What my debt to you is goes beyond all my power of estimating.

He was ever mindful of his father's expectations as he tried to settle on a career, and apologized for the delay ("I know what trouble I've given you at various times through my particularities.").[30] His respect for scientific fact, on the one hand, and the hope that he expressed to Ward that he might find a way of contributing to the welfare of the race, on the other, were both ingrained in him by his father. More important, even his episode of "panic fear" was something of a combined effort.

For his father had had a similar experience when *he* was in his early thirties—though it, like his son's, did not come to light for another thirty years. His harks back not to "self-abuse" but to the terrible accidental burning of his leg that occurred when he was a schoolboy of thirteen, and to the festerings and decay that necessitated not one but two amputations (without anesthesia, of course), the second reaching—finally, four years later—up to his thigh. The similarities between the two experiences of "panic fear" are striking: both Henry James Sr.'s experience and his son's took place in the evening; both were confrontations with abhorrent projections of their physicality; in both cases, the figures they came upon were squatting figures—the one a "fetid personality," the other, green skinned. The father was reduced to "almost helpless infancy," wanting to "run incontinently to the foot of the stairs and shout for help to my wife"; the son became "a mass of quivering fear," dreading to be left alone. The father's word for what he went through was "vastation," a Swedenborgian term suggesting a laying waste or (because Swedenborg had been a mining engineer) an excavation. The word also suggests (as does his use of the word "incontinently") what his son gestured toward when he spoke of awakening each morning with "a horrible dread at the pit of my stomach"— namely, a purgation, the self involuntarily emptying itself of all its filth. Both men had seen themselves as disgusting physical processes that were running on uncontrollably.[31]

The father interpreted his experience as proof of his abject sinfulness—his rotten, moral being—and he emerged from his crisis affirming God's goodness and mercy ("For truth is God . . . and who shall pretend to comprehend that great and adorable perfection?"). At the end of *his* account, the son spoke of using scriptural texts as stays against insanity and then, in a footnote, referred the reader to his father—"For another case of fear equally sudden, see Henry James: *Society the Redeemed Form of Man,* Boston, 1879, pp. 43ff." But he could not share his father's faith in the presence of the divine in nature, a presence (as William pointed out) that his father had simply posited in the first place. He could not understand "a *real* movement of return" to the phenomenal nature. Darwin and his own scientific studies had made that impossible.

After his father's death, in an effort to make amends "for my rather hard non-receptivity of his doctrines as he urged them so absolutely during his life," James went to work on *The Literary Remains of the Late Henry James* (1884).[32] In a long introduction, he spoke disparagingly of his father's "absoluteness," of his unrelenting insistence on man's sinfulness and the possibility of divine release: "With all the richness of style, the ideas are singularly unvaried and few," he said, adding with gritted teeth, "Probably few authors have so devoted their entire lives to the monotonous elaboration of one single bundle of truths." (Twenty years before, he had amused the family by producing a sketch of a man beating a dead horse and suggesting that it grace the title page of the father's latest book.)[33] His efforts to make Henry James Sr.'s views more widely known were loving, but they failed miserably. After six months, he wrote his brother Henry that only one copy had been sold.[34] The few reviews the book received ranged from cursory to savage.

William was not ready to hear what he called his father's single cry that "religion is real,"[35] but he listened carefully to another of the doctrines that invariably appeared in his writings. The father had spoken over and over again—in lectures, reviews, and essays—about the saving power of marriage, and the son attended. Here their strivings were more nearly one: William could not see God in the phenomenal world, but he was willing to adapt his father's language to his situation and imagine that as a faltering, if not a fallen, man he could be saved, as his father repeatedly declared, if he found the right wife.

The truth about Woman, according to his father, was that in her, more than in any good works, salvation lay. In fact, she was man's only escape from his fleshly, fetid being—or from his desirous, lustful self. She was created to show him the way out of his beastly state; in her, man could see the promise of his life, his otherwise "unseen spiritual manhood." By the elder James' reading of Genesis, man is "the rudest, crudest, spiritually least modified—that is most *universal*—form of human nature, representing the most base, earthly, material, centrifugal, *identifying* force in creation which is known as *selfhood* . . . that essentially evil, diabolic, or simply waste force in humanity." (One begins to notice what his son called the richness of his style. The sentences gather momentum, the father's voice swells. "What 'fun' it must have been to roll out his adjectives," Alice said when she read her father's *Literary Remains*).[36] Woman—Eve—by delightfully rendered and blinding comparison, was the

celestial counterpart of this vulgar deciduous Adam . . . his regenerate, *Divine*-natural, or individualizing soul, the dew of God's ceaseless, soft, caressing presence in human nature, full of indulgent clemency and tenderness towards the dull, somnolent, inapprehensive, unconscious clod with whom she is associated, and whom yet she is to educate and inspire by exquisite ineffable divine arts into the lordship of the universe, or marriage sympathy and union with the universal heart of man.

"Anyone with half an eye can see" that Adam's fall was no death. Rather, it was his rise "out of sheer unrelieved brutality" into self-consciousness, "*the recognition of his soul, or spiritual nature;* for this is what Eve signifies in reference to Adam."[37]

Henry James Sr.'s good friend Emerson once wrote that the "finest people marry the two sexes in their own person. Hermaphrodite is then the symbol of the finished soul," and wrote too that "a highly endowed man with good intellect and good conscience is a Man-woman and does not so much need the complement of woman to his being as another."[38] It was typical of him to elevate sex and gender distinctions above men's social experience—and appropriate that James, in turn, should think of Emerson as a superior being, so pure as to be unconscious of himself as either good or evil. "An unsexed woman," he called him.[39] But to Henry James Sr., in order for a man to be a "finished soul," he had to marry.

Man's fall, James argued, enabled him to recognize his separation from God, a separation he can then repair in holy matrimony. The only way man, "by nature . . . in himself unsocial," could enter that higher state was to marry, "to leave father and mother, and cleave unto the wife alone, that is, to a new manhood symbolized by woman." She was the "patient bondsman of the latter's necessities, the meek unresisting drudge of his lusts both physical and moral, so wooing him, and at last winning him, out of his grovelling egotism into the richest social and aesthetic dimension." Through her he could become "divinely human, or characteristically *social*."[40] James' readings of Charles Fourier and Emanuel Swedenborg drew his sights upward to where he envisaged woman patiently submitting to her husband in order that gradually she might build up "the family, the tribe, the city, the nation, and every larger or more universal form of human unity, until now at last her helpless nursling has become developed into THE PEOPLE."[41]

Henry James Sr.'s enthusiasms over the prospect of a society redeemed by the influence of Woman led him to some surprising views of marriage.[42] In introducing his translation of a Fourierist pamphlet titled *Love in the Phalanstery,* he spoke of "a hope for the eventual extinction of the present adulterous and promiscuous commerce of the sexes," by which he meant unions that were not forged by mutual preference, not inspired by true affection, but unions in which each spouse tried to own the affections of the other.[43] He later argued the case that the institution of marriage ought to be relieved by greater freedom of divorce. Otherwise a man would consider his wife his property, and though she was meant for submission, she would rebel, and he, in turn, would resort to "some vile and dastardly revenge." When it took the form of murder, he wrote in the pages of the *Atlantic Monthly,* the enraged husband would not be so much to blame as "the social constitution under which we live, inasmuch as that constitution makes the true sanction of marriage to be force, not freedom."[44]

When advocates of free love understandably started to claim him as an ally, he quickly and completely reversed his position. In 1853 there appeared a book on love, marriage, and divorce that contained his views on these subjects along with those of Horace Greeley, the editor of the *New York Tribune,* and Stephen Pearl Andrews, a leading proponent of free love. A later edition included a revealing—and embarrassing—letter in which James said, "The gospel of free love turns my intellectual stomach." He compared such love to the lascivious carrying-on of chimpanzees and monkeys and claimed that he had been saved from it by his marriage. He had discovered a divinity in his wife that was "the very opposite of everything I find in myself . . . a divinity infinitely remote from my own petty self, and yet a divinity in my very nature, so that I can't help becoming aroused to the meaning at last of living worship, worship consecrated by death to self." Free love turned his stomach; the state of matrimony set it right. It enabled him to spew out all that was decaying and nauseating in his system, to overcome the deadliest sin in his book—selfhood.

The reason he was so "aroused" to the meaning of living worship, which is to say, to the elimination of physical desire, was very simple: his wife no longer aroused him. "I marry my wife under the impression that she is literally perfect, and is going to exhaust my capacity of desire ever after," he explained, but "ere long," he said, "I discover my mistake." She could not meet his brutish demands. Lesser men might lead double lives; those who came after might benefit from more lenient divorce laws. In James' bosom there would be "a ceaseless conflict between law and liberty, between conscience and inclination," but he would never let on. His "good habits," his "good breeding," and his respect for his wife would prevent that from every happening. He would deny himself. "As for me," he concluded proudly, "I will abide in my chains."[45]

His wife, Mary, was a woman known for what her daughter, Alice, called her "extraordinary self-less devotion" to her family—a devotion that "embodied the unconscious essence of wife and motherhood."[46] But her virtuousness had its costs. It entailed high expectations and, in William's case especially, intolerance. She openly favored Henry, "the Angel" who did not cause her problems, and to him she openly criticized William for having always to express "every fluctuation of feeling, and especially every unfavorable symptom, without reference to the effect upon those about him." His was "a morbidly hopeless" temperament, she said. He had "such a morbid sympathy with every form of trouble or privation."[47]

Henry James Sr. elected to bind himself to his wife, Mary, and in the process happily deny his physical being. That way salvation lay. When his wife died, he was astonishingly true to his word: his worship was in fact consecrated by his death. Four months after Mary Walsh James succumbed to bronchial asthma, he wrote his son Henry about his purified yearnings: "She really did arouse my heart, early in our married life, from its selfish torpor, and so enabled me to become a man. . . . The sum of it all is, that I would sooner rejoin her in her modesty, and find my eternal lot in association with her, than have the gift of a noisy delirious world!" He longed to die, and he did so by denying *all* his body's needs. "He had no visible malady," Henry reported to William, after their father's death five months later. "The 'softening of the brain' was simply a gradual refusal of food, because he *wished* to die. There was no dementia except a sort of exaltation of belief that he had entered into 'the spiritual life.' "[48]

Henry James Sr. put himself in chains and abided in them until he died. He denied himself his "selfhood," his sensuality—ultimately his own body. Lacking his faith in future exaltation, his son did not go so far. He pressed on, all the while struggling to control his amatory and erotic feelings, holding himself in check. And all the while he dragged along the dead man chained to him. He was, that is to say, bound to have deadly, suicidal thoughts from time to time.

The Man—and Wife

James did not cut his earthly ties in order to enjoy the life hereafter, but he did follow his father's lead to the extent that he turned to marriage for the support he needed in order to carry on with his life. No one said so with his father's vehemence, but that was what was expected of a man. His son made the point himself—in his lecture titled "The Value of Saintliness" (1902)—from a later, more settled position. His celebration of the indifferent man, the man who valued poverty, included a stern warning to those who put off marrying:

When we of the so-called better classes are scared as men were never scared in history at material ugliness and hardship; when we put off marriage until our house can be artistic, and quake at the thought of having a child without a bank-account and doomed to manual labor, it is time for thinking men to protest against so unmanly and irreligious a state of opinion.[1]

Although James nowhere says so explicitly, his allusion to the obligations of his class, or "the so-called better classes," echoes crude warnings about "race suicide": men must marry early and thus get on with the task of producing children. Though they seemed to get lost in James' secular defense of marriage, there were religious reasons for getting married as well. Finally, as any contemporary medical text or manual would point out, and as James told his students, there was the simple fact that marriage was good for you. Marriage would allay a man's fears about his sexual potency. The way he put it in one course was that a disinclination to marry reflected an unwholesome love of luxury.[2] But of course he did not tell his classes about the hesitancies and anxieties of his own courtship and marriage.

In the mid-1860s, upon his return from Brazil, he had made a few half-hearted courting efforts. His most serious approach, to Fanny Dixwell of Cambridge, was blocked by Oliver Wendell Holmes Jr., a man who began as one of James' best friends but soon became stunning proof to James of his own differences from the more typically successful men of the period. Holmes was a year older and about to graduate from the Law School when James resumed his studies at the Medical School. The two young men engaged in friendly philosophical jousting, which continued in letters when James went abroad for his health and, upon his return, in meetings of a small "metaphysical club" that he proposed—one that was "to be composed of none but the very topmost cream of Boston manhood,"[3] he wrote Holmes. It was a group that included Charles Peirce, Chauncey Wright, and, when he was not out spreading a version of Herbert Spencer's Social Darwinism, John Fiske. But even in the late 1860s, while James was adrift, Holmes' interest in philosophical speculation was narrowing to study of the law—"nothing but the law," he wrote James in April 1868[4]—and their temperamental differences were becoming clear.

In the Civil War, Holmes fought for three years in what was known as the "Harvard regiment," and in spite of—or because of—having been seriously wounded, always thought of this experience as his "great good fortune."[5] He had proven his physical resiliency. He had settled on a career. Having done neither, James must have felt the cutting edge of the bantering way that Holmes explained his decision. "It has been necessary," Holmes wrote, "if a man chooses a profession he cannot forever content himself in picking out the plums with fastidious dilettantism and give the rest of the loaf to the poor, but must eat his way manfully through the crust and crumb—soft, unpleasant, inner parts which, within one, swell, causing discomfort in the bowels." The gastronomic imagery, the suggestions about the eating habits of more and less manly men, and about the embarrassing consequences—a lesser version of the violent turnings of the elder and the younger Jameses' stomachs—were potentially humiliating, but James managed to join in the spirit of Holmes' letter. "Wendell of my entrails," he replied from Dresden, and then went on to describe a woman on a balcony across the street, and a servant girl in a window just below her, and—still jocularly—to say "Excuse me!" while he had his breakfast. But he also confessed, "Much would I give for a constructive passion of some kind," and he acknowledged, "Your metaphysical industry and the artistic satisfaction you take in the exercise of it, gives you an immeasurable advantage."[6]

He also told Holmes that he considered him his best ally, better than Ward, who was "so deficient in power of orderly thought that intercourse with him hardly ever bears fruit," better than his brother Henry, whose orbit and his own "coincide but part way," and better than his father—who must not hear about his condition, he added. But it was not long before he found Holmes' resoluteness and aggressive virility repellent. His nobler qualities were poisoned by "cold blooded conscious egotism and conceit," he wrote his brother Henry.[7] A few years later, in 1876, he described Holmes in a way that set him up as the gruesome ideal of a mechanized and ruthlessly phallic age. Any idea of further fruitful exchange with him was shattered by his terrible image of Holmes as "a powerful battery, formed like a planing machine to gouge a deep self-beneficial groove through life."[8]

Holmes went on to abide by what he called, in a Memorial Day speech he gave at Harvard in 1895, "The Soldier's Faith," a faith that made James' struggles a month later—in "Is Life Worth Living?"—seem almost balletic. ("The measure of power is obstacles overcome," he assured his audience, "to ride boldly, at what is in front of you, be it fence or enemy; to pray not for comfort, but for combat.")[9] After reading about Holmes' exhortations to the Boston Bar Association about "life [as] action, the use of one's powers," James wrote Henry that Holmes had only that one speech. He occupied the highest judicial position in the state, but the speech was "too crude for a Chief Justice of the [Massachusetts] Supreme Court," James said.[10]

Holmes certainly did not set an attractive example of how to make contact with the opposite sex. The battery, the planing machine gouging its groove, was inhumanly masculine. And in fact, the relations with the wife he won were "grim." The word is Alice James', reporting from London. There Holmes was "flirting as desperately as ever." Of his wife she wrote, "There is something so grim as to be out of nature in that poor woman's life and character. What is there but ugliness in any relation between two beings which doesn't work to soften their hearts and open their minds to their kind. Solitude is surely a flowery path to that!"[11] The Jameses were wont to linger over moral subtleties. Holmes had complained that this tendency in William had thrown their philo-sophical discussion off course.[12] Had he known anything about his old friend's approach to marriage, he would have been totally dismissive.

James did not have to consider poverty as an ideal now that he was a member of the Harvard faculty, but as he confided to Ward, he did not think he was temperamentally suited to marriage. Insofar as he still believed that there were somatic sources for his depression and ill health, he thought he was literally unfit for it. "The greater part of the whole evil of this wicked world is the result of infirm health," he had told his brother Bob. Imagining that his "dorsal thing" was something in the family's blood, he dreaded the thought of fathering "unhealthy offspring."[13] Others might marry in order to keep their ranks well stocked; for that very reason, perhaps he should never make that leap.

Insofar as James imagined marrying, he assumed that it would have to be under very special circumstances, and to a most unusual woman. Given the theories and the example of his father, given his age's attitudes toward sex and marriage as they were pronounced in James himself, *his* marriage would have to be—emphatically—a spiritualizing arrangement.

When the women he pictured in the framed windows of Dresden assumed any shape, they appeared as mother figures, barely removed from the earth. He wrote the family, "The sight of the women here has strengthened me more than ever in my belief that they ought to be made to do the hard labor of the community—they are far happier and better for it." This particular observa-tion was a dig at "pampered Alice," as he called her. But he went on, "Seriously there is a great deal of good in it—and the ideal German woman of poetry (see Goethe, for instance) is a working woman."[14] He carried the image—the picture, the poetic figure—with him through the years. In 1882, he would tell his wife about seeing a peasant woman who, "in all her brutish loutishness," reminded him of a painting he had seen in Vienna. Her look of "infinite unawakedness," of "childlike virginity under her shapeless body and in her face," was such as to "make it a poem." He went on to describe peasant women dragging carts through the streets, oblivious of the stream of "luxury and vice, but belonging far away, to something better and purer." And he wept, he said: "All the mystery of womanhood seems incarnated in their ugly being—the Mothers! the Mothers! Ye are all one!"[15]

Though he would forget neither the triumphantly spiritual Eve his father envisaged nor the Earth Mother he celebrated, if he were going to marry, he would have to be more explicit about what he wanted in a wife—as he was, revealingly, in a review he wrote in 1869 of two books on women, one by Horace Bushnell, the most prominent theologian of the day, titled *Suffrage: The Reform against Nature;* the other, John Stuart Mill's classic *The Subjection of Women.* In airing his views on marriage, his father had already had *his* say on the specific subject of the "liberation" of women, and three months after his son had reviewed them, he too would write on Bushnell and Mill. Both articles appeared in leading intellectual journals, the father's in the *Atlantic Monthly,* the son's in the *North American Review.*[16]

In writing "Woman and the 'Woman's Movement' " in 1853, Henry· James Sr. had already provided a primer of essentialist thinking on the issue: a woman's place is in the home, and her calling is to be a wife; she could not love mankind; her task is that of helping and inspiring one man, her husband; reflection and learning do not become her; she lives in the present, in the realm of her senses, making the most of the life at hand. There are exceptions, of course—Queen Elizabeth, Catherine the Great, Marie de Medici—but their very success is proof of their being "unwomanly women." In sum, "woman is by nature inferior to man. She is inferior in passion, his inferior in intellect, and his inferior in physical strength." Inferiority is a fact, a decree of nature, no more deniable than gravitation or electricity. But of course therein lies her superiority: her "natural" inferiority is what spiritually exalts her above man, and is what enables him to transcend his defective, earthly being. Women exist in this world to perform this function. At times James describes them as no more than symbols of what is potential in man: "For woman is only the outward presentation of whatsoever is profoundest and divinest in himself. . . . She is the embodiment of his own ideal selfhood. She is his own better nature visibly incarnated."[17]

In his review of Bushnell and Mill, the Swedenborgian roots of Henry James Sr.'s thinking surface more clearly: the social significance of the relations of men and women transcends any meaning they may have for individuals. Marriage is now "a race-interest in humanity"; the family expands to include all mankind. Marriage is still a woman's apotheosis, but marriage not as Mill conceived of it—a just relationship, voluntarily entered into for the mutual benefit of the two individual parties—but rather as the means by which she enables man to spiritualize his natural instincts, to return to his divine source. He is the World, She the Church. When he enters this Church "the final *social* evolution of humanity" will have taken place.

William was not wholly enthusiastic about his father's articles on marriage and women. "I can't think he shows himself to most advantage in this kind of speculation," he told his brother.[18] But though he could not follow his father's arguments to their sanctified conclusions, he relied heavily on him as he him- self defined woman's position farther down the evolutionary scale. After ex- pressing his reservations about his style, William laid out Bushnell's version of the idea that women are "naturally" inferior creatures. Any kind of "adminis- tration," any exercise of authority is beyond them, Bushnell said, "most of all, the holding of political office, and the exercise of the suffrage." James' sum- mary of Bushnell's position is wry (the ellipses in what follows are his), but he agrees with it nevertheless:

This weighty conclusion is derived from a conception of the essential nature of woman and of government, expressed in an infinite variety of ways throughout the book. She is not "created" to mingle in any kind of strife, or "to batter the severities of fortune. . . . All government belongs to man. . . . Where agreement is impossible, one of the two clearly must decide, and it must be the man. The woman's law . . . . requires it of her . . . . to submit herself to his fortunes. . . . If he has no sway-force in him . . . . to hold the reins, he is no longer what Nature means when she makes a man." Women are "naturally subject," "subordinate," meant to yield to evil and violence, not to combat them with answering evil and violence.

All this, and then: "So far so good." But Bushnell had extended his argument in a way that gave James pause. Like Henry James Sr., Bushnell equated inferiority with superiority, asserting that women's "inferiority" gave them, "morally considered, the truest and sublimest condition of ascendancy," but his terms seemed to the son to smack of Catholic doctrine, and for this reason he objected: "Modern civilization, rightly or wrongly, is bent on developing itself along the line of justice, and any defence of woman's position on ascetic principles will fall with little weight on the public ear."

The secular "line of justice" is the one Mill took, and James was inclined to follow it. In fact, he ends his review by allowing for the possibility that *The Subjection of Women* will be "epoch-making . . . a landmark signalizing one distinct step in the progress of the total evolution." But for the present, James is no more willing to imagine society evolving in this direction than he was in believing it would ascend to its final resting place. He uses Mill to criticize Bushnell, but what he ends up with is a practical, dramatic version of Bush- nell's (and his father's) description of the woman as a subject creature. He appreciates Mill's call for "the morality of justice," but he thinks the abuses much less troublesome on this side of the Atlantic and—what he is really leading up to—American men will simply not subscribe to it. James is right about Mill: "Independence is Mr. Mill's personal ideal, and his notion of love confounds itself with what is generally distinguished as friendship." But James (or "we") has another ideal in mind: "We think that the ideal of the representative American is opposed to this. However he might shrink from expressing it in naked words, the wife his heart more or less subtly craves is at bottom a dependent being." James will not shrink from saying it: if the American man is ever going to assume his proper role as a married man, he will have to have a dependent woman.

"In the outer world [a man] can only hold good his position by dint of reconquering it afresh every day," James declares. It is the fall of 1869. We hear how little he thought stood between him and exposure, humiliation, and defeat. "Life is a struggle," he went on, "where success is only relative, and all sanctity is torn off of him; where failure and humiliation, the exposure of weaknesses, and the unmasking of pretence, are assured incidents." And so, a man

longs for one tranquil spot where he shall be valid absolutely and once for all; where, having been accepted, he is secure from further criticism, and where his good aspirations may be respected no less than if they were accomplished realities. In a word, the elements of security and repose are essential to his ideal; and the question is, Are they easily attainable without some feeling of dependence on the woman's side.

In other words: can a man trying to find his way in post–Civil War America do without the support and refuge that is Woman?

James says no in several voices. Bushnell is quoted at length as saying no, but saying it too dogmatically. Other, more judicious voices say no by saying yes to marriages that disallow autonomy and mutual respect. One voice defends love as "that flattering interplay of instincts," with egotism on one hand and "self-sacrifice on the other." Another points out that a "hierarchical arrangement" may not be what one expects in a friendship, but it is what one expects in a marriage. James cannot imagine things otherwise.

And then there was the question of sex. The father had objected to Mill's omission of it. Without sex there would be no "spiritual sanction" for marriage, no reason for a man to marry at all were it not for the possibility of his overcoming his animal nature by doing so. His son speaks of men's controlling their brutish energies by entering into a bizarre kind of social contract. Bushnell had described a state of affairs in which in exchange for little civilizing acts of "gallantry and chivalry," women agree not to try to change their status. We give our seats to ladies on the train, for example, on the understanding that they not interfere "in larger affairs." Were they to break that agreement, as

William James, c. 1890.
*Houghton Library, Harvard
University*

Extending the *frontier* by
rail and by wagon.
A. J. Russell, TRAIN ON
EMBANKMENT, GRANITE
CANYON, 1868–70. *The
Beinecke Rare Book and
Manuscript Library, Yale
University*

Striking workers versus the militia in poses that would serve in depictions of contemporary wars and athletic contests. GIVING THE BUTT, 1894. *Frederick Remington Art Museum*

Manhood and the Market. WALL STREET, 1915. *Paul Strand*

William James,
late 1860s.

Henry James, Sr.,
mid-1870s.

Alice James, c. 1870.

Oliver Wendell Holmes, Jr., 1872.
Harvard University Archives

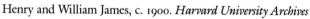

Alice Howe Gibbens, James' wife-to-be, 1872.
Houghton Library, Harvard University

Charles W. Eliot, the new president of Harvard. "We have a real captain at last," James Russell Lowell to Charles Eliot Norton, December, 1869. *Harvard University Archives*

Henry and William James, c. 1900. *Harvard University Archives*

"In memory of the sons of Harvard who died for their country." Memorial Hall, dedicated in 1874.

Hemenway Gymnasium, 1878.

Dudley Sargent, professor of physical training and director of the Hemenway Gymnasium.

Sargent's apparatus in the Hemenway Gymnasium.

Students' room at Harvard, 1870s.

Harvard University Archives photos

Going to the Harvard-Yale game, 1887.

Class Day, Harvard Yard, 1895. A few months earlier, James delivered his lecture, "Is Life Worth Living?"

IKEY—Ven ve die, vere do you t'ink ve shall go, Patsy?
PATSY—I'm t'inkin' we'll aich foller our noses, Ikey.
Diversity at Harvard. *The Harvard Lampoon* cover, January 11, 1900.

James puts it, "if they become our rivals in these latter, we shall no longer scruple to push them to the wall wherever we find them." It is a gruesome version of Bushnell's proposition. Bushnell says: I yield my seat to you on the train, and you agree not to ask to vote to seat people in positions of power. James adds: if you go ahead and ask, you could unleash "the mere animal potency of sex." Bushnell, like Mill, had left sex out. To James it is so disturbing, so ominous a force that the very existence of a woman precludes his ever fully expressing it—from ever pushing a woman to the wall. "An individual man, however his interests may clash with those of an individual woman, will always shrink from appearing personally like a brute in her presence." As a gentleman, instinctively he would never lose control over himself in the presence of a lady. This assumes that she remains a lady, a retiring, dependent being. Were she to be out in the world, intensifying the competition, depriving a man of security and solace, there is no telling what he would become, or what he might do.

However un-"Victorian" many Victorians may have been, James himself seems to have been extremely skittish about sex throughout his life. It was not something he talked about with any ease. What he called in *The Principles of Psychology* "the *anti-sexual instinct,* the instinct of personal isolation, the actual repulsiveness to us of the idea of intimate contact with most of the persons we meet" acted as a censor in him. The struggle may have been intense because of the very power of his sexual energy (the "strongest passion of all," he called it), but his *"anti-sexual instinct"* was every bit as strong. He devoted very little attention to sexual matters in his monumental opus. After a few paragraphs in the chapter called "Instincts," he said, "These details are a little unpleasant to discuss," and moved on. His only other consideration of sexuality in the *Principles* occurs in a paragraph on animal behavior in his discussion of the functions of the brain, a consideration that leads him to conclude, "No one need be told how dependent all human social elevation is upon the prevalence of chastity. Hardly any factor measures more than this the difference between civilization and barbarism."[19] Neither passage survived the transition from the *Principles* to the shorter, more popular *Psychology: Briefer Course,* which James published two years later.

As a teacher, James did take on the subject. Chapman reports of hearing him lecture on sex to his freshman class. What could a man say on that occasion, Chapman wondered in retrospect. He could not be "coldly philosophical," or humorous, or religious, or "purely scientific and medical." What he remembers of the occasion is a James who was "quite young then, and very severe." He "left on me a strong impression of stoicism," Chapman said.[20] In the *Principles,* James made chastity *the* measure of civilization. Surely his manner conveyed some such message to the freshmen. Hutchins Hapgood tells of being surprised many years later to hear James begin a lecture with the question "Why is it that a perfectly respectable man may dream that he has intercourse with his grandmother?" A stunning remark, but as Hapgood goes on to suggest, the recorded fact was left hanging in the air. James was too attached to the conventional: "in his conscious waking life, James seemed to be ruled, not only in his conduct but also in his moral values, by the conduct-standards of the community."[21] He was not one to analyze the meaning of such a dream.

In 1894, and then again in 1896, in his Lowell Lectures, published as *Exceptional Mental States,* James would respectfully notice Freud's early work on hysteria, but so far as we know, he never took any interest in what followed.[22] Temperamentally he could not have been open to Freud's ideas, or to put it historically, he was just too late. His student, and later combatant in the field of psychology, G. Stanley Hall, reported that James had called Freud "a dirty fellow."[23] In *The Principles of Psychology,* it was the recurrence of dreams that interested James, not their content; and he was too much the scientist to rely on symbolic readings of otherwise unverifiable experience.

As a young instructor—having found and learned how to follow the method, the "form," of his actions that would make a chaste and productive life possible—he was the more resistant to any interpretation of his dreams. And so, with his father's guidance, he made his way toward marriage. His father had provided the general definition of the ideal wife. When she appeared in real life, she did so in the most appropriate way imaginable: his father found her for him.

One evening, in the winter of 1876, Henry James Sr. came home from a meeting of the Radical Club on Chestnut Street in Boston and announced that he had met the woman his eldest son would marry. The club's membership included the more advanced Transcendental and Unitarian thinkers of the day. He himself had lectured to them on several occasions. When he had spoken on marriage, he had said of a suitable wife that she should be able "to quicken in [her husband's] heart a flame of chaste, interior, spiritual tenderness, such as no other sexual tie would ever have evoked."[24] When he met Alice Gibbens, she struck him as a woman who was eminently qualified to do that for his son. At the next club meeting, James was introduced to his future wife by his friend Thomas Davidson, and he went forward, assured by his father that if he would marry Alice Gibbens, financial support would be forthcoming.[25]

Alice Howe Gibbens was a stolid woman, twenty-seven at the time, who was a teacher at Miss Sanger's School for Girls, in Boston. She had long since proven her ability to take care of others. At the age of sixteen, her rakish father having died (presumably by his own hand) and her mother having totally collapsed, she had assumed responsibility for the welfare of her one remaining parent and her two younger sisters, guiding them first to Europe, where it was cheaper to live, and then back to Boston. Speaking of his parents' meeting, Henry James III later wrote, "Mother had never encountered anything remotely resembling his incandescent, tormented, mercurial excitability."[26] But she was prepared and more than willing to broaden the reach of her powers to save.

Their courtship lasted two years—or rather, having herself decided that she too had met her husband upon their first meeting, Alice persevered for two years while James came to terms with the idea of marriage. His first communication, dated March 19, 1876, is crammed on both sides of four postcards and a calling card. In it, James clearly described the parts husband and wife would play in marriage as he defined it. As his father had said again and again, Man was meant for spiritual regeneration, and it was Woman's calling to make that possible. He told her he himself was going against the conventional way of the world, the way "*officially* recognized by society," in wanting to marry her, because he did not meet "the standard of wholesomeness." One of the "crimes against the law" was "the marriage of unhealthy persons." But, he said, his thinking about marrying could be justified "by an appeal to some metaphysical world 'behind the veil' whose life such events may be supposed to feed."[27] He was overcoming his fears about his nerves, his back, about his "moral" being as he had probed it in his Diary a few years before. In two years he would be satisfied: Alice Gibbens enabled him to dispel his doubts about his body and his soul. "Every doctor I have ever spoken to has said that matrimony ought to be the best possible mode of life, for me," he told his brother Bob. "Alice Gibbens is an angel if ever there was one—I take her for her moral more than her intellectual qualities."[28]

In his first, long letter he described to Alice how she might assist him in a combined effort to enrich life "behind the veil." They would be wandering from "the outward order that keeps the world so sweet," and thus throwing themselves upon what he now called "the *Tragical*." To subscribe to what he would call "The Religion of Healthy-Mindedness" in *The Varieties of Religious Experience,* "to abandon [his] private spiritual advancement for the sake of obeying a natural average rule," would be "worse than a *crime* against nature"; it would be "a *sin* against the holy ghost—metaphorically speaking." He was not going to do that. "*Pereat mundus!* I say, I stand by my own soul," he wrote in the margin. So at the very outset he posed this question: was she prepared?

Now if the case come up with reference to matrimony, and I feel that it is a case of this kind, well and good for me! But if the other person through heedlessness, superficiality, or insensibility slide into the natural crime, without the imperative spiritual need which alone can make it be forgiven what thanks has she? She falls a prey to the Tragical, this time without atonement. Thus she must not take me unless she find it spiritually laid upon her as a tragic duty, to do so.

Were she to join him without a full appreciation of the stakes, it would be tragic in the more mundane sense of the word; if she understood, as he said in subsequent letters, she would be in a position to "serve the Universe."

From such exhilaration James lapsed in the following months into questionings about his venture, even about his mental stability. Longing for her, he would then absent himself, and then once away from her be drawn to her from a distance. When a friend of Alice's tried to lure her away on a trip to England in an effort to make her reconsider, he spoke harshly of the friend but then encouraged her to go. Few of us are at our best in the throes of love ("a monomania to which all of us are subject," James called it in *The Principles of Psychology*),[29] but James took his need for a "fight" and for the suffering it could involve to extremes. Of course he was excited when he fell in love with Alice, but six months later he seemed as thrilled by the prospect of being rejected by her—of the "negation" of him. "Blessed be the nature of things, blessed be misfortune that permits us to taste so really, so deeply the unfathomable Good!" If love was a disease, it would not poison him, but rather save his soul. His would not be a *Liebestod* but an embrace of his own death—"I will feed on death and the negation of me in one place shall be the affirmation of me in a better"—and he thanked her for her "undivided work" in making that possible.[30] We do not know how she responded to his gratitude, but however she did, he remained confident of his vision. She might not see things his way at first, she might detect "a certain aridity and bleakness of mind" in him, but, he said, "My thoughts have a *broader* scope than yours, so that it will take some time for me, especially as I am so awkward about it, to extricate them for you *as a whole*."[31] At one point he declared, "I should not scruple to sacrifice you," and then reviled himself for what had at first seemed "a masterly thing to contemplate."[32] When she tired of being positioned in his scheme of things, tired of what she perceived to be the oppressiveness of his and his father's theories, he wrote back telling her not to speak of her pain and her perplexities—"And do not speak of my *'doctrines,'* " he said; "they are only provisional perceptions of the facts of life."[33]

Just before their wedding, in a well-known letter, having established the terms of their future marriage, he provided her with a crystalline definition of himself. "The best way to define a man's character would be to seek out the particular mental or moral attitude in which, when it came upon him, he felt himself most deeply and intensely active and alive," he wrote in June 1878.[34] "At such moments there is a voice inside which speaks and says: '*This* is the real me!' " In his case the voice told of

an element of active tension, of holding my own, as it were, and trusting outward things to perform their part so as to make it a full harmony, but without any *guaranty* that they will. Make it a guaranty—and the attitude immediately becomes to my consciousness stagnant and stingless. Take away the guaranty, and I feel (provided I am *überhaupt* [generally] in vigorous condition) a sort of deep enthusiastic bliss, of bitter willingness to do and suffer anything.

The tension, he went on to say, translated itself into physical symptoms, into "a kind of stinging pain inside my breast-bone," and then, imagining her response, he cautioned her: "(don't smile at this—it is to me an essential element of the whole thing!)" It was "the deepest principle of all active and theoretic determination which I possess." And in fact, recourse to this letter can illuminate almost everything he wrote and did. It not only clarifies James' assumptions about himself as a man but also presages his death. As we will see, twenty years later the "stinging pains" took the form of lesions in his heart. The "deepest principle," the tensions and the struggles by which he lived, eventually killed him.

In his marriage, the required tension took the form of what James had referred to in his review of Bushnell and Mill as the "flattering interplay" of egotism and self-sacrifice. Around the first anniversary of their meeting, he wrote to her, "To have you recognize me, to have your truth acquiesce in my better self, form hence forward the only possible goal of my conscious life. You *will* do it—you will value me, care for me."[35] Five months later, he refined his definition of the role she had assumed. "I approach more and more the conclusion that the mission of your sex is not to originate but to judge—to distinguish the better from the worse when they have it offered them. . . . It shows how deeply a man needs the corroboration of the woman whom he respects, how something is missing until he gets it."[36] His summation of who he was in being married to her followed exactly from the way he situated her as his wife: putting it somatically, he said he was "that poor diseased boy whom you raised up from the dust"; putting it psychologically or spiritually, he said she had "redeemed [his] life from destruction."[37]

The modesty required of her precluded her ever saying she had saved his life, but in *her* summation of their marriage she came as close as she could. After James died, she told their friend Fanny Morse that she had tried "to make [her] life serve his, to stand between him and all harmful things."[38] She would never consider her "self-sacrifice" complete, but it was the ideal toward which she strove. Hers was "a quiet life of helping you," she told him in 1882.[39] She might fret when she compared herself to the "attractive, cultivated men and women" her husband associated with, but she was comforted by her reading of the apostle of Unitarianism, William Ellery Channing, who said that "elevation of soul can be had anywhere in any calling if we only work for it."[40] In January 1883 she declared, "I want to feel my responsibility a thousand times more keenly from *hour to hour,* not in general."[41]

James acknowledged and was deeply grateful for such caring, such generosity, but he also felt oppressed. He put the case directly to his friend Chapman. "As for will, freedom and the like, ask Mrs. Chapman," he wrote. "A young husband has neither will nor freedom."[42] He communicated this reading of marriage to Alice in a variety of ways. Whenever a child was born, and at Christmas and on other holidays as well, he fled to the Adirondacks or to Chocorua or abroad. If Alice went so far as to talk of joining him, she quickly withdrew the suggestion: "My idea of the quiet spot in which I should spend the summer with you in England or Wales as we used to plan sometimes is not worth seriously thinking about. It is true that it would make a dull summer for you."[43] Ten years later, she wrote to him in Germany, saying she would try to exercise more self-control, that she cared only for him, that she had grown so hard to live with, and then on the eve of Christmas, 1893, she put the situation in simple, conventional terms that she understood and accepted: "the lack of you is like missing the air I breathe, and just how keen a want it is I think you will never imagine because you are a man and not a woman."[44] In 1905, she told him of having dreams of "wandering in difficult places"—in the most recent, she had been making her way "over a trellis work built above the water"—and of always "carrying in my arms a baby, whose I know not, a weak ailing child whom I cannot get rid of or lay to rest." Typically, she took "this grief child" to be James or her family, and worried about what the dream might bode for them.[45] But we have to wonder how she felt about her own life, about the life that she could take so little time to nurture.

If the burden of their marriage weighed heavily on her, this was just how it should be, according to his father. And the son allowed himself to think: most women wanted it this way. Combating one or another illness at Bad Nauheim in the fall of 1900, he doubted that the latest water treatment was doing him any good, and wondered whether he was not enduring it solely for the pleasure of being obedient. James told their friend Fanny Morse about what he was feeling: "Just as in most women there is a wife that craves to suffer and submit and be bullied, so in most men there is a *patient* that needs to have a doctor and obey his orders, whether they be believed in or not."[46] The psychologist had taken people's enjoyment of submission one step further: he had observed that most women *craved* suffering.

It is not surprising that James greatly admired his brother's novel on "the situation of women," *The Bostonians* (1886). He had some of the trouble he often had with his brother's prose (the story might have been reduced to "a bright, short, sparkling thing of a hundred pages, which would have been an absolute success"), but he had read all five hundred pages, had read the novel "in the full flamingness of its bulk," and considered it "an exquisite production." No reader has ever been as appreciative of its poor, vapid heroine, the girl who is coached by feminists to be their most persuasive voice, but who succumbs, in the end, to the anti-feminist rhetoric of a former Confederate soldier named Basil Ransom. "There isn't a hair wrong in Verena," he said, "you've made her neither too little nor too much—but absolutely *liebenswürdig* [amiable]." He knew that the "moral situation" in which she had to choose between "Woman's rights and Ransom" was "deep," and he delighted in the outcome. He thought Ransom came alive "handsomely"; his *"fancy"* was "tickled by R.'s victory being complete."[47] He did not notice Henry's efforts to distance himself from his "very provincial . . . panting young man," but instead embraced Ransom's conclusions, not only his attacks on "the damnable feminization" of the age but presumably his brutal vows to silence Verena as well. James imagined none of the difficulties his brother had in trying to understand what he called "the most salient and peculiar point in our social life."[48]

In the presence of the two brothers, the worst of readers can resist reductive theories of sibling rivalry. But when it came to the question of men's lives, especially to the question of men's marrying, William was himself terribly reductive. In marriage, and about marriage, William was on the defensive. He resisted the encroachments of his wife and the entanglements of domesticity; on the other hand, he was critical of men who did not rise to the challenge of marriage—and of men, like himself, who delayed too long.[49] His brother Henry's novel was about the second civil war, the one that was going on between men and women as he wrote. It was a version of what George Fredrickson has called "the inner Civil War," the war veterans and non-veterans alike waged to preserve American manhood and to display it in everyday life.[50] Henry himself stood apart from it—amused, perplexed, ultimately inconclusive. But his brother William was in the thick of the struggle—proud, adamant, sometimes frustrated, sometimes angry, often militant, often in retreat.

Henry was quite sure that he would never marry. His response to William's announcement of his intentions was "I believe almost as much in matrimony for most other people as I believe in it little for myself—which is saying a good deal."[51] Their mother's vision of him in that state ("You would make dear Harry according to my estimate, the most loving and loveable and happiest of husbands")[52] can only have diminished the likelihood. Having taken the step himself, William was confirmed in his own mind that he was the more manly of the two. If there is any place where talk of their rivalry makes sense, it is in this arena—in James' assertions of the superior masculinity that was his for having married.

William tired of the family's referring to Henry as the "angel." When their sister did it, he told Henry he searched his imagination for "something very 'oriental.' " What that clearly means in *The Principles of Psychology* is: sexually perverse. "Modern Orientals" and "ancients" are fond of "unnatural vice," he said in the chapter on instinct—the notion of which "affects us with horror."[53] Alice appropriately greeted his implicit name-calling with "a tirade upon the petty jealousies of *men*."[54] The rivalry and the sexual innuendos were shrouded in jest, but when William's wife expressed the difficulties she had in getting to know her brother-in-law, William was more direct: "Yes, Harry is a queer boy," he intoned, "so good, and yet so limited, as if he had taken an oath not to let himself out to more than half of his humanhood, in order to keep the other half from suffering." He had taunted his younger brother years and years before with the fact that *he* played with boys. His message to his wife was still the same: Henry was less than a man, he did not live life the way *men* lived life. "Queer" may mean nothing but queer in his letter, but his attitude toward his brother had its physical, sexual undertones, as it did when he told his brother in 1892 that he had been thinking of their parents and of how little they had appreciated the difficulties of their lives. The moral was: "You skinny bachelors know nothing of the thickness of life."[55] Not that it was necessary, but the next year, in a letter to his brother, he made the gender implications of such comparisons specific. "There is a strange thinness and femininity hovering over all America," he wrote, "so different from the stoutness and masculinity of land and air and everything in Switzerland and England."[56] Assumptions about William's superior masculinity have prevailed ever since. Even the medical profession contributed with its physical "proof."*

In his lecture titled "Saintliness" (and with the kind of insight that has often prompted his readers to say that he too should have written novels), James reflected on a "mode of emotional excitability" that he thought was "exceedingly important in the composition of the energetic character." It took the form of "irascibility, susceptibility to wrath, the fighting temper," or, more subtly, "impatience, grimness, earnestness, severity of character." As if looking in a mirror, he generalized: "Earnestness means willingness to live with energy, though energy bring pain. The pain may be pain to other people or pain to one's self—it makes little difference; for when the strenuous mood is on one, the aim is to break something, no matter whose or what." And heaven be praised for such emotions, he says, for without them we drift. We take "a stern joy in the astringency and desolation" of these "sacrificial moods" in which "one's own inferior self and its pet softnesses must often be the targets and the victims." In a footnote he adds, "The career of a man beset by . . . an all-round amiability is hopeless."[57]

---

*A doctor whom Henry consulted declared that he had "an enormous amalgam of the feminine in his make-up; he displayed many of the characteristics of adult infantilism." It turned out that his "amatory coefficient was comparatively low; his gonadal sweep was narrow." *The Notebooks*, p. 328.

Not far below this surface image, we can discover the man who had taken an unusually long time deciding on a career, who would always be known for his geniality, who had channeled his energy, willed himself into action, and then, when he had finally married, had become the clearer about his need for greater effort in the face of more resistance. Should softnesses appear—his own or others'—sacrifices might have to be made, especially when one was in "the strenuous mood." "Softnesses" were easily sacrificed for the joy—the "stern joy in the astringency and desolation"—that one experienced.

Alice was inclined to castigate herself for draining her husband's energies or being hard to live with. The cost of standing up to him was great. When she did, their son reported, James "would pass from surprise to bewilderment, to excitement, to desperation." Sometimes he would explode, and "there was Mother, holding her ground in the face of thunder, lightning and universal disintegration, her face flushed, tears finally rolling down her cheeks."[58] On one occasion William brought home an oil painting which he thought had been a bargain, but which Alice considered an extravagance. "Oh, William, how *could* you!" she exclaimed, whereupon he took the scissors and cut the picture into shreds. William told their friend Elizabeth Glendower Evans about the incident, who calmly relayed it to readers of the *Atlantic* with no gloss on his final observation: " 'And will you believe me,' he said in telling me the story, 'that when I destroyed the picture Alice wept!' " Elizabeth Evans also told of Alice's objections to his upsetting their daughter by talking of an imminent departure in front of her. "When Peggy would go to bed, she would scream and scream with terror that she was to be left, she did not know when or where." When Alice pointed to the effects of his remarks, he would agree, but then say, " 'Well, Alice, that's the sort of people we are; so let's be hearty about it!' "[59] Their son Henry said of her, "she thought she had found the right way to consecrate herself to Father's welfare, and that made life seem holier and brought Heaven nearer." Accordingly, he ends his account of her with words on sainthood that *she* had copied out. "Why were the saints saints?" her quotation began. Because saints were cheerful and silent and agreeable when they wanted to be the opposite. "It was quite simple and always will be," the quotation ends, to which the young Henry added, "I have no doubt that she appreciated the irony of the final sentence."[60]

We know that at least once James released some of his erotic energy, for he confessed this to his wife. Out of the blue he had kissed Lizzy, the housemaid. To have repressed his feelings, he told Alice, would have seemed "churlish and inhuman."[61] But his expressions of interest in other women were more likely to be epistolary. Of the women with whom James corresponded, at least three seem to have been attractive to him, Elizabeth Evans and Sarah Whitman, both friends of his and Alice's, and Pauline Goldmark, a Bryn Mawr student whom he met in the Adirondacks in 1895. To the first he confessed he had "stirrings of romantic appreciation of [her] character,"[62] but as is often the case with James, he kills speculation with his frankness. (What Elizabeth Evans was doing publishing stories in the *Atlantic* like those above—publishing them, moreover, in an article on what she calls "the happiest and most harmonious family to be imagined"—is impossible to know.) There is talk of meetings in Sarah Whitman's letters to him, and his brother Henry thought of a story based on William's conviction that she ought to have left her "common, inferior" husband.[63] It all seems harmless enough, but when Alice became upset, he defended his "flirtation." He did so more out of impatience with her, it would seem—and perhaps with "Mrs. W.'s" natterings—than out of any need to cover his tracks: "You may say she's artificial, and an upstart, and what you like," he wrote, "but she has the real bottom thing in her, and in the long run I bet on her against the whole field, and I love her dearly—there!"[64]

James described Pauline Goldmark as "on the whole the finest girl I know, for general character," "quite my ideal," potentially "the best wife of any girl I know," and the like.[65] He was well aware that these were the dotings of a much older man, but that is also to suggest that they were more, rather than less, consuming than any other flirtations. More specifically, he always associated Pauline with the Keene Valley where they met—and where he and Alice had gone after their wedding. She was the spirit of the woods, the wilderness incarnate; in this role, though she was a Bryn Mawr student (and eventually secretary of the National Consumer's League), she appeared to him to be "ultra simple in mind."[66] He imagined her in both courtly (roseate) and sexual (bestial) terms: "I have been happy, *happy, happy!*—with the exquisite imperishable beauty of the place," he wrote his wife from Keene Valley. "Nature has made it for falling in love in, passing honeymoons and the like. There is a perfect little serious rosebud of a Miss Goldmark . . . who climbs like a monkey."[67] In the many letters he wrote Pauline over the next fifteen years, he imagined her being with him or his being where she was, he treasured mementos of her, and he invoked her invigorating energy, invoked it the more desperately as he feared that his was waning: *"keep me informed of your changes of address continuously and as soon as you know them yourself."* Towards the end of his life, he wrote, "How I wish, Pauline, that we lived nearer together, so as to meet everyday, as it were, and talk humdrumically."[68] The climax of their relationship came, as it came for Ibsen's Master Builder, when he tried to arrest time, to prove to the young woman that he was still a vigorous man. He was climbing mountains and not steeples (like Ibsen's Solness), but the result was the same.

In the summer of 1898, James invited Pauline and others of her family to join him for an ascent of Mount Marcy, the highest of the Adirondack peaks.

The night they all spent together at their meeting place was, he wrote Alice, "one of the most memorable of all my memorable experiences." The setting, the company, "the wholesomeness of the people round [him,] especially the good Pauline," the thought of his family and the Gifford Lectures coming up, all "fermented within [him] till it became a regular Walpurgis Nacht." He lay near Pauline for a while, but at about three he started wandering in the moonlight, imagining a meeting of the gods, thinking about "the intense inhuman remoteness of its inner life, and yet the intense *appeal* of it" and (ever the hostage of his racing intellect) thinking too about "its utter Americanism, and every sort of patriotic suggestiveness." Wordsworth's *Prelude* account of crossing the Alps figured in, as did, more importantly, the Witches' Sabbath to which Mephistopheles led Faust before his seduction of Gretchen. His thoughts reverted to his wife, and he concluded, "It was one of the happiest lonesome nights of my existence, and I understand now what a poet is."[69]

What did not survive his son's editing of the letter for publication was James' account of the "arduous 2nd day." On that day he had let his guide carry the young women's gear and so had added to his own load what the guide had been hired to carry. In noting his omission, Henry James III had two comments to make: his mother, who did not find Pauline Goldmark sympathetic in the first place, could never forgive her for this; and "this adventure was what first strained W. J.'s heart."[70] (He might also have noted that exactly a year later James got lost in the same setting and turned a three hours' descent into "a seven-hours' scramble" that he described to Pauline as doing him "no good.")[71] What his son meant by the first strain was that his father's overexertion caused a valvular lesion in his heart that would eventually bring about his death. What we can also say is that James' efforts to prove himself a man, a gentleman, an outdoorsman, and to prove himself in the presence of weaker figures, were bad for the heart.

Alice—the most fragile of the Jameses—and Henry were mutually devoted, but her relations with William were never simply supportive. His teasing over the years about her physical appearance, and about her chances of marrying, was disturbingly seductive. The fact that one of her severest breakdowns occurred when she realized he was going to marry Alice Gibbens may reflect his insensitivity; it may also indicate that she harbored expectations that could never be met, that her love was one that no brother could return.[72] But whatever the portioning of responsibility, in his expressions of affection and concern for his sister, William—in comparison with Henry—was clearly the more masculine as well as the older brother, the one she initially tried to emulate and later, when he seemed insufficiently attentive to her, the one she shrewdly and bitterly criticized.

"The constructive, without the imaginative," Alice once pointed out, "sometimes leads to the destructive." The occasion of her noting this was seemingly mundane—nothing more than William's handling of her furniture after she went to live in England. Whereas she had left specific instructions about which items to store, which to lend or give away, William had simply kept those that he could use and stored the rest. He had been inconsiderate, failing to give enough thought to her intentions and wishes, Alice wrote his wife. The reason he had been as "destructive" as he was lay in his being so "constructive"—which is to say, he worked so hard to make up the life he led that he ignored the lives of others.[73] Only families can move from arguments over small things like furniture to such large language, but the leap was made easier by Alice's intimate understanding of her brother's temperament. In the Diary that he kept during the crisis years, he had "posited" life and thereby made it real, posited it specifically as "the self-governing *resistance* of the ego to the world." She understood because she agreed: in 1890, in *her* Diary, she expressed her gratitude for having a "temperament" that saved her from the fate of those "who never find their bearings, but are tossed like dryed leaves hither, thither and yon at the mercy of every event which o'ertakes them . . . who never dimly suspect that the only thing which survives is the resistance we bring to life and not the strain life brings to us."[74] Even so, in her condition she was not about to assume that the manly resistance to neurasthenia that had worked for him would automatically work for her.

When he characterized her invalidism as "slowly stifling in a quagmire of disgust and pain and impotence!" and fell back on Carlyle (" 'Silence,' as Carlyle would say, must cover the pity I feel"), she threw his words back at him, noting that she and her companion Katharine Loring had had a good laugh when they received his letter, and asserting that she would manage very well on her own, thank you. "I consider myself one of the most *potent* creations of my time," she wrote. "Though I may not have a group of Harvard students sitting at my feet drinking in psychic truth, I shall not tremble, I assure you, at the last trump."[75]

At the end of her life she was even harsher. Again like him, she saw herself enacting her own life, her performance becoming the more interesting as her death approached. Foreseeing the end doubled its value, she wrote, "for one becomes suddenly picturesque to oneself, and one's wavering little individuality stands out with a cameo effect." But she thought William would not understand. She felt sorry for Katharine and her brother Henry because they would have to witness her performance, whereas she would only have to *feel* it. But she was not worried about them. They were taking her dying "like archangels," and cared for her "with infinite tenderness and patience." William was not to know about her condition, she wrote in her Diary: "Poor dear

William with his exaggerated sympathy for suffering isn't to know anything about it until it is all over." William's sympathies would be misplaced, she thought, they would be too principled, or redound too much upon himself, and this she could not bear. He was also wont to interject his "openness" to the idea of other states of being, the kind of thing he talked to his students about, and she was much too grounded in the here and now to think of such possibilities.

In fact, she relented. The day before she died, she whispered a message to Henry that was to be wired to William: "Tenderest love to all farewell am going soon." Even so, after her death, William wired back, warning Henry that Alice's death might be an illusion. As he later explained, "her neurotic temperament and chronically reduced vitality are just the field for trance-tricks to play themselves upon."[76]

During the crisis years, and adding to their gravity, another fragile young woman—the James' beloved cousin Minny Temple—died of consumption. On a page of his Diary, William blocked out a gravestone with her initials and the date of her death on it: March 9, 1870. On the following page he made a vow to her: "By that big part of me that's in the tomb with you," he would believe in the immediacy of death, and inspired by it, he would go out to meet the tragedy that was "at the heart of us" rather than dodge it or be run down by it. He concluded, "*Use* your death (or your life, it's all one meaning)." In the face of her death, the task of making something of his life was the more urgent, his physical and moral and practical failure up to that point all the more shameful. But it was the spring of 1870. He had begun to discover the bases on which he could move forward, and he had applied them to Minny. As she had reported to her friend John Gray just before she died, "Willy James sometimes tells me to behave like a man and a gentleman if I wish to outwit fate."

There was no irony in what she said, no irony at all. In fact, her adoration, like Gertrude Stein's twenty-five years later, knew no bounds. "What a *real* person he is!" she went on. "He is to me in nearly all respects a head and shoulders above other people." She said he was one of the few people in the world she loved, adding, "He has the largest heart as well as the largest head, and is thoroughly interesting to me."[77]

Nothing was ever further from William James' intentions than to be unsympathetic to anyone. Of all the essays he ever wrote, his favorite was "On a Certain Blindness in Human Beings." He recommended it to Pauline Goldmark, saying, "What horrifies me in life is our brutal ignorance of one another."[78] He wanted nothing more than to understand and cure people's insensitivity to each other—their lack of imagination. In a later chapter we will follow his thinking on the subject. Suffice it for now to repeat: in willing into being the kind of man he felt he had to be, in getting into fighting trim, so to speak, he was less imaginative about others than he knew he ought to be.

Reflecting on her anger over the furniture, Alice told her sister-in-law that she could easily imagine her brother's surprise. He had meant no harm, and she must have seemed, she said, "like some Fury descending into the blue of the serene and simple atmosphere which surrounds all his personal relations." He cared deeply for others, and he was loved and admired by almost everyone who knew or read him. He worked so hard at being virtuous that to many he was something of a saint. But there are costs to any man who is as intent as James was on working out his own salvation. As Orwell reminds us (in speaking of Gandhi), all saints are guilty until proven innocent. And in fact, James himself knew how far he was from sainthood. Wittily, insightfully, he observed upon his retirement in 1907 that he had spent his entire life trying to be good, but that he had succeeded in becoming only great.[79]

Insofar as he *was* a saint, he was what John Jay Chapman called him: "a saint in chains."[80] What Chapman meant was that the light of Christianity could penetrate James' metaphorical cell only through a few chinks that he himself had made. But as we have seen, the metaphor goes way back to when James was working out a more existential salvation, trying to free himself from the prison of his recalcitrant body, from indecision, from despondency and despair. God might help, but only after James had disciplined himself to become a particular kind of man and thereby proven himself worthy of support.

He was in distinguished and powerful company as he worked out his fate. He represented the institution that he served, and it, in turn, worked out a most influential way to prepare students to be "men of the world." On many occasions, Harvard recognized James' contributions. When Charles William Eliot and Harvard celebrated the twenty-fifth anniversary of his presidency, for example, James wrote him a congratulatory letter. Recalling how James had been a chemistry student of his at the Lawrence Scientific School, Eliot began his reply: "You carry me back farther than anybody else—to 1861." Eliot went on to acknowledge that at the time he already had some of the powers he now possessed but that he had "little range of observation, no breadth of experience, and small capacity for sympathetic imagination." It was as if they had been walking a common path, a path that he knew did not go straight into the minds and hearts of others. But Eliot now thought that they had "the same fundamental reason for being moderately content with the years that are past." After reflecting on the university and his own role in its development, Eliot turned James' compliment around: "Your coming to the

University and your career as a teacher and writer have been among my most solid grounds of satisfaction."[81]

We will return to James' career at Harvard, but first we must consider the educational developments that occurred at the institution itself during the years of Eliot's presidency, developments that contributed mightily to the making of modern American manhood.

2

Teaching Men Manhood at Harvard

IN SEPTEMBER 1902, for his last column as University editor of the *Harvard Graduates' Magazine,* Albert Bushnell Hart of the History Department chose to write on "Harvard manhood." "Teaching men manhood," he said at the outset, was a difficult subject to discuss, because it was "not a matter of record on the College books." But elusive as it was, it was clearly an important and nameable topic, and Hart approached it from several angles. By the end of his short piece, having cast his eye back to the year 1875 (when he himself had entered Harvard as a freshman), he could assure his readers that while the culture was undergoing momentous transformations, their alma mater had succeeded in strengthening "Harvard manhood."[1]

Of all the changes, the first that he noted was numerical. In 1875, there had been about 750 undergraduates, 141 of them in the senior class. Not everybody graduated in those days. In his inaugural address six years before, President Eliot had warned, "It must not be supposed that every student necessarily graduates. . . . More than a fourth of those who enter the College fail to take their degree."[2] In 1902, the undergraduate body had grown to about 2,000, with around 450 in the graduating class.

Nationally, increasing numbers involved—most dramatically—increasing numbers of immigrants. At Harvard the influx found expression in a population that came from strikingly diverse backgrounds. Whereas 135 members of the Class of 1875 had "unmistakable English names" (and three of the others "were probably of English-speaking families"), in the class of 1902 you would find Germans, Irishmen, Scandinavians, "and some Slavs and Latins"—which is to say, too, many Catholics and Jews. (You could also find African-Americans—in fact, probably the best student Hart ever had was W. E. B. Du Bois—but he did not mention them.) The number of students coming from homes with little or no "tradition of intellectual life"—from homes where financial and social survival was more important than learning—had also increased, but among these newcomers many had distinguished themselves at Harvard, Hart said, and he was confident that they would "take their places in the world" and then send their sons to Harvard. In spite of the changes in the ethnic and social composition of the student body, in other words, things remained essentially the same. Harvard was successfully responding to the enormous social changes taking place in post–Civil War America. The faces and the names may have been different, but the prevailing manner and purpose of a Harvard education were not.

From Hart's vantage point, though much had changed since he and his readers were undergraduates, Harvard was fulfilling its essential mission: it was still producing men of sound moral character. "The moral quality of the Harvard man is sound and hopeful," he said. To him that meant, more specifically, that Harvard was continuing to produce gentle, or cultured, men. Hart made the point by focusing on one professor—Charles Eliot Norton of the Fine Arts Department. Students were still taking his courses, coming to hear him discourse not just on the fine arts but, as the title of his most famous offering had it, on "the history of the fine arts as related to society and general culture." Norton felt that the goal of education could not be directly reached through anyone's teaching. It was "the consummation of all studies," he wrote in 1895, "the final result of intellectual culture in the development of the breadth, serenity, and solidity of mind," ultimately "in the attainment of that complete self-possession which finds expression in character."[3] It was a matter of deportment, of all that one knew and, more important, of how one carried one's knowledge and oneself. Though he might not be able to teach whatever it was that made a man educated, Norton could represent it. He was cultured, he was a gentleman, and he would address his students as gentlemen—and then he might add (for he loved to tease), "As I speak these words the realization comes over me that no one here has ever seen a gentleman."

Norton was a popular and renowned figure.[4] In 1892, while an undergraduate, Edwin Arlington Robinson considered him "by all odds the greatest man in America."[5] He had translated Dante, edited the correspondence of Carlyle and Emerson and Lowell, and published the letters he himself had received from Ruskin. In the more public sphere, he was an editor of one of the leading quarterlies of the day, the *North American Review,* and he was one of the founders of the *Nation.* He stood firmly against imperialism and urged his students not to enlist in the Spanish-American War. Never mind that students flocked to his lectures in part because he had a reputation for being easy. Norton had made it known that he would like "to see an increase in the number of these idle persons" who came to hear him. The more sweetness and light he spread, the better for the country. Nothing about manhood was recorded in the catalog or any official "College books," but citing Norton's ability to attract students, Hart could be emphatic: the fact that "a high standard of life appeals to Harvard students is shown by the great influence of Prof. Norton during a quarter of a century."

But in order for Hart to present Norton as a model for Harvard manhood at the turn of the century, some major alterations were necessary. Norton was of an older generation, class of '46. As Hart said, many of the students were sympathetic to him, but his inclination to dismiss all art after 1600 was something of a joke. So too were his protests against the ugliness and rawness of an America that was industrializing and expanding westward. He was forever deploring the vulgarity of American taste, especially as it was represented by Harvard's buildings. He vowed never to teach in the new one that housed his own department—and then relented. The students imagined his complaining upon his arrival in heaven—"So overdone! So Garish! So Renaissance!"—but then preferring to stay rather than spend eternity in Harvard's own Appleton Chapel.

James acknowledged Norton's kindness "to struggling talent" in his field, and his generosity in parceling out his thirty-four-acre estate just north and east of Harvard Yard—he, along with Royce and Frank Taussig of the Economics Department, was among those professors who benefited—but he deplored what he thought was, ironically, the "crudity" of Norton's own aesthetic judgments.[6] He and his brother Henry agreed that Norton's opinions were distinctly homegrown and merely snobbish. Hart had to adjust Norton's version of the gentleman to accommodate people like the Jameses; more generally, he had to situate the Harvard gentleman in the postwar world.

The College had grown, and to the casual observer been "subdivided into sections." It was no longer as likely that "one vigorous young man" would influence large numbers of his classmates. But it was still the case, Hart said, that "the student who has something to contribute to the body academic, who is going to be a centre of influence throughout his later life, readily finds friends, opportunity, and power at Harvard College." The leaders, the most popular and most honored men, were men of "strength, decision, and high standards." The language had changed to fit the times: Hart now spoke of vigor, of bodies, power, and strength. In 1902, athletics was so prominent a part of college life, and had filled so many pages of organs like the *Harvard Graduates' Magazine,* that Hart did not even have to mention it, but clearly his gentleman has spent time either on a playing field or at the gym. And the way this gentleman marshals his energies, the way he moves from opportunities to decisions, indicates that he is prepared to enter a newly subdivided, newly structured and rationalized world. He seems to move not just among class-mates and friends but among future associates as well.

Having presented this newly fashioned Harvard man, Hart went on to cite two reasons for his existence. He was offered a curriculum that fitted his needs, and—it followed—he was *treated* as if he were a man. What Harvard offered him, and what most immediately distinguished a Harvard education during this period, was an elective system, a system that was proving an efficient means of social discipline—"the protection and defense of good order." Not being in college against his will, the student no longer had any excuse for being boisterous; the teacher could expect "the courtesy of quiet behavior." There had probably never been a time, Hart said, "when there was so little necessity for severe discipline: in Harvard College, from the standpoint of the Dean, students seem on the whole to accept the responsibility of manhood."

Neither Hart nor Norton, nor James, spoke for Harvard University. They were even less likely to be speaking for each other. But they could agree on at least two things. The first was the central importance of the students. To varying degrees, all of them were still in loco parentis. For all the differences in their ideas and beliefs, in their personal and pedagogical styles, they were all intent upon converting youths into the kind of gentlemen who could meet the challenges of a world that had suddenly become large and complex and all but godless. The second point of agreement was the fact of Harvard's greatness. Any of them could have said, and been proud to say, as James did in 1903, "From the point of view of education, Cambridge is first-rate."[7]

"First Citizen of the Republic": Charles William Eliot

In fact, there *was* one man who could speak for Harvard University. That was Charles William Eliot, who became president in the fall of 1869, while James was in his darkest moods, and retired in 1909, two years after his most illustrious and successful appointment stopped teaching.[1] James never warmed to Eliot—then again, nobody did—but he would not have disputed his right to the title of "First Citizen of the Republic," which Theodore Roosevelt bestowed upon him,[2] or questioned Learned Hand's impression of him as "the most majestic and moving" of all the eminent men he had known.[3] Tributes tended toward the imperial: James' friend John Jay Chapman called Eliot "the Pope during this epoch."[4]

Eliot belonged somewhere in between the Christian and the classical worlds—which is to say among the Unitarians, along with most Brahmins of his day. He had been born in Boston and gone to Harvard, graduating in the class of 1853. What was unusual about his qualifications—unprecedented, but appropriate to post–Civil War America—was his background in the natural sciences. He had been a tutor in mathematics at Harvard, then head of the chemistry laboratory of the Lawrence Scientific School, and a faculty member at the Massachusetts Institute of Technology before returning to Harvard as president, at the age of thirty-five. Harvard had turned to a layman for its president long before—President Josiah Quincy, in 1829—but never before had they elected a man who knew his way around the City of Man so well as Eliot. In his inaugural address, he spoke of how the university "serves Christ and the church," and then went on to transform *his* university into something like a global empire.

Eliot was psychologically as well as academically equipped to lead Harvard into the everyday battles that lay ahead. Nothing had had more effect on his growing up than the ugly, swollen birthmark that covered much of the right side of his face. As a youth, he had been hooted off the Boston Common because of it; he learned early not to be unnerved by the opinions of others, to "look outward and not inward, forward and not back." As his biographer put it, "he developed a callous protective shell and accustomed himself, too young, to discourage familiarity." Symbolically, in almost all his photographs he turns his left side to the viewer. When he was once asked what quality he thought was most essential to the success of a college president, he answered, "The capacity to inflict pain," a remark that spoke not only to his ability to make hard decisions but also to his empathy with those who were made to suffer.[5] He knew all too well what lay behind men's protective shells. His nephew by marriage tells the story of his having to leave a meeting with the parents of an undergraduate whom he was expelling lest they see his tears.[6]

In acknowledging James' tribute to him on the occasion of his twenty-fifth-anniversary celebration, he expressed his appreciation for James' use of the phrase "devotion to ideals." So many people had measured his accomplishments in terms of buildings and numbers of students and dollars that he feared he would be remembered as a Philistine.[7] In truth, he was the ideal man to lead Harvard into the industrialized and professionalized future. In the judicious words of Oswald Garrison Villard, Eliot was "a great thinking machine with a completely balanced mind—and his heart was not cold or indifferent, not at all, but a heart controlled and never permitted to run away with him."[8] His Stoic manner made him ideally suited to the task before him. He knew even better than James that if he and the institution were to go forward, both would have to be strictly disciplined.

Eliot had not been the overwhelmingly popular choice of the Harvard Overseers—many held out for the acting president, Andrew Preston Peabody, professor of Christian morals, and for the values he represented—but whatever else people said about him, they could not deny that in contrast to his predecessors, he had quickly established himself as a leader. Dr. Oliver Wendell Holmes reported that in a very short time, Eliot had "turned the whole University over like a flapjack."[9] Eliot's efficiency pleased James Russell Lowell no end. "Our new President of the College is winning praise of everybody," he wrote Norton. "I take the inmost satisfaction in him, and think him just the best man that could have been chosen. We have a real Captain at last."[10] The most famous story that went the rounds had it that Dr. Henry Bigelow, an entrenched power at the Medical School, had asked Eliot why it was that his faculty had gone on for eighty years doing just fine, "and now, within *three or four months,* it is proposed to change all our modes of carrying on the School?"—to which Eliot had calmly replied, "I can answer Dr. Bigelow's question very easily: there is a new President."[11]

At his first commencement, Eliot said, "We mean to build here, securely and slowly, a university in the largest sense"; in his forty years, Harvard would firmly establish itself as America's leading educational institution. Even before he became president, Eliot asserted that America should not look to Europe for models. Its own elite could provide. In 1869, writing on the theme "The New Education: Its Organization" in the *Atlantic Monthly,* he said, "When the American university appears, it will not be a copy of foreign institutions, or a hot-bed plant, but the slow and natural outgrowth of American social and political habits, and an expression of the average aims and ambitions of the better educated classes."[12] Upon Eliot's retirement—and on American terms—Harvard would be among the world's great universities. In 1882, after visiting several universities in Europe, William James told his wife he was readier to believe that Harvard was "one of the chosen places of the Earth." The instruction and the facilities were "on the whole superior to anything" he had seen. He wrote his brother Henry, "Nowhere did I see a university which seems to do for *all* its students anything like what Harvard does. Our methods throughout are better."[13] Twenty years later, in the opening words of his Gifford Lectures at the University of Edinburgh, he tactfully pointed out that whereas it had always seemed natural for him and his colleagues "to listen whilst the Europeans talk," he looked forward to more exchanges now that "the current . . . [had] begun to run from west to east."[14]

When Eliot took office as president, Harvard Yard was not bounded on all sides. Within its eventual confines there was Appleton Chapel, a laboratory, and the library, Gore Hall, and beyond that the land rose slightly to Quincy Street, whose stately dwellings (their backs to the Yard) were occupied by President Eliot, by faculty members, and by a few interlopers—most notably, between 1866 and 1882, by Henry James Sr. and his family. Cambridge was only a large town, with a few shops in Harvard Square, and detached homes standing on lawns or small fields. Farmers drove their cattle through the thoroughfares; horsecars had recently started to provide transportation into Boston.[15] Expansion occurred while Eliot was president, many buildings were added, but when he spoke of a university "in the largest sense," its physical plant was about the last thing he had in mind. Eliot said nothing about buildings in his inaugural address, except at the very end, when he announced that in the near future "a noble monument" would be erected in commemoration of those who had died in the recent war. His was a gesture that Henry James might have had in mind when he had Basil Ransom say of Memorial Hall (in *The Bostonians*), "It stands there for duty and honour, it speaks of sacrifice and example, seems a kind of temple to youth, manhood, generosity." Eliot's last words were about "the manliness" that had been nurtured on the site, and about Harvard men's having dispelled any doubts that "gentlemen would in this century prove as loyal to noble ideas as in other times they had been to kings." He was thinking of an institution that would create gentle warriors, prepared to strengthen the new union with the same vigor and honor that their forebears had displayed in the Civil War.

The number of students was important, if for no other reason than that the College's main source of income was tuition. Harvard continually compared itself to other institutions and worried when enrollments leveled off after the turn of the century, but whatever the size of the student body, during all the years Eliot was president, Harvard was no larger than what we now think of as a small liberal arts college. Only about 3 percent—or about 250,000—of the nation's 18- to 24-year-olds were resident students at colleges and universities in the country as a whole. The small number of students enrolled at Harvard—fewer than 2,000 at the turn of the century—had the potential of wielding enormous influence.

Largeness was most evidently a matter of the men Eliot appointed—and again, not the number he appointed. When he started, there were 23 men teaching at Harvard; in 1890, what had become the Faculty of Arts and Sciences numbered 62; when he retired in 1909, though the number had ballooned to 164, it was still smaller than Amherst's or Williams' faculty today.* When writers speak of Harvard's "Olympian Age" or "Golden Age," their pages are devoted to what they consider the ruling deities in the Philosophy Department, and to Hart, Norton, Shaler, Wendell, and a few others. What they have in mind is the influence of a relatively small number of men. Largeness during these years was a matter of presences.

In his inaugural address, Eliot pointed out that teaching was attracting "very few men of eminent ability," so he went out on his own to find some.

---

*Oscar Handlin says 21 in 1869, and 123 when Eliot retired, in "A Small Community," *Glimpses of Harvard Past* (Cambridge, 1986), p. 112. According to Donald Fleming, the numbers are 45 in 1868–69, 90 in 1888–89, and 194 in 1908–9—presumably with the professional school faculties included. "Harvard's Golden Age?" ibid., p. 77.

Usually he appointed these men and, in his first years, appointed them without consulting anyone, for when he began, there were no established procedures for consultation, and no departments with which to consult. (In 1873, he announced that he would begin consulting with others, but throughout his years as president, his was the final word no matter what advice he received.) He asked his first cousin Charles Eliot Norton to teach fine arts. He persuaded Henry Adams to teach medieval history, though Adams had never taught before and professed to know nothing about the subject. Eliot remembered James from the small chemistry class he taught at the Lawrence Scientific School in the early 1860s, remembered him as a man with a delicate nervous system but as a man who possessed "unusual mental powers, remarkable spirituality, and great personal charm,"[16] and his proposal arrived just as James was vowing to take some action that would energize him and begin to put his mind at ease. He persuaded Charles Franklin Dunbar, the former editor of the *Boston Daily Advertiser,* to come out of retirement and teach political economy, which up until that time had been taught as a branch of moral philosophy. Remembering the brilliant conversation of a young law student named Christopher Columbus Langdell, whom he had met in a friend's room while he himself was a junior, Eliot found him in an obscure New York law firm, and then hovered over the first recorded meeting of the law faculty while its members agreed to hire Langdell. Soon after—to Eliot's increased satisfaction—they made him dean.

Citing low pay as a primary reason for the shortage of good men in the profession, Eliot immediately saw to it that his faculty received the first of what would be several salary increases. In his earlier years, no institution's faculty salaries came close to competing with Harvard's. And in Eliot's view, with a Harvard appointment as professor came tenure. In 1880, he established a pension system that covered special cases (by 1899, it would cover all men who had served for twenty years) and a system of sabbatic leaves at half-pay as well.[17]

Eliot was not in a hurry to develop graduate programs or, in spite of what we now think of the essential characteristic of a university, to facilitate research. "The prime business of American professors in this generation must be regular and assiduous class teaching," he said in his inaugural address. Teaching was what professors did, research was what students did. Eliot had published an important chemistry manual; textbooks rated high in his estimation of a faculty member's publications. When he delayed the promotion of George Santayana, he gave as a reason the fact that Santayana did not write "school-books." One of the most prominent and lasting results of the elective system (and thus the abolition of large required courses) would be the freeing up of teachers to do research, and Eliot would eventually honor and defend their independent work before all else. Eventually, too, he would respond to the challenge of other institutions, Johns Hopkins University in particular, with its emphasis on graduate research. Whereas he did not stir in response to Hopkins' attempt to lure James after he had lectured there in 1878, in 1904, when James spoke of retiring, Eliot was ready to play the game. "We want your name," he told James. The next year, when James proposed resigning while he taught for a year at Stanford, Eliot protested, saying that in the public eye this would detach him from Harvard.[18] But throughout his presidency, even as he developed Harvard's professional and graduate schools, Eliot wanted Harvard undergraduates to be generally educated. At the outset at least, he also wanted them to have the best men he could find devote the majority of their time to accomplishing that end.

During his first years, Eliot spent much of his energy raising the standards of the professional schools. The year Eliot became president, William James received his medical degree after a ninety-minute oral examination that culminated with a difficult question in anatomy, posed by Dr. Oliver Wendell Holmes. Hearing the correct answer, Holmes said, "If you know *that,* you know everything; now tell me about your family and the news at home."[19] Divinity students could go three years without being examined; law students, three terms. Eliot tightened the testing procedures required of a man to graduate, and—as we heard in the words he uttered in 1908, at his last commencement—he made the admission process more stringent as well by instituting the requirement of a bachelor's degree.

At whatever juncture of his long career, and whatever his aims, Eliot was prodigiously efficient. In his inaugural address, he spoke of organizing the institution along lines followed by governmental agencies, "manufactories, and all great companies," and he devoted a third of it—that is to say, about thirty-five minutes—to an exposition of the relationships among the faculty, the seven-man Corporation, which supervised finances, personnel, and other matters, and the much larger Board of Overseers, which ratified the Corporation's decisions. He went on to create many standing faculty committees and a network of deans who reported to him. William James was among those on the faculty who warned that serving on committees might overwhelm "the lives of men whose interest is more in learning than in administration," and reluctantly, in time, Eliot acceded to the faculty's desire to let administrators administer so that faculty members themselves could learn.[20]

As Harvard grew, it reached out to its alumni and others through several publications, of which the *Harvard Graduates' Magazine* was the most impressive—"the pioneer publication of this kind in the world," by its own account.[21] In 1899, the road between Harvard and the "real world" was further paved by the establishment of a career-counseling service.[22] Given the increased amount of administering taking place at Harvard, one almost expects to happen upon the founder of "scientific management," Frederick Winslow Taylor, in histories of the Harvard of Charles William Eliot, but Taylor succumbed to the pressures that were building up during these years *before* he got there. He passed the entrance examinations, but in 1874, having developed what appears to have been psychosomatic eye trouble, he went on directly to the Midvale Steel Corporation to engage in factory, rather than academic, work and administration.[23]

Most of Eliot's accomplishments cost money, and he was a master at raising it. He kept his eye not only on enrollment figures but on the endowment as well—which trebled in his first twenty years, and then trebled again in his second. The ties that already bound Harvard to Boston's great cultural and medical and financial institutions were strengthened under Eliot.[24] Boston's elite was only too happy to support this man who had affirmed Harvard's preeminence and had proven himself to be a trustworthy trainer of their sons and of the men who would work for them upon graduation. Leaders in the various professions supported their own particular schools. Men gave portions of their fortunes to build dormitories in their names. Although he worried momentarily about their monies not being wholly pure, Eliot accepted gifts from barons like John D. Rockefeller. He considered prosperity a reward for a man's good works, as "the fruit of character," for, as he put it, "it is energetic, honest, and sensible men that make prosperous business."[25]

Eliot's prominence, his greatness, was inextricably connected to changes in American education that coincided with and shaped the country's meteoric growth in the years after the war. His institution was enormously influential in defining and producing the kind of man who could manage, the man who could run things, in the Gilded Age and thereafter. Eliot was a man who unified, who "set a standard," Chapman said, and he added—drawing on still other ideals and images that (as we will see) were being developed at Harvard—he was one of those men who "brand wild cattle and build fences." Chapman felt that Eliot was so right for the times that he was no *man* at all: he was just a "force," "a one-man machine," "one of the figureheads of the age," an age that he thought was deadening men's spirits.[26] Santayana made the point a little less tendentiously: Harvard was to him "a very large machine serving the needs of a very complex civilization."[27] But before we can judge, we must know more about the kind of man Eliot and Harvard produced, and about how they did it.

The Harvard Aristocracy

In writing about "Harvard manhood," Albert Bushnell Hart had offset his information about how things had changed with assurances that Harvard's mission—and therefore the Harvard man—remained essentially the same. It was a rhetorical feat that reflected the reality of the successful conversion of difference into sameness, multiplicity into unity, subdivisions into a whole, which occurred during the Eliot years.

In antebellum America, a young man would typically go from his years of elementary schooling to work. Whether that work was on the farm or at the shop or in one or another office determined the age at which he would start (the more physical the task, the earlier he would begin) and the socioeconomic level at which he would settle (the less physical the task, the higher he might rise). Any schooling he received in law or medicine or engineering did not precede but rather supplemented the work he did as an apprentice. Not until Eliot arrived would anyone argue for his having to have a college degree before seeking professional knowledge and accreditation. Before the Civil War, a boy went directly on to learn and do men's work.

If he were rich and his parents were so inclined, the youth might go to a college for diversion or for "finishing." Having lost its reputation for instilling piety in its students well before any comparable institution, Harvard was especially vulnerable to the criticism that all colleges did was allow boys to be boys, and possibly teach them some manners. After the war, few of the men who were building America and amassing fortunes in the process paid any heed to what was going on in institutions like Harvard. Those genuinely interested in pursuing knowledge might do so on their own, or through institutions like the American Academy of Arts and Sciences, the Museum of Comparative Zoology, or the Institute of Technology, which were incorporated independently. Johns Hopkins was founded in 1876, and Clark University in 1889, as havens in which serious, advanced students could do research. The idea that youths in their teens could be inspired to learn and to be responsible for their own learning, the idea that learning mattered as preparation for citizenship in the first place, was anything but commonplace when Eliot assumed office. Thus it was to their learning that he attended first.[1]

Eliot took the lead, and he provided what he knew the age demanded. Learning was advancing at an unprecedented rate and becoming increasingly specialized; educational institutions were growing in numbers and in size. No one would yet argue that a young man *had* to attend one in order to establish himself in society, but it did appear that if he spent three or four years in college, he would improve his chances of succeeding in this world. "The savage, terrible hordes of America waked up in 1870, to the importance of education," John Jay Chapman wrote in his essay on President Eliot. "As the Frankish tribes in the sixth century submitted to Rome, so the Americans submitted to Massachusetts." As pope, Eliot was instrumental in answering the momentous questions that followed: just who was to be saved? and how would that be accomplished?

In response to the first question, Eliot wanted Harvard to be as democratic as possible, and of course everything hinged on how he defined "democratic." In working towards their goal, he and Harvard answered questions about geographical representation, financial resources and family background, and what ostensibly mattered most—a young man's desire and ability to learn; their conclusions helped determine what kind of men would end up in positions of distinction and leadership. Education suddenly *mattered,* and mattered to more citizens, and to a more diverse citizenry, than it ever had before. Would this change mean that ideally "the people" had unprecedented opportunities? Or would it mean that the same people would more surely remain in positions of authority and power? In 1869, in "The New Education," he assumed that the American university would express "the average aims and ambitions of the better educated class." Memorial Hall was going to honor "gentlemen," Eliot said.

From such beginnings, what chance was there that the American university would evolve in response to the influence of—or even admit—the sons of the uneducated or the less well situated? In time, Eliot would speak of "the better educated" and of gentlemen in relatively flexible terms, of "a real gentleman" as one who was "also a democrat," implying that those among the privileged who did not share his meritocratic ideals might not remain real gentlemen. Eventually he would outstrip his faculty in his effort to make Harvard more truly democratic. But throughout the years of his presidency, as Harvard did become more democratic, it did so in such a way as not to weaken the aristocracy that had ruled it before he arrived. In 1902, the year that Hart reported on the "new nationalities" and their effect on the composition of "Harvard manhood," Eliot articulated the principle in a speech titled "American Democracy": "The democracy preserves and uses sound old families," he said; "it also utilizes strong blood from foreign sources. . . . Democracy, then, is only a further unfolding of the multitudinous human nature, which is essentially stable."[2] In other words, the old Harvard aristocracy would be strengthened by an infusion of "new blood." In diversifying, it would continue to rule.

Greater geographical representation was both inevitable and desirable. In 1869–70, as much as 80 percent of the student body came from Massachusetts. In 1880, two-thirds of the student body of about eight hundred came from within a hundred-mile radius of Cambridge.[3] As enrollments and incomes increased, as memories of the war faded and Southern students considered Harvard once again, as the fact of Harvard's lack of piety became more tolerable, and as travel improved, students came from farther and farther afield. When they became alumni and gathered in the South or out West, they reported in the pages of the *Graduates' Magazine* that their region would benefit from having more of its young men educated at Harvard. Harvard reached out and its alumni pressed in, with the result that by the turn of the century about half of the students came from out of state. At the commencement of 1908, slightly more than half of them did.

But however sweeping Harvard's effort to find students was, and however far its alumni ranged, in Eliot's rhetoric Massachusetts continued to possess enormous centripetal force. In 1903, the *Graduates' Magazine* "publicly proclaimed" that all of the principal embassies in Europe were occupied by Harvard graduates. Noting this fact in a speech to the alumni in Boston, Eliot protested that the publicity was regrettable; and then he went on to address the issue of alumni representation.[4] Members of his audience wanted more say in the University's affairs. He could understand that, but he asserted that Harvard was the embodiment of what he called "the Massachusetts spirit," and that "Massachusetts must practically govern Harvard University." He pointed out that the alumni could elect a few members of the Board of Overseers, and he argued that Massachusetts residents were more likely to show up at commencement, but his main defense—in keeping with Governor Guild's claim about Harvard and America—was that Massachusetts had itself become nationally representative.

The energy that radiated out of Massachusetts affected the composition of the Harvard faculty and student body as well, according to Eliot. Men of many different races had recently emigrated there, and they were "all infected with the Massachusetts spirit. It is wonderful how pervasive and penetrative that spirit is." Governor Guild had recently appointed two judges, graduates of the College and the Law School, and both of them were Irish Catholics. There was a young instructor on the faculty whose father was a shopkeeper on Hanover Street. "Some of you know what that means," Eliot said—meaning he came from the most impoverished section of Boston.

As Eliot went on to say, Harvard proposed "to welcome all the new races and to do its best for them," and in fact, when he retired in 1909, the "diversity" of the student body was quite extraordinary. Out of the 2,100 or so students, there were surprisingly few of Italian descent (8), given the population of Boston, but there were, as there had been for decades, a large number of Catholic students. There were 5 Negroes, 56 students of Jewish descent, and 50 of Irish, and among those who came from abroad, there were 33 Russian Jews and 19 Chinese. Being situated in the heart of cities, Columbia and Pennsylvania were slightly more hospitable to "all the new races"; the student populations at Yale and Princeton were markedly more homogeneous.[5]

But however varied the nature of the Harvard community, its "spirit" remained the same. The admissions process that evolved during these years was more democratic, but the result was finally a more diverse group of gentlemen—gentlemen with more liberal attitudes and gentlemen from different places, to be sure, but still gentlemen. For one thing, from wherever they came, only a select few could *afford* to come to Harvard. Tuition remained at $150 all the years that Eliot was president—at Yale it was $155—which is laughable now, but when Eliot started, that was more than a laborer's yearly income, and financial aid was only gradually made available. If only for economic reasons, most Harvard students came from middle to upper enclaves in Boston, New York, Philadelphia, and beyond.

But Eliot gave little thought to the issue of class. In his speech "American Democracy," he said that one of the things it meant was "sensuous luxury for those who want it, and can afford to pay for it." He also said that the luxury of "the wise rich" could include "promoting public objects by well-considered giving." That was to say, they could give their money to Harvard.

Eliot resisted the idea of increasing tuition, because he did not want to see too wide a gap open up between the students, but a gap there always was, one wide enough to make Harvard look to many like "a rich man's college." In the first issue of the *Graduates' Magazine* it was reported that a quarter of the students spent between $450 and $650 a year, half between $650 and $975, and a quarter over $1,250.[6] It did not say how much over. Five years earlier, in 1887, George Herbert Palmer noted that one student might spend $400, another $4,000, a year.[7] To take what may be the most dazzling example, while in one year Eliot himself spent $5,000 keeping up two homes, entertaining, and sending two sons through Harvard, Theodore Roosevelt, of the class of 1880, spent half that much on clothes and club dues alone.[8] According to Charles Eliot Norton, in 1890 about 125 students received financial assistance, their scholarship awards averaging $236.[9]

The housing situation obviously reflected divisions of social class, the more obviously because as Harvard expanded, it let private capital do a lot of the deciding for its students. Beginning in 1876, smart money converted old boarding houses into dormitories with suites whose amenities would not be found in some of the buildings in the Yard for thirty years—central heating and plumbing above basement level, for example, not to mention swimming pools and squash courts. As well-appointed buildings spread along Mt. Auburn Street, it came to be known as the Gold Coast. One of them, Claverly Hall, was so sought after that freshmen had to be elected even to be candidates for its rooms. At the other end of the social spectrum, space being limited in the College's facilities, many students who could not afford these relatively luxurious quarters had to fend for themselves in town.

Election to Harvard's clubs also—and for the most part simultaneously—distinguished a social elite. The man who could afford the one could usually afford the other. The interlockings and relationships among the clubs, and the processes by which a young man moved from one to another, were so Byzantine that Harvard's all but official historian, Samuel Eliot Morison, resorted to speaking of "the Institute-Pudding-waiting club-final club crowd" to describe the aspiring socialites among the undergraduates.[10] During the Eliot years, about a third of a class was elected to a society that featured lectures and debates called the Institute of 1770. Those in the Institute with the requisite talent would also be enlisted for theatricals that were the pride of the Hasty Pudding Club. Students would be elected in groups of ten, the first group chosen selecting ten in the class below it, which would then pick ten of its classmates, and so on; as late as 1904 the results, the very order of election, would be printed in the College and Boston papers. The top six or seven or eight "tens" would automatically become members of the D.K.E. (or the "Dickey")—"to which everybody of consequence belonged," Santayana wrote in his novel, *The Last Puritan*—and from their numbers would come those who were elected to the chapters of national fraternities (that had usually gone local), which were called waiting clubs. Around the turn of the century, several "waiting" clubs would declare that they themselves were "final"—but until then, from among their ranks a select few would ascend to the top by becoming members of Alpha Delta Phi or, most prestigious of all, the Porcellian Club.

The rituals and general behavior of club members were cause for concern among those who cared about Harvard's reputation; they also drew national attention, especially in the 1880s. Critics of the system pointed to elaborate and lengthy initiation rites, to hazing, and to the dissoluteness that was assumed to be characteristic of Harvard students' life. Ten years before Thorsten Veblen caustically described the "manly" drinking habits of "the leisure class," one Aleck Quest, in "The Fast Set at Harvard" in the pages of the *North American Review*, ran down "the scale of 'manly pleasures' " to the dissipation that he said was "of the sort that modern refinement exalts as 'gentlemanly.' " "A fast Harvard man when in his cups," Quest wrote, "is proudly conscious of the fact that he is still a gentleman." What distinguished a Harvard man was that he was better dressed and paid more for his vices than the ordinary man, but he was still a disgrace. Quest spoke of the gambling that went on, and of the tutoring and the local cram schools that enabled the students who could afford them to get through Harvard with the least disruption of their social schedules. It was serious criticism by a man, calling himself Quest, who expected more of Harvard. It was aimed at Harvard's pretensions to being democratic, and at all those boys who were supposedly men.

In a rejoinder in the next issue, "One of the Fast Set" acknowledged that there were abuses of privilege, but he said that they were exceptions (he knew of only about six cases of cheating at poker), examples of fallen human nature that could be found on any college campus and that at Harvard had lost others' respect. Then he concluded with a gesture that was hardly geared to silencing Harvard's critics. He assured Quest, "We are glad we are rich."[11]

"The fast set" was clearly monied. The social elite need not have been. For all the laxity of student life, Eliot expected more of the undergraduates than did his predecessors, and thus a large portion of them (two-thirds in his first years, about half in 1900) came to Harvard by way of schools founded to prepare students for college, some founded to prepare students for Harvard specifically—St. Paul's in 1856, Groton in 1885, Middlesex in 1901. Youths now came to Harvard at eighteen, not at fourteen, as had been the case before the war, and they came with friends. The social mix was further enriched, once they had established themselves at Harvard, by Boston society, which required the right sort of Harvard men to make it work. That sort was not *just* rich, or at least money did not guarantee social success, and a young man of modest means and background might be elected to a club, or be invited to Boston or the North Shore on the weekends. As Eliot had said—and as William Dean Howells rendered the dynamic most memorably in *The Rise of Silas Lapham* (1885)—old money might require and welcome, or even seek out, infusions of new energy.

The social elite at Harvard was not exclusively or crudely a financial elite, but it set a tone that could not be ignored. Harvard would always differ from Princeton or Yale in its heterogeneity. Its social elite would not set *the* tone. But during this period, an exceptionally large portion of the students were connected—or aspired to be connected—to the business world, and this group knew full well that it helped to be *well* connected. In the 1860s, half of the students at Harvard came from families that were in business—of the twenty-two millionaires in Boston, only five did not send their sons to Harvard—and business was the second most popular career of the seniors (behind law). In the 1890s, 40 percent of the graduates were going into business, 22 percent into the law, and 3 percent into the ministry.[12] In 1907, a lead editorial in the *Crimson* asked that more prominent men of industry be invited to speak to the seniors about the principles and ideals that had led to their success.[13] Those headed for business far outnumbered their counterparts at Yale, for example.

Though Eliot regretted the situation, though he regretted the extent to which the student body was divided along class lines, he would do very little about it. He had every expectation that it would right itself. In his annual report for the year 1901–2, he said, "For some reasons one could wish that the University did not offer the same contrast between the rich man's mode of life and the poor man's that the outer world offers; but it does, and it is not certain that the presence of this contrast is unwholesome or injurious. In this respect, as in many others, the University is an epitome of the modern world." He was intent upon educating Harvard youths for the changing, modern world where such divisions persisted; the sooner they learned about them, the better prepared they would be and the greater the likelihood that they would be socially responsible and not just scramble after wealth.

Eliot set an example, as did James, for the way a young man might address the issue of money. Legend had it that he had spurned the offer of a lucrative job at a textile mill in Lowell, Massachusetts, in order to continue teaching chemistry, saying that he had no desire to be rich, and that it would be "unmanly" to exchange "a direct usefulness for an indirect one." This was only a legend. In fact, his mother had heard about the opening, but because Lowell seemed so far away and because Eliot did not see how he could use his expertise, he did not pursue the matter (though knowing how the story could benefit him, he allowed the prospect to be discussed).[14] But Eliot was known for, and he preached the virtues of, restraint in financial matters; he saw it as a means of unifying the student body and the country. As an undergraduate, he had turned down Porcellian because of what he considered the dissipation of its members.[15] In his inaugural address, he said, "The poverty of scholars is of inestimable worth in this money-getting nation. It maintains the true standards of virtue and honor." He considered wealth "divorced from culture" disastrous for the nation; he wanted it chastened or elevated through contact with the less fortunate. In performing this function, the less fortunate would in turn be influenced by conceptions of virtue and honor that nobody at Harvard wanted to see lost. Matthew Arnold would have said that the social elite was educating its future masters, but no one at Harvard was so explicit.

Eliot imagined that in college a young man would make choices, he would exercise his will, and he would thereby realistically create a life for himself. Given his assumptions about the gentlemanly ideals of his institution, Eliot rarely dwelt on its difficulties or injustices. The results—the ideal men he envisaged—were much more inspiring to contemplate. From the ranks of both the rich and the poor would emerge what he defined in his inaugural address as an American aristocracy,

the aristocracy which excels in manly sports, carries off the honors and prizes in the learned professions, and bears itself with distinction in all fields of intellectual labor and combat; the aristocracy which in peace stands firmest for the public honor and renown, and in war rides first into the murderous thickets.

Harvard's expectations of the men who would graduate after the Civil War were clear from the beginning of Eliot's reign: they would be prepared for a world that Eliot knew would be increasingly professionalized, one in which intellects would no longer work apart but would contribute to and vie with other laboring forces; this aristocracy would work to clean up government and, if need be, would saddle up and go off to war again. His listing of what the Harvard undergraduate would have to confront is remarkably prescient.

Eliot began with "manly sports," but he did not foresee how great a part athletics would play in the creation of the modern American man. Although he did everything he could to oppose, or at least to slow down, the development of intercollegiate athletics, they advanced along lines that he himself laid down for the evolution of Harvard's social and curricular life. In each sphere, boys were left to their own devices with the expectation that however diverse their backgrounds, interests, and characters, at Harvard they would become honorable, disciplined, and self-possessed individuals and also members of a harmonious elite. They would become the kind of men who would bring glory to the institution and to the nation.

Many would join Eliot in deploring the fact that Harvard's greatness could be reduced to a victory over Yale in football, but many more at the College, and soon all over the country, seized on Harvard's teams as proof of the virtues of Harvard men. Eighteen years after Eliot retired, Morison surveyed the culture and concluded that "the desperate desire for notoriety and victory . . . still trails its slimy track over American intercollegiate athletics."[16] Were he writing today, he would allude not to mere trailings but to ecological disasters. But whether for good or ill, during the years in which Eliot was president of Harvard, "manly sports" became the most obvious and popular means by which a youth would be tested for his potential manliness.

"Manly Sports"

In no context does the word "manly" appear more often and more insistently than in the context of discussions of athletics during this period. All the prominent figures connected with Harvard voiced their opinions on the subject. All of them agreed that athletic activity engendered manliness, and therefore, to varying degrees, all of them approved of it. Their disagreements arose over questions concerning which athletic activities ought to be emphasized, how much emphasis should be placed on them, how each ought to be conducted, and who ought to be allowed to participate or to watch. Their disagreements were heated, since they all started from the premise that what was permissible and encouraged would greatly affect the kind of man they considered ideal. What each deplored was the influence that he thought would tarnish that ideal.

The moral quality of the Harvard man remained "sound and hopeful," Hart reported to the alumni in 1902. Though the definitions that his audience might assign to the word "moral" differed, all of them would have taken "sound" to imply "physically fit" as well as dependable, and most of them associated one or another sign of physical imperfection or weakness with a characterological flaw. More than one of them intoned, *"mens sana. . . ."*

Given the prevailing thinking, it is not surprising to find the 1893 Phi Beta Kappa speaker, Francis Walker, talking on the subject "College Athletics," or to find him downplaying the life of the mind in the course of his speech.[1] To begin with, Walker was an ideal spokesman for his era. A brigadier general during the Civil War, he was a professor at Yale's Sheffield Scientific School, and then president of the Massachusetts Institute of Technology (the post he held as he spoke), but he was most influential as an economist—"the apologist of the Gilded Age," he has been called.[2] The steps from war to science to the economy seemed naturally to lead to "college athletics," even on an occasion honoring academic achievement. "No theme is to-day of greater consequence to the colleges and universities of our land," Walker began.

Walker proceeded to contrast an image of the college hero in the days before the Civil War with a postwar model. The earlier specimen was "a young man of towering forehead, from which the hair was carefully brushed backwards. . . . His cheeks were pale; his digestion pretty certain to be bad." And inevitably it followed that "he was self-conscious, introspective, and indulged in moods, as became a child of genius"—a fairly accurate description of William James in the 1860s, incidentally. But this young man, with his literary and debating societies, his cloistered religion and "morbid transcendentalism," and his fashionable contempt for "mere bigness," had been superseded by men of action, and by muscular Christians, who knew that "it is a glorious thing to have a giant's strength." The war had everything to do with the transformation: "it showed how much nobler are strength of will, firmness of purpose, resolution to endure, and capacity for action, than are the qualities of the speechmaker and the fine writer, which the nation had once agreed chiefly to admire." The honorable man of the present age would be strong, firm, resolute, active.

Walker's subject was "college athletics," but what he was most interested in was physical education. In fact, he spent an appreciable portion of his speech on the *dangers* of athletics, on excessive training, the inclusion of players from the professional schools, and "the unsportsmanlike system of organized cheering," which was "unfair to the visiting team." He had a courtly image of the ideal Harvard man. He imagined his treating the visitors within his gates with "something like the grace of antique chivalry." Walker's ideal man was attentive to his studies, and—as set out in a rousing and surprising peroration—he appreciated great art. Or at least he appreciated the beauty of the male body as rendered by the Greeks.

Walker's ultimate concern was men's bodies. His scorn for the prewar student was based on the phrenological evidence of a "towering forehead." His hopes for the future were rooted in a widely held faith in the miraculous results of proper bodily conditioning. If the muscular Christians exaggerated when they claimed that you could literally sweat out evil, nonetheless they had "got hold of a great truth," he said. "Hearty physical force" might be consistent with "vicious desires," he acknowledged, but mainly it worked to combat them. His hopes were echoed and grounded a few years later when G. Stanley Hall—whose doctorate in the field of psychology (awarded by Harvard's Philosophy Department) was the first of its kind in the country—reported the results of his research on "student customs." He too was excited about the potential influence of athletic and gymnastic activity. *His* image of students of an earlier era was of seminarians who led ascetic and sedentary lives, and who were therefore "prone to reaction in forms of revolutionary violence." He agreed that had they been allowed to develop their muscles, there would have been less vice. But now, what with "athleticism"—which he considered "one of the most happy but new fashions of academic life"—the institution had "a safety-valve for exuberant animal spirits." He said, "As a respectable topic of conversation, athletics have been a godsend."[3] Prospects for social order were much improved.

So too, in the minds of many, were the prospects of world order, or of the domination of distant lands and peoples by those with sound, fit bodies. Such ideas must have been on Francis Walker's mind. He was a Social Darwinist with race theories that he put into practice as an official of the U.S. Immigration Service. Such theories would be the burden of a long report by an alumnus of the Scientific School of research done on Harvard University oarsmen that was published in the *Graduates' Magazine* in 1904. After all the evidence was in—life expectancies, occupations, insurance acceptances and rejections, pulse rates, urine analyses—the good news was that men who had rowed for Harvard were on the average more likely to get married and to have more than their share of children. Harvard oarsmen, in other words, were "superior in the matter of perpetuating the best elements of the American race," especially in matters relating to "the question of race decline."[4]

The chief apologist for physical education and gymnastics was Dudley A. Sargent, for forty years the director of the Hemenway Gymnasium at Harvard, and for ten of those years also assistant professor of physical training. Sargent graduated from Yale Medical School, but he started out life as a circus performer. Wanting not to practice medicine but to direct a physical education program instead, he opened up his own gymnasium in New York, where Eliot found him in 1879 and appointed him director of the gymnasium that was under construction at Harvard.[5] Walker and Theodore Roosevelt were undergraduates at the time. He consulted at length with Roosevelt (and perhaps Walker) as he developed his plans for creating ideal physical and moral men.

Sargent too thought that you could successfully attack neurasthenia, and all that ailed the body politic, if you started with men's muscles. First the muscles, then the organs of respiration, circulation, and nutrition, then the brain, "not to attain bodily health and beauty alone, but to break up morbid mental tendencies, to dispel the gloomy shadows of despondency, and to insure serenity of spirit," he wrote in the *North American Review*.[6] To serenity of spirit he would add "the manly virtues" of "energy, strength, courage, alertness, persistency, stamina, and endurance" in one publication,[7] "courage . . . coolness, presence of mind, and the rapid and responsible exercise of judgment under trying circumstances, which are so desirable in the 'battle of life,' " in another.[8] He too turned for his model to the perfectly developed, perfectly symmetrical body sculpted by the ancient Greeks. Against it he measured and charted Harvard students ("In the Harvard man there is a greater development of the chest-muscles; while the Yale man has a larger chest-girth, though the lower border of the pectorals is hardly discernible"), and the results of his efforts—"strength tests," they were called—were a regular feature in the *Graduates' Magazine*.

Believing that "the great mental and moral disturbances which sometimes threaten the stability of a government may be traced to physical causes,"[9] he envisaged the men he trained establishing calm and order in the state. Imagining that the purity of the race was threatened, he could see their superior circulatory system flushing out the "large infusion of foreign blood of an inferior quality [that] has undoubtedly impaired the physical status of our people as a whole."[10] In "The Hemenway Gymnasium: An Educational Experiment," he said that a man's ultimate motive, his mission, was higher than any engendered by athletic competition. A man had a duty to improve his physical condition in order to be able to "bear his burdens in the world, and help to advance the condition of the rest of mankind by improving the stock and raising the average."[11]

He also believed that class or club teams could prevent a young man's becoming too self-absorbed, and that "our youth may even be taught to play football and basketball and still be gentlemen."[12] Throughout his long career, Sargent had an ideal man in mind who is, by now, immediately recognizable: a gentleman who was well balanced and self possessed, and who could bring order to a nation recently divided within by war and currently threatened by invading immigrants from without. Sargent thought this man could survive and temper and redirect the bombardment of new stimuli which, like George Beard, he saw as coming from the media, the telegraph, the press, the rapid transit system—and from the shakiness of the class system and the prevalence of fortune making as well.[13] Ideally he wanted to require physical education at Harvard, but that was hardly possible in an institution in the process of abolishing curriculum and even chapel requirements. At the very least, he wanted the institution to allot funds with some sense of proportion. Funding was heavily weighted toward team sports. The $112,000 spent on fewer than 200 members of athletic teams seemed hardly fair when compared to the $12,000 he received for a gymnasium that was meant to serve an entire student body of just under 2,000.

But Sargent could not buck the cultural tide. The discrepancy in funding was just another indication of the commercialization of the country—of a piece with the establishment of gate receipts, the hiring of coaches, and, worst of all, the gambling that "outside elements" brought into the athletic picture at Harvard. In the realm of "manly sports," competitive athletics were taking over, and many feared that they would compromise Harvard's ideals. Sargent argued that they were ruinous to the bodies of its students. Oarsmen and football players scored badly on his tests because their musculature had been developed only for particular purposes. But it was the competitiveness that was most insidious. It led "to madness and destruction," Sargent wrote towards the end of his career at Harvard. "We have allowed the fighting impulse, represented by the spectacular side of athletics to get the better of the educational and developmental side. In other words we have lost control." Competition was the "crying evil of the age," and "the arch-enemy of all true culture, mental as well as physical."[14]

But by then the battle had been lost: Sargent's ideal of a Harvard gentleman was becoming all but unrecognizable. As a member of the three-man Faculty Committee on the Regulation of Athletic Sports, formed in 1882—the other members were Charles Eliot Norton, chair, and John W. White, professor of Greek—Sargent had exerted considerable influence. Competition against professional teams was not allowed, nor was the hiring of professional coaches. The metaphorical fence that these men erected around the "amateur" and gentlemanly play of the undergraduates took physical form when they had the athletic fields enclosed—in order, they said, to "protect the grounds and exclude objectionable persons." They defended the Oxbridge tradition of "a gentleman amateur [hired] to assist in the gymnasium and superintend games"; having witnessed what was markedly *un*gentlemanly behavior on the football field, they sought to have the sport banned. They were supported by the president and the faculty and, on one occasion, by the Board of Overseers, but eventually they were overruled by the Corporation.[15] Sargent's original five-year appointment was renewed in 1884. In 1889, Eliot recommended to the Board of Overseers that he be promoted to the rank of professor of physical training. To some on the board, he had not exerted enough control; to others he had exerted too much. In its response to Eliot's proposal, the Corporation stripped Sargent of his faculty rank altogether.

In Sargent's story, in his views about the shape a man's body ought to assume and the purpose to which it ought to be put, and in the fate of his views, we can read an important segment of the history of the ideal that was being developed for American men's lives during this period. Sargent wanted men's bodies to be well proportioned, strong, poised; to be capable of persevering, and, though self-contained, capable of functioning with others and, if need be, of leading them. By the end of the century, this idol would not be entirely smashed—the gentleman would survive—but like it or not, he would have to specialize, develop this muscle or that skill. He would have to compete, and once in the competition, he would have to win.

Those whose views prevailed wanted an athletic program that was, like Sargent's model gymnast, strong, well balanced, and influential, a program that would develop young men's mental and moral beings as well as their bodies, and that would have an effect on morale in the classroom and on the general social life of the College and beyond. The difficulty was that they expected these characteristics and results to derive from a program that also included the competitive, intercollegiate athletics that Sargent distrusted. With *them* came a host of influences on students' athletic activities and on their lives generally that Eliot was in the habit of calling "evils." Few resorted to loaded, moral terms, but almost everyone who was intent upon educating gentlemen deplored, or at least wanted to control, the excesses of intercollegiate athletics.

Sargent was so busy defending his own territory that he was not about to celebrate the benefits that accrued from Harvard's sports program. But everyone agreed, to begin with, that exposing a boy to the relatively benign tutelage available in *this* school of hard knocks enabled him to grow out of boyhood. "If a boy is ever to get away from his mother's apron string, he must take his chances against other boys," was one faculty member's version of the familiar argument.[16] Admittedly, he pointed out, any sport that was "capable of teaching courage and manhood" involved an element of risk. Football was obviously the worst, but rowing, yachting, coasting, and even golf were also hazardous. (Just how golf could be hazardous—whether because of poor sportsmanship, or incredible lack of coordination, or stray balls—we do not know, but along with twisted knees the author cites "broken teeth" as one of golf's perils.) By participating in one or another athletic activity, a youth who entered Harvard would come out of himself—and enter "the real world" as a real man.

Some took this developmental argument to the very end of the line: competitive sports prepared a man for the hardest knocks of all, for war. They prepared a young man to meet not just life but death. In his speech "The Soldier's Faith" (1895), Oliver Wendell Holmes Jr. enthusiastically embraced that prospect. He told his audience that he recognized a gentleman by his willingness to give up his life ("that is what the word has meant"), and that he himself prayed for combat. As he looked around at what he called the "snug, over-safe corner of the world" in which he was speaking, he celebrated the only version of war he could discover. There were no battlefields in sight, but there were playing fields, especially the thirty-one acres—Soldier's Field—that Major Henry L. Higginson had given in 1890 in memory of six of his classmates who had died for the Union cause. At least when looking out at them, he could rejoice. Young men were at play, and the rougher their play the better. "I rejoice at every dangerous sport which I see pursued," Holmes said.[17]

Henry Cabot Lodge is usually credited with the most sweeping and simplistic articulation of the argument for sports as a substitute for or—as he actually had it—a preparation for war. Though preferring solitary rowing and, occasionally, boxing when he was himself an undergraduate, at the commencement dinner twenty-five years later, in June 1896, he boosted the idea of team sports at Harvard because they conditioned men to be victorious.[18] "I want Harvard to play the part which belongs to her in the great drama of American life," he said. "Therefore I want her to be filled with the spirit of victory." To him it was a matter, literally, of conditioning. Just as Muscular Christians, or advocates of physical education like Walker, Hall, and Sargent, expected physical development to make for moral improvement, Lodge expected an athlete's training and practice to produce a deep commitment to winning, a commitment—by his further reckoning—that necessarily subordinated the individual to the group, and enabled the group, "whether it be a college or a nation, to achieve great results and attain to high ideals." Those results and those ideals were for him, as they were for his friends Theodore Roosevelt and Walker, nothing short of world domination. The calculus was simple, the virtues of competitive sports obvious: learn to take your lumps on Soldier's Field, and you will someday rule the world. "The time given to athletic contests," Lodge said, "and the injuries incurred on the playing-field are part of the price which the English-speaking race has paid for being world-conquerors."*

What with the rules of football still in flux, and anything like adequate protective equipment a thing of the distant future, the sport was in fact extremely dangerous. Injuries were frequent and severe. Although no one died on a Harvard athletic field during Eliot's time, in 1895, in his twenty-fifth annual report, he cited several fatal football accidents that had occurred elsewhere, and warned that "in every strenuous game now played . . . there is the ever present liability to death on the field."[19] Though the figures seem hard to

---

*Or defenders, as the then Boylston Professor of Rhetoric and Oratory at Harvard argued in 1918: "this war," he said "has come nearer [to] justifying our methods in intercollegiate athletics than we had thought possible." LeBaron Russell Briggs, "Intercollegiate Athletics and the War," *Atlantic Monthly,* CXX (September 1918), 304.

believe, it is said that during the 1904 football season, twenty-one players died nationwide, eighteen in 1905, and thirty during the 1909 season.[20] One would think that not even Holmes' gentleman would delight in such statistics, but a look at the most popular Harvard fiction of the day suggests that, at some level, many men were thrilled at the idea of violent sport.

Published in 1893, Waldron Kintzing Post's *Harvard Stories: Sketches of the Undergraduate* was in its fifteenth edition by 1899. It is a modest book for which Post made modest claims. The stories were "only yarns and pictures of us boys"—us boys at play. One story begins with Dick Stoughton tossing his John Stuart Mill aside, picking up his "Mary Jane," lighting her "affectionately," and after a few puffs, going off to "the Pudding" for beer and companionship. In another, Stoughton helps the central figure, Jack Rattleton, make it through finals by humiliating the man who is proctoring the exam. Otherwise, Post's pages are filled with non-academic matters, with pranks, skits, personal rivalries, minor mishaps, and, in one instance (for which Post asks his reader's indulgence), a maudlin rendering of Class Day. The two stories that are clearly intended to engage us most, though, are about war and about rowing—linked celebrations of men's suffering and self-sacrifice.

The first, "In the Early Sixties," is given over to an old grad who mesmerizes Stoughton, Rattleton, and their crowd with reminiscences of the war. The moral of his story is that deep down a Harvard man is a valorous and a gentle man, whether fighting on the Confederate or the Union side. (One of them is Robert Gould Shaw, the "fair-haired boy of five-and-twenty, and the most sunny lovable gentleman that ever left the ballroom for the battle-field," who died "in front of his niggers in that terrible charge on Fort Wagner.") The old grad's narrative is suitably contrasted to the views of war of the effete and dilettantish Gray, who appropriately tries out for coxswain but does not make it. Even "little Digges, 'Nancy' Digges, the quiet, shy, little pale-faced student who looked as if he would blow away in a strong wind, and whom no one had thought was good for anything but grubbing for Greek roots," is promoted for bravery. Though unpopular while an undergraduate, another contemporary proves he too "had breeding" after all, proves he has "at least the hard part of a gentleman," by getting killed trying desperately to rally his scattering men.

But *self*-sacrifice is not the highest achievement of these men. They can sacrifice each other. Jim Standish is in prison. The narrator can't see him, but he can procure pipe tobacco for him, and he can delight in a correspondence taken up by news of classmates. And then, given a Hardyesque coincidence in which, as officer in command, he shoots Jim as he tries to escape, he can find fulfillment in his friend's death:

> "As I leaned over the dearest friend I ever had, we recognized each other and he smiled. I took his head in my lap and he died holding my hand."

If to Poe the greatest of poetic subjects was the death of a beautiful woman, on the training ground of men, there is nothing more inspiring than a mortal wounding of—or by—your best friend.

The most exciting news Jim had to report was not about the war. It was the news from Harvard that the crew had beaten Yale. The race is what the last (and longest) story, "How River's Luck Changed," is about. Obviously the story is not about the simple business of winning, but neither does it pay the usual tribute to how—win or lose—gentlemen play the game. Charlie Rivers, the hero, was a football player in the first story, but it is appropriate that he fulfill the noble destiny of his name: an oarsman Charlie Rivers on the Charles River. Post is clear about the athletic hierarchy:

To the layman there is in tennis and base-ball four times the skill and pretty playing that there is in foot-ball, and in rowing there is none at all. Yet a tennis match excites the least interest of all college sports, base-ball comes next in the rising scale, and both of these combined do not rouse a quarter of the enthusiasm provided by a foot-ball game. But at the head and front of all athletic contests is rowing—because it hurts the most.[21]

Mindful of the criticism that too much emphasis was being placed on athletics at Harvard, Post gives the opposition a hearing, but dooms the argument by putting it in the mouth of the woman. It is the woman whom Rivers loves who asks Rattleton, "Is it not a little childish to make an athletic contest the aim of a man's life?" and "Do you think the only pluck worth admiring is that which goes with muscle?" Speaking of educated men, she asks, "Should the manliness of the athlete be any more patent to them than the higher courage of the students?" Rattleton acknowledges she may be right, but argues that though manly qualities may evidence themselves in several fields, they are most easily recognizable in athletics. Writing in the year Walker gave his Phi Beta Kappa address on college athletics, Post has Rattleton point out that all the presidents in the last seventy years have been soldiers, and that while warriors have always been honored, "other men, who have hammered away all their lives with long-winded pluck and perseverance, must content themselves with secondary honors." Besides, Rivers "has been so strong and patient and loyal,—oh! such a *man*." Implicitly she comes around, and in his own voice Post makes the point that so long as women come to watch their men "hurt themselves . . . this republic will never fail from the effeminacy of its young men."

The scene is thus set for another eerie climax. Halfway through the race, something goes amiss, and Rivers is ostensibly to blame. He has gradually given up, to the point where at the race's close he is doing nothing except "being carried over the line by the crew he had ruined." But it turns out that Rivers' sliding seat had broken and that for half the race the steel tracks on which it rode were cutting into him at every stroke. ("There is no fiction about this," Post writes in a footnote. "It was done by a Harvard oarsman.") He is lifted from the blood-stained shell, taken to Rattleton's uncle's yacht, where he recuperates and then, come fall, marries his true love in Newport. Those who expressed their reservations about "manly sports" at Harvard by pointing to the risk of injuries had to contend with a very well-worked-out apology for manly sacrifice.

But competitive athletics, football especially, introduced another element that was not so easily assimilated. What concerned many about intercollegiate athletics was "foul play," and "foul play," in turn, often involved another concern: the new diversity of students. Sometimes the "problem" was just boys from Boston, poorer boys (those coming from greater distances being much more likely to be rich and drawn to lighter physical activity). In the speech he gave upon the occasion of his dedication of Soldier's Field, Higginson had spoken of "the Princeton and the Yale fellows" as brothers, and had asked that it be understood that Harvard men would try to "beat them fairly if we can, and believe that they will play the game just as we do."[22] But the pages of Harvard periodicals during these years confirm just how frequently at least one side in any given contest thought the other side was not playing fair. Infractions of the rules were rampant; charges and countercharges resounded in the air. A few years later, in 1893, the *Graduates' Magazine* pointed out that America had no tradition of "sportsmanship" and that now, with "the sudden influx of students in the past twenty years, there had come "a large proportion of young men whose breeding and antecedents have not made them gentlemen."[23]

In 1903, the head of the athletic committee, Professor Ira Hollis of the Engineering Department, tested football by the standards of an idealized Middle Ages—tested it for the presence of *gentilesse,* we might say. If intercollegiate athletics were our modern chivalry, he asked, how much "valor, fairness, courtesy, and moderation under all circumstances" were to be found in the men who played football? After going through a litany of abuses—the injuries, the foul play, the cheating, the commercialism, the suspiciousness, the incivilities—he had to conclude, not much. Football had become all too similar to war: "We have succeeded in developing a war game wherein it is the business of each side to take every possible advantage."

There had been a decline of learning too. "Everything must give way to the ambition for commercial supremacy," Hollis wrote. "The students come from homes saturated with the worship of material success." Hollis did not single out one "element," or if he did, he did so more subtly than the writer who was worried about "the sudden influx of students" without breeding. Some students and their families had to worry more about material success than others, but what he called "the tendency of the times" was ultimately responsible, not just the presence of poorer students.

In Hollis' eyes, athletics, football in particular, was only a symptom of the end of the era of the gentleman. But football still had its uses: "It teaches some of the manly virtues admirably, and it exercises a moral restraint upon a large body of youths who might without it drift into all kinds of dissipation." If football had ushered in a more savage age, it might enable Harvard to deal with the savages, both the scholarship students and the "fast" ones who belonged to clubs and drank too much. "Our chief hope is that it is steadily growing better in spirit."[24]

But it was hard to hope in the face of another of the "evils" of intercollegiate athletics: increased professionalism, which literally introduced a commercial element into games, and figuratively encouraged students to value success above all. Athletic committees sought to elevate the spirit in which intercollegiate athletics were played by forbidding competition against professional teams, and by barring men with any professional experience (which was sometimes hard to detect). Men from the law and other professional schools were barred as well, for some were subsidized by eager graduates, never bothered to attend classes, and simply left Cambridge after the Yale game. What had to be preserved, if possible, was the amateur—the man who played a sport for the love of sport, the way the men at Oxford and Cambridge presumably did.

The question of coaching was particularly thorny. Harvard had enjoyed considerable success in rowing and baseball over the years, but Yale and other institutions had long since hired coaches, and if Harvard did not, Harvard would fall behind. At Oxbridge, competent and knowledgeable former oarsmen considered it an honor to be invited to come back and coach the undergraduates. Harvard did the best it could under the circumstances: in 1896, it invited a Cambridge graduate who had coached the Oxford crew, Rudolph C. Lehmann. Lehmann represented "the best ideal of English sportsmanship": he was a gentleman, a true sportsman, someone who had "a wholesome scorn of tricks, subterfuges and ruses," a man for whom victory was not "the best thing." After their first season together, a mass meeting was held at Sanders Theater in Memorial Hall to honor the new coach and his crew. When Lehmann was introduced, he received "one of the greatest receptions ever given a speaker at Harvard." In the course of his speech, he told his audience about an Oxford oarsman: "His was the spirit of a true gentleman, of a true sportsman, I take it,—strength without aggression, confidence without self-assertion, cheerfulness without ostentation, and endurance to the end."[25] For the moment, Harvard had found the ideal representation of the kind of manhood it was trying to teach: not a scholar and a gentleman but a sportsman and a gentleman; a man whose strengths (and pains) are well contained; a reserved but strategically responsive man. And this man was also winning. In 1897, Harvard awarded Lehmann an honorary degree.

Football presented many more problems than did rowing. There was, to begin with, a record of defeat that not even the most ideal "sportsman" could tolerate. As Morison put it, during this period "Harvard felt a certain loss of manhood in not winning a single football game with Yale in the eighties and only two in the nineties."[26] Even Henry Adams was upset. "You must have put real genius into discovering how not to win," he wrote a correspondent in Cambridge after a third consecutive loss.[27] Something had to be done. Here, Harvard could not look to England, but among its graduates there was the obvious choice of William Reid Jr., class of 1901, who had led Harvard to one of its two victories over Yale in the nineties. Reid also symbolized a slight changing of the social guard: he was club material, but he protested against unearned social privilege, objecting specifically to the possibility of one John Hallowell's being elected football captain solely on the basis of his name. At the team's invitation, he stayed on to coach, and was again successful: Harvard went undefeated, beating Yale by a larger margin than ever before. The next year, Reid married and returned to California to teach at his father's school, and Harvard went back to its losing ways. The players, now supported by the Graduate Football Association, lobbied—and were willing to pay $3,000— for Reid's return, but the College's athletic committee held out for amateurism. After one more humiliating loss, though, it agreed to an offer of $3,500. When Reid turned them down, the committee allowed the alumni to add another $3,500 for "extraordinary expenses," and in the spring of 1905 Reid came on at a salary that was about a third more than that of any faculty member and only slightly less than that of President Eliot. Harvard had given its blessings to big-time football.[28]

In Reid, Harvard had an administrator whose efficiency rivaled even Eliot's. Looking at the task before him, Reid concluded that no one was to blame for Harvard's losses, which were only "the natural result of a failure to conduct our football on rational business principles." With those principles in mind, he transformed the athletic scene. He gathered a staff of coaches around him, he recruited and scouted, he had the names of every Harvard student and their potential as players on file, he procured tutors for students who were in academic trouble (and assured his players that if they showed up at class and appeared interested, they would never be in serious trouble), and he went more than the extra mile to retrieve those who withdrew. Once he sent a message by horseback to a sheep ranch in Idaho where one of his best players had gone. He set up training and dieting and hygiene programs, he tried to find the perfect way to catch a punt or take the snap from the center, he devised special equipment (leather ribbons on a kicking shoe, for example, to create just the right spiral), and he went to New York to obtain a copy of the order that Yale had placed with Spalding's sporting goods store and then to New Haven to buy samples of what his arch-rivals would be wearing. He tried to manipulate game schedules and to hire officials he thought would favor Harvard, and he recorded everything in a diary that, covering the period from his arrival at Harvard to the end of his first fall season, went on for over a thousand typewritten pages.

His explanations of the rational business principles by which he operated could have inspired James Thurber. Here he is, writing on the recruitment problem, in his article "The Football Situation": "Some of the men are too beefy to use—others have impossible temperaments, while others are susceptible to injury. . . . The beef must be active, teachable, and intelligent." Institutions with lower academic standards and a higher tolerance for professionalism exacerbated the problem: "Fellows of small means are secured good jobs at market prices."[29] Ninety years have only refined the system that he put in place.

But after two years Reid resigned. In his two seasons at Harvard, he lost only three games, but two of them were to Yale, and he thought of himself as a failure. By the end of his tenure, he had worked himself into a state of nervous paralysis, had lost weight, was drinking and resorting to drugs to help him sleep. One hesitates to speak of a neurasthenic football coach, but his physical collapse does parallel that of others who succumbed to similar pressures—pressure to discipline the body, pressure to order one's life, pressure to succeed at work. There was also the pressure to be a man in the eyes of his wife. After leaving Harvard, he became a bonds salesman and was, relatively speaking, a failure there too. "I know that you want a masculine man," he wrote his wife in 1911, "and that it must be a humiliation to you to see other's [sic] earning so much more."[30] Manhood was no more than victories and sales, and Reid could point to neither.

In the 1880s, the costs of football were calculated primarily on the basis of the injuries and of the dirty play that caused them. Adding these things up, the original athletic committee that included Norton and Sargent had tried to abolish the sport. Subsequent committees—committees that included alumni and student, as well as faculty, representatives—would not propose such radical measures, but some of the faculty did not abandon its cause, and the athletic committees retained control. In 1895, when the faculty voted to drop the sport, the athletic committee promised to introduce reforms. Though nobody seems to have taken the possibility seriously, Ira Hollis floated the idea of abolishing just the Yale game. In 1905, the faculty once again tried to get rid of the sport, this time with the support of the Board of Overseers. In the commencement speech he gave that June, Theodore Roosevelt (now President

Roosevelt) went on record against "brutality": "Brutality in playing a game should awaken the heartiest and most plainly shown contempt for the player guilty of it," he said, "especially if this brutality is coupled with low cunning."[31] Careful monitoring was necessary. But by then the abolition of football was unthinkable.

In 1895, Roosevelt had stated categorically that he "would a hundred fold rather keep the game as it is now, with the brutality, than give it up."[32] His response to Eliot's call for abolition was that it would be doing "the baby act." After his commencement speech, through the offices of the headmaster of Groton, Roosevelt summoned representatives of Harvard, Princeton, and Yale to the White House to encourage reforms in the way the game was being played. Reid was among the delegates (and Reid would be called to Washington two more times to give his account of specific nasty incidents). Two years later, in another speech at Harvard, Roosevelt restated his basic position: "As I emphatically disbelieve in seeing Harvard, or any other college, turn out mollycoddles instead of vigorous men I may add that I do not in the least object to a sport because it is rough."[33] What threats to the game remained were defused by a cagey Reid, who gathered his staff together and released a letter condemning exactly what he knew Eliot objected to, and doing so "with a manner of expression," he confessed twenty years later, "as close to his own as we dared use."[34]

In the relatively early days of his presidency, Eliot descended to the rhetoric of manhood on which so many discussions of collegiate and intercollegiate sports would be based. He too could implicitly attack the arty types, the dissipated and the idle ones, anyone whom he imagined avoiding the gym and the playing fields. He could join the chorus that declared that "effeminacy and luxury are even worse evils than brutality."[35] And he extended the defense of bodily exercise out into the rough-and-tumble world of business. It was a common argument. Even reading the College's most impressive literary magazine, the *Harvard Monthly,* you would learn (in an article by A. T. Dudley titled "The Mental Qualities of an Athlete") that athletic participation prepared a man for business because it made him more reliable and added to "the coolness and confidence with which he attempt[ed] any task in later life."[36] In 1881, Eliot sounded that note too. "Games and sports" helped, he said, "not only because the ideal student [had] been transformed from a stooping, weak, and sickly youth into one well-formed, robust, and healthy," but because of what automatically followed: "the perseverance, resolution and self-denial necessary to success in athletic sports turn out to be qualities valuable in business and other active occupations of after life."[37]

But finally Eliot stood apart. Year after year, in his annual reports, he attacked football as the embodiment of everything that compromised the ideal man who made the most of his time at Harvard. "Games and sports" might have been beneficial to a young man in the earlier, more decorous stage of his development—he himself had rowed as an undergraduate—but over the years they had assumed monstrous forms. In a section headed "The Evils of Football," in his 1903–4 report, he noted that given "the moral quality" of the game, "worse preparation for the real struggles and contests of life can hardly be imagined." Clinging to language that befit a gentleman, he wrote,

Civilization has been long in possession of much higher ethics than those of war, and experience has abundantly proved that the highest efficiency for service and the finest sort of courage in individual men may be accompanied by, and indeed spring from, unvarying generosity, gentleness, and good will.[38]

He was especially incensed by the war analogy. In his report for 1898–99, he had given the lie to the simple-minded notion that scholars were men with poor builds, and to the equally simple-minded notion that athletes were more likely to go to war. He had gone to the records, and they proved otherwise. He also pointed out that nothing could be further from actual fighting than the bodily contacts of football.[39] Even at West Point and Annapolis, the conditioning was more subtle than that. "One of the most cheerful things" about the education offered at those institutions was, he said in 1899, "the systematic provision of dancing."[40] So opposed to football was he by then that in his mind it had become war's immoral equivalent. At least officers displayed some gentlemanly social grace, which was more than he was willing to say for a football player.

Although Harvard's and the nation's athletic programs grew without Eliot's support and in spite of his objections, he affected their development. One could trace the various efforts at reform back to him, for whether they were successful or not, everyone knew where the president stood. His presence must also be partly responsible for what came to be known in the 1880s as "Harvard indifference"—that subtle but unmistakable pose which the Harvard man struck in order to tell you he didn't really care all that much about his team's winning. But still, the athletic program grew. No one could prove that it actually produced the model businessman or the conquering hero that orators evoked in its defense. All we can say is that the rhetoric they used to defend intercollegiate sports was the same as the one they used to describe the prerequisites for success as they understood it. Athletes were levelheaded, and calm under pressure, even as they made the quick decisions a businessman had to make. Athletes were capable of persevering, of enduring physical hardships, which has always been true of victorious warriors. Athletics were imagined, in other words, in the terms that many saw befitting America—expanding, competitive, ultimately victorious in its economic, political, and military struggles—and inasmuch as Harvard was expanding and changing in response to the times, it was bound to develop the athletic program that the boosters and leaders of the country called for.

The rhetorical circle is complete. Escaping from it, we can say, more concretely, that as Hollis and G. Stanley Hall and others pointed out, intercollegiate sports made for a more orderly student body. Rallies, parades, cheering (dutifully rehearsed beforehand at the Harvard Union), victory celebrations, and the like were mob scenes, but scenes in which the mobs were choreographed. They were a means by which students' energies were contained by the institution. What with the issue of social control becoming more and more serious, and the student body expanding and diversifying, administrators and governing boards were more and more supportive of athletics. It had the makings of an effective opiate. But because Eliot was more interested in individual achievement, he was as "indifferent" to this salient characteristic of an athletic program as he was to who won and who lost.

Around the turn of the century, the athletic issue divided Harvard men neatly along generational lines. None could avoid addressing it. Among those who were clearly of the nineteenth century—Eliot, James, Norton, Sargent, for example—the most venerable representative was the geologist Nathaniel Shaler, "the best loved man in our university," James once called him.[41] He was in many ways James' kindred spirit. From his earliest years, he was afflicted by mysterious ailments that struck his nervous system and ruined his digestion, and like James, he had broken down when he was about thirty and went abroad to take the waters. As a boy, his nerves had been so delicate that rather than be subjected to any formal schooling, he had roamed the woods around his home in Kentucky and been privately tutored in the classics and the philosophers that interested him. Later, when he came to Cambridge, he too found relief studying with Louis Agassiz—or, more exactly, settled his nerves, as James had, by learning to concentrate and thus to develop his genius as a naturalist.[42]

In reaction to the neurasthenic in him, Shaler lumped together and scorned the mere "tenderfoot" and the mere "professor," and looked to the Kentucky woodsmen, the St. Lawrence seamen, and the miners whom he met in his work as models for the grounded, practical, trustworthy life of the mind he himself wanted to exemplify for his students. "This type of strong uneducated man, while he had little learning," he said, "often had more light than those bred in academic places."[43] Shaler flourished before the age of specialization. He fancied himself a social critic (as we shall see); he wrote a five-volume (not act, but volume) "dramatic romance" on the history of the reign of Queen Elizabeth; and he taught a geology course that was, like Charles Eliot Norton's fine arts course, a gut—"all the geology necessary to a gentleman," he said.[44] As he was about to retire, he speculated that he had taught almost half of the young men who had been at Harvard during his thirty-nine years of service. A few months before his own death, after reading Shaler's posthumously published *Autobiography,* James said, "Of all the minds I have known, his leaves the largest impression, and I miss him more than I have missed anyone before."[45]

As a child Shaler watched soldiers mustering for the Mexican War, and as he grew up watched family members and friends settle affairs of honor in duels. During the Civil War, he commanded a Union regiment from Kentucky. But counting the losses, in duels as well as in battles, he never imagined men's lives coming to any glorious end in either way. "The grown men who glory in the images of war are led thereto by their sense of their own timidity," he said in his *Autobiography.*[46] On Memorial Day, 1898, in a speech titled "The True Measure of Valor," he dwelt on the ideals of the commonwealth and men's willingness to preserve them. The true soldier was to him a man who saved his breath for action, and the real hero was one who "from the essence of his nature, is a critical and generally a rather pessimistic man."[47] Again, we think of James, dragging his ailments and anxieties through life without complaining, or even letting on.

All these interests and opinions were reflected in Shaler's attitude towards athletics. In 1903, Harvard awarded honorary degrees to both him and James. At the commencement dinner, Shaler spoke about athletics. Boasting that he was the only member of the faculty who went to the Hemenway Gymnasium on a regular basis, he said he was especially justified in protesting, as he had for the past fifteen years, against the increasing emphasis on athletics at Harvard. As a naturalist, he had carefully observed the students over the years. He was happy to report that their moral life had improved (there was less drinking and gambling), but he had to say that they were less capable of steadfast work. They were distracted by all the games and everything surrounding them, distracted too by misleading talk about athletics and its relationship to war. Like so many of his contemporaries, he summed up his opposition with a gesture that evoked images of alien strains attacking the supposedly purer student body that was English: "The malady, my brethren, has its seat in the disease of athletics which is ravaging the educational system of our English people."[48] The old system of fighting the demons within, of keeping the body healthy so that the mind's focus did not blur, had worked for him. As James said, "Full of excesses as he was, due to his intense vivacity, impulsiveness, and imaginativeness, his centre of gravity was absolutely steady."[49] But as he spoke, Harvard was gearing up to pay a twenty-six-year-old football coach a third as much again as it was paying Shaler after almost four decades of teaching and research.

The best place to discover James' views on the subject is in his essay of

1899 titled "The Gospel of Relaxation."[50] It is one of three "Talks to Students" that he included in his *Talks to Teachers* that same year. Without actually citing *"mens sana . . . ,"* he held up "the ideal of the well-trained and vigorous body," and placed it "neck by neck with that of the well-trained and vigorous mind as the two coequal halves of the higher education for men and women alike." The athletic activities for women that he mentioned were the skiing and snow-shoeing that Norwegian women had taken up, and "the tennis and tramping and skating habits and the bicycle-craze which are so rapidly extending among our dear sisters and daughters in this country." Thanks to their exercise, to "the new order of muscular feelings" they had developed, Norwegian women were no longer "sedentary fireside tabby-cats," but rather leaders "in every educational and social reform." In this country, women's activities were sure to lead to a "sounder and heartier moral tone."

But the ideal he had in mind had already been realized throughout England. Attributing "the strength of the British Empire" to the "strength of the individual Englishman," James sounded momentarily like his more belligerent students, but then his vision expanded more democratically. "That strength," he was persuaded, "is perennially nourished and kept up by nothing so much as by the national worship, in which all classes meet, of athletic outdoor life and sport." Ultimately, like Eliot and Shaler and other supporters of physical education, James was interested in what the Englishman could teach the young American male who was trying to find his way in his much less settled culture. There were traditions of sportsmanship and of fair play, traditions that prevented men from being disrespectful of the law or greedy in the marketplace (even as they eventually served to justify extending Her Majesty's power around the globe). But there were also things that he could tell these men from his own experience.

What was wrong with Americans? what was the cause of our dis-ease, "this absence of repose, this bottled-lightning quality in us Americans?" James knew that everyone had read Beard on "American Nervousness"—"The explanation of it that is usually given is that it comes from the extreme dryness of our climate and the acrobatic performances of our life, the hard work, the railroad speed, the rapid success, and all the other things we know so well by heart"—but he wanted them to plumb more deeply. Consequently, he led his reader to what he knew was the psychological source of Americans' malaise— knew because he had been there. It was the state of mind he had experienced thirty years before, the mind turning in on itself, doubting itself, finding no relief in action. Now, "stated technically, the law is this, that *strong feeling about one's self tends to arrest the free association of one's objective ideas and motor processes.*" In times past, one escaped to Europe. "We say that so many of our fellow-countrymen collapse, and have to be sent abroad to rest their nerves," he wrote. But that was probably "an immense mistake." The remedies were nearer to hand. There were the popular self-help books of Annie Payson Call, books like *Power through Repose* and *As a Matter of Course,* which told the reader how to free himself "from the inhibitive influence of reflection" and helped him not to care. And there was exercise, muscular activity, which saved a man from looking and acting like this: "gigantic domes of our crania, arching over our spectacled eyes, and animating our flexible little lips to those floods of learned and ingenious talk which will constitute our most congenial occupation." Without exercise, in other words, he would be another version of the grotesque intellectual that Francis Walker had derided in his Phi Beta Kappa address on college athletics a few years before. With it, with an amount of exercise proportionate to the amount of intellectual energy expended, the student, the institution, even the race, James assured his reader, would have "calm for its ideal, and for their own sakes [love] harmony, dignity, and ease." And who would perform best in class? Often, James said, it would be "those who are most indifferent." The attitude that had taken him so long and been so hard for him to assume was precisely the one that Harvard was ingraining in students as they were coming into their manhood.

James observed the change in Harvard's attitudes towards athletics at even closer quarters: his son William Jr. was a member of the Harvard crew. In 1901, he started on the four-oared crew and won over Yale while the varsity lost. His father was in Bad Nauheim when he received the news, depressed not only about his health but about the sudden death of a colleague. He had no trouble putting his son's victory in perspective: "Yale beat the University race *[sic],*" he wrote his brother Henry, "*but* Bill's four beat the Yale four. On such things is human contentment based."[51] The next year Bill rowed bow on the varsity, and the year after that he was elected captain. But he resigned instead and went abroad. His father kept his uncle informed as to just what was involved. Bill was, he wrote,

fairly sick at heart at the prospect of another year of politics and publicity and exterminating physical training, with no opportunity for inner leisure or advance in study, and all for the sake of an end so essentially childish as spending 20 minutes a year hence rowing a few seconds faster than a crew from Yale. It takes a more primitive kind of being to regard such an end as seriously worthy of the sacrifice of a year.

He went on to say he would probably have to step in "between him and this incubus" and send his son away.[52]

In December 1903, an essay by Bill titled "Sport or Business?" appeared in the *Graduates' Magazine.*[53] Again, his father's hand is admittedly evident ("I helped him out a little bit," he told Henry),[54] but in this instance it is clear that his son spoke with his own authority as well. Not that he didn't agree with his father and his father's friends. His essay was a plea for the retention of

the spirit of amateurism. He declared that more important than Harvard's
rivalry with Yale is "the checking of its fierceness and bitterness by the graciousness of gentlemanly feeling," and went on to say that although it may be
costly in business or in politics not to finish what you start, the same need not
hold true in athletics. Something was wrong when a man played (or rowed)
not because he enjoyed the sport but because he felt it was his duty to represent
the College against Yale. He would rather see Yale beat Harvard "incessantly
if the business and hysterical elements of the thing could be left out," and he
concluded by listing the sources of those "elements": they came "from outside
pressure, from the papers, the graduates, the non-athletic undergraduates, the
crowd of betting toughs who turn up at every important game, and, in general,
the false 'friends of sport.' " They came from everywhere except the athletic
man himself. Business interests—those who looked at the gate receipts, the
media, even the gamblers—had joined those who could only watch, and together they had reduced the sporting life to a matter of winning or losing. For
them, the outcome was at best profits or psychological compensation. For the
athlete, it was a diminution of his manliness.

It takes a brave man, Faulkner once said, to quit while he's behind. William James Jr. was able to do that and to speak out in the name of sport and of
the manhood his father represented, one in which the body's health did not
support the country's domestic or foreign enterprises, but rather kept a man's
mind and "soul" alive and clear. Curiously, in the same issue of the *Graduates'
Magazine,* there appeared the first mention of his uncle's work. It took the
form of a scathing review of the most minor of his efforts, *William Wetmore
Story and His Friends* ("It is artificiality prepense, literary foppery,—grimaces,
gestures, powdering, and rouging done before a mirror").[55] It also included a
picture and a detailed description of the gigantic, Coliseum-like stadium that
was under construction on Soldier's Field. There was nothing subtle about the
kind of manhood that would be taught on the various fields of physical education in the future.*

Among the younger faculty who put the best face on the things that were
to come were two of James' colleagues in the Philosophy Department, Josiah
Royce and George Santayana. In their philosophies, both men managed to
transform athletic fields into sites of spiritual regeneration. Royce was well
known for his writings on the question of loyalty, a subject that lent itself
nicely to the ongoing discussion of athletics. It was his topic—lost in the

---

*One other James must be heard on the subject. In November 1903, Bill's brother Henry James
III, then in his third year at the Law School, wrote to the *Crimson* to protest against what he
thought were the editor's excessive efforts to drum up support for the football team. "The fun of
the game will be spoilt for all," Henry said. The author of the editorials was Franklin Delano
Roosevelt '04. Frank Friedel, *Franklin D. Roosevelt: The Apprenticeship* (Boston: Little, Brown,
1952), pp. 62–63.

unprepossessing title, "Some Relations of Physical Training to the Present Problems of Moral Education in America"—when he was invited to address the Boston Physical Education Association.[56] In his speech, he did not attempt to elevate the spirit of the students' games (what Ira Hollis had wished for football); he tried instead to define what he called the "maximal experiences" available to those who played, and to inspire the members of his audience "to find [their] way to the high places of the Spirit" through their work as physical educationalists and coaches.

The "maximal experience" was one of loyalty, loyalty as it was initially (and one expects for the occasion) *physically* expressed. ("It is useless to call my feelings loyal unless my muscles somehow express this loyalty," he claimed.) Royce then situated loyalty in the usual terms of conventional apologies for physical education. The ideal man who began to emerge combined the virtues of the athlete and "the moral hero" in ways we readily recognize from our readings of Sargent, Shaler, and—especially—James:

To hold on to one's self at the moment of greatest strain, to retain clearness, even when confronted by tasks too large to be carried out as one wishes, to persist doggedly despite defeats, to give up all mere self-will and yet to retain full self-control,—these are requirements which, as I suppose, appear to the consciousness of the athlete and to the consciousness of the moral hero in decidedly analogous ways. And in both cases the processes involved are psycho-physical as well as physical, and are subject to the general laws of physiology and of psychology.

We also know how to take the next step in the argument: there is no place in athletics for "thoughtless individualism"; athletic activity is primarily social and moral because it takes a man out of himself. What is quintessential Royce is the belief that competitive games train a man to be loyal and, what is more, to love loyalty even in his opponents. A man must love their loyalty to their cause (or love thieves who honored each other), even when it inspires deeds that one must oppose out of loyalty to one's own cause. "Fair play" is loyalty in action, he said, but "this active and practical honor for the loyalty of your opponents is no mere external ornament of the chivalrous virtues." It is nothing less than "the very essence of all the highest virtues." Accordingly, the idealist Royce envisioned loyalty working to reform the worlds for which other enthusiasts had imagined athletes being trained: "If a man is loyal to the loyalty that he has seen . . . he ought to be helped toward that loyalty to unseen loyalty which constitutes the soul of rectitude in great business enterprises, the heart of honor in our national and international enterprises."

Royce traced his young man's development from physical exercise to competitive athletics all the way to international relationships without wishing the young man was an English gentleman, but he still had trouble with the people who were getting involved in athletics. "The unsound social conditions which have been allowed to surround and to attend both the intercollegiate and the interscholastic games" made the fulfillment of his ideal very difficult. He deplored the press and the crowds, "the presence of excited and cheering multitudes" that interfered with the moral education of America's youth. "Nobody can learn loyalty from mobs," he said. "The Harvard Stadium is an admirable place when it is not too full of people."

Santayana made no effort to reconcile the spirit that he could see being elevated by athletics with the crowds surging into Harvard Stadium. In "Philosophy on the Bleachers," published in the *Harvard Monthly* in 1894, he allowed a spectator to imagine what is permanent in sport without fear of the incubus that so troubled James and others.[57] More than that, it allowed him to view sport not as preparation for other ways of life but as itself the realization of what is best in men. Seated there in the stands, watching "some well-conceived contest, like our foot-ball," Santayana saw what no one else at Harvard had seen: "The whole soul is stirred by a spectacle that represents the basis of its life."

Santayana paid no homage to gymnastics. Because he viewed the athletics he loved to contemplate as an end in itself, he considered "the valetudinarian motive" of physical education alien to what he was extolling, relatively harmless only because its scope was relatively limited. When he came to the standard comparison to war, he did not dismiss the analogy but turned it around instead. "The relation of athletics to war is intimate," he said, "but it is not one of means to end, but more intrinsic, like that of drama to life." In small American communities, as in ancient Greece, sports were not enjoyed because they trained men for war. Quite the contrary: games come into being in times of peace, allowing men freely to express their beings, their "martial energy," in "beautiful and spectacular forms." Plato wanted young men's bodies to be developed for their minds' sake, but he allotted seven years to the athletic trainers as well as seven to those who taught art. He wanted the body to be cultivated not just in order that a man become morally sound; equally important, he wanted him to be beautiful.

Santayana was sitting in the bleachers in Cambridge in the final years of the nineteenth century. Like many of his contemporaries, he looked to England for inspiration, and like theirs the ideals he imagined for the students were shaped by his understanding of what constituted true manhood. In the England that he invoked, a young man's whole existence was schooled, his teachers sharing in his social and athletic life. The sight of a master at Eton, a clergyman as well, running along the towpath beside the crew was neither unusual nor undignified. English colleges had "a value which cannot be compensated or represented by any lists of courses or catalogues of libraries,—the value of a rounded and traditional life." That life was totally and happily male, and anyone who appreciated its games, Santayana said, had "one more chamber in his memory, one more approach to things, and a manlier standard of pleasures and pains."

That appreciation united "vitality with disinterestedness," and that was "the chief claim which athletics make upon our respect." It freed up "the spontaneous and imaginative will" that in America was likely to atrophy in moral servitude. America had regained its political and religious freedom, Santayana said, but it had yet to value its moral freedom—the freedom that James had struggled so hard to gain, the freedom that Santayana so effortlessly defines as "the faculty and privilege of each man under the laws to live and act according to his inward nature." Athletics therefore might be—and Santayana knew this would "seem a ridiculous thing to say"—the culture's best weapon against the Philistines, "the most conspicuous and promising rebellion against this industrial tyranny." Turning specifically to the students, Santayana characterized their usual fate with a stylistic grace that is itself a protest against that tyranny: "We sell our birthright for a mess of pottage, and the ancestral garden of the mind for building lots."

So to Santayana there was nothing excessive in all the athletic activities at Harvard. To him it meant "infinite potentiality" and "some inward rebellion against a sordid environment," and when all was said and done, all the attention paid to athletics might have made excellent educational sense. Young men's bodies were maturing during their undergraduate years, while "the intellectual part [was] too immature to bear much fruit." Perhaps the body was the place to start; perhaps the sense of freedom and play that athletics engendered would lead a man to demand or create a better life than any represented by his elders. At the end of his essay, Santayana describes himself as filling up "the waits at a game, while the captains wrangle," and in his mind's eye imagining "greener fields" than the ones he could see from the bleachers—a latter-day Wordsworth, watching the children sport upon the shore.

Having other designs on the young men of Harvard, Santayana's colleagues were not prepared to grant them as much freedom as he was. When the athletic committee came to the question of students' authority in 1897, it meted it out cautiously—phrase by phrase. Undergraduates, they said, "under careful general restrictions, ought to be given so far as possible, a free hand in the management of their sports and in the choice of their advisers."[58] Three years later, the committee that Hollis chaired introduced a clause that corralled them even more: "It is at present the settled policy of the Athletic Committee to leave the management of sports and contests in the hands of students so far as it is compatible with good behavior and good scholarship."[59]

But no one disputed the fact that sports were themselves educative and that they ought to be an integral part of the life of a Harvard man. However much one teacher or committee's rhetoric differed from another's, everyone conceived athletic activity as vital to a young man's development, a means of strengthening him and his position in American culture. As for the development of his mind, the means would be, most famously and influentially, the elective system.

"Scholarly Manliness"

In 1889, when a nephew in California was thinking of applying to Harvard, Josiah Royce warned him that Harvard was "unquestionably a decidedly trying place for a young man, as indeed it ought to be, and is proud of being." Life at Harvard was "a great but also a very serious test and training of one's manhood, courage, ability and moral fibre." There were over a thousand students enrolled now, students with varying backgrounds, characters, and talents. His nephew should remember that the East, and especially a great college like Harvard, could be "at first very imposing, and a little overwhelming in its bigness and its dignity of new life"—and he added, "I speak as a California boy myself." If his nephew was serious about coming, he should first come East for some preparatory schooling, and to that end, Royce recommended that the boy seek the advice of W. T. Reid, an alumnus who had founded a school in Belmont, California (and who was the father of Harvard's future football coach). "What you want is the *best* schooling, even if it loses you a year or even two of time. Unless you want the *best* preparation, it isn't worthwhile to think of Harvard."[1]

Royce had described the situation at Harvard very well—which may be why, for all we know, his nephew never came east. In his talk of testing and training, of courage and moral fiber, he was presumably telling his nephew what he might expect in Harvard's classrooms, but his language could easily have been lifted from any number of descriptions of the nature and purpose of Harvard's athletic program. It lent itself to either, and to the social scene as well. In whatever situation a young man found himself at Harvard, it would be "a very serious test and training of [his] manhood."

A month before Royce sent his letter, writing in the *North American Review,* Shaler also conjoined remarks about young men's behavior and their education in the same gendered terms.[2] Addressing the subject of "Discipline in American Colleges," he proposed that any problems having to do with students' conduct be solved, as at Harvard, by arousing their "manly, dutiful sense" of their educational opportunities and responsibilities:

Every youth who is fitted to be a student in our higher colleges or universities will quickly respond to the stimulus he feels in passing from the disciplinary conditions of childhood to those which are fit for men. If he be in spirit capable of scholarly manliness, we may be sure that his imagination has forerun the conditions he has met in his lower schooling. He has longed for something like the independence and responsibility of manhood; for an advance to the place of trust to which he is bidden.

President Eliot had made the point more succinctly in his inaugural address twenty years before: "The best way to put boyishness to shame is to foster scholarship and manliness."

Eliot himself was too much of a worldly democrat to make the connection explicit, but hovering in the air was also the idea that the young men who could wean themselves from a predigested, prescribed curriculum and face the challenge of the elective system were America's elect. Shaler, on the other hand, was not reluctant to sanctify the numbers and the selection process. "Remember," he wrote, "that few are called to the peculiar work for which the university trains men. The places it undertakes to fill are not suited to more than perhaps one in twenty of our young men." In his praise of the system, George Herbert Palmer, the senior member of the Philosophy Department, was even more definite. "A student forced, as the routine education of the past attempted to force him, is no student at all," he wrote in his autobiography. "Men of independent intelligence are therefore trained here today to a degree unknown of old." By his rendering, they were not doing God's work; rather, they were doing exactly the kind of work God Himself did: "Our Father in Heaven had been using the elective system long before we discovered it."[3]

Eliot did not invent, or even introduce, the elective system at Harvard— experiments with electivism had taken place on many campuses, including Harvard's, over the years—but the way he presented it has shaped debate about undergraduate education ever since. The process of its establishment was long and at times difficult. There were strong opponents in every constituency except the student body; in 1885–86, Eliot's advocacy of the system actually prompted the Board of Overseers to look for a replacement for him. The trend was reversed in his later years—some requirements were reintroduced—but Eliot was surely justified when he said in 1894, "The development of the elective system . . . has proved to be the most generally useful piece of work which this university has ever executed."[4]

Up until the 1870s, American undergraduates would typically study a limited number of required subjects in a strictly limited way. At Harvard, all freshmen would take Latin, Greek, mathematics, French, elocution, ethics, and Duruy's *Histoire Grecque*. As sophomores they would have to take physics, chemistry, German, elocution; they would write themes and pore over "twenty chapters of Gibbon's 'Decline and Fall' and 'about 350 pages' of Dugald Stewart." They also had to take eight hours of classes a week from a list of course offerings limited to Latin and Greek, mathematics and Italian, and English. The same balancing of requirements and a few electives continued in their junior and senior years. Their choices were restricted further by the fact that each course was identified with a particular class, so that however well prepared a student might be, he would have to wait until his junior year, say, before he could study what was offered to juniors. A student coming to Harvard already proficient in Greek would have to wait until his senior year before he could read *Antigone;* he could have had eight years of Latin and still not be allowed to study Juvenal until his junior year.[5]

Colleges enjoyed and strengthened the illusions that they knew and could teach what ought to be known about the world. The system was further tightened by the prevailing belief that growing boys possessed certain faculties or powers that were to be sequentially developed, if not literally exercised. What has since been called a "core curriculum" offered a young man what he needed to know, and developed the means by which he would need to know thereafter. Knowing the course of empires as exemplified by the fate of the Romans, for example, would have been considered a necessary part of a young gentleman's education. A young man would trace and learn the ways of history by ingesting twenty chapters of Gibbon, and ever after, that man would live confidently in the knowledge that the experience of peoples proceeded according to the principles exemplified by that set text.

The Civil War was a great shock to men's confidence that they could predict history's course. By the end of the century, only the most pious could believe that the culture lent itself to but one interpretation that could be arrived at by one route. But Darwin had already called their beliefs about men's mental and moral makeup into question. Of more immediate, or at least ongoing relevance to what went on in the classroom was the rise of experimental psychology in Germany, and its importation into American thinking by men like James and Hall. It made it increasingly difficult to retain the belief that all men possessed specific powers of judgment and feeling that could be strengthened in specific uniform ways. What James demonstrated experientially, what he knew from his readings of Emerson, and what he went on to recount in his writings was that ultimately each man had to define and determine the nature of his own individual existence. What James struggled with in the late 1860s—his body, his mind, the relationship between the two—became a focus of scientific inquiry. It was his student E. L. Thorndike who dealt the death blow to the idea of a uniform set of laws that the mind obeyed, with his proof that skills developed in one function do not operate in others. Memorization or recitation did not necessarily lead to greater attentiveness or accuracy in one's thinking about anything other than what one was memorizing or spouting back.[6]

At other institutions reform came slowly. Sounding a bit unsportsmanlike, Eliot declared in 1880, "The manners and customs of the Yale Faculty are those of a porcupine on the defensive." In fact, it was President Noah Porter—not his faculty—who held out for mental discipline. When Yale did allow its students freedom to choose—by 1901, that meant all upperclassmen—their choices were still limited to sequences of courses, and they had to meet distribution and concentration requirements as well. At Princeton, Presidents James McCosh and Francis Patton were even more conservative (the latter citing Calvin, Augustine, and Saint Paul as his authorities well into the 1890s), but by the end of the century, the last two years of the Princeton curriculum were completely elective.[7]

In his inaugural address, Eliot gestured towards the "accurate general knowledge of all the main subjects of human interest" that Harvard would enable its students to gain. But his speech made clear that general knowledge was not his primary concern. The students would be only "acquainted" with it, "acquainted in a general way with the accumulated thought of past generations." What he cared most about was a young man's developing his own interests. "Every youth of eighteen is an infinitely complex organization, the duplicate of which neither does nor ever will exist," he said in a later talk titled "Liberty in Education." Provided he had been well instructed, such a youth could select "for himself alone—a better course of study than any college faculty, or any wise man who does not know him and his ancestors and his previous life, can possibly select for him."[8] Between the very months when William James (then almost thirty) cursed himself for the "dead drifting" of his own life and determined to "believe in [his] individual reality and creative power," President Eliot declared in his inaugural address that "a young man of nineteen or twenty ought to know what he likes best and is most fit for"—adding with feigned impatience, "If he feels no loves, he will at least have his hates." The schools would have given a boy training that was "sufficiently wide." By the time he came to Harvard, he would know "whether he [was] most apt at language or philosophy or natural science or mathematics," and his appreciation of his own talent, or "genius," as James was calling it at the time, was cause for celebration:

When the revelation of his own peculiar taste and capacity comes to a young man, let him reverently give it welcome, thank God, and take courage. Thereafter he knows his way to happy, enthusiastic work, and, God willing, to usefulness and success.

In his 1884–85 report, drawing on the sartorial image that Carlyle had put into circulation, and preparing the way for Henry Adams' use of it in the preface to his *Education*, Eliot said, "Groups are like ready-made clothing, cut in regular sizes; they never fit any concrete individual."[9] Harvard was interested in the individual and would help him tailor his education to fit his own, not any group's, needs and abilities.

Eventually, Harvard would offer a multiplicity of courses from which a student could freely choose. In the very first words of his address, Eliot said that Harvard would recognize "no real antagonism between literature and science." There would be no choosing between "mathematics or classics, science or metaphysics." He spoke of poetry, and of the dismal condition of the English language, of languages ancient and modern, and of the "indispensable" natural and physical sciences. Out of loyalty to his cousin Charles Eliot Norton, he got specific and also warned, "We cannot afford to neglect the Fine Arts." In sum, "We would have them all, and at their best."

Not only the individual but the state would benefit—"for the State, it is variety, not uniformity, of intellectual product, which is needful." To underscore the point, he turned to a production site few, if any, college or university presidents were likely to turn to in 1869. Well aware that in science and technology America was moving on, Eliot pointed to the "thousands of years between the stone hatchet and the machine-shop." There had been dizzying change in the sciences, and a Harvard education would make it hard for a young man to ignore that fact. It would focus his attention on the realities of contemporary American life. On the other hand, it would be a liberal and not a vocational education. No subject would be explored for its mere utilitarian value. No subject would be introduced in order "to promote the material welfare of mankind. . . . Truth and right are above utility in all realms of thought and action."

Within a few years, Eliot saw to it that courses were listed according to the area of their offerings, rather than by class, with numbers and instructors' names for quick identification. Eventually a student would be able to take any course at any time, provided he could prove that he was qualified. Starting at the top, with the seniors, Eliot chipped away at curricular requirements. By 1884, there were none, other than freshman English and French (or German), sophomore and junior themes and forensics, and two routine half-year lecture courses in physics and in chemistry. Starting the same year, freshmen were allowed to elect courses freely. Gradually all requirements (with the exception of English) were dropped.

Soon after the demise of the freshman Latin and Greek requirement, Harvard stopped requiring Greek for admission. The classics were no longer such trustworthy guides as to justify being required subjects of study. "By the later years of the eighties," Edmund Wilson has written, "the industrial and commercial development which followed the Civil War had reached a point where the old education was no longer an equipment for life. It had, in fact, become a troublesome handicap."[10] As an admission requirement, Greek disqualified students who did not have the advantage of attendance at elite preparatory schools, students whom Eliot wanted to attract to Harvard. The chagrin caused by the elective system as a whole came to a head when the presidents of eight New England colleges begged the members of the Corporation to reverse Harvard's decision to drop the Greek requirement.

Freed from the burdens of classical studies, a young man would be able to gain what Eliot described as "a minute and thorough knowledge of the one subject which each [student] may select as his principal occupation in life." He might discover his own heritage and gain a general knowledge of "all the main subjects of human interest"—but how he might do one or the other Eliot did not say. His focus was on the individual young man and on his ability to specialize. He even recommended how he might more efficiently spend the hours of his day—eight hours of sleep, three for meals, two of exercise, one for "social duties," and ten hours for study, he told the assembled freshmen in 1894.[11] The emerging man was to go through a harder day than the one that his equally well-organized predecessor Ben Franklin had scheduled for himself. If Eliot had anything to say about it, he would not engage in competitive sports. He would exercise instead, the body's health being integral to his realization of himself as a man. But whereas Ben Franklin had allowed for "diversion, or conversation" between seven and ten in the evening, Eliot imagined the Harvard undergraduate tearing himself away from his studies for just one hour, and even then only out of a sense of obligation to his classmates.

Of course, under the elective system there was the distinct possibility that he might gain little or nothing from his education. Without the support of a prescribed curriculum, forced to take on the burdens of choice himself—choice of his "occupation of life," choice of the courses that would prepare him for his occupation—he might collapse under the pressure. Wilson goes on to speak generally of the "appalling demoralization" of members of the college classes of the eighties, and of "the rate of failure and insanity and suicide." The breakdowns and neurasthenic episodes of almost every figure whom we have met bear Wilson out.

More likely was the possibility that they would indulge in a life that required no constructive effort whatsoever, that they would merely gather evidence for later claims that these were the best years of their lives. Behind all the criticisms of Harvard as "a rich man's college," behind all the "Harvard Stories," was the assumption that the Harvard undergraduate did not have to work very hard. If at all. He could hire men (poorer students, or former students who had set up shop in town) to write his papers for him, or to tell him what went on in classes he never attended. The *Crimson* regularly ran ads for such services. There were stories about one or another young man who simply headed south (to Havana, in the one most often cited) for the term. The institution tightened its attendance policy, and some professors scheduled exams at strategic times. In 1889, the *Harvard Monthly* reported that James had scheduled an exam on the Saturday of a Princeton game, only to cancel it the day before in response to his students' consternation.[12] Much was made of an advising system that saw to it that the students were not left helpless or allowed too much freedom, but glaring abuses remained. It was one thing for Santayana to "cut" all the lectures of his Latin class except the first and come away with a 90 for the term, but quite another—as was the case—for 55 percent of the class of 1898 to take nothing but elementary courses during its four years at Harvard.[13] Eliot had spoken of students spending ten hours a day studying, but in 1903 it was discovered that they spent more like fourteen hours a *week*.[14] There was ample reason why the Faculty of Arts and Sciences was sometimes called the "Faculty of Larks and Cinches."[15]

But shocking as the situation appeared to the public and to many of Eliot's fellow educators, he himself was not concerned. In 1885, he claimed that the faculty was of the unanimous opinion that "more and better work [was] got from this class of students under the elective system than was under the required." Whether that was true or not, he remained certain of the wisdom of creating a situation in which young men could test and develop their own capacity to function as mature men in a complex and demanding society. Like James, he imagined a moral life for his students in the sense that he wanted their lives to be willed, directed from within. As Nathaniel Shaler put it in his article "Discipline in American Colleges" in 1889, under the elective system, "the young men are made ready for the work of the world." The very process of electing courses was educational: "This repeated choice is, as a feature in education, worth more than any other instruction which [the student] receives in the college, for the reason that it brings him at once into contact with the problems of life."[16]

In 1886, Harvard became the first American institution of higher learning to abolish required chapel. Allowing students more freedom in their social lives, Eliot shrunk the College rule book from about forty pages to five. A shrewd psychologist in his own right, when the rowdier element took to setting bonfires in the Yard, he told the proctors to ignore them and thus deprive them of much of their childish motivation. The fires died down. On a more principled level, he believed that "the moral purpose of a university's policy should be to train young men to self-control and self-reliance through liberty." As for the less intellectually mature, Eliot felt they would not behave all that differently under stricter conditions and, moreover, might be inspired by a teacher to whom they were drawn for their own reasons. He also knew what Hart had pointed out in writing about manhood at Harvard, namely, that given their freedom of choice, those who complained of not being interested, or acted out their lack of interest in a class, were on much shakier ground than they would have been had attendance been required. Harvard was for disciplined, *self*-disciplined, men. "It really does not make much difference what these unawakened minds dawdle with," Eliot said.[17]

Whether or not they abused their privilege, student after student sang the praises of the elective system. "I found freedom of the spirit all about me. . . . I unfolded as a flower unfolds when the physical conditions are right," Hutchins Hapgood wrote.[18] "If there could be a place intellectually more attractive than Harvard University toward the end of the Nineteenth Century, my imagination does not give it form," his brother Norman (like Hutchins, a journalist and prestigious social critic) said.[19] Robert Morss Lovett, man of letters and professor of English at the University of Chicago for forty years, testified to the "stimulating and broadening effect" of the elective system, even as he spoke of Harvard as an "intellectual cloud-cuckoo land."[20] When he looked back on his days at Harvard in the 1890s, Monroe Trotter, the first Negro to be elected to Phi Beta Kappa, folded praise of the elective system into praise for all that Eliot hoped it would represent:

Harvard was an inspiration to me because it was the exemplar of true Americanism, freedom, equality, and real democracy. Harvard was a place where all races, proscribed in other sections, could find carried out in a practical way the policies and ideals that all beings want. Each individual was taken on individual worth, capability, and ambition in life.[21]

But in spite of Eliot's praise of the elective system, the faculty was *not* unanimously in support of the system. In 1900, in "Some Old-Fashioned Doubts about New-Fashioned Education" in the *Atlantic,* Eliot's own dean of students, LeBaron Russell Briggs, questioned the freedom of the system and asked whether the natural sciences had proven as successful in training young minds as classics and mathematics.[22] Joining him on the "Committee on Improving Instruction" two years later was Professor A. Lawrence Lowell, who, having set his sights on succeeding Eliot, had already begun to criticize the system many years before.

The most provocative opposition—in print, if not in the corridors of power—came from Irving Babbitt, an assistant professor of French at the time. Like Eliot and so many others, Babbitt focused on his students' manhood, and in fact the man he wanted to see emerge from Harvard was much like the one Eliot had in mind. But Babbitt had nothing but scorn for Eliot's methods. According to his acerbic summation of Eliot's eighteen-year-old and the system that catered to him, "The wisdom of the ages is to be as naught compared with the inclination of a sophomore."[23]

Like Eliot, Babbitt deplored the rise of competitive athletics. They had become an end in themselves, success in them had become everything, as it would in the realm of business the students entered upon graduation, and the adulation of the athlete had produced the worst kind of snobbery. No one was to be fooled by the numbers of students from public schools or working to pay their way through school. It was not "worship of family or of wealth," he said, but "athletic prowess" that had become the source of the "real snobbishness" prevailing among college students. "Indeed, the American has suffered more seriously in his humane standards by his pampering of the athlete than the Englishman by his truckling to the lord." Though Babbitt could agree that some kinds of athletic activity were needed "as an offset to certain enervating influences of modern life," and that without some physical education an undergraduate would turn out to be no more than a pale copy of a man, the ideal man the students were looking up to was only a brute. So by the standards of the day, one was forced to choose between two indefensible positions, "to oscillate between effeminacy and brutality, and at the same time miss the note of real manliness." By his more "humane standards," Babbitt would have educators sound and listen for that "note of real manliness."[24]

His standards were those of the Greeks, his man not just the sound-bodied, healthy-minded figure idolized by physical educators, but rather the reasonable man in whom opposites—sympathy and judgment, thought and feeling, unity and diversity, the absolute and the relative—were reconciled. His hazy definitions of this man became somewhat clearer in his criticisms of the modern world. He thought it a specializing age, in love with facts, a scientific, efficient age. He called himself a humanist, one devoted to the perfection of the individual man, but all around him he saw humanitarians—men concocting schemes to elevate mankind as a whole—holding sway. Babbitt thought students were being encouraged to limit their studies on the basis of a particular interest or talent, and to get on with the business of living and earning too quickly.

Beginning in the early 1880s, Harvard had made it possible for students to graduate after only three years if they gained extra points on their entrance examinations or took extra courses during the term or over the summer. Some defenders of the policy said their talents were needed in the world, and that they would marry earlier and have more children for the race's sake.[25] By 1906, over a third of those graduating with a B.A. were taking advantage of the three-year option. Babbitt noted with dismay that whereas at Oxford the less able students departed after three years and the better ones stayed on and worked for honors, Harvard was rushing the better ones out, while "the inferior or idle student who remains is labored over by a humanitarian faculty in accordance with its great design of leavening the lump and raising the social average."[26]

Babbitt also pointed to the beginnings of a dichotomization of courses on the basis of familiar stereotypes of men. He saw that in an age that honored the athlete on the field and the specialist in the academy, young men would flock to courses in the "hard" sciences and be ashamed to take literature seriously: "The literature courses, indeed, are known in some of these institutions as 'sissy' courses. The man who took literature too seriously would be suspected of effeminacy. The really virile thing is to be an electrical engineer." Throwing up his hands over the feminization of literary studies, Babbitt said he could already envisage "the time when the typical teacher of literature will be some young dilettante who will interpret Keats and Shelley to a class of girls."[27] In his bitterness, Babbitt used this gendered caricature to revile the culture, which meant, though, that he relied on its language. He only wanted to turn it around. *His* men, he argued, were the manlier for addressing the range of serious questions raised by literature. Whereas someone like Hugo Münsterberg of the Philosophy Department contrasted the more masculine, or "productive," scholars with his more passive, or feminine, colleagues who merely "distributed" the findings of others, Babbitt's ideal scholar was the one who made "that effort of reflection, virile above all others, to coordinate the scattered elements of knowledge, and relate them not only to the intellect but to the will and character."[28]

Babbitt's students Wallace Stevens and Van Wyck Brooks (both graduates after three years) also felt compelled to construct and defend an image of the lettered man as masculine. "Poetry and Manhood" was the title Stevens gave an entry in the journal he kept as an undergraduate:

> Poetry and Manhood: Those who say poetry is now the peculiar province of women say so because ideas about poetry are effeminate. Homer, Dante, Shakespeare, Milton, Keats, Browning, much of Tennyson—they are your man-poets.[29]

The ideas about poetry that were in the air were those of R. H. Stoddard, Richard Watson Gilder, E. C. Stedman, Henry Van Dyke, G. E. Woodberry—men long since forgotten, but influential critics, editors, and anthologists of the fin de siècle. Poetry was to them a renunciation of the world and all its "getting and spending," the means by which the soul ascended to purer realms. The writing or appreciating of poetry was clearly incompatible with making one's way among men in the "real" world. Keats was their representative poet. Stevens would use what he claimed was a manly Keats for his own poetic purposes, and he would succeed as an insurance executive in America's supposedly more masculine business culture while writing poetry. Like Babbitt's, his thinking bore the imprint of the stereotyping that emerged during these years. It is evident, for example, when he revealed the "great secret" to his future wife that he was gathering together "a little collection of verses"—"There is something absurd about all this writing of verses; but the truth is, it elates and satisfies me to do it. It is an all-round exercise quite superior to ordinary reading. So that, you see, my habits are positively lady-like"[30]—or when, many years later, he gave a lecture titled "The Figure of Youth as Virile Poet."[31]

Brooks sat at the feet of Professor of English Charles T. Copeland—or "Copey," as he was commonly and affectionately called—whose chambers in Hollis Hall were always open "Wednesday evenings after ten." He listened while Santayana brushed aside American poetry with the *mot* "We poets at Harvard never read anything written in America except our own compositions," and he sipped sherry while Charles Eliot Norton read from the *Paradiso* at his home on Shady Hill. But he was devoted to none of them. Brooks found Copeland too enamored of the merely journalistic and unappreciative of his style, he preferred the canine to Santayana's feline manner, and he never felt entirely at ease at Norton's house. But these were the circles in which he traveled, and he was ready to confront anyone who thought that those who appreciated the arts were nothing but limp-wristed aesthetes. In an article on "the so-called 'aesthetic' side of college" that he published in the *Advocate*, Brooks started out cautiously but proudly, saying, "I desire first of all to make plain that the word 'aesthetic' indicates not a flabby, purple and altogether repulsive state of mind, but the outlook on life of certain clear and sensitive persons who are quite honest and straightforward and by no means effeminate." There were posers of every stripe—posing aesthetes, posing democrats, posing athletes. When you came right down to it, he said, "I rather think it is less harmful to pass one's self off as a person of exquisite taste than to pass one's self off as a 'fine manly fellow'—when one is, after all, merely average in both respects."[32]

Their parents' financial situations figured in both Stevens' and Brooks' decision to graduate in three years, but more important in Brooks' case was the fact, underlined in *An Autobiography*, that *"the university is the very worst place possible for a man with literary ideals."*[33] Men of letters abounded, and he had no trouble finding sympathetic friends, but like Babbitt (the teacher who influenced him most), he thought that the institution did not take literature seriously enough, and that Eliot and the elective system were to blame. Eliot called those courses whose utility he could not immediately discern "culture courses."[34] By 1904, with half of the graduating class planning to go into business,[35] and with no means of making him think otherwise, the average undergraduate would be inclined to accept the implied message that courses in literature were peripheral. The masculinist ethos prevailed. Under the elective system, a student was encouraged to follow whatever path he wanted, but some were obviously considered straighter than others.

Babbitt had shaped many of Brooks' attitudes, but the trouble was that Babbitt himself was unapproachable. He was an exasperated and a dogmatic man, miscast as a teacher of French ("a cheap and nasty substitute for Latin," he called it), and though he possessed, Brooks said, some of the "masculine virtues" that he admired in critics, he had none of the "feminine virtues" that he despised, so that his pronouncements about "poised and proportionate living" were unconvincing. For all his interest in the whole man, Babbitt himself was no model. Nor was his division between the humanitarian and the humanistic, as Brooks discovered when he actually *read* Babbitt. The world was changing fast, there were peoples who had a right to be heard, retreat was no strategy for a young man who cared about literature and its relation to "the actualities of modern living."[36]

Looking back on his days at Harvard, Brooks saw himself as too immature to appreciate what the men in the Philosophy Department had to offer; he regretted most not having studied under James. He had fallen in with those who "looked backward in time and across the sea" instead. Only later did Brooks come "to admire and love this enemy of all despair, of authority, dogma, fatalism, inhumanity, stagnation."[37]

Brooks may have been too immature, but he was also too late. He had come at the end of an era—the era, specifically, in which one learned at the feet of men. The Harvard that had with its elective system concentrated its efforts to educate independent-minded men who would be recognized as leaders in the world was, according to the opposition, finding it difficult to monitor what it was doing. Writing in 1889, Shaler had said that Harvard's educational system required a large number of instructors, enough men to watch over and be responsible for students' conduct and learning, even as they required students to make choices on their own: "The method of work must be such that the teachers come in very close contact with the students. The relation between officers and students must not be very remote, as under the unhuman system common of old, but one of man to man."[38] In 1900, when G. Stanley Hall joined Dean Briggs and Professor Lowell and others in criticizing Harvard's "method of work," what worried him most was the widening of the gap between the faculty and its students. According to his long account, "Student Customs," the spirited, even savage boy who went off to a college found outlets for his energies in his songs and in his cheers, in the rituals of his clubs, in debate, and in athletic activity, but (turning specifically to Harvard) because of the loss of class unity, he could no longer comfortably learn humility, or docility. By the same token, the elective system could lead to "premature independence [which] is always dangerous and tempts to excesses." The students were on their own, and their teachers had withdrawn. "Our typical young professor," Santayana had observed in 1894, "wishes to be a scholar, and is a teacher only by accident." Whatever the explanation—the pressures of professional advancement, the numbers and the unruliness of the students, the faculty's own felicific calculus—"teaching itself," as Hall put it, had "degenerated to a trade."[39]

Bigness was winning out. "The bigger the unit you deal with, the hollower, the more brutal, the more mendacious is the life displayed," James wrote in 1899.[40] What was most distressing to Brooks was the "unhuman" state of faculty-student relationships. They had been "Germanized and depersonalized into a pure intellectualism," he said. The learning that Harvard encouraged had become more and more specialized, its faculty more and more professional, more and more likely to withdraw in order to "do its own work." There was no one left for a student to work with "man to man." Brooks wondered if he had learned anything at Harvard that he wouldn't have learned just as easily had he stayed home.[41]

"Man to Man": The Faculty and Students at Harvard

In his inaugural address, Eliot asserted that a college is the safest place for a young man to be "during the critical passage from boyhood to manhood," and that what made the passage not only safe but successful was the presence of his teachers. Colleges served to socialize a boy, he said. No "sloth, vulgarity, and depravity," or "shams, conceit, and fictitious distinctions," could survive in the "exuberant activity" that characterized college life. There was, in other words, strong peer pressure. But what more surely guaranteed a student's emergence into manhood was the presence of the right teacher. In an uncharacteristic display of emotion, Eliot encouraged students to express their gratitude to whatever man it was who had made their intellectual maturity possible:

When you feel a true admiration for a teacher, a glow of enthusiasm for work, a thrill of pleasure at some excellent saying, give it expression. Do not be ashamed of these emotions. Cherish the natural sentiment of personal devotion to the teacher who calls out your better powers. It is a great delight to serve an intellectual master. . . . If ever in after years you come to smile at the youthful reverence you paid, believe me, it will be with tears in your eyes.[1]

The presence of one's fellow undergraduates, and the code of manliness they silently upheld, could be oppressive in stifling "genuine sentiment." The otherwise stoical Eliot told students to forget that code when their thoughts turned to their mentors.

When he began in 1869, nothing had been more important to Eliot than teaching. One of the first points he made in his inaugural address was that "[t]he actual problem to be solved is not what to teach, but how to teach." Jettisoning requirements, abandoning faith in the existence of faculties that needed exercising, meant—among other things—no more recitations, and this meant that students could think on their own and their teachers not just drill and correct, drill and correct. The system required more courses and more teachers (for which Eliot immediately found the funds), who would teach more of what they, as well as the students, wanted. The change called for more independent research on the part of the faculty, but Eliot welcomed it on the correct assumption that a teacher would be more likely to inspire his students if he himself was in pursuit of further knowledge. At the outset, Eliot said it was his firm conviction that "the prime business of American professors in this generation must be regular and assiduous class teaching." This was his conviction even as he determined to establish a system that would make teaching secondary in the generations that followed.

But at least until the turn of the century, there were men who had watched over and in a variety of ways nurtured the Harvard undergraduate. For all their differences, they did so with a sense of common purpose. Teaching was *not* a trade, George Herbert Palmer later wrote, but rather a profession, an end in itself, involving self-fulfillment and service to others. To him it was the best of the professions—a "prophetic" activity that presented "a type towards which all organized society moves." It beckoned men to a society in which "the mad scramble for personal profit will cease to enslave us," in which men will find their own "best opportunity for personal self-expression" and consider their neighbor's needs inseparable from their own. Through their devotion to these ideals, teachers constituted what Palmer called a "consecrated brotherhood."[2] Writing for *Scribner's Magazine* an article called "The Life of a College Professor" in 1897, Bliss Perry betrayed just how privileged this brotherhood was when he said, "Your life-long associates will be gentlemen." But like Palmer, like all of his colleagues at the time, he considered professors men who were setting an inspiring example for their students and the world.[3]

Ideally the students were face to face with the kind of men they were to become. They chose their courses more and more freely and, with Eliot's encouragement, more and more on the basis of the men whom they thought worthy of emulation. They learned their manner as well as what they taught. Indeed their manner was what they might be most likely to remember. When required chapel was abolished, a program of morning prayers took its place. It proved to be a vital program not only because it was voluntary but also because of the initial presiding preacher to the University, the Reverend Phillips Brooks. "When Phillips Brooks preached," it was said upon his death in 1893, "men listened, for the most part, not to the sermon, but to him." He aimed "directly at the heart of his hearers," giving them not theology but "the presence of a strong, loving, aspiring, and believing soul."[4] In similar fashion, James and his colleagues—Briggs, Copeland, Norton, Palmer, Royce, Shaler, Wendell, and, slightly later, Santayana—presented themselves as guides and examples.

Going back a few years, one can see—in spite of the protective irony with which he later surrounded his experience—that the method Henry Adams employed in teaching history at Harvard between 1870 and 1877 was ideally suited to the educational process that Eliot had in mind.[5] With a metaphor that would have fit right into Adams' *Education* (1907) almost forty years later, Eliot had characterized lectures as "useless expenditure of force"—useless because while the lecturer poured forth knowledge, the student sat passively, retaining very little. "The lecturer pumps laboriously into sieves," Eliot said. "The water may be wholesome, but it runs through. A mind must work to grow." Adams worked up and delivered lectures in many of the courses he taught at Harvard, but he had objections to lecturing that overlapped with Eliot's. He had "no fancy for telling agreeable tales to amuse sluggish-minded boys, in order to publish them afterwards as lectures." It was not his lectures but his small seminars that distinguished his work at Harvard.

He had been one of the first men Eliot had asked to join the faculty. Initially he refused, protesting that he knew nothing of the history he had been asked to teach (anything "between the dates 800–1649"), but Eliot convinced him that he knew as much as anyone else and that he could teach it better than anyone else they could find. Adams' knowledge of his ignorance and his concern about the way his students learned made him the teacher that he was. Though many professors might know what it was they wanted to get across, or at least did not know that they were frauds, Adams knew *he* would be one if he told romantic tales or developed evolutionary (or anti-evolutionary) theories of history. He knew history to be "in essence incoherent and immoral," and knew that it would be falsified if it were taught otherwise. It would have been ideal, he later wrote, to have "a rival assistant professor" in the room, opposing everything he said. But according to Adams, Eliot and Harvard would not go that far. They could not tolerate "contradiction or competition between teachers." Not that they insisted on any particular theory of history or on procedures by which one or another faculty would be strengthened, but at the very least there were attitudes that they wanted to ingrain in the undergraduates. They were not training men to *oppose*.

Adams ought to have been grateful to those who entertained large audiences—Norton, for example, or Shaler—for they made small courses like his possible. But he did not think they were educating the students. He thought large numbers stifled or leveled discussion; in his most famous class, he would have no more than six. He had his handful come down "through the Salic Franks to the Norman English," concentrating on legal institutions. They "worked like rabbits," he said, digging holes all over the field, burrowing into legal documents, in unknown languages. He attacked every proposition in the texts he assigned and encouraged his students to do likewise. When they reported individually on their readings, he engaged them in argument "by the hour." His mind, said one admirer, was "robust and virile," rather than "sub-tle"; in dialogue with him, his students came to believe in whatever talent they themselves possessed. "As pedagogy," Adams said, "nothing could be more triumphant."

By titling the relevant chapter in the *Education* "Failure," Adams was not just being characteristically sour. He was referring to his and his students' fate in the larger context of Harvard's educational system. Eliot wanted experi-enced men who would teach not from books alone, and he wanted students who, inspired by the example of such men, would find their own way in the world. But "try as hard as he might," Adams said of himself, "the professor could not make [his subject] actual." He had created a situation in which students had come to believe in their ability to learn, but in the context of their other courses, there was no way to put their talents to use. "What was the use of training an active mind to waste its energy?" he asked. His method led nowhere: "they would have to exert themselves to get rid of it in the Law School even more than they exerted themselves to acquire it in the college." They could learn only the way they participated in athletic activities—that is to say, "as far as possible," "so far as it is compatible," with what the institution considered good scholarship and good behavior. Some critics have related the triumph of the elective system to "industrial and business divisions of labour" and read Adams' classic as a satirical rendering of the development of capitalist education, one in which specialists emerge triumphant and "play into the nervous hands of corporate bosses who do the 'integrating' in their own interests."[6] Whatever the reading of the context within which Adams' students learned, to him that context was overwhelming. He considered failure inevita-ble. The system "could lead only to inertia."

What redeemed teaching for Adams was the students themselves. Having asked one of them what he thought he could do with the education he had received, the student replied, "The degree of Harvard College is worth more money . . . in Chicago." But the answer did not dampen Adams' enthusiasm or admiration. The students he knew were "cast more or less in the same mould, without violent emotion or sentiment," ignorant of all that men had ever known or imagined, he said, "except for the veneer of American habits," but they were quick, energetic, tireless, and touchingly committed to the idea of education. He made it a rule, he reported to his friend Charles Milnes Gaskell, "to ask questions which I can't myself answer. It astounds me to see how some of my students answer questions which would play the deuce with me."[7] He set aside a "study table" in the library for his students, and in what may be the earliest example of a "reserve" shelf, he gathered books that would be placed there for the exclusive use of his class. They met in the library of his Back Bay home. Throughout his teaching years, "he found them excellent company." Ideally, Adams imagined a teacher's knowing what a student thought of himself, his studies and his teachers, how much he knew and how well, in what spirit he approached his work and his teachers approached him. By this, "the true historical method," students' diaries would have been important sources of information. Adams did not go that far, but had there been more situations like the ones he did in fact create, he might have considered his students' Harvard education a "Success."

It is how LeBaron Russell Briggs would have labeled almost anything having to do with Harvard education—his later reservations about the elective system notwithstanding. Adams' seminars fulfilled Eliot's pedagogical ideals; Briggs' every move was taken to be a realization of some Harvard ideal. Beginning teaching at Harvard the year after Adams stopped—1878—he taught English for several decades, and served as dean of the College between 1891 and 1902, when he became president of Radcliffe College. A graduate of Harvard in the class of 1875, he was also dean of the Faculty of Arts and Sciences and the Boylston Professor of Rhetoric and Oratory during the presidency of Abbott Lawrence Lowell. Upon his retirement, he could justifiably say that few men could have cared more about the College. From all reports, no one cared more for the students. He was the legendary "friend for life," the man to whom students went when they were feeling far from home. The poet Conrad Aiken called him "one of the very few genuine saints that Harvard College has produced."[8] He was the ideal dean: because he was so liked, no one seriously questioned his authority, or protested even when asked to leave the College.

At the heart of the enterprise, as he conceived of it, was the inculcation of "self-discipline." His message to new students was a heartening one: the purpose of the College they had come to was "not so much intellectual as moral; and her strongest hope [was] to stamp her graduates with an abiding character." Their teachers, he said, would be the ones who would leave the strongest imprint; they would do so not as intellects but as models of manly character themselves.

Those were Briggs' priorities. He had gone to Germany upon graduation from Harvard, but more because that was becoming the thing to do than from any desire to study. Subsequently, like Babbitt and many others, he used the Germans as a foil. Stereotyping it all as Dryasdust, he said, "Of all scholarship theirs is the easiest to attain."[9] So far as he was concerned, "the teacher's first business is to teach—writing is a secondary affair." His ideal teacher was the schoolmaster "whose preparation consists first in manliness, and secondly in only a moderate amount of learning."[10] His ideal student was the familiar young man who engages in athletic activity but not too much athletic activity, and who studies but does not lose himself in thought. In apportioning the energies of this ideal undergraduate at Harvard (and on this occasion, Rad-cliffe), Briggs could summon up his auditors' Puritan heritage:

In the twentieth century what we call the Devil, who is never behind the times, assails the better men and women through their depressed nervous systems till some of them say, "We are tired. What does it come to? Let it go." This is the temptation of the scholarly and the sensitive.[11]

Even into the 1920s, he was still defining education in the context of the manly ideal that Harvard had been upholding in its golden age. On the subject of "The American College and the American University," he observed, "The ideal of sound and strong manhood is big, simple, noble, practical. Some men realize it without college training; but college training is in men of the right sort an inspiration to it."[12]

Briggs' close friend and colleague in the English Department, Barrett Wendell, exerted a comparable influence on the Harvard of these years—and he was even more of a legend. He was one of those who believed we murder to dissect, and so in class he would simply read literary texts and then, after a suitable silence, ask, "Isn't it beautiful?" He had a trim red beard, wore spats, carried a walking stick aloft on his little finger, and affected something like an English accent in what Briggs called "a roaming, high-pitched voice," and what others heard as "whinnying." At home he was known to bark like a dog and crawl up the stairs on his hands and knees to bed.[13]

Because he was so obviously not one himself, he was the more insistent upon honoring the typical man about campus. From his earliest days, he was one of those youths that James and Sargent and a host of others pointed to as a warning. By his own account, he was "morbidly self-conscious and pettily ill-tempered," and it followed—as they would have immediately pointed out—that he "disliked physical exercise." He started with the class of 1876 at Harvard, but what he called his "probably hysterical paralysis" forced him to withdraw to travel for a year. Before entering Harvard in 1872, he had written plays about figures he hoped would invigorate him, plays about "Raymond of Caen," "Red-wing the Pirate," and the like; as an undergraduate, he was one of the founders of the *Lampoon;* after graduating, he tried his hand at novels. He also went through the Law School, but he failed to pass the bar exam. Comparing notes with a fellow would-be man of letters, he suggested that if his friend ever thought of writing a novel about him, its title ought to be "A Study of a Failure." "A good motto for it," he went on, "would be the epitaph I have lately composed for myself: 'He lacked the courage to do good or evil.' " When his father died, he interpreted his sizable inheritance as his father's response to his not having "quite the robustness of temper which is demanded for success in the stress of American life."[14] If he needed any assurance that he was not robust enough, that he was not the man the prevailing rhetoric of

Harvard was defining, he had only to look at his younger brother Evert, who was a remarkable athlete and "a born leader,"[15] or later at his son, who was captain of the baseball team the year James' son was elected captain of the crew.

Thanks to the smallness of the world of Harvard, Wendell ended up teaching English, beginning in 1880. When he ran into his old teacher Adam Hill and expressed his frustration with the law, Hill asked him what he would rather be doing. What Hill himself did was the response, and Hill signed him on to read sophomore themes. In time, he became a professor and published frequently, but like his friend Briggs, he never considered himself a scholar. Looking back on his life, he said, "Now nobody knows better than I that I am no scholar—and therefore of no consequence to learning." On the other hand, that was never his intention:

My task as a Harvard teacher was to give glimpses of literature to men who would generally not be concerned with it in practical life. That I never forgot. Any scholar can help make scholars; but lots fail in the process to humanize. My real duty, as I saw it, was not scholarly but humane.[16]

To accomplish this task, he performed for the students.

Though their relations were cordial, Wendell's mannerisms, his endless socializing, and, more specifically, his drinking were too much for William James. Santayana was more sympathetic toward Wendell. In his tantalizing summation of Wendell's life at Harvard, we can detect something quite distinct from the masculinist ethos that dominated the place. "His force spent itself in foam," Santayana said. But insofar as Santayana was inclined to struggle against that ethos himself, he saw that, at least in principle, he and Wendell "were on the same side of the barricade."[17]

Wendell struggled to be different, but at the same time he nervously capitulated. His opinions could be so conservative as to seem frivolous. While Santayana might flippantly say that the only American writing he and his circle read was their own, Wendell wrote a whole *Literary History of America,* all the while giving the distinct impression that he did not think American literature worth anyone's serious, critical attention. In presenting a copy to James, he characterized it as "Tory, pro-slavery, and imperialistic; all of which I fear I am myself."[18] His Toryism, his protestations about good family and the importance of being a gentleman found their silliest expression in *The Privileged Classes,* a book in which he complained about taxes and about how hard it was to get things fixed, and defensively cited as "privileged" the workingmen who sprawled across two seats of a streetcar, leaving a citizen such as himself to stand.[19] When Walter Lippmann attacked it in the pages of the *Monthly,* William James went to his room to congratulate him, after which the two met weekly for tea.[20]

Wendell's affectation of such attitudes was interwoven with worries about the possible feminization of America's young men. The trouble with American writers generally was that they were "of little lasting potence." In an 1893 lecture, he did single out six New England writers for serious consideration, but he found them "emasculate," even while honoring "the great purity of their lives."[21] Casting around for more manly texts, he found them in the sixteenth century. As for the nineteenth, it was all "introspection . . . idealistic inaction." Regrettably, the Puritans had ushered in a tradition of self-consciousness and questioning, and Harvard had perpetuated it. "It is not deliberately taught," he wrote in the *Monthly* in 1889. "Indeed, I am mistaken, if many of the teachers would not suppress it," he added, but the results were undeniable: "the Harvard undergraduate is deplorably given to 'crying baby.' " In an ironic and sad turn on himself, he mounted a defense of the Philistines:

A man who goes through life without playing an active part is a failure. He may be a noble one; but his life is a real tragedy. To me there seems to be more and more truth in what I used to think the vulgar commonplaces of Philistia. . . . [A]ction is the ideal that we should keep before us—an active struggle with the life we are born to, a full sense of all its temptations, of all its earthly significance as well as of its spiritual.[22]

Wendell was arguing for no more than some way to describe introspection that would make it seem more "active" or more "strenuous," for a pugilistic account of "the dialogue of the mind with itself" that Arnold had said the nineteenth century ushered in. And finally, he knew he was doing so out of what he considered to be his own inadequacies. He said as much in correspondence with Robert Herrick—chronicler of modern, urban life in some fifteen novels and countless stories—who had been inspired by Wendell's teaching. The writing that Herrick had sent him came as a "great bewildering surge," Wendell said, "if only for its endless energy." He wished that when he was younger he had had "the luck and the pluck to give and take in a world where something was a-doing." As it was, he was left with only the urge to compensate: "Muscularity isn't my trait, now, I fear; so I love the trait far more than it may be worth by the standards of the eternities."[23]

There he was, surrounded not by those who stood aloof but by "muscular men," the hundreds of representative young men he was trying to humanize. In a piece called "Social Life at Harvard," Wendell characterized that group as one of "honest, self-respecting gentlemen, alive in rare degree to the best ideals of the time." You would recognize them anywhere, he said. They were not what Wendell called "the unwholesome book-worm once described as the 'long-haired grind,' " nor did they display "aggressive eccentricity." They might not be brilliant, they might even lack "the uncompromising vigor that the cant of our day describes as practical"—in other words, they might seem "indifferent"—but together these young men of Harvard constituted as ideal a society as Wendell could imagine.

Among Wendell's creative efforts, his first, a novel titled *The Duchess Emilia,* is of most interest because it hints at what he was hiding behind his manly front. In the safety of the Gothic tradition, or its American version by way of Hawthorne, Wendell toyed with the possibility that in the soul of a man there dwells a woman. Such is the case with his aptly named hero, Richard Beverly, who enters the steamy Roman atmosphere of intrigue and murder surrounding one Cardinal Colonna, and cleanses it with his death. What he has to purge is the murder of the Cardinal's brother by the Duchess Emilia, who is the Cardinal's lover. Beverly is a boy whose mother suppressed "the robustness that was really in his nature." Later, his ambiguous "nature" is touched on by a friend who is a painter: "A queer thing has happened to Beverly after the fashion that queer things have of happening to queer people. . . . [O]ur ideas of the common-place are only the quintessence of our own peculiar sort of queerness."[24] Whether or not the word "queer" can bear any of the weight we now put on it, Beverly, having been born the moment the Duchess dies, may in fact *be* her, which sends something of a shiver through those scenes in which the Cardinal recognizes her as the Duchess and is attracted to him. At the very least, the story represents an odd detour off the straight road that went from "Raymond of Caen" and "Red-Wing the Pirate" to Wendell's incessant defenses of the manly.

None of these men was nearly as interesting as William James in his representation—both his account and his embodiment—of Harvard's efforts to make men out of their young charges. Only George Santayana came close.

His description of the institution as "a very large machine serving the needs of a very complex civilization" comes from an article on the World's Columbian Exposition, held in Chicago in 1893, and its relation to what he called "The Spirit and Ideals of Harvard University."[25] At the exposition, Harvard was assigned 5,000 square feet of space in the Manufacturer's and Liberal Arts building. Its exhibit, according to the *Official Guide,* could in and of itself be considered "an historical review of the development of universities in America." (Yale mounted a much smaller exhibition; Johns Hopkins was represented by twenty-five framed facsimiles of pages from various of its university publications.)[26] It was good advertising—an opportunity for Harvard to present itself as being admirably responsive to the challenges of the age. Accordingly, its displays were predominantly scientific: examples of what was being studied in the Medical School, at the astronomical observatory, or—with many photographs of Professor Sargent's best specimens—at the Hemenway Gymnasium. A visitor to the exhibit could see that Harvard was abreast of every technological and scientific advance. Noting a reluctance on the part of the organizers of the exhibit to single out individuals, with the exception of "a few of its distinguished dead," Santayana imagined a visitor leaving with "the conviction that Harvard was scientific, that it was complex, and that it was reserved."

The last of these qualities was not so easy to illustrate, so Santayana devoted the final pages of his article to a description of the subtler attitudes of the student body. There were the "grinds"—the brightest students (often the poorest as well), who had little time for student activities and who, in turn, were respected but not really valued by their classmates—and there were the eccentrics who held themselves aloof. But the bulk of the men at Harvard were those on teams, on publication boards and literary societies, and in clubs. It was in those circles that "college life" gathered. "This complex social organization," Santayana said, "which the undergraduate takes very seriously . . . explains a good deal of that reserve and exclusiveness, that non-conductiveness and apathy, which is noticeable in the typical Harvard man." Everybody knew about the Harvard man's supposed "indifference" to the results of athletic contests; in his article, Santayana converted it into the typical Harvard man's overall "mental maturity and balance." The elective system had thrown each man upon himself, enabling him to develop self-reliance, self-restraint, "a habitual and constitutional choice of the nobler thing in conduct and in feeling," and withal, a sense of proportion, a tentativeness—in sum, a reserve that was fitting, given the absence of any "definite faith." By the end, he credited Harvard with catching "the spirit of the age" in this man who "worthily represents both its successes and its problems."

Many years later, in *Character and Opinion in the United States,* he described the students in terms that Henry Adams might have used. They were "intelligent, ambitious, remarkably able to 'do things.' " And yet: they took only the vaguest interest in political and religious questions, but rather got their education from their own "absorbing local traditions," those of their athletic and social life as undergraduates. They were "keen about the matters that had already entered into their lives, and invincibly happy in their ignorance of everything else." Unlike Henry Adams, he accepted the situation, adding that "teaching is a delightful paternal art." It was an art akin to the actor's, rehearsed and performed just once before an audience that was summoned and released by bells, an audience that must not be bored or perplexed or demoralized. He knew his lines. Up there on stage, he said, the lecturer could not reveal the best that was in him unless he felt the support of knowing he was "the vehicle of a massive tradition." In the absence of such support, he could not "speak in his own person, of his own thoughts," without diffidence. He was forced to speak graciously, letting science or humanity speak through him lest he sound "bitter, or flippant, or aggressive."

Acknowledging that what he might want to teach was incompatible with his students' capacities and expectations, Santayana acted out his part. The very fact that philosophers should be professors was anomalous to him: "free reflection about everything [was] a habit to be imitated, but not a subject to expound." Accepting the situation involved a heavy responsibility, and the cost of assuming it was high, but between 1885 and 1910 "the academic environment" offered no alternative:

> Now the state of Harvard College, and of American education generally, at the time to which I refer, had this remarkable effect on the philosophers there: it made their sense of social responsibility acute, because they were consciously teaching and guiding the community, as if they had been clergymen; and it made no less acute their moral loneliness, isolation, and forced self-reliance, because they were like clergymen without a church, and not only had no common philosophic doctrine to transmit, but were expected not to have one.[27]

So the philosophers and professors spoke to their charges about a rapidly changing world, tried to provide them with knowledge and demonstrate useful skills, and, above all, tried to instill values that may have had little divine authority behind them, but that nevertheless had vital civilizing power. And they felt personally responsible, even drawn to their students. They sat in the bleachers, watching while they played their games, and they welcomed them into their rooms or homes. They were enlivened by these men. As for what their teaching was accomplishing, they might have to content themselves with Adams' memorable statement "A teacher affects eternity; he can never tell where his influence stops."

The way Santayana responded to the pressure to be masculine during these years is especially illuminating. As an undergraduate in the 1880s, he was very much a part of the club and literary scenes. He served on the board of the *Lampoon* (his publications included fifty-one cartoons), was one of the founders of the *Monthly,* and joined the O.K. Society, a club that encouraged debate and drinking, the Institute of 1770, the Hasty Pudding, and several other clubs. As a young instructor, he retained his membership in a few of them, but he also joined a small group of students that took Harvard "indifference" to its limits. With Robert Morss Lovett and the Hapgood brothers, he formed the Laodicean Club. Languishing about, sipping weak tea, the members vowed not to take the religion and philosophy they discussed seriously. They elected Santayana pope. When it came time to name their saints, they recommended Horace, Goethe, Omar Khayyám (of course), and God (Santayana's choice), but having vowed to disband if they ever reached a quorum, they did so after their second meeting.

Ostensibly a joiner, Santayana more nearly resembled those whom he described in "The Spirit and Ideals of Harvard University" as remaining aloof. While an undergraduate, he sought relief from his classmates in the social life of Boston, and when he later became a faculty member, he sought refuge from his colleagues and the socialites of Boston by befriending undergraduates. Walter Lippmann remembers his "preferring to pass his leisure in the company of handsome athletes rather than with colleagues or Boston matrons."[28] He was most comfortable among the Harvard men he had celebrated in his essay, the exclusive ones, the reserved ones, whom he considered typical, even as his Spanish heritage, his Catholicism, and his relative poverty meant he could never really be one of them.

Santayana carefully walked the line between what Harvard considered morbidity and what it considered health. There were those who overstepped it. Shirley Everton Johnson, class of 1895, described them in *The Cult of the Purple Rose: A Phase of Harvard Life,* a slim volume that he published in 1902 at his own expense. "No Harvard man will take this book seriously," Johnson said in his preface. "It deals solely with the doings of a few extremists." The book recorded the activities of those undergraduates who imagined themselves working for "the advancement of art," and who looked to Max Beerbohm, Oscar Wilde, Aubrey Beardsley, and *The Yellow Book* for guidance in their efforts to make their lives "beautifully irregular."[29] To them Johnson was faithful.

Much to the displeasure of everyone at Harvard, another member of the class of 1895, Charles Flandrau, described a darker side of Harvard life—and with none of Johnson's disclaimers. In the early pages of his *Harvard Episodes* (1897), Flandrau ironically introduced "the conventional idea of a college" as consisting of "a multitude of lusty young men linked together by the indissoluble bonds of class and college, all striving shoulder to shoulder, for the same ends." He has a graduate ask a would-be man on campus, "Do you think that Harvard is fair, and do you think that it is American?" The graduate provides his own answer: whether it is fair or not, it is American, that is to say, typically American in seeming to be nobly fraternal while in fact being distinctly layered by class. What Flandrau calls "the 'hale-fellow-well-met-God-bless-everybody' ideal" is obviously a fiction, but nevertheless, there are a few men who have it in their power to "compose it" and run things as they see fit. "Fortunately," he adds wryly, "their ideas are good ones,—clean and manly."

The *reality* Flandrau's stories give us is of an institution that is undemocratic and sick. Almost all of the men who "compose" social life at Harvard live in Claverly Hall and belong to the right clubs, where they retire to drink beer and smoke pipes, while others are taking notes or even writing theses for them. There is a future magna, or even summa, cum laude in their midst, an occasional contributor to the *Monthly* (of which Flandrau was an editor) and the *Advocate,* and, of course, an athlete. But it is not their merits that bind them together. If anything, the distinctions they have earned are held against them. Only the bright lad cares what degree he earns; the athlete is away at practice all too much. What matters is their common background and their present agreeableness. "The system was scarcely broadening," Flandrau writes, "but it was very delightful."

What it supports, though, is the likes of "Wolcott the Magnificent," a bully and a snob who is tolerated, it seems, primarily for his bodily presence: "His was an exceedingly muscular, well-developed posture indeed. . . . [H]e really was magnificent. Everybody who knew about arms, and legs, and chests, and things, agreed that he was." Or Bradley, your average carouser, or, taking Wendell's hero's name one step further, Beverly Beverly, who is so persistently hounded by a woman of "abundant tonnage" in "The Class-Day Idyl" that he imagines every punishment for her short of killing her. Contrasted to Wolcott is his tutor, the "grind" who wears Wolcott's hand-me-downs and is in the end humiliated into acknowledging Wolcott's munificence. And there is— most gruesome of all—another "grind," who simply wastes away and dies of pneumonia in his digs on Kirkland Street. The student who has managed to drag some of his reluctant classmates to the funeral service muses at the end, "It was such a queer waste, his having lived and come here at all."

Flandrau's stories questioned the soundness of what Wendell and Santayana and others took to be the core of Harvard's social life, and he recounted what happened on its edges. He questioned the very myth of "the typical Harvard man," saying at the end, that it amounted to no more than that he is not ill dressed or ill bred, but rather "always a distinctly presentable young person." When *Harvard Episodes* came out, everyone was dismayed. "Why publish such unpleasant things?" the *Lampoon* asked.[30] The *Graduates' Magazine* had no trouble arriving at a verdict. "Harvard men are not habitually brutal of speech, nor unmanly, nor unemotional," they declared. The greatest failing of *Harvard Episodes* was, quite simply, that "so many of its types are unmanly."[31] Flandrau's own *Monthly* declared, "We are none of us pleased with the book, and we have said so, and our reputation as gentlemen is at stake in the manner in which we speak."[32] When Flandrau followed it up with a much less cynical *Diary of a Freshman* four years later, the *Monthly* greeted it with relief—"perfectly healthy," they called it.[33] But the *Episodes* wouldn't go away. In 1907, in the course of arguing that "the Harvard spirit is pre-eminently reverent," Dean Briggs said, "It is not to be judged by select paragraphs from 'Harvard Episodes' or by the less sensitive pages of the *Lampoon;* it is to be judged by the lives of the great body of Harvard men."[34] That "body," insofar as it was defined by Harvard's most influential men, would obviously reject Flandrau's insinuations.

Santayana's bill of health was much cleaner than Johnson's or Flandrau's, but he raised questions nevertheless. In 1894, he published a small volume of sonnets and other poems that, like Shakespeare's sequence, deliberately obscured the identity and the sex of their subject, but some of them specifically, and others presumably, commemorate the death of Warwick Potter, a student who graduated in 1893 and died of cholera shortly thereafter. Santayana described Potter as "plastic, immensely amused, a little passive and feminine," and said that his "dominant trait . . . was clear goodness." Towards the end of his life, he looked back and concluded, "Though seven years younger than I, he had been a real friend, and as I now felt, my *last* real friend."[35] These lines from "To W.P." are typical:

> In my deep heart these chimes would still have rung
> To toll your passing, had you not been dead;
> For time a sadder mask than death may spread
> Over the face that ever should be young.[36]

They are just appropriately sad and staid late Victorian performances, but from quasi-official Harvard came the warning that Santayana's volume showed signs of "morbidness." "There is a mild disease, common among a certain class of cultivated men to-day, and which we may call Walter Paterism," the reviewer for the *Graduates' Magazine* wrote. "Many mistake it for culture, but wrongly, for culture means health."[37]

Many years later, Santayana remarked to Daniel Cory, his confidant and secretary, that he supposed that A. E. Houseman was "really what people nowadays call 'homosexual,' " and that he himself "must have been that way in my Harvard days—although I was unconscious of it at the time."[38] He was certainly justified in being skeptical about the labels. Sexologists were just then introducing the terms "homosexuality" and "heterosexuality" into the language, and categorizing people rather than acts is simplistic and potentially inhumane at any time. But how disingenuous Santayana was being (or how protective Cory was) when he claimed such ignorance about his attraction to Potter and other young friends is hard to say. What *is* clear—and what matters here—is the way he felt he had to carry himself, whatever were his feelings for his student and his friends during his Harvard days. He was certainly justified, in other words, in worrying about what people thought of him.

It was one thing for him to play "the fastidious Lady Elfrida" in the Hasty Pudding show. Members did that kind of thing. So too did the members of the Dickey, when, for example, they formed a ballet troupe in their club's version of *Alice in Wonderland*. Pictures of men in flowing gowns or tutus appeared in respectable journals of the day.[39] To be sure, there were those who worried. G. Stanley Hall, for example, asked if "a truly manly nature [could] thus devirilize himself and take on so naturally all the secondary quali-

ties of the other sex without evincing either defective masculinity or else tend-
ing to induce femininity." In his essay "Student Customs," he confidently
stated, "We know too from the sad and unspeakable new chapter of psychology that deals with aberrations in this field that the passive pediast has special
gifts or abilities in the line of acting female roles."[40] But there was nothing
unusual about undergraduates engaging in such theatricals.

Still, Santayana sensed he was not playing the role expected of him. As
Cory paraphrases him, "various people at Harvard (he did not mention any
names) must have suspected something unusual in his make-up," and he felt
"acutely at times their silent disapproval." The clearest signs came from on
high, from Eliot himself. He had accosted Santayana early on in his career at
Harvard, and asked him how his classes were going. Accordingly to Santayana,
when he started to tell Eliot about his students and their progress, Eliot
interrupted him: " 'I meant,' said he, '*what is the number* of students in your
classes.' " Opposite the professor with his strange airs and social habits, his
"pessimistic, old-fashioned verses," and his unusual way of ranging through
literature and philosophy, Eliot played Gradgrind: "we should teach the *facts*,"
he told him, "not merely convey *ideas*."[41] We know that Eliot, speaking to the
mother of an undergraduate, defended Santayana's speculations about sexually
motivated behavior in the name of academic freedom, but we also know that
Santayana's presence on the faculty made him uneasy. In 1898, in expressing
his hesitation about promoting Santayana, Eliot pointed to his failure to write
textbooks (or "dig ditches, or lay bricks," he said) and his reluctance to take
part in "the everyday work of the institution." But basically, Eliot's problems
were with the man himself. "I suppose the fact to be that I have doubts and
fears about a man so abnormal as Dr. Santayana," he wrote Santayana's senior
colleague, Hugo Münsterberg. After Münsterberg assured him that Santayana
was really a "strong and healthy man," and (nice irony) "a good, gay, fresh
companion," Santayana's promotion went through.[42]

Whatever Santayana's actual feelings towards other men, he knew that he
was not perceived as meeting the prevailing standards for Harvard men. He
was not one of those who embodied "the spirit and ideals of Harvard University," not one of those whom he watched from the bleachers. What makes his
situation the more telling is that he thought to consult Harvard's own authority on matters psychological—his former teacher William James—but then
thought better of the idea.

Santayana had felt a tension between the two of them ever since his arrival
back at Harvard at the beginning of his sophomore year, after a visit to his
father in Spain. He had contracted smallpox on his trip and, he said, "must
have appeared rather weedy and unpromising to James." Unpromising as a
philosopher, Santayana meant. James' response to his interest in the subject

had been "You don't really want to go in for philosophy, do you?"[43] Over the years, for all their differences as philosophers, James developed the greatest respect for his colleague; and though he could never join Santayana on the other side of the barricade, there was a part of him that sympathized with him, for James considered himself something of an outsider too. But when James took up a central position on the faculty and in the Harvard community at large, he was bound to sense or to put some distance between them. Even as James supported him, he managed to convey a feeling that there was something missing in Santayana. In recommending him to M. Carey Thomas for a temporary appointment at Bryn Mawr in 1889, he placed the emphasis carefully in his description of him as "the best *intellect* we have turned out here in many a year." In 1896, his defense of him to Eliot was that, yes, Santayana was not an active man—"a spectator rather than an actor by temperament"—but "apart from that element of weakness," he was a man "of thoroughly wholesome mental atmosphere." It was the same argument Münsterberg would make for Santayana's promotion. What James said to Eliot on that occasion was oddly debonair. He said that Santayana's "type of mind" was "a rare and precious type, of which Harvard University may well keep a specimen to enrich her concert withal."[44]

If it really was a question of "homosexuality," it was clear where James stood. In *The Principles of Psychology* he had written that he imagined most men might "possess the germinal possibility" of being sexually attracted to other men, but as we have seen, he went on to say that the idea of anyone's acting on the possibility—"the ancients" and "modern Orientals" were his examples—"affects us with horror." In doing so, James explained, such men's instincts were inhibited by their habits. The sexual instinct, natural though it was, was subject to inhibitions, to various temperamental conditions and impulses. It had to contend with shyness, for example, or with "the *anti-sexual instinct*" that caused a man to be repulsed by "the idea of intimate contact with most of the persons we meet, especially those of our own sex." What had happened to "the ancients" and "the modern Orientals" was that they had gotten into vicious habits and thereby suppressed their "natural" inhibitions. James was instinctively repelled by their practice; therefore, it was unthinkable to him that they acted on instinct, or acted "naturally": "We can hardly suppose that the ancients had by gift of Nature a propensity of which we are devoid." It was unthinkable that what he knew to be true of a few unfortunate souls was "natural" to a whole culture. It couldn't be that the ancients "were all victims of what is now a pathological aberration limited to individuals," he argued.[45]

But there was no need for technical labels. Words like "abnormal," "weak," "spectator," and "specimen" were enough, and besides, what Santayana *was* mattered less than what he wasn't. He was not manly, not what James and others had worked so hard to be, not what they represented to their students. Santayana existed in their minds primarily as someone unlike them. His depiction of himself in that situation—in James' presence specifically—is shrewd and moving enough to be quoted at length:

I, for instance, was sure of his goodwill and kindness, of which I had many proofs; but I was also sure that he never understood me, and that when he talked to me there was a manikin in his head, called G.S. and entirely fantastic, which he was addressing. No doubt I profited materially by this illusion, because he would have liked me less if he had understood me better; but the sense of that illusion made spontaneous friendship impossible. I was uncomfortable in his presence. He was so extremely natural that there was no knowing what his nature was, or what to expect next; so that one was driven to behave and talk conventionally, as in the most artificial society. I found no foothold, I was soon fatigued, and it was a relief to be out again in the open, and alone.[46]

Santayana knew the conventions as they had been established at Harvard by men like James, and he knew what they dictated. He knew the understandings that men had of themselves and of their relations to other men, and that those understandings precluded what he had in mind to share with James.

Not surprisingly, he was much more comfortable with Henry James. He met him only once, in England, just before he died. "Nevertheless in that one interview," Santayana later wrote, "he made me feel more at home and better understood than his brother ever had done in the long years of our acquaintance."[47] Whether or not they even talked about Harvard, James had, over thirty years before, in *The Portrait of a Lady,* rendered the men of Harvard in terms that Santayana was bound to have found compelling, and that are—for us—neatly summary.

In Caspar Goodwood, Isabel Archer's relentless suitor, James portrayed the representative Harvard man, one who had been educated and trained to become a representative industrialist. At Harvard, "he had gained renown rather as a gymnast and an oarsman than as a gleaner of more dispersed knowledge." From individual, bodily achievement, he went on to the more communal activity of rowing, and thence to the cotton mills, where he developed the art of "managing men." Someone who "liked to organize, to contend, to administer," he was "by character and in fact a mover of men." You could read as much by looking at him: "His jaw was too square and set and his figure too straight and stiff: these things suggested a want of easy consonance with the deeper rhythms of life." He reminds Isabel Archer of figures in museums she had visited, or portraits she had seen, armored figures "of supremely strong, clean make . . . naturally plated and steeled, armed essentially for aggression." In sum, he is a phallic nightmare, looming up as if "to deprive her of the sense of freedom," James writes. "There was a disagreeably strong push, a kind of hardness of presence, in his way of rising before her." His polar opposite is the novel's other Harvard graduate, Ralph Touchett. The one, good hard wood; the other, a delicate touch. The one, a muscular wonder; the other, sick and dying. The one, intently focused, uninterested in dispersal in his studies and in his dealings with men; the other, "inclined to adventure and irony, indulg[ing] in a boundless liberty of appreciation," who goes on to further study at Oxford.[48]

Surely one prefers Ralph, but tough readers have criticized James for having Isabel flee Caspar's sexuality, and sometimes, it has seemed to follow, have criticized James himself for fleeing the country. Theodore Roosevelt, for example:

> Thus it is for the undersized man of letters, who flees his country because he, with his delicate, effeminate sensitiveness, finds the conditions of life on this side of the water crude and raw; in other words, because he finds he cannot play a man's part among men, and so goes where he will be sheltered from the winds that harden stouter souls.[49]

Calling him a "miserable little snob," Roosevelt flared up, it seems, at the very thought of Henry James. Like Santayana, James clearly did not fit the image of what Dean Briggs called "the great body of Harvard men." They were not manly presences. They made many Harvard men nervous.

John Jay Chapman on the Spirit of the Age

One of the men who best represented—both embodied and described—the quest for manhood during this period was John Jay Chapman, who first tore himself apart trying to live up to Harvard's standards and then, with what he salvaged, railed against what he saw as the corruption of those standards in American politics, society, and education—at Harvard especially. On whichever front he fought, he did so on the masculinist terms that his alma mater and the culture set. He could not be the kind of man the age honored—his nerves would not allow it, and he objected on principle—but he found no other kind of man to idolize. His struggles, both as a writer and as a man, were heroic—and they were futile.

What was said of Chapman in his efforts to reform government could be applied to his character in general. He was a man who had "no element of compromise in his nature." And so, inevitably, he lost. He may have proceeded in something of a self-destructive spirit, but once engaged, he often brilliantly illuminated the way his contemporaries thought and felt and lived their lives. Another motto for his life could be his own declaration "All life is nothing but passion."[1] He was the kind of man who would passionately defend his ideas at the lectern, leap down off the platform in order to collar a heckler—and later stand him a drink.

But his deepest passions were repressed. His father was an especially dark version of the distant patriarch. When Chapman lay close to dying of pneumonia at the age of fourteen, his father had nothing to say to him; and yet, having recently rescued a stray dog, he created a home for it in their house and tended it night and day in the belief that his son's fate was bound up with the dog's. He was a drinker and, according to his son, "a man of suppressed emotions . . . more or less inarticulate." But on one subject he had no trouble at all making his views known: he was a man, Chapman said, of "granite chastity." Chapman's mother, meanwhile, so confused him as a boy—now indulging him, now fiercely opposing him—that he seemed, he said, "never to have had an intimate relation to her." His strategy was to be "conscientious in entertaining her and nevertheless retaining a sort of incognito so far as [his] inner self was concerned." He kept her at bay by writing to her frequently up until the time she died in 1921. In the heat of his courtship of his first wife, Chapman said he hated his family, hated "just about everybody," but he also confessed to her that it was "second nature for me to deceive people about my own feelings." He had ample reason to think of himself as "a shy, oppressed person." To others—not surprisingly—he appeared to be a "smiling tempest."[2]

Reading Chapman, one detects a whirling that suggests a dynamo's gathering energy, but Chapman was a dynamo that kept breaking down. In 1876, when he was twelve years old, he was sent to St. Paul's School, where a puritanical version of Thomas Arnold, the Reverend Dr. Henry A. Coit, deepened his hatred of his body and his fear of God, and where the physical and social environment turned him against institutions for life. Coit and St. Paul's humiliated him spiritually and physically. The very sound of Coit's low voice and the touch of his hand on his shoulder invariably brought on tears, Chapman said. Inept at all sports, he once fell into a prayer-like stance while batting in a cricket game—which the school played instead of baseball, for its "English" influence. There were rumors that he performed religious rites at his own woodland shrine. He was sent home twice, once with pneumonia, brought on by the freezing temperature of his attic room, and a second time because his general behavior had become so odd. He was "very morbidly conscientious," Dr. Coit told the Chapmans, as he summoned them to take their son home. Chapman later wrote that "a jail, a lunatic asylum, a summer school—community life of any sort, is a sanitarium," adding that he couldn't bear to drive by a high school.[3] In one of his last letters to William James, he encouraged him to turn down an academic honor offered by the French, adding that if he "had had an ounce of manhood" in him, he would have told them, "The first principle which morality inscribes upon the heart of man is contempt for institutions."[4]

Finishing his tutoring at home, he went on to Harvard, where ostensibly he was more successful at fitting in, but though he was a member of the Dickey and later the Hasty Pudding and Porcellian clubs, he tried to democratize their constitutions and to establish a place where clubmen and those who did not belong to any club could meet. His social life spilled over into properest Boston, into the homes of Cabots and Lawrences and Lowells, and into the salons of Mrs. Gardner and Sarah Whitman, while his father's business failed and he was forced to tutor to meet his expenses. He was like one of those characters in Waldron Post's *Harvard Stories* whose high station in life is supported by the social elite, but with the passing of the years he was increasingly uneasy with the privileges he enjoyed. Belatedly rebelling against the religious tyranny of his youth, he skipped enough chapel to have his diploma withheld a year. In 1885, he entered Harvard Law School, where he took his meals with his friend from St. Paul's, Owen Wister, and others who rented a house on Appian Way that they called "The Palace."

But he took to law school no more easily than he took to any other institution. He developed eye trouble that seems to have been psychosomatic. The summer of his first year, he tried farming as an antidote to too much reading and reflection, but the "real life" of digging post holes and cherry picking did not suit him any more than did the manly activities of "sport, athletics, or muscular development." After graduation, he spent the 1890s in New York, working for political reform and writing extensively on American civilization as it manifested itself in its politics. When he married a second time (his first wife having died), he married into financial security, but told his wife,

It is not so easy to keep the keen vision which an empty stomach lends, if you have a footman. I fear a footman. I tremble before a man with hot water. . . . Let's keep the New Testament open before us. The losing of wrath is to be feared. . . . If I become classed with men at ease about money, the Lord protect me. It is a steel corslet against the heart of mankind and the knowledge of life.[5]

In 1901, he suffered a nervous collapse, obviously from overwork, but surely too from causes that lay in the darker recesses of his personality. Imagining he had lost the use of his legs, he remained bedridden in a dark room at his wife's family estate on the Hudson for a year.

Chapman's most famous collapse had occurred during his first courtship. Not surprisingly, he was at first repelled by women and protected himself against them by taking anti-feminist and cruder misogynistic positions. The first reminiscence that really bit him, he said in looking back over letters from his Harvard years, was of a woman the University employed who was, he noted, so ugly that it was not just an error but a crime that she had been hired. At the other end of the social scale, his reaction to the young women of Boston society was to agree with Milton—"women were not meant to be learned." Those who *were* intelligent were to him like the feminists Henry James had satirized in *The Bostonians*. He said that he had yet to "see a girl who is a human being, with a good mind well filled, yet no spectacles, no woman's rights."[6] When he fell in love, he fell completely.

The summer before he entered Harvard Law School, in Tuscany, he encountered what he later called "the two handsomest women" he had ever seen, the one "a Juno" he glimpsed opening the shutters of a window, the other, standing in the marketplace of Florence with her husband, "both of them large, dominant, stupendous creatures—savage as the hounds of Thessaly." In Minna Timmins he met their reincarnation. The daughter of an Italian widow and a Boston Brahmin, she and her sister had been brought to Boston by her aunts when their brother, her father, died. Her appearance was sibylline and her temperament "leonine." Her good friend Sarah Whitman called this shadowy and powerful figure "Ombra." An independent spirit, Minna had a studio of her own and, in stark contrast to Chapman, "a passion for manual work of any sort and for open-air exercise." The two read Dante together in a bare and quiet room on the top floor of the Atheneum in Boston all one winter when he might have been studying the law. In their communings, when she told him of her painful early years in Milan, he played Desdemona to her Othello. As he put it, "An onlooker might have said, 'You loved her for the tragedies of her childhood and she loved you that you did pity them.' " When another man came between them—or rather when Chapman interpreted the innocent attentions of Percival Lowell (brother of the future president of Harvard and of Amy) as proof that another man had despoiled Minna—he went berserk. Accosting Lowell after a party at the Brookline home of Mrs. Walter Cabot, Chapman beat him with his walking stick. When Minna explained his mistake and insisted he apologize, he went back to his Cambridge digs, thrust the offending hand into his coal fire, and burned it so badly it had to be amputated.[7]

For over a year, Chapman poured forth letter after letter to Minna and to friends who he hoped would intercede on his behalf. He had not known what to do with his desires. "I was ashamed to impose my instincts or personality on her and went through hell rather than do it," he told one woman; "I denied myself the being a man even *[sic]*." The teachings of his father and Dr. Coit had left him feeling confused and guilty, he had not declared his love, and, given his view of sex, he had assumed the worst about Lowell's intentions. When he confessed to Minna that there was another woman whom he could consider having for his mistress but never his wife, Minna wrote a letter that burned away everything Chapman's father and Dr. Coit had taught him about the relationship of body and soul. What with their beliefs about the sordidness of the one and the sanctity of the other, none of these men, it seemed, knew the first thing about passion. "How crude and undeveloped you have been of nature's instincts," she said:

Don't you see it, don't you feel it, the very root of the matter—this the temple of love in every pore of one's body. The appetite of love is that very whirlwind of passion, making it a true, open reality, sublime, the primary force that lies beneath all. I do not believe in wife if she be not the mistress also.

Chapman came back again and again to his terrible conviction that he was not man enough for Minna, and he meant exactly what he said. In his confusion, he thought he lacked the most essential passion of all. "I want to die," he said in one letter,

not figuratively, but literally because the system of life, which makes life worth while— the reproductive system got destroyed and burnt up and pulled out of me. . . . I am in no sense sick, but in the true sense dead. The passion of life is gone out of me. Do you know that all passion is sex?

He had feared impotence all along, feared that he could not give Minna children; after what he had done, there was nothing left of him or his love:

I think I should have done something with that love of you. It raised me so high. The beginning now is great and terrible. My spirit sickens and collapses. In the night I wake feeling my loins empty.

In a letter to an older woman who was his confidante, he pushed himself over the line: "God has used me as a clinical demonstration. Like a woman. My soul was like a woman's in many ways."

In Chapman's wild imaginings, Minna had proceeded to make his humiliating emasculation complete by having the quintessential masculinist, Oliver Wendell Holmes Jr., visit him in the hospital. Having tried herself and been discouraged from seeing Chapman, she thought their friend might play the part of go-between, but of course Chapman saw him only as another man, a man whom Minna trusted, and therefore a man who had usurped his position. Thus while Holmes extended his manly, helping hand, Chapman seethed at the thought of him. "This man—this man whom I had told and told you I did not like nor sympathize with," he wrote Minna. "Still Holmes seems to sit in my mind. I do long to kill him for a parasite and hypocrit [sic]." And all the while, neither knew what was on the other's mind.

"I hope we have seen the last of that unfortunate young man," Minna's uncle and guardian said, as he planned and subsidized her travel for two years, but Minna was determined to bring Chapman back to life. "Try to live a little in others," she wrote him. "You always strike me as being disposed to live in yourself entirely." In time, she released him from the prison of his obsessions about his failure as a man. In 1889, upon her return, they were married. Minna gave birth to two children, and then, in 1897, a month after a third was born, she suddenly died.[8]

So unruly a sensibility and so dramatic a life as Chapman's cannot be described solely in the terms of the rhetoric of masculinity prevailing in his day, but it is nevertheless true that he judged himself in those terms at the most climactic juncture of his life, and true too that in the years that followed he often couched his opposition to his culture in just those terms. He thought the trouble with American civilization was that the men in it were not man enough.

In 1892, he satirized Münsterberg and Royce in *The Two Philosophers: A Quaint and Sad Comedy.* He scorned bickering academics and Ph.D.'s. The teaching of literature was "woman's business."[9] A classicist himself, in his later years he pronounced the Attic mind "abnormal"—calling the *Symposium* "the sulphurous breviary of the pederast," for example—and updating his homophobia with an attack on the "preciosity of style" of the Neo-Hellenists. He also recommended that students be on the lookout for "some modern professor of Greek who had struck as manly a blow against pederasty as the barbarian Lucian had dealt the monster in the Age of the Antonines."[10]

Some of his best writing is to be found in *Causes and Consequences* and *Practical Agitation,* small collections of essays on American's social and political behavior in the 1890s. At the heart of them lies Chapman's intense faith in the individual, his belief that any time a man accommodates himself to the opinion of others, he necessarily diminishes his being. In a long and resonant appreciation of Emerson—another piece that he wrote in the 1890s—one hears him spurring himself on: "His works are all one single attack on the vice of the age, moral cowardice"; "It was the cause of character against convention"; "It is as if a man had been withdrawn from the earth and dedicated to condensing and embodying this eternal idea—the value of the individual soul—so vividly, so vitally, that his words could not die, yet in such illusive and abstract forms that by no chance and by no power could his creed be used for purposes of tyranny."[11]

In *Causes and Consequences* and *Practical Agitation,* Chapman's exhortations were less abstract. In them he protested against the money grubbing that ground men down to dullness and sameness: "America turns out only one kind of man. Listen to the conversation of any two men in a street car. They are talking about the price of something." The Emersonian individual was nowhere to be found. Men spoke and acted not sincerely or freely but merely out of the "desire to please, which has so much of the shopman's smile in it." This was the terrible fact of life in all classes:

The dandy at Newport who conscientiously follows his leaders and observes the cab rule, the glove ordinance, and the mystery of the oyster fork, is governed by the same law, is fettered by the same force, as the labor man who fears to tell his fellows that he approves of Waring's clean streets. Each is a half-man, each is afraid of his fellows, and for the same reason. Each is commercial, keeps his place by conciliatory methods.[12]

And what was most distressing to Chapman was the thought that the same was true of Harvard as well.

Chapman's attacks on Harvard were vehement and witty—even joyous, he told his son. As he readily acknowledged, he could not have proceeded in life had it not been for Harvard. His alma mater had supplied the "light and liberalism—hardly elsewhere to be seen in America"—that made his criticisms possible. So admiring was he of Harvard and of what he called the "miniature nationalism" of nearby Boston that he once said, "Every young person in the United States ought be sent to Massachusetts for some part of his education."[13] Conversely, his criticisms are all the more scathing because he thought Eliot had extinguished the light that New England, Emerson, and Harvard had kept aflame.

"What is the most important thing in education?" Chapman asked in his essay on Eliot.[14] He agreed with Eliot's judgment in his inaugural address: "It is the relation between teacher and pupil. Here is the focus of the whole matter; this tiny crucible must boil or your whole College will be cold." But he thought that everything at Harvard had boiled down to money during the Eliot years: "The Business Era chilled this heart-center of University life in America." The corrupting ingredients were athletics, the curriculum (the elective system, the emphasis on science, the "Puritan dread of the Humanities"), a sense of class (what Chapman called "ethnic loyalty"), and, most important, identification with America's deeply monied interests. "The money question is the key to Doctor Eliot's career, merely because it is the key to his epoch," Chapman stated. "He cared nothing for money; he cared merely for power. But power in the United States between 1870–1910 meant money power: therefore Eliot's nature took on a financial hue."

Chapman recalled a man named Dyer who had been at Harvard in the early 1880s, when he was an undergraduate. Dyer was, like Copeland or Shaler, like Wendell or even James, a man who used "to make himself personally agreeable to the students" and to invite them to his rooms. But even then, the Harvard air was growing cold, "the glacial age" of which Eliot was "the spiritual father" was setting in, and Dyer was forced out. Chapman admitted that even he had patronized the man. In the last years of the century, ladies' teas and young men's Christian associations came into being as a result of Harvard's effort to warm the atmosphere, but according to Chapman, the machine ground on, "crushing talent." His ideal bright young instructor might, for example, have thoughts about the new gymnasium which opposed the views of "the Control." Were he to voice them, he would be doomed. "How then can we advance him? His advancement would put our whole administration in jeopardy," Chapman imagines "the Control" saying. Ignoring all the democratization that had made for or accompanied change at Harvard, Chapman argued that "a true University" could not "rest upon the will of one man," but rather ought to abide by the wills of "many divergent-minded old gentlemen," who "growl in their kennels." But Harvard *did* rest upon one man's will and for a very simple reason: he determined those men's salaries. The system "attacked the soul of the individual instructor through its control over his livelihood."

When the time came to think of Eliot's successor, Chapman vented his spleen to James. He had received his share of mailings from the College, and he had no trouble seeing the relationship between money and athletics, and between them and recruiting on the open faculty market:

I cannot bear to be called "a loyal son of Harvard." This chest-thumping, back-slapping, vociferous and cheap emotionalism, done to get money and land money, is too much like everything else. . . . Everything seems to be a baseball team—jollying, rough good-feeling, and a thorough-going belief in money and *us*—and it's bad form to be accurate about anything except cash. Harvard is a baseball team, and they'll bid high to get the best man they can, even if they have to outbid the Sioux City Nine.

Maybe he didn't understand Harvard, he said, maybe all he had been exposed to was "the boom-side of it," but he found that side intolerable. "Eliot has boomed and boomed—till we think it's the proper way to go on," he said. "Why not a man who does not boom? Is boom the best thing in life? Is it all boom?" and finally: "If Eliot is a great man, I want a small man."[15]

Chapman appreciated—understood and enjoyed—the fact that his views were both limited and overstated. He knew that his candidate for president would get "50 blackballs out of 51 votes." Albert Bushnell Hart wrote to tell him that his writings were "jammed full of assumptions and wild guesses and reckless statements . . . just inexpensive bosh," but he didn't need to be told that. Nor did he need Hart to remind him that Harvard men were playing important roles in the nation's life.[16] In other moods he might himself stress Harvard's contributions to the culture, or admit that Eliot has "done wonders,"[17]—or recall that it was Eliot who had stepped in and found a way to help him when his father's business failed. But we cannot expect Chapman to expatiate on the democratization of higher education in America, or on the modern university's role in advancing mankind's knowledge. Chapman was upholding a venerable tradition by speaking out; and in the process he nicely dramatized the processes by which Harvard shaped the men of whom Hart and Harvard were so proud.

Ultimately, Chapman recognized that the forces he was opposing would roll right over the likes of him. To put it crudely, he could literally afford to protest all he wanted, but meanwhile, the individual man whom he idolized would proceed to train and learn and court and deal with an eye on the reactions of others. Chapman might continue to growl, but he knew that there was a time when silence was more appropriate. True to his recommendation to James about accepting honors, he blocked Harvard's attempt to award him an honorary degree. He did agree to address the Phi Beta Kappa Society in 1912. On that occasion, he read a long poem in which he advised Harvard to "drop behind the age," to "seek silence; walk in shadow and disgrace."[18] There is no record of anyone's taking him seriously.

But Chapman was appreciated as a gadfly, and by no one more than William James. Once, when the Jameses and the Chapmans were visiting at the country home of Sarah Whitman, James came into Chapman's bedroom, put his hands on his shoulders, and said, "Jack Chapman, you talk like an angel."[19] "The only reincarnation of Isaiah and Job," he called him on another occasion.[20] James could never speak like Chapman, and for that very reason he admired him. Chapman's voice lent encouragement and support to the oppositional in him. He counted on Chapman's criticism and cited him often in his writings. Psychologically, there was a bond between them as well. When she read the essay Chapman had written about her late husband, Alice James wrote him, to say, "I doubt whether you know how he valued you, how he delighted in you, how he sympathized with and understood, ah, *how* he understood,—your nervous temperament."[21] Both men had broken down, both had been nursed back to health by their wives, both were what James called "sick souls."

Elizabeth Chanler, the second Mrs. Chapman, recognized the affinity too. "My wife says she now sees why I desire to see you," Chapman wrote James in 1908. "It is because we both desire to lock arms and groan."[22] Ten years before, in *Causes and Consequences,* Chapman had argued that for all the changes brought about by science and technology, "everything depends as completely on personal intercourse as it did in Athens. The real struggle comes between two men across a table, my force against your force."[23] If James admired and appreciated Chapman, Chapman idolized James. He was his ideal man, a man after his own heart and of his generation—an arm wrestler. Chapman wrote Elizabeth Chanler in 1897 that James was "the only man [he] had struck yet in the U.S. . . . simply the only man who wasn't terrified at ideas, moonstruck at a living thought, but alive himself."[24]

And it followed that James was one of the few men Chapman could imagine making a difference at Harvard. But of course, given Chapman's temperament and expectations, not even James could satisfy him. In a late piece titled "Harvard's Plight," in the voice of an "old friend," he complained that though James was highly gifted, highly educated, "he wouldn't oppose Eliot." If he and Royce and Palmer had gone to the Corporation, Chapman wrote, and insisted that one or two men of purely intellectual interests be made fellows, the course of history might have been changed, but the philosophers were dedicated "to philosophy and to things much larger than Harvard." They couldn't see that it was "their business to fix the kitchen stove."

This old man's argument was the masculinists' argument, one that James himself had invoked at times: reflection was not enough for a man; the reflective man was not man enough. "There are truths as deep as the truths of contemplation which only fighters know," Chapman said. "No matter how great or how good you are, there is a force that only comes to you through fight." But Eliot appointed these men, the old man goes on. He couldn't have been the demon Chapman made him out to be. In his own voice, Chapman replies, " 'Oh, I'm not talking of demons, but of the Spirit of the Age.' "[25]

3

William James' Teaching

The "Undisciplinables" and the "Pass Men" at Harvard

IN THE SPRING OF 1873, William James began his teaching career at Harvard by offering an undergraduate course in anatomy and physiology in the Department of Natural History. On April 10, he recorded in his Diary that he was satisfied with his work, and that just the day before, he had informed President Eliot he would accept his offer of a full year's appointment for the following academic year. Though his "deepest interest" would always be in "the most general problems," the experience of the previous years had made it clear that he could not dwell on such problems. To address them as a philosopher—which also meant to address questions about the workings of the mind that was questioning—would plunge him right back into what he called "the abyss of horrors":

I came to this decision mainly from the feeling that philosophical activity as a *business* is not normal for most men, and not for me. To be responsible for a complete conception of things is beyond my strength. To make the *form* of all possible thought the *matter* of one's thought breeds hypochondria. . . . [T]he dream conception, "maya," the abyss of horrors, would spite of everything grasp my imagination and imperil my reason.

By contast, "the concrete facts in which a biologist's responsibilities" lay provided some stable reality to lean upon, something on which he could "passively float, and tide over times of weakness and depression." Given such support, when "the gallant mood" was on him, he might hope to address universal questions, but for the present, he knew he did not have the makings of a professor of philosophy.

Four years later, in 1877, he began his shift into psychology and philosophy. Thereafter he taught large introductory courses on various combinations of the two: "Logic and Psychology" in 1887–88, for example; a course based on *The Principles of Psychology* in 1890–91; and in 1894 a course (or rather the third of a course) that introduced the field of psychology, the other two segments, introductions to philosophy, being taught by Josiah Royce and George Santayana. He also offered smaller, philosophy courses, including "English Philosophers" and "Descartes, Spinoza, and Leibnitz," and he taught graduate seminars titled "Pleasure and Pain," "Metaphysics," and "Questions in Psychology" or "Questions in Mental Pathology," some of the seminars being the contexts in which he directed graduate students in their research. In his thirty-five years as a professor at Harvard, he eventually taught a great deal of philosophy, but he was never entirely at home in the "business." Santayana said, "Philosophy to him was rather like a maze in which he happened to find himself wandering, and what he was looking for was a way out."[1]

Considering the variety of subjects James taught and the settings in which he taught them, generalizations about his teaching are suspect. What could Theodore Roosevelt's experience in James' course on the comparative anatomy and physiology of vertebrates possibly have in common with Santayana's experience studying "Taine on Intelligence," or Du Bois' when he took "Logic and Philosophy"? Not to mention the incalculable differences among these men, could even James himself be the same man in such different situations? But almost from the beginning of his teaching years, right through to the testimonials that accompanied his retirement in 1907, James' teaching was praised in remarkably similar terms.

He was known for his learnedness, of course, but also for his ability to make whatever he taught accessible and relevant to his students' lives. The *Crimson* commended his course "Physiological Psychology": "Dr. James's course, dealing as it does with Herbert Spencer's principles of psychology and with the latest investigations on the functions of the brain, supplies a want that is felt by every student of philosophy."[2] In 1880, the *Advocate* gave two reasons why those who had missed his physiology lectures would want to arrange their next year's electives so as not to make the same mistake again: one was that "physiology is a subject of which no one should be ignorant"; and then, of course, "Professor James's faculty of making a subject interesting is so well known."[3]

But James did not just make his subjects accessible. He was *himself* humanly present for his students. In the words of the *Monthly,* he was "one of Harvard's most brilliant teachers and America's greatest philosopher,"[4] but at the same time he appeared before his students as just another—albeit older and wiser—man struggling to find and create meaning in his life. That is what he thought it meant to be a philosopher.

What set William James apart from Copeland or Briggs or Wendell, from most of the teachers who were known for making themselves available to their students, was that he was professional as well as personable. The others were dilettantes by comparison, often explicit in their admissions that they were not

The Harvard Varsity Football Team, 1898. Bill Reid, the future coach, is to the left of the captain.

The Harvard-Yale game, November 23, 1901.

Harvard Stadium under construction, 1904–5. At the time, it was the largest poured concrete structure in the world.

Coach Bill Reid, 1905.

Henry Adams, professor of history, c. 1875.

Le Baron R. Briggs, professor of English, c. 1880. Briggs went on to be president of Radcliffe College from 1903 to 1923.

Nathaniel Shaler, professor of geology, 1880s.

Barrett Wendell, professor of English, late 1880s.

John Jay Chapman, Harvard '84, as an undergraduate. *Harvard University Archives*

George Santayana, professor of philosophy, c. 1910. *Harvard University Archives*

William James, 1907. *Houghton Library, Harvard University*

Gertrude Stein, Radcliffe '98, as an undergraduate. *Beinecke Rare Book and Manuscript Library, Yale University*

James and Josiah Royce, Chocorua, New Hampshire, 1903. *Harvard University Archives*

Frank Norris, center right, and fraternity brothers at the University of California in 1893, the year before he came to Harvard. *The Bancroft Library, University of California, Berkeley*

PARTNERS AT LAST. *Harvard Lampoon*, December, 1893.

Below, THE USURPER, the *Lampoon*'s rendering of the partnership three years later.

W. E. B. Du Bois, front row right, among the speakers at the commencement of 1890. *Special Collection and Archives, W. E. B. Du Bois Library*

Teddy Roosevelt, Harvard '80, in his senior year. *Harvard University Archives*

Owen Wister, Harvard '82, the father of the *Western*, as he appeared in a theatrical performance his freshman year.

"Mr. Roosevelt in the Title Rôle Fails to Please the Gallery." The *Lampoon*'s version of Roosevelt's speech, "The College Man," at the Harvard Union, February, 1907. The profiled faculty member on the right is probably meant to be James.

Eliot and A. Lawrence Lowell at Lowell's inauguration, 1909.

scholars. "James's spirit and temper do good to whoever comes within their range; and it is as much through their affections as through their intellects that his disciples are attracted to him," Charles Eliot Norton wrote a friend in 1908.[5] Years later, the philosopher Wittgenstein said simply, "That is what makes him a good philosopher; he was a real human being."[6] James' colleague George Herbert Palmer told him he fulfilled the "common and delusive dream that the professional man's output is but the completed expression of his private life." Readers liked to imagine that "every Tennyson or Browning must be as romantic or heroic as his own verses," Palmer wrote, when James first began to think of retiring. Of course it was "an unreasonable fancy. Professionalism has its own exactions which often run quite outside the personal element." But in James' case the dream had come true. In him the two, the personal and the professional, were "largely united and the big man expand[ed] undistorted into the solid professional."[7]

Palmer's reference to Tennyson and Browning, rather than to, say, a pair of prominent philosophers or academicians, as the basis for his judgment, was appropriate because another thing that made James distinctive in everyone's eyes was his inspirational power as a writer. Santayana and Shaler and Wendell might in fact publish poems or fictions, but none was so appreciated for his ability and potential as a writer of literature as James. Indeed there were occasions when praise for James' virtues as a stylist suggested he was not truly a philosopher or a psychologist after all. One reviewer said that "one sometimes suspects that it is Dr. James's luminous style, and not the content of his thought, that has given Pragmatism its great vogue," and another spoke of *A Pluralistic Universe* as the work of a poet and wondered, "Perhaps it may turn out that Mr. James's Pluralism is the latest fashion in Subjectivity."[8] Much more common, however, were appreciations of James' ability to make philosophy so readable, so comprehensible. A more sanguine reading of James' *Pragmatism* had it that it was "probably the most delightfully written philosophical work ever published." The reviewer agreed with James when he said that pragmatism "*unstiffens* all our theories," and he saw the volume as climactic evidence of James' "deep sympathy with those who feel the pains of mortality." It fit Wordsworth's definition of poetry: "His is a book in which man once again speaks to man."[9] Some people wondered if James mightn't emulate, or even rival, his brother. Inspired by "the wide and genuine sympathy" he found revealed on every page of *The Will to Believe,* the reviewer for the *Monthly* was prompted "to repeat the wish we have often heard expressed, that he would some day write us a novel."[10]

James fit no mold. As one admirer said, it was "the unacademic qualities of William James" that made him "our leading academician."[11] Palmer's tribute to his significance is exactly right:

It is a vast contribution you have made to our Harvard life, ennobling and intelligizing it just at this time of transition when, but for influences like yours, it might easily have become chaotic. You have given seriousness without humbug, rationality without dilettantism, daily courage without rudeness.

James was proof that Harvard was meeting the demands of post–Civil War culture, that learning not only need not but must not be pretentious or evasive, that it had to be grounded in the complex realities of everyday life at the turn of the century. At the same time, James showed that though the struggle for survival and success in the world required that a man be bold and assertive, there was no need for "rudeness."

What Palmer said of him—that in him the personal and the professional were one—James believed to be true of the thinkers he most admired. "A philosophy is the expression of a man's intimate character," he wrote in "The Types of Philosophic Thinking" (1908).[12] In *The Varieties of Religious Experience,* he carefully distinguished between what he called *"existential judgment,"* or inquiry into the nature or origins of anything, and *"spiritual judgment,"* or inquiry into its importance or meaning, and warned that "neither judgment can be deduced immediately from the other." That Saint Paul once had something like an epileptic fit, or that George Fox was a psychopath, or that Carlyle "was undoubtedly auto-intoxicated by some organ or other," in no way invalidated each man's religious beliefs, James maintained. His was an "empiricist criterion." Allowing himself to be uncharacteristically folksy, he said, "By their fruits ye shall know them, not by their roots."[13] In his readings of more worldly thinkers, he smudged the line between origins and meanings. A man's philosophical beliefs might reveal the struggles he had undergone in order to arrive at them. In "The Present Dilemma in Philosophy" (1907) he said, "The books of all the great philosophers are like so many men."[14]

Certainly the conjunction of the personal and the philosophical that students easily recognized in James accounted for his great popularity as a teacher. "Life is confused and superabundant, and what the younger generation appears to crave is more of the temperament of life in its philosophy, even though it were at some cost of logical vigor and of formal purity," he said at the beginning of his essay "A World of Pure Experience" (1904).[15] That was what he provided—"more of the temperament of life." Accordingly, in his thinking and in his teaching he proceeded relatively informally. His lectures were not meticulously worked out beforehand. "Prepare yourself in the *subject so well that it shall be always on tap;* then in the class-room, trust your spontaneity and fling away all farther care," he advised teachers.[16] He talked or chatted with his students rather than lecture to them. Sometimes he might even stop in mid-sentence and ask, "What *was* I talking about?" if he lost his way, or dismiss the class altogether.[17] Robert Morss Lovett told the story of James putting syllogisms on the board that did not work and then calling out to the young man who took attendance for him (and tutored his children) to come up and take over.[18]

More seriously, his students sensed that he was struggling with questions and ideas alongside of them, and would settle for no neat solutions. He knew too much about the world, and had suffered too much, to accept any conclusions that had been abstracted from the complexity of lived experience. As Josiah Royce said, "he never could teach what he had not himself experienced."[19] Knowing full well what it was like to be confused by life's "superabundance," Robert Frost came to Harvard as a special student in 1897, specifically to study under James, but because James was on sick leave that year, he had to content himself with going through the abridged version of *The Principles of Psychology* in Hugo Münsterberg's classes. And so he was later fond of saying, "My greatest inspiration when I was a student, was a man whose classes I never attended."[20]

Professionally, the life of the mind as James embodied it appeared not to be bound by invidious or petty distinctions. No departmental label would suffice—he was not just a scientist or psychologist or philosopher—nor was his intellect in need of accreditation. The academy was producing more and more Ph.D.'s, and the men in it were, like professionals outside it, forming their guilds (the historians in 1884, the economists in 1885, the political scientists in 1899, and so on). As of 1884, only nineteen members of the Harvard faculty had earned their doctorate;[21] but the battle against administrative enforcers was doomed to be a losing one.

Nevertheless, in 1903, in an essay he titled "The Ph.D. Octopus," James waged it.[22] In the name of what he considered true scholarship, and in "recognition of individuality and bare manhood," he went after the deadly, inkspraying Ph.D. His effort was an example of what five years later the governor of Massachusetts would call "Patriotic manhood," for he did it for his country's sake as well. Comparing America to countries in the Old World, where titles counted, he intoned, "Let us pray that our ancient national genius may long preserve vitality enough to guard us from a future so unmanly and so unbeautiful!"

In his essay, James acknowledged that the awarding of higher degrees had at first stimulated scholarship and justly rewarded the ambitious with jobs, but he deemed making the doctoral degree a requirement for teachers yet another instance of the dehumanizing effects of Bigness: "the institutionizing on a large scale of any natural combination of need and motive always tends to run into technicality and to develop a tyrannical Machine with unforeseen powers of exclusion and corruption." A sign of the times, the academy had turned into a machine, into a business, advertising itself by means of its titled elite and its catalogs all decorated with "baubles." Opposing this transformation were "bare human beings," "bare manhood," "essential manhood," "bare personality," now marked by what he called (echoing Shakespeare) its "outcast state." In his rhetorical scheme of things, the American innocent was falling.

Reading such sentences, we might think that we were approaching ground where Walt Whitman also stood, but it is the differences between James and Whitman that are instructive. Both evoke a common figure, that of beautiful manhood, stripped of the meaningless trappings of rank, but James put it to much more modest use—as a metaphor for his ideal students, the ones with independent minds, the ones who tested their learning with their lives. He attracted students because he really believed (in Whitman's words) that "he most honors my style who learns under it to destroy the teacher," but his ideal men were of a certain class, educated, and unambiguously masculine. If James had said, echoing Whitman, "I am the teacher of athletes," he would have been referring to men who worked out, or to men on teams. And whereas Whitman challenged his readers to set out on their own journeys of self-discovery, and warned them that reading his poems could do them as much harm as good—perhaps involve actually touching another man, in fact[23]—James carefully fashioned a particular image of manhood for his audiences that was at once familiar and ideal, one that stretched but did not burst the limits of the world as they knew it. He gave them themselves in the most decent form imaginable. Hutchins Hapgood could be exhilarated at the celebration of openness all around him at Harvard, and say, "The most remarkable in that respect was William James. To him each student had the highest possibility." But Hapgood could also go on to say of James that "in temperament he was a Puritan, and subscribed to all the orthodox conventions of the community."[24]

Granting that James' openness did not rival Whitman's, his tolerance of others was nevertheless as legendary among his contemporaries as his manliness. Walter Lippmann's testimonial is typical of the many that exist. Fresh out of college, in 1910—in his first signed article—he said that James was "perhaps the most tolerant man of our generation. . . . He listened for truth from anybody, and from anywhere, and in any form. He listened for it from Emma Goldman, the pope, or a sophomore; preached from a pulpit, a throne, or a soap-box; in the language of science, in slang, in fine rhetoric, or in the talk of a ward boss."[25] James was interested in everyone and everything. Justice Learned Hand celebrated the range of his sympathies in sentences that are themselves notably generous:

his mind and his nature were so rich and varied that he was apparently able to harbor harmoniously what others with less gifts of conciliation found mutually rebellious. It always seemed to me that the angels must have visited his cradle and bestowed on him whatever was charming and understanding and helpful and beautiful.[26]

The *Lampoon* once listed a number of professors and the plays that had supposedly influenced them; when the editors came to James, they abandoned any attempt at humor and simply said, "Humanity."[27]

James was famous for defending and appealing most to the outsiders among the students at Harvard, those whom he called, in a speech titled "The True Harvard" (also 1903), "our undisciplinables."[28] They were the students whom he thought of as "our proudest product," for they gave Harvard its "preëminent spiritual tone." Any college could foster "club loyalty." At Harvard, "mere animal feeling for old schoolmates and the Yard and the bell, and Memorial and the clubs and the river and the Soldier's Field" was understandably strong, but Harvard—any institution—required "something deeper and more rational." The men James was honoring were so private, so little present as to be all but invisible. They often came from great distances, without school or social connections; they were special students, graduate students, students likely to be on scholarship. According to the "Harvard Stories" of Waldron Kintzing Post, or the claims of the administration, such men usually ended up within the fold, but James' exemplars did not. "They seldom or never darken the doors of the Pudding or the Porcellian; they hover in the background on days when the crimson color is most in evidence." Nevertheless, James said, their loyalty to Harvard was "deeper and subtler and more a matter of the inmost soul than the gregarious loyalty of the clubhouse pattern often is." Only "in the souls of her more truth-seeking and independent and often very solitary sons" was the "true Harvard" to be found. What made Harvard special, what kept it "in the van," was that it protected these "independent and lonely thinkers." At a lesser institution they too would somehow be infused with their school's spirit, but not at Harvard: "The day when Harvard shall stamp a single hard and fast type of character upon her children, will be that of her downfall."

If we think back to the typing of the student body engaged in by Briggs and Santayana and Wendell, James was holding out for the men whom they— even Santayana—had happily peripheralized in the name of the social and athletic mass. Typically, according to Santayana, out of the "charity and breadth" of his mind, James was defending Harvard's loners, the "lame ducks and neglected possibilities,"[29] the men whom others were inclined to criticize for being too self-absorbed—or just plain odd. It is one of the most attractive aspects of his character. It is what impelled him to befriend Charles Peirce, for example, who managed to offend everyone, including James, and to arrange for him to lecture at Harvard against Eliot's opposition (in a private home, as a compromise); to embrace Josiah Royce—"one of James's cranks," as he called himself;[30] and to pay special attention to the young W. E. B. Du Bois. In 1907, in an address called "The Social Value of the College-Bred,"

James called those men who stood apart from ordinary college life "intellectuals," men committed to the disinterested development and exchange of ideas, "intellectuals" being those men, he said in 1899, who preserved "our precious birthright of individualism" from the corrupting influence of institutions.[31]

But James himself was not really an outsider. Though he would never wholeheartedly join those who looked askance at men who were not club material, or who were not seated in the cheering section, he often took their side. Subtly but tellingly, he could sound like those who insisted on mere manliness in a man. In fact, he did so even as he was defending the "undisciplinables."

The occasion of his definition of "the true Harvard" was the commencement dinner the year he and Shaler received honorary degrees. Among the outsiders whom he defended were men like himself who had not gone to Harvard College and who would therefore never feel as comfortable at commencement as, say, his friend Barrett Wendell. In doing so, he associated himself by name with other friends—with Hollis and Royce and Shaler—who had not gone to Harvard and who (whether he thought of it at the time or not) had all raised questions about the effect of Harvard's aggressive entry onto the national athletic scene. It was on the same occasion that Shaler spoke out against what he called "the disease of athletics."[32] Only a few months had passed since his own son had resigned his captaincy of the Harvard crew. "I wish to use my present privilege to say a word for those outsiders with whom I belong," he began. But then he went on to prove himself very much of an insider when it came to the gathering he was addressing:

Many years ago there was one of them from Canada here—a man with a high-pitched voice, who couldn't fully agree with all the points of my philosophy. At a lecture one day, when I was in the full flood of my eloquence, his voice rose above mine, exclaiming: "But, doctor, doctor! to be serious for a moment . . .", in so sincere a tone that the whole room burst out laughing.

And so they must have at the dinner. While defending the solitary sons of Harvard, James was also giving himself over to an occasion in which man-to-man relations seemed to exclude them. Not high-pitched voices but deep laughter was the order of the day.

It is an isolated moment, but one that is symptomatic of James' attitudes towards his students and their education. To take another example, in the year that he retired, James delivered his lecture "The Social Value of the College-Bred," in which he told his audience that the best thing a college could do for them was to *help you to know a good man when you see him.*"[33] Acknowledging the possible irony of making such a pronouncement at a meeting of the Association of American Alumnae at Radcliffe College, he assured his audience that what he had to say was neither a joke nor "a one-sided abstraction": "The best claim we can make for the higher education, the best single phrase in which we can tell what it ought to do for us, is, then, exactly what I said: it should enable us to *know a good man when we see him*." He knew that his ideas and his words were vague, but he insisted that their meaning was "unmistakable." And indeed, after considering his description of the technical or professional school graduate as "a crude and smoky kind of petroleum, incapable of spreading light," and his characterization of the college graduate as redeemed, well-bred, and "lit up" by "a lasting relish for the better kind of man, a loss of appetite for mediocrities, and a disgust for cheapjacks," his meaning is quite apparent. His is a version of the argument—imported from Matthew Arnold and applied by President Eliot (among many others) to America's more democratic situation—for the "saving remnant," for the "alumni and alumnae of the colleges [who] are the only permanent presence that corresponds to the aristocracy in older countries."

In James' version, suggestions of class superiority give way to images of victory in a gendered, biological war. What colleges should not do, he says, is cultivate the kind of "sterilized conceit" and feebleness and "priggishness" that you might find in drawing rooms "near Cambridge and Boston," and in the publications of those who frequented those drawing rooms. (In fact, he spent relatively little time in that society, his friendship with Sarah Whitman being an exception.) The mission of colleges was to condition their students against such effeminacy: "every good college makes its students immune against this malady, of which the microbe haunts the neighborhood-printed pages. It does so by its general tone being too hearty for the microbe's life." Much is at stake: "If democracy is to be saved," he says, "it must catch the higher, healthier tone."

Knowing stylist that he was, James noted, " 'Tone,' to be sure, is a terribly vague word to use." But to him there was no other: "this whole meditation is over questions of tone," he said. "By their tone are all things human either lost or saved." In these late utterances, the sounds and rhythms of his sentences, the metaphoric life stirring in them, create the manly, the gentlemanly presence that was so appreciated at Harvard and that, as we have seen, Harvard was so intent upon producing. James gave into it, we might say. His tone captured in its simplest form what he called—for Pauline Goldmark's benefit—"the entire striving ideal life."[34]

Sympathy for the solitary thinkers who had sequestered themselves here and there at Harvard and in the town of Cambridge would not be enough. A part of James would always resonate to them, but another part willingly embraced the great body of Harvard students who banded together socially. When he engaged in stereotyping exercises of his own, he could draw the lines in a way that erased the important "little difference" that distinguished him from them.

He did so—most evidently—in the debate over the "three-year course" that took place in the early 1890s.[35] In his contribution to it, the "undisciplinables" translated as the "theoretical" students, the "honor men," and the "specializers"; all the others were the "pass men," the "general-culture-men." The distinction between the two was, James declared, "founded in the nature of things." In "The True Harvard," he said the former were what gave Harvard its "preëminent spiritual tone." James would never consider the latter more important to Harvard than the solitary souls, but in reflections titled "The Proposed Shortening of the College Course," he described them as "the backbone of the country," and as such, they were men who were equally impressive to him.

There was never any doubt in James' mind but that, as he says, "the leaders of every generation should as far as possible be college-bred men," and it seemed abundantly clear, in 1891, when he shared his thoughts on the "three-year course" with readers of the *Monthly,* that the conditioning that future leaders were getting at Harvard was just about ideal. Harvard had become more "mature," more "efficient." The "more strenuous and professional sort of ideal" that all of Harvard's reforms had tended to consolidate had proven to be a far better "agent in the formation of *character*" than the amateurish ideal that was prevalent when James started teaching. None of this is surprising—neither James's characterization nor his enthusiasm. What is surprising is the spirit in which he defends the reform under consideration and, by extension, the strength of his commitment to the masculinist ethos of the institution and the culture.

In his article, James honored the more independent thinkers among the students, but he also observed that their intellectual life seemed "unreal and fastidious" to most students—and, he had to admit, the majority's response was contagious. In characterizing the average students' needs, he becomes rhetorically vicious:

These excellent fellows need contact of some sort with the fighting side of life, with the world in which men and women earn their bread and butter and live and die; there must be the scent of blood, so to speak, upon what you offer them, or else their interest does not wake up; the blood that is shed in our Electives, fails to satisfy them very long.

It seems that the hunt for courses, and for interest in them, can stir the blood of the Harvard man for only so long. The solution is to educate him for three years—long enough to impress him with the "reality" and the seriousness of what went on in the academy now that it had become professionalized—and then to let him go free. More than three years, and the potentially mandarin nature of the institution will become apparent and "these excellent fellows" will become contemptuous. Or it might be that they will go on thinking, and their resistance to the disease of "priggishness" will get dangerously low.

As is true of so much of James, this is a version of Emerson, in this case the Emerson of the famous 1837 address to the Phi Beta Kappa Society at Harvard: "The American Scholar." Behind James' accommodation of the average Harvard student lies Emerson's praise of the active, heroic thinker—"Man Thinking"—who will not content himself with the instruments of learning, with others' transcriptions of experience. "Only so much do I know, as I have lived," Emerson declared. We have heard James echo the sentiment many times. But the bloodied figures of speech are James' own, distillations of Emerson's ideas into terms appropriate to the Harvard that was becoming the country's leading educational institution during the decades following the Civil War.

In a talk given to the Yale Philosophical Club called "The Moral Philosopher and the Moral Life" (also in 1891), James presented this full-blooded man who might graduate in three years as an ideal believer—an ideal believer and, at the same time, proof of religion's worth. Looking forward to more famous dichotomies to come—the "sick soul" as against the "healthy-minded," the "tough" as against the "tender" minded—James argued that the "deepest difference, practically," in the moral life as James presents it in this talk, "is the difference between the easy-going and the strenuous mood." One is the result of our avoidance of trouble; the other is inspired by "the wilder passions," by "big fears, loves, and indignations; or else the deeply penetrating appeal of some one of the higher fidelities, like justice, truth or freedom." Whereas "the solitary thinker" inclines toward indolence, James' moral philosopher is aroused:

the strenuous mood awakens at the sound. It saith among the trumpets, ha, ha! it smelleth the battle afar off, the thunder of the captains and the shouting. Its blood is up; and cruelty to the lesser claims, so far from being a deterrent element, does but add to the stern joy with which it leaps to answer to the greater.

Though there can be no proof of God's existence, men postulate Him in order to release such energy. They postulate Him "simply as a pretext for living hard, and getting out of the game of existence its keenest possibilities of zest." Sounds of the playing field and the battlefield echo in James' rhetoric. Finally, in his summation of this athlete-warrior-believer's role in history, we may hear an echo of what James once said a man would do to the woman who moved into public life: "the strenuous type of character will on the battlefield of human history always outwear the easy-going type, and religion will drive irreligion to the wall."[36]

"Because of men like you," Palmer wrote him in 1900, "Harvard is now taking a chief place in shaping the ideals of this country."[37] In the Phi Beta

Kappa address that he delivered the year after James' death eleven years later, Royce claimed that their colleague's influence was more direct. Whereas Palmer had acknowledged James' instrumental role in the development of Harvard and of its reputation, Royce called James himself "our national philosopher" and "the prophet of the nation that is to be." He situated him at the center of their age:

He belongs to the age in which our nation, rapidly transformed by the occupation of new territory, by economic growth, by immigration, and by education, has been attempting to find itself anew, to redefine its ideals, to retain its moral integrity, and yet to become a world power.

Royce saw James as "representative," not just recounting how the nation was expanding westward and across the seas, but doing something more immediate and intimate. He was introducing Americans to themselves as they went through these trying times: "For the philosopher must not be an echo. He must interpret. He must know us better than we know ourselves, and this is what indeed James has done for our American moral consciousness." He had done this not by standing apart in order judiciously to analyze, but rather by his example—by being the man he was. What was true of the age was true of him:

Was not he himself restlessly active in his whole temperament? Did he not love individual enterprise and its free expression? Did he not loathe what seemed to him abstractions? Did he not insist that the moralist must be in close touch with concrete life? As psychologist did he not emphasize the fact that the very essence of conscious life lies in its active, yes, in its creative relation to experience? Did he not counsel the strenuous attitude towards our tasks? And are not all these features in harmony with the spirit from which the athletic type of morality just sketched seems to have sprung?[38]

Active, enterprising, realistic, creative, strenuous, athletic. He is the same man whom Gertrude Stein had so admired sixteen years before—"He is a strong sane noble personality reacting truly on all experience that life has given him"[39]—only now his character is of national and not just local significance. A large order, but one that James could see himself filling. "Some of us are in more favorable positions than others to set new fashions," he wrote knowingly in one of his "Talks to Students." "Some are much more striking personally and imitable, so to speak."[40]

In essays and in public lectures, James passed on what he had learned about the relationship between his own mind and body during the crisis years of the late 1860s and early 1870s. In 1895, in his talk to the Boston Normal School of Gymnastics called "The Gospel of Relaxation," he recommended relatively mild forms of exercise as a means of combatting the deleterious effects of "floods of learned and ingenious talk which will constitute our most congenial occupation.[41] Ten years later, in "The Energies of Men," the man whom James imagined functioning most efficiently was less inclined to such talk. "The Energies of Men" was the presidential address to the American Philosophical Association, but in it James explicitly eschewed ideas one might hear discussed in philosophical or "laboratory circles" in favor of a conception used by "common, practical men,—I mean the conception of the *amount of energy available* for running one's mental and moral operations by." It was a lecture that kept pace with America's technological and imperialistic advances, a lecture on human hydraulics, filled with calculations of the best means of tapping men's "unused reservoirs of power," of "throwing them into gear," or carrying them "over the dam," and establishing an "efficiency-equilibrium." The means were *"excitements, ideas, and efforts,"* ranging from Yoga exercises to the "classic" emotions (love, anger), to "the dynamogenic effects of a very exalted political office," to war. "Wars, of course, and shipwrecks," he said, "are the great revealers of what men and women are able to do and bear."[42]

Although we might wish we detected a hint of playfulness here, it is only James giving voice to a belief that he had often expressed before and that would be pivotal in his essay "The Moral Equivalent of War," written in the last year of his life. We heard a version of it in his brief for "the cheerfulness that comes with fighting ills" in his lecture "Is Life Worth Living?" And in his Gifford Lecture titled "The Value of Saintliness" he said that in an age that worshiped "material luxury and wealth," an age therefore threatened by "effeminacy and unmanliness," the obvious remedies were "athletics, militarism, and individual and national enterprise." War was especially appealing, because war, "the school of strenuous life and heroism," was both "congruous with ordinary human nature" and "universally available." It prevented men "from treating themselves too tenderly." But he was opposed to war, so his was a continual effort "to discover in the social realm . . . the moral equivalent of war."

In the context of his lecture on saintliness, he proposed poverty as a solution, not a war on poverty, but poverty itself, for "poverty indeed *is* the strenuous life."[43] In his more famous essay, the moral equivalent of war was war "against *Nature*."[44] Again James assumed that "we inherit the warlike type," that thousands of years of peace would not breed "pugnacity" out of us, and he was grateful that such was the case. Were it not for men's warring instincts, alien forms of being would, it seemed, take over the planet. Microbes, bespectacled creatures with large heads, even "Roosevelt's weaklings and mollycoddles," might end up "making everything else disappear from the face of nature." But there was always "militarism," which was "the great preserver of our ideals of hardihood, and human life with no use for hardihood would be contemptible." There was no sense—no sense at all—in opposing the warlike in man. He agreed with his friend Chapman: one had to "enter more deeply into the esthetical and ethical point of view" of those who favored war and *"then move the point."* Men would always love to fight, but they might be made to cease warring on each other and to take on unformed Nature instead:

The military ideals of hardihood and discipline would be wrought into the growing fibre of the people; no one would remain blind as the luxurious classes now are blind, to man's real relations to the globe he lives on, and to the permanently sour and hard foundations of his higher life. To coal and iron mines, to freight trains, to fishing fleets in December, to dish-washing, clothes-washing, and window-washing, to road-building and tunnel-making, to foundries and stoke-holes, and to the frames of sky-scrapers, would our gilded youths be drafted off, according to their choice, to get the childishness knocked out of them, and to come back into society with healthier sympathies and soberer ideas.

James targeted privileged young men—the pass men, the general-culture men—and imagined how they might be conditioned to assume positions of social responsibility.

Although he never forgot the cranks and the lame ducks, the misfits and the solitary sons of Harvard, the more celebrated William James spoke for the more manly men of Harvard, those who would be "the backbone of the country." His own experience suggested that endless reflection could lead to what he called in the *Varieties* "anhedonia," or "mere passive joylessness and dreariness, discouragement, dejection, lack of taste and zest and spring." Whatever the constitution of others at "the true Harvard," he himself had been as neurasthenic as any in his neurasthenic generation, as alone with his thoughts, and as fearful of physical and moral breakdown. All the more reason for his rousing defense of Harvard manhood. Given his own "great dorsal collapse" in 1870, and his fears lest it denote a moral collapse as well, all the more reason for his encouragement to those who provided backbone, and for his urgings and recommendations about how to relax, how to release energy, and to maintain one's balance and poise.

He was obviously one of "the sick souls" of whom he wrote most movingly in the *Varieties*—nor would he have had it otherwise. Those with whom he contrasted them, "the healthy-minded" (to whose ranks he relegated Whitman), were pale copies of humanity—"more often feminine than masculine, and young than old, whose soul is of this sky-blue tint, whose affinities are rather with flowers and birds and all enchanting innocencies than with dark human passions."[45] He himself spoke as one familiar with dark passions and abysses, as the hero he defined most memorably in a passage whose stirring and summary nature justifies quotation at length:

If the "searching of our heart and reins" be the purpose of this human drama, then what is sought seems to be what effort we can make. He who can make none is but a shadow; he who can make much is a hero. . . . When a dreadful object is presented, or when life as a whole turns up its dark abysses to our view, then the worthless ones among us lose their hold on the situation altogether, and either escape from its difficulties by averting their attention, or if they cannot do that, collapse into yielding masses of plaintiveness and fear. The effort required for facing and consenting to such objects is beyond their power to make. But the heroic mind does differently. To it, too, the objects are sinister and dreadful, unwelcome, incompatible with wished-for things. But it can face them if necessary, without for that losing its hold upon the rest of life. The world thus finds in the heroic man its worthy match and mate; and the effort which he is able to put forth to hold himself erect and keep his heart unshaken is the direct measure of his worth and function in the game of human life. He can *stand* this Universe.[46]

This is William James in 1890, in mid-career, writing on the Will in his magnum opus, *The Principles of Psychology*. It is the image of a man who, having curbed and disciplined his own will, his body upright once again, can now fearlessly face the sinister and the dark. It is both a self-portrait and the expression of an impersonal ideal that was enormously useful to the culture.

"The Fullness of Living Itself"

The most popular lesson James ever taught was on "habit."[1] Over time, he would be universally appreciated for his defense of men's and women's religious beliefs against all that science had to say about them; as a philosopher, he would ultimately be internationally recognized for the version of Pragmatism he developed in several volumes after the turn of the century; but as a lesson, nothing that he wrote compares to his essay on habit. It was first published in 1887 in the *Popular Science Monthly;* it was integral to *The Principles of Psychology* three years later, and then to the subsequent *Psychology: Briefer Course;* it was reprinted in his *Talks to Teachers* in 1899, and thereafter in anthologies with titles like *College and the Future: Essays for the Undergraduate on Problems of Character and Intellect.*[2]

Speaking from his own experience, addressing his readers with more urgency than usual, James did not just talk *about* "the gilded youth" of Harvard and America; instead, he addressed them directly, especially the younger—and therefore the more educable—ones among them. He was eager to pass on the things that he'd learned that had—as he would say—paid off. "The great thing in all education is to *make our nervous system our ally instead of our enemy,*" he asserted in the physiological language he still spoke in 1887. And then shifting to the language that the culture spoke more fluently: "It is to fund and capitalize our acquisitions, and live at ease upon the interest of the fund. *For this we must make automatic and habitual, as early as possible, as many useful actions as we can.*" In whatever language, the message was simple: form good habits before it is too late. The critical years for the formation of "intellectual and professional habits" were those between twenty and thirty. It was a proposition all the clearer to him because of the difficulty he himself had experienced in settling on a career. Though he'd been a little over thirty when he accepted Eliot's offer, he had succeeded, and with relief could say, "It is well for the world that in most of us, by the age of thirty, the character has set like plaster, and will never soften again."

But he did not explicitly focus on himself. Instead—in the kind of passage that prompted readers to think of his becoming a novelist—he spoke of habit as "the enormous fly-wheel of society, its most precious conservative agent." With majestic sadness, he observed:

It alone prevents the hardest and most repulsive walks of life from being deserted by those brought up to tread therein. It keeps the fisherman and the deck-hand at sea through the winter; it holds the miner in his darkness, and nails the countryman to his log-cabin and his lonely farm through all the months of snow; it protects us from invasion by the natives of the desert and the frozen zone. It dooms us all to fight out the battle of life upon the lines of our nurture or our early choice, and to make the best of a pursuit that disagrees, because there is no other for which we are fitted, and it is too late to begin again.

As if imagining a Dickensian composition-to-be, he went on to note "the little lines of cleavage running through the character, the tricks of thought, the prejudices, the ways of the 'shop,' " that distinguish the traveling salesman, the doctor, and the "counsellor-at-law." And then he went back in time to speak of "the period below twenty" as "more important still for the fixing of *personal* habits." He said we should "guard against the growing into ways that are likely to be disadvantageous to us, as we should guard against the plague." If there was anyone who had to deliberate before rising or setting out to work, for example, James exhorted him: "If there be such daily duties not yet ingrained in any one of my readers, let him begin this very hour to set the matter right." Seventeen years before, he had set down this resolution in his Diary:

Recollect that only when habits of order are formed can we advance to really interesting fields of action—and consequently accumulate grain on grain of wilful choice like a very miser—never forgetting how one link dropped undoes an indefinite number.

In "Habit," he cast his determination to take control of his life in more starkly gendered terms:

When a resolve or a fine glow of feeling is allowed to evaporate without bearing practical fruit it is worse than a chance lost; it works so as positively to hinder future resolutions and emotions from taking the normal path of discharge. There is no more contemptible type of human character than that of the nerveless sentimentalist and dreamer, who spends his life in a weltering sea of sensibility and emotion, but who never does a manly concrete deed.

"Woe to him," he continued in the sermonizing mode, who can recognize the good that men should strive for only in its "pure and abstract form." Woe to those, for example, who are too taken by the arts: "The habit of excessive novel-reading and theatre-going will produce true monsters in this line." A "final practical maxim" followed: *"Keep the faculty of effort alive in you by a little gratuitous exercise every day."* In a metaphor that could be traced back either to Watt or to Onan—either to scientific advances of the age or to its prudery— he said that physical education or conditioning would produce more nearly "normal discharge." Along with other forms of self-discipline involving "habits of concentrated attention, energetic volition, and self-denial," physical exercise would produce the kind of man whom he would later consider to be "the backbone of the country." Such a man would "stand like a tower when everything rocks around him, and when his softer fellow-mortals are winnowed like chaff in the blast."

In 1899, in his address "On Certain Limitations of the Thoughtful Public in America," delivered at Vassar College, Josiah Royce told his audience about his discussing this "wonderful chapter on Habit" with a young woman who was a student of psychology—this chapter, he said, that was "so full, as some of you may know, not only of theoretical wisdom, but of wholesome practical advice about the formation and control of habits." She had said ("with adorable naïveté," according to Royce) that "she had found this chapter full of advice which must be very valuable indeed 'for the young men for whom it was intended.'" Royce deduced from her remark that she had "certainly observed part of the significance of Professor James's chapter," but also that she was exemplifying just the kind of "limitation" that Royce was deploring in his lecture—namely, what he called "too abstract thoughtfulness" and an "overfondness both for mere formulas and for abstract arguments about complex practical issues." Royce said he had noticed this tendency in "some educated women, some women who enter public life as reformers, and perhaps too many college-bred women." They were examples of the kind of thinkers who "try to reform all the world, or even any great region of our complex lives, by insisting upon any one set of phrases, of human conceptions and words, which the individual himself has found somehow dear to his own consciousness."[3]

We recognize the situation: a relentlessly gendered text; a woman's reading of it that may emanate either from an even more sharply defined sense of the different social situations of the men and women who might read it or from a desire for a *less* gendered conceptualization of the issue; the counterclaim that no, common human experience is all that James has in mind here—a claim that incorporates the suggestion that the gendered reading is naive, perhaps adorably so, and merely formulaic. Royce's habits of mind and expression are so ingrained—so set in plaster, James would say—that there is no chance of his imagining the Vassar student's position. Ultimately we should read James' essay without "overfondness for mere formulas," but we cannot write off this woman's reaction to the masculinist culture which it reflects and supports as just "somehow dear to [her] own consciousness."

James' essay was sure to prove valuable to typical young Victorian men. Still—as everybody recognized—James was different. Though we can find many examples of his manhood on display, those who knew him insist upon the range of his sympathies. He was known for his refusal to take anything for granted, for his attempts to imagine "foreign states of mind," and for his attraction to alternatives. Such traits made his relentless psychical research more understandable; they accounted for his defense (in 1894) of faith healers and mind curers against a Massachusetts legislature that was being pressured by the medical profession to prohibit them from practicing; they made for his love of misfits and "undisciplinables," for his apparent interest in each and every student and for everything he had to say.

James' most interesting and lasting expression of his temperamental and philosophical commitment to openness occurs in the section headed "The Stream of Thought" in *The Principles of Psychology*—or as he renamed it in the *Briefer Course* two years later, "The Stream of Consciousness."[4] It precludes our ever reducing James' utterances to apologies for his culture.

Generations of anxious readers of Joyce or Woolf or Faulkner have acknowledged James' insights—if only by invoking the famous phrase "the stream of consciousness"—but of course what James (and, later, the modernists) illuminated was not just a technique but rather what that technique served to approximate or re-create: namely, the condition in which we live and use language. What James gives us is a world in which men are cut off one from one another in their essential individuality. "The breach from one mind to another is perhaps the greatest breach in nature," he said. "Absolute insulation, irreducible pluralism, is the law." He makes brilliantly clear how we conceive of and use language in ways that diminish ourselves and others as individuals— how, as he put it, "language works against our perception of the truth." What he suggests—and no more than suggestion, or evocation, is possible, given the unalterable limitations of language—is the indeterminate, the ready, the expectant attitude toward experience that he was known for as a teacher.

James begins with a pair of elementary postulates: *"thinking of some sort goes on,"* and thinking is part of an individual's consciousness. He then defines consciousness in terms of the metaphor of the stream—not of the chain, or the train, he is careful to point out, but, more appropriately, the stream: "It is nothing jointed; it flows. A 'river' or a 'stream' are the metaphors by which it is most naturally described. *In talking of it hereafter, let us call it the stream of thought, of consciousness, or of subjective life.*" The very care he exercises in his choice of metaphor reflects his awareness of the further fact that any such descriptive term will be—must be—only metaphorical. Heraclitus' terms serve him best. Experience, James says, is forever reshaping us; our reactions are the ongoing result of our accumulated experience up to the moment; the objects to which we react may be the same, but no experience can be the same as any that precedes or succeeds it. "There is no such thing as repetition," Stein would say. The procession that we personify as I or me, or the self, moves on, changing constantly. Thus, James says, "It would certainly be true to say, like Heraclitus, that we never descend twice into the same stream."

That is the "truth" which language works against. But James' is no mere romantic *cri* over those limitations. Words, he wrote in "Pragmatism and Humanism," plunge us forward "into the stream of our experience."[5] Some— "Fatherland" or "Science" or "Liberty"—have tremendous "energy-releasing" power, as he pointed out in "The Energies of Men."[6] At the other end of the scale, the words *"and"* and *"if"* and *"but"* and *"by"* signify moves of our streaming consciousnesses and the feelings that accompany those moves:

> There is not a conjunction or a preposition, and hardly an adverbial phrase, syntactic form, or inflection of voice, in human speech, that does not express some shading or other of relation which we at some moment actually feel to exist between the larger objects of our thought.

Our language represents rich life going on. There is a potential novelist in us all. But we only half attend. We ought to recognize the feelings of *"and"* and *"if,"* but we do not: "so inveterate has our habit become of recognizing the existence of the substantive parts alone, that language almost refuses to lend itself to any other use." We are what James called us in "The Will to Believe"— "slouchy modern thinkers"[7]—and so we look for names and labels, phrases and systems, for linguistic ways to arrest or climb out of the stream of life. We content ourselves with "the mythological formulas," with patterns of speech that offer us confidence and control over our own lives and the lives of others. In "The Will to Believe," James' example of our laziness is our resistance to Latin. In "The Stream of Thought," he gestures towards the classical languages, "the agglutinative languages," as better guides than English, because "names did not appear in them inalterable, but changed their shape to suit the context in which they lay." But as it is, we confuse the objects of our thought with the shifts and movements of our thinking, we persist in our belief in static and venerable "ideas," and much of life is lost on us. "Concepts, first employed to make things intelligible," he wrote in *A Pluralistic Universe,* "are clung to even when they make them unintelligible." Then, "Instead of being interpreters of reality, concepts negate the inwardness of reality altogether."[8]

James' interests, his curiosity—certainly his knowledge—seemed to know no limits. Still, he pursued them *within* limits—the limits of language, the limits of his temperament. In his philosophy, he tolerated some alternatives, some attitudes and ideas, more than others, and many that he himself expressed did not differ radically from those conventionally favored by most Harvard men. The men who wanted to position themselves centrally and comfortably in the culture had no trouble finding much in what James had to say that would prove inspiring, even as the best among them were—like James himself—constantly imagining possible alternatives.

The place for any of them to start would have been *Pragmatism: A New Name for Some Old Ways of Thinking,* the lectures that James began giving in 1905, that appeared as *Pragmatism* in 1907, and that would be reprinted eight times before his death in 1910. (It would have been an especially appropriate place for Harvard men to start because—by one witty reading—it was "the Harvard elective system applied to the universe.")[9] It was "a very 'sincere' and, from the point of view of ordinary philosophy-professorial manners, a very unconventional utterance," he told his brother Henry, but it was momentous nevertheless—"quite like the protestant reformation," he said, in its questioning of authority. He knew it was not an entirely original work, but he felt it had "just the amount of squeak or shrillness in the voice that enables one book to *tell,*" and that in ten years—given his prowess as a stylist—it would be considered "epoch-making."[10]

Pragmatism is the volume of lectures with which James is most readily associated and—it is fair to say—that most obviously establishes him as a man of his time. It is also his philosophical writing at its most accessible. ("Popular Lectures on Philosophy" is its second subtitle.) In his opening paragraphs, James said he knew that the philosophy that had most meaning for most people was what he called "popular philosophy"—"not a technical matter," but rather "our more or less dumb sense of what life honestly and deeply means"—and that although he would have to linger over technical matters in his lectures, what he had to say would still be engaging because philosophy, as he understood it, was inevitably engaging. It was sometimes repugnant in its manners, "its doubting and challenging, its quibbling and dialectics," but it was also able to "inspire our souls with courage." Enamored of rhetorical figures like that of the backbone or the tower, this time James used the image of the lighthouse to enhance his readers' sense of the abiding and comforting power of philosophy. He claimed that "no one of us can get along without the far-flashing beams of light it sends over the world's perspectives," and that its illuminations created "an interest that is much more than professional"; and characteristically, he located its influence in the temperaments of its sources.

Although philosophers offered "impersonal reasons" for their conclusions, it was their temperaments, and not their "more strictly objective premises," that shaped their arguments. Men wanted "any representation of the universe" that suited them, and considered philosophers "of opposite temper" incompetent, "even though they may far excel . . . in dialectical ability."[11]

Never known for taking his ideas to their logical conclusions himself, James constructed a philosophical world that suited his temperament. In his first chapter, "The Present Dilemma in Philosophy," James set out on his most extended and famous typological tour, the one in which he contrasted the "tender-minded" and the "tough-minded." The former he characterized as "rationalistic (going by 'principles')," "idealistic," "monistic," starting from wholes and universals, and inclined to make "much of the unity of things." The latter was "empiricist (going by 'facts')," "materialistic," "pessimistic," starting from parts, "and not averse to calling itself pluralistic." He said, "The rationalist finally will be of dogmatic temper in his affirmations, while the empiricist may be more sceptical and open to discussion." The attentive reader of James goes down his lists of temperamental characteristics, noting that James possessed some in each column—and is thus happily prepared for his "solution": "I offer the oddly-named thing pragmatism as a philosophy that can satisfy both kinds of demand. It can remain religious like the rationalisms, but at the same time, like the empiricisms, it can preserve the richest intimacy with facts." He thought that the age was "almost religious" in its dedication to empirical knowledge. He was trained as a scientist himself, and became "the most gifted scientific observer America has produced,"[12] but throughout most of his teaching and his writing life, he tried to keep men receptive to the presence of divinity in the post-Darwinian world in which they lived. Although the word "pragmatic" now evokes images of men in boardrooms, high up over the city, making hard-nosed decisions—images that one can easily trace back to the Gilded Age in which James began to write—his ultimate aim in developing a pragmatic philosophy was not to empower men in their worldly pursuits but to encourage their belief in the existence of a transcendent order of things without their being dogmatic or smug or hopelessly behind the times.[13]

Pragmatism was a means, "a method only," James insisted. It was the way a man tested his ideas. His opening (and most labored) example is of a squirrel scrambling around a tree to keep out of sight of a man who is pursuing him. The question that he poses is: does the man go around the squirrel, or not? It is obvious that both go around the tree, but does the man go around the squirrel? "Which party is right," James argues, "depends on what you *practically mean* by 'going round' the squirrel." If you mean passing from the north of him to the east to the south and so on, then the man goes around him, but if you mean being in front, then to the right, then behind, he does not. "Make the distinction, and there is no occasion for any farther dispute. You are both right and both wrong according as you conceive the verb 'to go round' in one practical fashion or the other." Though ostensibly an example of "quibbling," this example does show how pragmatism tests ideas for their practical consequences, or their instrumental value, rather than for their referential validity. We find truth in our ideas and not in the world. As Coleridge said in the *Biographia Literaria,* "we are all collectively born idealists, and therefore and only therefore are we at the same time realists."[14] Moving quickly from squirrels to religion, James says that theological ideas, abstractions even, are valuable, "so long as you get about among particulars with their aid and they actually carry you somewhere." Again: *"If theological ideas prove to have a value for concrete life, they will be true, for pragmatism, in the sense of being good for so much."*[15]

Though it is typical of a James to encourage us to contemplate such an ambiguous relationship as this between man and squirrel, as one reader has noted, it is typical of William to show us a way to clear it up: "In William's pragmatic approach, one can use knowledge to make choices fearlessly and without regret; in Henry's view, knowledge is always imperfect, and some loss is inevitable."[16] When James comes to the "real" issues (those issues involving life's meaning, the issues Jamesian philosophy intends to address), he makes his choices clearly and with energy and determination. Having satisfied his desire for different perspectives, he is eager to harmonize.

What men want, James asserts, is order in their lives. An early and seminal version of this proposition is contained in his two essays titled "The Sentiment of Rationality" (1879, 1882). James focuses not on men's abstract reasonings but on their feelings about the reasonable, and then explores not their efforts to discover simple unifying conceptions of experience but rather what he assumes to be their insistence on being clear about experience in detail. To settle for the former would be to enjoy what he calls "the philosopher's logical tranquility," which "is in essence no other than the boor's." The man who did would be worse than "tender-minded"; he would be less than a man, for he assumed that "the impulse to take life strivingly" was—like the martial impulse—"indestructible in the race." As would be the case in his handling of the types of mind in the opening pages of *Pragmatism,* James' effort in "The Sentiment of Rationality" was to describe the conditions of "most favorable compromise," and, again, there is no mistaking the direction in which his thinking moves.

Rephrasing the difference between "the need of unity and the need of clearness" as one between idealism and materialism, James says in "The Sentiment of Rationality" that "all sentimental natures, fond of conciliation and intimacy," tend towards idealism. A few sentences more and this type of person becomes neurasthenic and effeminate: "Now in certain sensitively egotistic minds this conception of reality is sure to put on a narrow, close, sickroom air. Everything sentimental and priggish will be consecrated by it." By contrast, we have "every strong man of common-sense," who resonates to a reality that James conceives of in familiar, swashbuckling terms, one that "calls forth powers that he owns—the rough, harsh, sea-wave, north-wind element, the denier of persons, the democratizer."[17] James' intention is to mediate between these two kinds of "mental temper," these two "true"—because usefully, inspiringly imagined—versions of experience, but when he lapses in fact or in his imaginings in the direction of the sickroom, his defenses of the active man become aggressively hearty.

But his inclination towards the "strong man" is not a full commitment to him. "Denier of persons" James could never be. Nor, certainly, could we be asked to admire the amusing version of this man found in the *Varieties of Religious Experience*—"your robust Philistine type of nervous system, forever offering its biceps to be felt, thumping its breast, and thanking Heaven that it hasn't a single morbid fibre in its composition."[18] When confronted with men whose reactions against the brute fact of the world took the form of Bigness—of amassing big fortunes or power in big institutions, or lording it over struggling peoples in the Philippines—James would embrace those who were disengaged or vulnerable. The alternatives and the tension between these two understandings of the truth about the world constitute James' temperament. He was himself the mediation.

In sum, we might think of him as "the entire man" of the first version of "The Sentiment of Rationality," the man who "will take nothing as equivalent for life but the fullness of living itself." "Weary of the concrete clash and dust and pettiness," he will "refresh himself by a bath in the eternal springs, or fortify himself by a look at the immutable natures"—but he will do so only as a visitor. It is James speaking feelingly after six years as a teacher at Harvard: "he will never carry the philosophic yoke upon his shoulders, and when tired of the gray monotony of her problems and insipid spaciousness of her results, will always escape gleefully into the teeming and dramatic richness of the concrete world."[19] Given his sense of "what life honestly and deeply means," James had to re-immerse himself in the world—in his philosophy, at any rate. The sentiment of rationality required the right balance of idealism and materialism, of tender- and tough-mindedness. But even this would not be enough for him. The Arnoldian overview, seeing the world fully and seeing it whole, would not be enough. James also had to be envisaging a better world, ever better, and ever more nearly resembling some transcendent ideal order of things that he felt had to be, even though in the late nineteenth century no creed or church could be trusted to define it. By envisaging it, he thought he would be doing his part in the creation of that ideal order.

Such thinking—as the title of one of his more popular essays had it—was "What Makes a Life Significant." In this essay, James pairs off men's ideals and their active virtues, and, with a kind of glee verging on the manic, he lights into men's notion of the ideal as represented by "the middle-class paradise" he had come upon the assembly grounds at Lake Chautauqua. The Chautauqua Literary and Scientific Circle, formed in 1878, was the most popular adult education program of the period, offering reading and lecture courses to upwards of 35 million people by 1920. A mecca for those who would improve themselves, it was—according to Theodore Roosevelt—"the most American thing about America."[20] James lectured at one of the CLSC's summer sessions for a week in 1896. Recounting his experiences in his lecture, he said that he had found no resistance there. None was possible in a world "without a sin, without a victim, without a blot, without a tear," and so there had been no significance:

This order is too tame, this culture too second-rate, this goodness too uninspiring. This human drama without a villain or a pang; this community so refined that ice-cream soda-water is the utmost offering it can make to the brute animal in man; this city simmering in the tepid lakeside sun; this atrocious harmlessness of all things—I cannot abide with them.

"In this unspeakable Chautauqua," he writes, warming further to his subject, "there was no potentiality of death in sight anywhere, and no point of the compass visible from which danger might possibly appear." There was no opportunity for "the sterner stuff of manly virtue" to prove itself. Metaphorically, there was no war, there were no competitive sports: "The ideal was so completely victorious already that no sign of any previous battle remained, the place just resting on its oars." Speaking at least for himself, he said that "what our human emotions seem to require is the sight of the struggle going on."[21]

James' struggle was what Blake called a "mental fight," a struggle for the richest possible understanding of the world. His fight was also, more practically, an effort to build Jerusalem, or some earthly paradise, out of all of the elements of human experience. He believed, as he said in *Pragmatism,* that the "need of an eternal moral order is one of the deepest needs of our breast,"[22] and the order he had in mind would deny none of the hardships or the evils of the world. In his "Conclusions" to *The Varieties of Religious Experience,* he even hesitantly put forward the "over-belief" that that order existed in *other* realms of consciousness and that those other realms "must contain experiences which have a meaning for our life also."[23] Inevitably, being a professor and not a Blake—or a Wordsworth or Byron—he paid relatively little attention to the revolutions and to other concrete attempts to establish moral order taking place around the world—although he noticed more than most of his colleagues, as we will see. He paid much more attention to the philosophical means by which men could fight for moral order in their thinking.

"No particular results then, so far," he wrote in "What Pragmatism Means," "but only an attitude of orientation, is what the pragmatic method means. *The attitude of looking away from first things, principles, 'categories,' supposed necessities; and of looking towards last things, fruits, consequences, facts.*"[24] In "Pragmatism and Humanism," he said that, for Pragmatism, reality is *"still in the making, and awaits part of its complexion from the future."*[25] The truth of a man's thoughts, in other words, lies in the thoughts and ideals towards which they tend. "The belief creates its verification," he wrote in "The Sentiment of Rationality." "The thought becomes literally father to the fact, as the wish was father to the thought."[26] James' beliefs tended towards man's greater humanity and, ultimately, as his final lecture, called "Pragmatism and Religion," made clear, towards the Absolute. Making use of these ideas was not so easy a matter as making use of the idea that the man went around the squirrel, but James maintained that in a man's moral and spiritual life too, his belief in an idea created the truth of it—if he truly believed.

There could never be satisfaction this side of the grave, presumably, but was there ever any respite? "What a curse philosophy would be if we couldn't forget all about it!" James exclaimed to Santayana on one famous occasion.[27] James did speak of "moral holidays," of times when one dropped one's intellectual burdens and just believed, but as the phrase suggests, such "holidays" were like those periods of relaxation that were condoned because they enabled one ultimately to be the more active and energetic. One took a break, but on the understanding that one's valiant efforts to scale the heights of faith might then be more nearly successful.

But there seemed to be moments of complete escape as well—to the Adirondacks, to the White Mountains. (Santayana noted that even while conducting a class, James "liked to open the window, and look out for a moment.")[28] Yet returns or escapes to nature had to be rich subjects for inquiry in themselves—at least to William James, whose stream of thought was not likely to dry up, even on holiday. In fact, in the late nineteenth century, it would be under precisely those circumstances—and not in any church—that a would-be believer would hold out what hope he had of arriving at "a complete conception of things." His scaling of Mount Marcy with Pauline Goldmark was one such occasion—that "most memorable of all my memorable experiences," he told his wife.[29] Another was the earthquake that hit San Francisco in 1906.[30]

Before he had left to teach at Stanford, a Californian friend had said he hoped James would be introduced to that "Californian institution," the earthquake. The introduction took place on April 18—it lasted forty-eight seconds—and later James personified the force he had met: "it was *the* earthquake of my friend B.'s augury"; it came "directly to *me*"; it pointed back "to a living agent as its source and origin." When James asked around, he discovered everyone talking about "It"—what "It" did, or what "It" intended—and that led him to conclude, "To me, it wanted simply to manifest the full meaning of its *name*. But what was this 'It'? To some, apparently, a vague demonic power; to me an individual being, B.'s earthquake, namely." There were newspaper reports of looters, some so eager for valuables that they chopped off fingers, and of the drunkenness of troops sent in to restore order, but James either didn't read them or ignored them.[31] He felt only "pure delight and welcome," because at that moment it seemed to him that the word had become the thing and, moreover, that it had done so as if with purpose.

He also marveled at the way people quickly set about reconstituting their lives together ("the rapidity of the improvisation of order out of chaos"), their determination ("like soldiering," he said, "always latent in human nature"), and their "universal equanimity," their "cheerfulness or, at any rate, [their] steadfastness of tone." That people had satisfied their need for order, "naturally," and that they had behaved like warriors, both under such trying conditions, was exhilarating enough, but the earthquake's being what its name signified—"B.'s earthquake, namely"—made the experience a climactic one in James' life. He would never experience the Word's being God, as the Gospel according to Saint John has it, but for any natural phenomenon to embody what it was called had to be for William James a religious experience. One clear indication of the extraordinary, incomparable impact of this experience is his later reflection that it was "too overwhelming for anything but passive surrender to it." In any other situation one can think of, James would imagine improvement, and would encourage man's active efforts to bring it about.

"It is clear that pragmatism must incline towards meliorism," he said. It was so clear to James that anyone who disagreed with him ended up in very sorry company. "The pragmatism or pluralism which I defend has to fall back on a certain ultimate hardihood, a certain willingness to live without assurance or guarantees," he wrote in "The Absolute and the Strenuous Life." "To minds thus willing to live on possibilities that are not certainties, quietistic religion, sure of salvation *any how,* has a slight flavor of fatty degeneration about it which has caused it to be looked askance on, even in the church."[32] In "Pragmatism and Religion," he asked his auditors to imagine being asked if they wanted to take part in the salvation of the world with the dual understanding that salvation would be dependent on each agent's doing his "level best" to bring it about, and that there was no guarantee of safety—"a real adventure, with real danger, yet it may win through," he said. He asked them if they could imagine turning down the opportunity, and quickly answered his question for them: "Of course if you are normally constituted, you would do nothing of the sort." And then down onto the heads of those who could even contemplate refusing, down on the "abnormal," came these rhetorical figurings of unmanliness: the "morbid minds" for whom "only a fighting chance of safety" had no appeal; the "prodigal son" who would like to fall on his father's neck "and be absorbed into the absolute life as a drop of water melts into the river or the sea"; "the hindoo and the buddhist," who are "simply afraid, afraid of more experience, afraid of life"; those who in "their last sick extremity" find absolutism their "only saving scheme"; and finally, the cringing cowards. To put these dastards down, James resorted to the melodramatic: "Pluralistic moralism simply makes their teeth chatter," he said; "it refrigerates the very heart within their breast." James' final gesture of mediation between extremes could leave his audience of only one inspired mind: "Between the two extremes of crude naturalism on the one hand and transcendental absolutism on the other, you may find that what I take the liberty of calling the pragmatistic or melioristic type of theism is exactly what you require."[33] How could anyone not resolve to obey the doctor's order?

Differences with Others

The year that *Pragmatism* came out, James retired from the Harvard faculty. In the pages of the *Advocate,* Van Wyck Brooks celebrated his Olympian presence over the years by calling him "our greatest teacher." But anxious students can be retrospectively hard on their influential teachers. Twenty-five years later, Brooks still thought James stood preeminent. He was still "that golden man and poet whose every personal trait . . . was lovable and magnetic"—in his lifetime he had become the intellectuals' "acknowledged master"—but now Brooks thought that, as their master, what he best represented was the *betrayal* of the intellectuals. Specifically, Brooks said, James had carried his pragmatism, his tolerance for any man's will to believe anything, to the point where he had rendered any elevating and unifying defense of values impossible. Like other detractors, he pointed to the example of Mussolini. What was one to make of the fact that Il Duce had said that James' pragmatism had been of great use to him in his political career?[1] Pointing out that James was himself a "sick soul," Brooks said James' whole life had been an effort to achieve "healthy-mindedness,"

an effort also to reconcile himself, to bring himself into rapport with a busy, practical, "tough-minded" world, an effort in which, in order to play the game, he gradually and unconsciously surrendered his belief in the final importance of any values superior to those that were current in American society of his day.

In a world in which one man's sense of how the game ought to be played was as good as any other's, the only way for the game to proceed was for everyone to play by the existing rules. With his pragmatic philosophy, James had destroyed all independence, "all honesty of mind."[2]

He was echoing the criticism that his former teacher Irving Babbitt had leveled against James' pragmatism even as James was presenting it in his lectures. Other colleagues objected on firmer philosophical grounds, none more strongly than Charles Peirce—"the most original and versatile of American philosophers and America's greatest logician," he has been called.[3] He had known James longer than any of them, the two having first met in 1861 at the Lawrence Scientific School, where they studied chemistry together. Peirce spent thirty years as a research scientist in the Coast and Geodetic Survey and held temporary academic positions at Johns Hopkins and Harvard—the latter negotiated by James. Peirce's biographer calls Royce and not James "his one real student," but Peirce recognized James as his one true friend. Although James confessed to not understanding a word of the Lowell Lectures on the philosophy of science that Peirce gave in 1866, and to finding another course that he gave at Harvard in 1869 "incomprehensible," and furthermore, although he spoke of him as "so thorny and spinous a bedfellow," James knew that Peirce was a genius, and he did everything in his power to help him. In 1907, James set up a fund to sustain him financially. In turn, after having known him for almost fifty years, Peirce wrote that no one could have been more nearly his opposite than "the world's highest respected and closest beloved philosophic soul, William James," but that for that very reason, he could claim to be an authority on James' understanding of men: "He so concrete, so living; I, a mere table of contents, so abstract, a very snarl of twine." No one understood "the mainspring of my life" better than James, Peirce said. In appreciation, the year before James died he added Santiago—Saint James—to his own name.[4]

In the early 1870s, both men were members of "the Metaphysical Club" in Cambridge. The most significant work to emerge from their Sunday meetings was the paper that Peirce read on pragmatism in 1872—even if its significance resided primarily in James' distorted version of the philosophy it introduced. Peirce thought that philosophy should be an exact science; the aim of his pragmatism was to determine how concepts could be used to investigate objects of conception in a laboratory setting or to establish an ethical ideal. It was a theory of the signs, or symbols, that constituted the entirety of men's thinking. All that men knew about the world, he argued, they knew by abstraction and inference after the fact of their sensations or their thoughts. According to Peirce, a concept had no meaning in the sense of affecting their feelings about or their conduct in the world. It is *"nothing more* than the concept, not of any concrete difference that *will* be made to someone, but is nothing more than the concept of the *conceivable* practical applications of it."[5] James had applied Peirce's pragmatism first in the psychological realm, asking what propositions made for a man's truth in the sense of being useful to him, and then converting pragmatism into a philosophical theory about the nature of truth. Whereas Peirce used language to define and promote a conception of the good life that reflected the stability and harmony of things, James explored the ways that conceptions could help men in their individual, existential struggles.

Peirce personally chastised James for his failings as a logician, and at one point offered to make a mathematician out of him. James had carried pragmatism too far, he told him, adding, "Pragmatism solves no real problem. It only shows that supposed problems are not real problems." Questions about immortality or the relation of mind and matter left one completely in the dark. To misuse words, to speak of what we cannot speak, Peirce wrote James on another occasion, is "downright bad morals . . . for it prevents philosophy from becoming a science."[6]

James' relationship with Josiah Royce was more sustained and intimate, but it followed the same pattern: the two men were opposed as thinkers but extremely close personally, and in his gratitude and love for James, Royce too was more than willing to overlook their philosophical differences. Whereas Peirce was the son of a distinguished Harvard professor of mathematics and had gone to Harvard himself, Royce came from a small California mining town, and made friends only with characters in books until he went to college at Berkeley. There he met his first intellectual father figure, the geologist Joseph LeConte. If, as Royce said, his early years in California prompted him to center what he called "his deepest motives and problems" on "the idea of Community," LeConte was the first to inspire him to look beyond the material world for the realization of that idea. LeConte's theory of evolution—grounded in that of Herbert Spencer—had it that God was an "all-pervading force" working through Nature in a process that culminated in the creation of man. He believed that "Man alone, of all the objects of Nature, is the child of God." In Man the spirit of God came to independent life.[7]

After study in Germany and at Johns Hopkins, Royce came to Harvard, first for the summer of 1877—during which, legend has it, he worked in Harvard Yard as a member of the grounds crew—and then, five years later, as a temporary replacement for James. Temporary it was supposed to be, for he had been teaching English at Berkeley. But he came to Cambridge with his wife and child, intending to stay, there being in his mind no other place where he belonged. His first meeting with James had sealed his fate. "James found me at once," he said at the unveiling of James' portrait in 1910,

made out what my essential interests were at our first interview, accepted me, with all my imperfections, as one of those many souls who ought to be able to find themselves in their own way, gave a patient and willing ear to just my variety of philosophical experience, and used his influence from that time on, not to win me as a follower, but to give me my chance.[8]

Royce was James' colleague for almost twenty-five years—his most valued colleague—and his neighbor for most of those years.

James embraced Royce as a friend more warmly than he did any other man. He protected him, the way an older brother might. (He was thirteen years Royce's senior.) Royce's needs were obvious. In the first place, what with his flaming red hair and his giant skull, which seemed to sink down into his short, squat frame, he seemed oddly out of place physically. James associated his face with illustrations from medical books. He was a social misfit as well, likely to talk nonstop when asked the simplest question. Chapman said he had an "infantile look like that of an ugly baby," but loved the way he babbled on. "A benevolent monster of pure intelligence," he called him, "zigzagging, ranging, and uncatchable. I always had this feelings about Royce—that he was a celestial insect."[9] James furthered his career, he helped out financially (giving money to a trust fund set up for a son who had to be institutionalized at the age of twenty-five), as he did with Peirce, but Royce was more grateful and graceful than Peirce in accepting James' charities.

Women were not so tolerant of him. His wife enjoyed comparing her husband's work to a game in which you hid a doll in an attic trunk, asked everyone where the doll might be, turned the house upside down, and then finally asked, "Do you suppose it could be in that old trunk?"—after which you went up and found it. Her marriage, she said, was "just like being married to any other fellow when you didn't know what he was talking about." Once, while standing next to W. E. B. Du Bois at a reception, she gestured towards her husband, who was on the other side of the room, talking excitedly, and said, "Funny-looking man, isn't he?"[10] Whatever specific form *James'* wife's antipathy toward Royce took was so overt that Royce felt compelled to comfort James in his embarrassment: "I haven't been an odious little creature all these years without fully knowing the fact," he wrote, "and I think of none so highly as I do of those who share my appreciation of the odiousness in question."[11] As he said of James in his speech in 1910, "He was good to me, and I love him."[12]

His feelings were returned—in the form of what Shelley called "intellectual love." While composing his Gifford Lectures at Bad Nauheim, James wrote Royce that he was "the centre of my gaze, the pole of my mental magnet," and then—in an extraordinary flourish—said, "I lead a parasitic life upon you, for my highest flight of ambitious ideality is to become your conqueror, and go down into history as such, you and I rolled in one another's arms and silent (or rather loquacious still) in one last death-grapple of an embrace."[13]

He compared the experience of teaching a course with Royce to a love affair between Siamese twins.[14] The figure is another of those that bring out how intensely and entirely these men imagined their professional and personal lives together. On a philosophical plane, it makes graphic their sameness and their differences. Both were—loosely speaking—idealists, believing in man's capacity to transcend his mere earthly existence in the attainment of individual virtue and—more in Royce's philosophy than in James'—salvation as a social being. But they were idealists only up to a point, after which each had very different readings of the ways men proceeded, and of the odds of their success. In one of his earliest essays, "Remarks on Spencer's Definition of Mind as Correspondence," James spoke of a man's setting up "his private categorical imperative of what rightness or excellence in thought shall consist in," or "different ideals," which then, rather than "entering upon the scene armed with a warrant—whether derived from the polyp or from a transcendental source—appear only as so many brute affirmations left to fight it out upon the chess-board among themselves." The winner—"the true one"—would be the one with "the most massive density," he said. "But this is a point which can only be solved *ambulando,* and not by any *a priori* definition."[15] In his later writings, James would turn away from polyps in the lab and look for more religious confirmation of the "rightness or excellence in thought," and the fight to reach the source would resemble sports more physically challenging than chess, but in his imaginings he would still focus on the individual, questing man, and he would never grant him any more than the temporary satisfaction of knowing he was on the right track because for the time being he seemed to be making progress.

James pointed out on more than one occasion that the Absolute probably had a much better time being Josiah Royce than being William James. Determined that the Absolute existed—or, James would have argued, temperamentally requiring that He exist—Royce posited His existence, whereas James could only describe the many ways that a man's will to believe *might* confirm that He did in fact exist. James appreciated Royce's "manlier" monism, but it was still monism, and monism itself, be it the determinism of the materialists on one hand or the idealism of the rationalists on the other, implied relatively passive thinking. Thus, as the metaphors fell out, Royce appeared to James to be something of a lightweight. "In spite of the great technical freight he carries, and his extraordinary mental vigor," he wrote D. S. Miller in 1900, "he belongs essentially among the lighter skirmishers of philosophy. A sketcher and popularizer, not a pile-driver, foundation-layer, or wall-builder."[16]

In turn, Royce, like Peirce, was dismayed by how little philosophical effort James had made in *Pragmatism*. Now it was James who seemed to be shying away from the struggle. In 1879, in "The Sentiment of Rationality," James had written that the "man" would refuse to "carry the philosophic yoke upon his shoulders." Twenty-eight years later, Royce told James that such a refusal made *Pragmatism* "in large part a splendid joke,—a brilliant *reductio ad absurdum* of all attempts at serious grappling with any philosophical issue." But Royce knew that was not James' intent. It was just a matter of "the externals,—the mere setting and style," he said, and he assured James, "No criticism of mine is hostile." That would be impossible, given his appreciation of their labors and their relationship. "Life is a sad long road, sometimes," he concluded. "Every friendly touch and word must be preciously guarded. I prize everything that you say or do, whether I criticize or not."[17]

Santayana would not come so close to James, but he too had much in common with him. They were more like two magnets than like Siamese twins—mutually attracted, potentially allied, and yet turned the wrong way temperamentally, and so forever bouncing off in different directions. Santayana had been James' student; recalling Whitman's definition of the ideal student—"He most honors my style who learns under it to destroy the teacher"—it is tempting to say he was James' best. But insofar as he tried to undermine James, he did not do so with James' manner. As was the case in his relations with Peirce and Royce, James was the more comfortably situated. He was older—more than twenty years older—and an even more forbidding, masculine presence than he was to either Peirce or Royce. From his loftier position, he did not entirely succeed in imagining Santayana's foreignness—and thus, as we have seen, Santayana shied away from him—but James was still the more generous of the two men.

James recognized Santayana's genius, as he had Peirce's and Royce's, but to an extent not true in their cases, he also enjoyed Santayana's way of "doing" philosophy. While Santayana was pursuing graduate study abroad on a Walker Travelling Fellowship, James tried to prepare him for the scrutiny—"the literal eyes"—of his colleagues in the Philosophy Department. What he had seen so far showed too little evidence of the kind of "considerable research done (or undertaken) in the way of scholarship"; it seemed "a little too much like a poem." Santayana was insouciant. "I confess I do not see why we should be so vehemently curious about the absolute truth, which is not to be made or altered by our discovery of it," Santayana wrote in one letter.[18] Being a foreigner and coming from a rather different intellectual and moral *milieu*," he wrote in another,

I have a lighter and less conscience-stricken way of taking things, which produces the impression of idleness and frivolity in the absence of ocular proof that after all I do as much work as other people.

James had misread him, he said; he had taken him "rather too seriously":

I was drawn to philosophy in the beginning by curiosity and a natural taste for ingenious thinking and my attachment to philosophy remains as firm as ever. . . . These things never came to me as a personal problem, as a question of what was necessary for salvation. I was simply interested in seeing what pictures of the world and of human nature men had succeeded in sketching.[19]

But he also said, "What I shall write will certainly not smack so much of a professorship of philosophy as if it were on the normal jerk of the knee-pan," and that of course was bound to please the future author of "The Ph.D. Octopus." In 1905, after having had him as a colleague for many years, it was James who was writing from abroad, complaining about "the gray-plaster temperament of our bald-headed young Ph.D.'s, boring each other at seminaries," and appealing to Santayana: "Can't you and I, who in spite of such divergence have yet so much in common in our *Weltanschauung*, start a systematic movement at Harvard against the desiccating and pedantifying process?"[20]

After reading Santayana's *Interpretations of Poetry and Religion* in 1900, James wrote Palmer to say that while he rejected Santayana's Platonism, he had "literally squealed with delight at the imperturbable perfection with which the position is laid down on page after page." Being at work on his lectures for *The Varieties of Religious Experience,* he had to have taken heart at the way Santayana blurred the lines between poetry and religion, but what he stressed in his letter to Palmer was Santayana's "thickening up of our Harvard atmosphere," by which he meant Santayana's having enriched the "philosophic universe at Harvard" and thus increased the possibility of "open conflict and rivalry of the diverse systems" represented in the department. The philosophy was "fantastic," James said, adding scornfully, "as if the 'world of values' *were* independent of existence," but he loved how Santayana had presented it. He himself was among the "barbarians . . . in the line of mental growth," he said, "and those who do insist that the ideal and the real are dynamically continuous are those by whom the world is to be saved," but it was, nevertheless, good that "the other view, always existing in the world," had found "so splendidly impertinent an expression among ourselves." Moreover, there was his marvelous prose: "He is certainly an *extraordinarily distingué* writer." James asked Palmer to show Santayana his letter, his opinions being the "more free-spoken and direct" that way, and he concluded, "Thank him for existing!"[21]

It is in the context of this letter that James said he finally understood Santayana. And in it we find his famous statements about the "perfection of rottenness" in Santayana's philosophy and the "moribund Latinity" of Santayana himself. What might otherwise seem withering comments are expressions of pleasure. James is almost giddy with the sense of the department's greatness and of coming frays within it; he is grateful for one more alternative to his own philosophy, one that will not let it rest, but rather put it to another and a harder test: "It is refreshing to see a representative of moribund Latinity rise up and administer such reproof to us barbarians in the hour of our triumph."

Though James may have intended to please, in speaking about "perfection of rottenness" and "moribundity" his aim was clearly off. Having learned of James' characterization of him, Santayana wrote to James, "Apart from temperament, I am nearer to you than you now believe." But first he had to have *his* say in the matter of temperaments. "You tax me several times with impertinence and superior airs," he said. "I wonder if you realize the years of suppressed irritation which I have passed in the midst of an unintelligible sanctimonious and often disingenuous Protestantism." Because they were not grounded in reason, his "Catholic sympathies" didn't justify his speaking out, but his study of Plato and Aristotle did. Though he agreed with James that philosophy could not be departmentalized, that it should provide a way of life, he let others know that he thought James' "excursions" into the field were too often "in the nature of raids," his manner too "haphazard." He was made uncomfortable by James' "incalculableness and jumpiness."[22] Whereas to James, truth was "nothing but a happy use of signs,"[23] Santayana asserted that *he* sought to prove the objective existence of goodness and beauty and reasonableness.

There was James' loose grip on reason, his unintelligibility, yes, but what Santayana found most intolerable was what he thought was James' sanctimoniousness—the spirit in which James carried out his mission as a teacher. As he later put it in *Character and Opinion in the United States* (1920), "A slight smell of brimstone lingered in the air" at Harvard. The professors were Protestants, doing their duty. They were "clergymen without a church," and, like Americans generally, they were driven by only "native good-will, complacency, thoughtlessness, and optimism." They believed they could think what they wanted, so long as they were dedicated to "the common task of encouraging everybody and helping everything on," Santayana said. As for James him-self, he "fell in with the hortatory tradition of college sages"; he turned his psychology "to purposes of edification"; his writings on habit and will and faith were "fine and stirring, and just the sermons to preach to the young Christian soldier."[24] Many years after that, in *The Last Puritan* (1936), Santa-yana relegated James to the company of "Charley" Copeland and Barrett Wen-dell, calling the three of them "sentimentalists." "What else can good men be without the Faith, and seeing only the wrong side of the tapestry?" he asked.[25]

In the summary portrayal of James found in his memoir, *Persons and Places* (1945), Santayana paid tribute to James' perceptiveness and his "picturesque words," and to the "naturalistic temper" that his medical training produced. He spoke once again of James' "masculine directness." All this, he said, added up to "his American sense of being just born into a world to be rediscovered." And then he produced a magnificent image of James as a tethered bird. He said that James was "really far from free," that he was "held back by old instincts, subject to old delusions, restless, spasmodic, self-interrupted: as if some impetuous bird kept flying aloft, but always stopped in mid-air, pulled back with a jerk by an invisible wire tethering him to a peg in the ground."[26] It was a more sympathetic picture than the one of James the preacher.

Unbeknownst to Santayana, James had used the image himself, years before, in a letter to his wife-to-be—used it, implicitly, about himself. He was trying to prepare her for his need for freedom in their marriage. Heroic individuals, he said, "let their bird fly with no strings tied to its leg."[27] ("We love the things we love for what they are," Robert Frost would say in "Hyla Brook.") But James could never allow himself that freedom.

Others have stressed how much he succeeded. Chapman speaks of his "playfulness." In our own time, one critic has called James' vision "comic": "If the very heart of comedy was to highlight how mean suffering was and to find and display ways to overcome things that impeded human joy," he writes, "James's vision was comic."[28] It is a reading arrived at through Santayana's appreciation of James' "radically empirical and radically romantic" philosophy, the philosophy that opened up "a new philosophical vista" for Americans, as Santayana said. James' tolerance, his openness, his keen awareness of the necessity for linguistic flexibility, seem forever to hold out such promise. But not, I think, for joy.

For thirty-five years, James was on the faculty of an educational institution bent on providing the intellectual and social and physical training required of America's leaders. He embodied and defined the manly ideal to which those men would aspire, having developed it for his own survival and well-being before he arrived. And that ideal grounded him—both gave him strength and prevented him from soaring. He wanted to fly "aloft," but he was held back by the masculinity he perfected, in the environment that was encouraging him and learning from his example. Yet he was still the most prominent member of that extraordinarily distinguished faculty, pointing the way to more openness of mind and spirit than he could ever reach.

4

On a Certain Blindness

IF MANHOOD was considered a necessary component of a man's humanity during this period, then it had to be that the unmanly were not wholly human. Women, of course, were often construed as dwelling above the realm of men, therefore capable of transforming whatever brutishness resided in men's nature and of elevating their society beyond the merely human. Not that being endowed with such virtue and responsibility would always prove a blessing—having placed her on such heights, men often felt compelled to bring her down. Still, all that was womanly was honored in a woman. But when men discovered womanliness in their *own* kind, their judgments and the measures that they took were summary. At least when the Harvard men to whom manhood was of primary concern contemplated what men were making of themselves, they almost certainly deplored whatever trace of womanliness they found.

"The American woman of the nineteenth century will live only as the man saw her," Henry Adams wrote in *The Education*.[1] When we think of the men who are the subject of this study—the men, in effect, about whom Adams is writing—the women in their lives enjoyed only as much social and political and economic freedom as men allowed, and as Adams said, what a man allowed a woman was dependent on how he imagined her. She would live as he saw fit. She might well conceive of herself in ways that differed vastly and variously from the ways in which he imagined her, but the quality of her life was largely determined by his perceptions of her. The same was true of many "others," of African-Americans, of immigrants, even of the African-Americans and the sons of immigrants who were coming to Harvard in small but increasing numbers during these years. Insofar as ideal manhood was represented as active, healthy, and gentlemanly—which in turn usually meant of higher station and having something called "Anglo-Saxon" origins—then not only women, and not only the passive, sickly types, but also those whose racial or national origins were obviously *not* "Anglo-Saxon" would be thought of as less than ideal men.

Known himself for the reach of his compassion and understanding, James was as aware as anyone of the limitations of men's sympathetic imaginings. He addressed the subject most famously in what to him was a pivotal essay, "On a Certain Blindness in Human Beings" (1898).[2] When it was included, along with "The Gospel of Relaxation" and "What Makes a Life Significant," in *Talks to Teachers on Psychology: and to Students on Some of Life's Ideals* the next year, he wrote his French colleague Theodore Flournoy that it was the essay for which he had "a partiality." More sweepingly, he told his friend Elizabeth Evans that it was "really the perception on which my whole individualistic philosophy is based."[3]

Typically, he framed the problem in terms of men's activities. "We are practical beings," he said, "each of us with limited functions and duties to perform. Each is bound to feel intensely the importance of his own duties and the significance of the situations that call these forth," and thus, he went on, bound not to be sympathetic to the "vital secret" of others, just as they were bound not to take any interest in ours. "Hence the stupidity and injustice of our opinions, so far as they deal with the significance of alien lives." Active or not, man is pathetically self-centered, sharing no more with his fellow man than with his fox terrier. "Take our dogs and ourselves," James wrote,

connected as we are by a tie more intimate than most ties in this world; and yet, outside of that tie of friendly fondness, how insensible, each of us, to all that makes life significant for the other!—we to the rapture of bones under hedges, or smells of trees and lamp-posts, they to the delights of literature and art.

The outsider's, "the spectator's judgment," as James calls it, "is sure to miss the root of the matter and to possess no truth."

In his rendering of these bleak human conditions, James never specifically considers the blindness of men imprisoned in their concern for manhood. He is himself too blinded to do that. He is so exemplary of the subject that he cannot, himself, make his own blindness—or his own gendered self—his subject. In addressing the issue of men's vision generally, though, "On a Certain Blindness" suggests that even the best of men may not be able to see very far into the life of others. Coming from the man who was legendary for his appreciation of the richness and the sanctity of others' lives, the essay is a surprisingly limited performance.

The way out is simple, and thus—if we recall the distinction James made in his essay "The Sentiment of Rationality"—not very clear. It lies in what he variously describes as "the feeling of the vital significance of an experience," in "feelings of excited significance," in a "higher vision of an inner significance," or "wherever a process of life communicates an eagerness to him who lives it." Carrying in his head the titles of other essays written at about the same time, James says that it is on such occasions that "life becomes genuinely significant," and that "life is always worth living if one have such responsive sensibilities." As it turns out, such significant or worthwhile experiences occur, for the most part, in the presence of "non-human natural things," of what James says is "mysterious sensorial life." He gives many examples—from Senancour's *Obermann*, from Wordsworth and Emerson and Whitman, and from more contemporary and popular writers such as Richard Jefferies and W. H. Hudson. He gives so many examples that in its notice of the essay the *Graduates' Magazine* said little more about it than that it was mostly quotations.[4] Taken all together, they present us with the James who was inclined to turn on his own kind, and to denigrate abstract thinking and the comfortable life of a professor, in the name of some immediate experience, some "pure sensorial perception"—an earthquake, for example—to come. "We of the highly educated classes (so called)," he says, "have most of us got far, far away from Nature. We are trained to seek the choice, the rare, the exquisite, exclusively, and to overlook the common. We are stuffed with abstract conceptions, and glib with verbalities and verbosities." Small wonder that "our" perceptions of alien others are stupid and unjust. "The remedy under such conditions is to descend to a more profound and primitive level." For the "over-educated pessimist" that means imprisonment or shipwreck or forced enlistment in the army, for others loafing (with Whitman as inspiration) or drastically reduced circumstances (with Tolstoy's Pierre Bezuhkov as a guide). In other words, if we could simplify, simplify, as Thoreau had said (though James seems to have quoted *him* only once, in *The Varieties of Religious Experience*), and appreciate the very fact of life, we might then be able not necessarily to understand what mattered to others but at least to spare them our projections. "Hands off," James concludes: "It is enough to ask of each of us that he should be faithful to his own opportunities and make the most of his own blessings, without presuming to regulate the rest of the vast field." What James concentrates on in "On a Certain Blindness in Human Beings" is the familiar challenge of ordering and settling one's own life. As for the promise of his title, all that is revealed to us about others is that ideally they will make the best of their lives too.

What James does see of others adds up—according to one interpretation—to the figure of Pauline Goldmark, with whom he was enjoying the rigors of Adirondack climbs around the time that he was composing his essay.[5] To James, Goldmark was "the symbol of a mood, a region, a way of life," her sister later wrote. Just before he died, he himself told her, "Lose no chance during all these young years to live with nature—it is the eternal normal animal thing in us, overlaid by other more important human destinies, no doubt, but holding the fort in the middle as the security of all the rest." It seems too neat to have Goldmark represent the humanity to which he was trying to open men's eyes in his essay, but we know how enthralled he was on that "Walpurgis Nacht" that he spent with her and her friends on Mount Marcy, and in his essay he does quote Emerson on those experiences of "higher vision" to which we "ascribe more reality . . . than to all other experiences," using as his own examples "the passion of love" that he says "will shake one like an explosion, or some act [that] will awaken a remorseful compunction that hangs like a cloud over all one's later day." And it has always seemed amusing that he began his next talk in the series ("What Makes a Life Significant") with those more familiar hill climbers, Jack and Jill, and attributed to *them* extraordinary empathic powers—forgetting what is surely the greater truth about the relationship between love and blindness. But that there is some connection between James' feelings about Goldmark and his belief in the humanizing effects of "sensorial" experience seems evident. When "On a Certain Blindness in Human Beings" appeared in his *Talks to Teachers,* James wanted her to read it even if she read nothing else in the volume, "because," he said, "I care very much indeed for the truth it so inadequately tries, by dint of innumerable quotations, to express, and I like to imagine that you care for it, or will care for it too."[6]

The one human encounter that occurs in the essay takes place in the mountains of North Carolina; in this instance James turns the idea of a return to Nature around. Coming upon a settler's clearing—all charred stumps and a rail fence to keep the pigs and cattle out—he exclaims, "Talk about going back to Nature!" All he sees is "unmitigated squalor," "a sort of ulcer," "denudation." But after hearing the settler's tale of his family's struggle and ultimate victory over the natural environment, he draws this moral: "I had been as blind to the peculiar ideality of their conditions as they certainly would also have been to the ideality of mine, had they had a peep at my strange indoor academic ways of life at Cambridge," and from there he jumps to his individualistic, and pluralistic, philosophy: "Wherever a process of life communicates an eagerness to him who lives it, there the life becomes generally significant." Inspired oneself, one is the more likely to acknowledge that others are inspired in their lives too, but James says nothing about any impulse or need to imagine much about the source of their inspiration, nor about what might happen should the inspirations or truths of different lives come into conflict. It is not hard to imagine the settler's being fairly clear about the benefits of a professor's life, or at least to imagine one or another social theorist's being quite precise about the social context in which each made his living, but to James it is enough that each count his own blessings and not compare.

He ended his companion piece, "What Makes a Life Significant," on a similar note.[7] Bearing in mind the rash of strikes and lockouts during the Depression of 1893—thinking, perhaps, of the Pullman Strike of 1894 in particular (which eventually cost thirty-four lives)—James reminded his audience, "We are suffering from what is called the labor-question." The conflict—the suffering, the chasm that separated rich and poor—was "unhealthy and regrettable," but "only to a limited extent," he said. Wealth doubtless had to be distributed more equitably, but eventually it would be: "such changes have always happened, and will happen to the end of time." What James regretted was people's failure to appreciate each others' humanity: "the unhealthiness consists solely in the fact that one-half of our fellow-countrymen remain entirely blind to the internal significance of the lives of the other half." It is the "solely" that is telling. It leaves no room for how, say, Jacob Riis had presented the results of half the population's blindness to the other half in *How the Other Half Lives* (1890) or *The Children of the Poor* (1892).*

In introducing the "labor-question," James said to the students, "When you go out into the world, you will each and all of you be caught up in its perplexities." They would also, as Henry Adams put it, find Karl Marx waiting there, ready to offer his explanations.[8] But while they were at Harvard, the challenges they faced were those presented by the new sciences, by philosophical debate about the relations between an autonomous self and ideal societies, and, if economics interested them at all, by "his Satanic free-trade majesty John Stuart Mill" when Adams was there and, later, by the "ultra-gradualism" of Harvard's leading economist, Frank Taussig.[9] Having graduated in 1893, Oswald Garrison Villard considered staying at Harvard to teach, but moved on, instead, to follow in the footsteps of his uncle, William Lloyd Garrison, and, in 1909, to join W. E. B. Du Bois in the founding of the NAACP. He thought that at Harvard "one was too safe, too sheltered, too at ease." It was, he said, "like sitting in a club window and watching the world go by on the pavement outside."[10]

James' writings characteristically turn inward, providing the means by which one could understand the nature of an imagined self and prepare it for as various and effective a life as possible. He had not just the club but humanity at heart, and he attended more than most of his colleagues to the new array of

* On the other hand, Robert Park has written movingly of the inspiration he received from James, specifically of the profound effect of hearing James read "On a Certain Blindness in Human Beings" when he was in James' class. As a result of James' words, Park took "a new interest in the study of the Negro and the race problem," spending seven winters roaming through the South from a base at Tuskegee Institute and eventually becoming a power behind Booker T. Washington's throne there. With James' essay in mind, he also addressed men's failure to understand women. "In fact men have felt in the past and," he says, writing in 1950, "still feel in some obscure way, I suspect, that women, no matter how interesting, are not quite human in the sense and to the degree that this is true of themselves." See his *Race and Culture* (Glencoe: Free Press, 1950), pp. vi–vii, 50.

forms it took at the turn of the century—to immigrants and (somewhat) to the labor questions to which they gave rise, and to the peoples of Cuba and the Philippines. But though distinguished and exceptionally intent upon "seeing," like any other individual at any other time, he was still relatively blind.[11] Later generations, led by others, would see more deeply into the cultures of others, whatever the losses of insight they might experience in doing so.

To take a sharp example, in March of 1888 James went with W. E. B. Du Bois—his student at the time—to visit Helen Keller at the Perkins Institution for the Blind. She was then twelve years old. He brought her an ostrich feather, saying that he thought she would like it, for it was "soft and light and caressing." On that occasion, and again twenty years later, when she sent him a copy of her *The World I Live In,* they talked about how little people differed from one another "in [their] problems and processes of thought." In acknowledging her gift, he wrote, "You live in a world so indistinguishable from ours. The great world, *the background,* in all of us, is the world of *our beliefs.*" Everyone's relations with "the permanencies and the immensities" were verbal, he said. Whether the "content of our verbal material" was optical or tactile mattered little.[12]

By contrast, what struck Du Bois about Helen Keller on that occasion and thereafter was that she was—in his sense of the term—color-blind. After she had spoken out against "the iniquity and foolishness of the color line" in 1936, in her own state of Alabama, he wrote, "This woman who sits in darkness has a spiritual insight clearer than that of many wide-eyed people who stare uncomprehendingly at this prejudiced world."[13]

The point is not to feel superior to James at this (or any other) moment. Du Bois certainly doesn't. Rather, it is that the sameness that James saw was different. He and his colleagues were less open to the complexities of racial—and gender, and class—differences than later observers would be. Their obsession with constructing and living up to their own specially gendered kind of humanity limited their vision. Given the ideal against which these men measured human beings, they would either resolve racial and gender and other differences on some barely accessible abstract plane or else (as we now go on to see) they would envisage and define those differences in such a way as to reinforce the standards by which they held themselves accountable.

"As the Men Saw Her"

Between the end of the Civil War and the beginning of the First World War, nothing challenged men's conception of themselves and their place in the world more than the woman's movement—"the emancipation of women, giving them the suffrage, releasing them from bondage, co-educating them with men, etc.," as Henry James defined it in 1883. "The situation of women, the decline of the sentiment of sex, the agitation on their behalf" was, he noted, "the most salient and peculiar point in our social life."[1]

In *The Bostonians,* the long and unruly novel that he went on to write, the haughtiness towards the movement that one detects in "releasing them from bondage" prevailed through the first of the three volumes and then subsided into deep skepticism. Though he was determined to write "an American story," and to take this most important one seriously, and though his attitudes towards his combatants Olive Chancellor and Basil Ransom are complicated, he was, like William, his father's son: finally he regretted "the decline of the sentiment of sex" that occurred during the second Civil War, the one waged between men and women. James' manner precludes our simply appreciating or deploring his satirical portraits of the desexualized or masculinized women of the movement, whatever our political sympathies. By the end, James would have us be moved by Olive's superior self-knowledge and by the martyrdom that he has her masochistically embrace. But so far as he can tell, no woman can be both a woman and interested in women's emancipation. There is no such being as an effective, admirable feminist in his novel. On the other hand, though William and his friends delighted in Ransom's victory, from Henry's point of view no man who wholeheartedly resists the movement can be very sympathetic either. Some of Ransom's lines, especially those he utters in Memorial Hall, prompt one momentarily to think that indeed "the masculine tone is passing out of the world," and to regret the fact, but the way he lures Verena away from Olive and the woman's movement proves not only that masculinity is far from extinct but that it has assumed new and brutal form. "If he should become her husband," James writes of Ransom, "he should know a way to strike her dumb"; having won Verena over, having convinced her that "the idea of giving herself to a man [is] more agreeable . . . than that of giving herself to a movement," James says of Ransom that "he found means to deepen this illumination, to drag her former standard in the dust." In *The Bostonians,* neither sex is good for much.[2]

At the Harvard College depicted in the novel, the few who pay any attention at all to the movement do so mockingly. To the undergraduates, Mr. Burrage and Mr. Gracie, Verena is an attractive curiosity, a redheaded "townie" whom they would have liked to have come and speak, "to save [a] Harvard College" whose students are "sunk in ignorance and prejudice," according to Mr. Gracie—which is to say (as Olive tries unsuccessfully to point out to Verena), in order that they might be amused.[3] At Harvard itself, in the 1890s a Massachusetts Man Suffrage Association was founded for the express purpose of opposing woman's suffrage. Villard gave what he called his "maiden" speech on woman's suffrage while still an undergraduate; in 1911, he would be among the eighty or so men who marched in the first joint suffrage parade.[4] But supporters of the idea would not organize a Harvard Men's League for Women's Suffrage until the end of the first decade of the new century. During this period, the agitation on women's behalf in and around Harvard did not emanate from concern about issues so obviously political as the vote.[5]

One glaring exception was the stir caused by Charles Peirce's wife, Melusina (or Zina) Fay Peirce, who argued that women should not wait to be given the vote but should organize committees and proceed to make policy in the fields of education, health, and welfare on their own, and who even more radically not only proposed but set up a system of what she called "co-operative housekeeping," whereby husbands were made to pay for their wives' housework.[6] She did in fact glare, as Alice James reported to her brother William after she first met her. "A nice woman," Alice wrote, "if she would only refrain from throwing up her head and glaring at one like a wild horse on the prairies." But as Alice also suspected, Zina Peirce was "very intelligent and energetic."[7]

Between November 1868 and March 1869, she published a series of five articles in the *Atlantic Monthly* that described how women could regain a control over their own lives that she posited they had enjoyed in colonial times. In buildings where they would have their kitchens and their sewing and supply rooms, they would form cooperative societies; set apart in their own work places, they would wear short skirts and trousers instead of corsets; the fees that they would charge for "domestic" work would make them economically self-sufficient. Peirce placed men and women in wholly separate spheres. "Men are very fond of twitting us women with desiring to leave our own 'sphere' in order to lord it over theirs in a high-handed manner," she wrote, but if anything, the opposite was true:

I believe that nothing would induce the majority among us to enter their dusty, noisy, blood-stained precincts; but we should be exceedingly obliged if they would just step out of ours. Back, sirs, back! For shame! this unmanly intrusion into the women's apartments.

Though this does not at first blush seem a prescription for an ideal marriage (and the Peirces' ended in divorce in 1883), that is precisely what it was. A woman so fulfilled, so little reduced to merely pleasing men, would be in a position to insist on men's virtue:

knowing her own worth, she will come to demand worth in him. The dignity and sacredness of wise and gracious womanhood will at length assert itself; and as the maiden gradually rises into a true aid and companion for man in his advanced intellectual and material condition, so the youth will have to make, and will rejoice in making, greater moral sacrifices to win her,—will scorn all baser passion, and fling himself a stainless knight at his shining lady's feet.

In a conclusion to which Henry James Sr. also might have come, she wrote, "Then no more will girlish hope and freshness fade, or manly ardor and purity perish while waiting until they can 'afford'—O lamentable word!—to marry; but early marriage, the crown of human bliss, the safeguard of society."[8]

What with five articles in the *Atlantic*, Zina Peirce had to be taken seriously. In Cambridge, in May 1869, she chaired the first meeting of the Co-operative Housekeeping Society at her in-laws' home on Quincy Street, a few doors down from the Jameses. Whether or not Henry Sr. attended, we do not know, but many Harvard faculty members and administrators came with their wives, as did William Dean Howells and his wife. By the end of the year, the society had rented its own house; six months later, the laundry was in operation and breaking even.

But clearly, this would never do. In the spring of 1871, the society disbanded, ostensibly because Peirce had agreed to go with her husband to witness a solar eclipse in Sicily the previous fall—because, in other words, her leadership was essential—but obviously too because few people in Cambridge or anywhere else could imagine that there might be a connection between autonomous women and a blissful marriage or a safely guarded society. There was interest in the idea, but very little sympathy with it. It is presumably no coincidence that in 1870 Howells, Charles Peirce, and several other men who had attended the first meeting of the society established an all-male supper club that met once a month at each others' homes.

Nathaniel Shaler, for example, wished Zina Peirce well, but though his attitude towards women was, as his wife once wrote, "exceedingly chivalrous," he would never have considered throwing himself down at the feet of the kind of woman Peirce had written about. Mrs. Shaler goes on:

so far as he was concerned, women only existed in a generalized way and not as objects of definite personal interest. There was a time in his life when he was apt to take the absence of beauty in a woman as a personal affront, and if one of his "boys" married a plain girl he was indignant. Farther along, however, this, in a measure, ceased to be the case, he was content to find in their faces a good, motherly, feminine expression.[9]

William James would not meet Alice Howe Gibbens until after the demise of the Cambridge Co-operative Housekeeping Society, but it is doubtful that he would have supported the wife of his friend Charles in this venture. We have seen how dependent he was on Alice's angelic presence in his house. He was not likely to support the idea of women setting themselves up in the business of housework. One of his few criticisms of Stanford was that the faculty were not paid enough to allow them to get away or to have servants who would relieve their wives of "domestic drudgery."[10] Alice herself had no patience with the fact that Josiah Royce was "being worked at home" as a result of his wife's refusal to hire help.[11]

"HUSBAND-POWER," Zina later angrily wrote, "is very apt to shut down like an invisible bell-glass over every woman as soon as she is married."[12] For all of these husbands a woman's place was in the home, or if not in the home, somewhere, doing something that would relieve or ultimately elevate the quality of home life. The Cambridge Co-operative Housekeeping Society, no, but there were activities that Zina Peirce and many other Cambridge and Harvard women engaged in on women's behalf that were tolerable—even encouraged. There was, for example, the Female Humane Society, whose members also helped women earn money—but indigent women, women who made clothes out of fabric other members donated. Among its members were Zina, Elizabeth Agassiz, Alice James and her mother, and women of the Dana, Lowell, and Norton families. And there was the Society to Encourage Studies at Home, a correspondence school, founded in 1873, that offered courses in history, art, English, French, and German literature, and—thanks to Elizabeth Agassiz—natural science. Alice James worked with this woman's organization too, in the history division, under the woman who would be her lifelong companion, Katharine Peabody Loring. William had no trouble seeing the value of such work. Having tried to find her a job at the Museum of Comparative Anatomy, he was happy for her, reporting to Henry, with what would seem to be only the slightest hint of irony, that "Alice has got her historical professorship which will no doubt be an immense thing for her."[13]

As might be expected, in Cambridge and at Harvard the woman's movement was primarily a movement in education. Insofar as it caused any agitation, it did so not because of any "society" activity but because of the presence of women at the "Radcliffe Annex," more specifically, because their presence there raised the unnerving possibility, in Henry James' phrase, of "coeducating them with men." The history of Radcliffe is interesting in itself, but as Virginia Woolf once remarked, "The history of men's opposition to women's emancipation is more interesting perhaps than the story of that emancipation itself."[14] The resistance of the men of Harvard to the idea of coeducation—even to the very idea of higher education for women—is a case in point. It provides us with a new and especially clear version of the story of Harvard's commitment to educating men for manhood.

The terms of Harvard's resistance were originally and powerfully set in 1873 by Edward H. Clarke, a professor at the Medical School and later a member of the Harvard Board of Overseers, in a small book titled *Sex in Education; or, A Fair Chance for Girls*. It was reprinted seventeen times in thirteen years, threatening at least a generation of educators. M. Carey Thomas said apropos of the founding of Bryn Mawr in 1888, "We did not know when we began whether women's health could stand the strain of education. We were haunted in those days by the clanging chains of that gloomy little specter,

Dr. Edward H. Clarke's *Sex in Education*."[15] In Clarke's scheme of things, women's health, women's bodies, were basically what was at issue, but by the time he had finished making his argument against coeducation, he had constricted a culture's thinking about men's and women's roles for years to come.

The question of "sex in education," Clarke maintained, was not an ethical or a metaphysical but simply a physiological one. Men and women were different and should be educated differently. In the case of young women, "nature has reserved the catamenial week for the process of ovulation, and for the development and perfection of the reproductive system"; therefore their "whole education and life [should] be guided by the divine requirements of her system." If they were not, if she were to devote those years to uninterrupted studying—in other words, "to study just as boys do"—she would turn into one of the many nerve-wracked grotesques described in the third of his book that Clarke called "Chiefly Clinical." She would became neurasthenic and qualify for the entombment, the "rest cure," devised by "one of our most eminent American physiologists" (as Clarke described S. Weir Mitchell)— incarceration in a dark room, complete and interminable inactivity punctuated by massage and low-level electric shock, and adherence to a strict diet that featured milk.[16] A few years later, in 1881, George Beard cited "the mental activity of women" as one of the five characteristics of American civilization that made it especially susceptible to "nervousness and nervous diseases."[17] By the lights of all three authorities, the source of life resided in women's bodies, and therefore the proper life for women was domestic life. Women might benefit from education too, but education that abided by the dictates of their bodies; constant thinking on a woman's part would lead to nervous collapse; should that occur, measures would have to be taken to bring her body back to its natural, biorhythmic state; and that, in turn, would enable her to fulfill her appointed role as the source of life.

"Periodicity characterizes the female organization, and develops feminine force," Clarke wrote. "Persistence characterizes the male organization, and develops masculine force." It followed that different educational systems for boys and girls, for men and women, were essential. If they were adhered to, much more would happily follow. Again, it all made simple, common sense: "Educate a man for manhood, a woman for womanhood, both for humanity," Clarke said. "In this lies the hope of the race."

But considering women in all walks of life, Clarke found "numberless pale, weak, neuralgic, dyspeptic, hysterical, menorraghic, dysmenorrheic girls and women"—the very names, it would seem, designed to frighten a reader— that he considered proof of his thesis. Not that "disregard of the reproductive apparatus" was the sole cause, and not that all female graduates were "pathological specimens," but there were enough who were "permanently disabled" to cause alarm—which was to say, already, in 1873, the race showed unmistakable signs of being suicidal. If the race did not abandon the idea of coeducation, "the wives who are to be mothers in our republic must be drawn from trans-atlantic homes," Clarke predicted, and "the race will be propagated from its inferior classes. The stream of life that is to flow into the future will be Celtic rather than American: it will come from the collieries, and not from the peerage."

Clarke's argument was based on physiology, but once set in motion, the language of the body drifted into the realms of ethnicity and class, and the perfect sense that was then made was easily substantiated by further rhetorical moves into the marketplace. Educational policy that ignored women's bodies not only led to race suicide, but it was also bad economic policy: "Income derived from air, food, and sleep, which should largely, may only moderately exceed expenditure upon study and work, and so leave but little surplus for growth in any direction." Women's studying without a break was analogous to men's masturbating in that both were spending their vital energies. Both activities frayed the nerves—or worse. Both stunted growth—individual physical growth, but also economic growth—and if American bodies grew weak and the American economy failed to keep up, the lords and ladies of America would be replaced by Irish and European miners with teeming families.[18]

The composite is a familiar one. The particular physical, racial, social, and economic ideal that rises out of what is Clarke's supposedly basic physiological concern is of a piece with the ideal towards which Harvard's educational policies moved. Both Clarke and Harvard posited as ideal an American civilization in which robust and well-situated Anglo-Saxons were in positions of power and influence. If that ideal was to prevail, as women ventured into the academy—and they did so slowly, constituting less than a fifth of those who graduated from college at the end of the century[19]—they would have to retire periodically while men pressed on, pressed on in their studies and in their social and athletic activities. When women were educated otherwise, "Amazonian coarseness and force" resulted, Clarke said, and as if that were not enough, he went on, "Such persons are analogous to the sexless class of termites," and then "a closer analogy than this . . . exists between these human individuals and the eunuchs of Oriental civilization."[20] We may recall James' image in the *Psychology* of "modern Orientals" and their "forms of unnatural vice, of which the notion affects us with horror."[21] Following the decline of the sentiment of sex right down to the bottom, it seems one ended up in China.

We should not be surprised to find such seemingly different men as Clarke and James thinking about manhood and womanhood in similar terms. Edward Clarke was professor of materia medica at the Harvard Medical School when

James was one of a relatively small number (170) of students there;[22] his *Sex in Education* was published the year James began teaching physiology at the College. James' greatness lay in his power if not to transcend then to imagine worlds richer and more various than the one he lived in. To put it negatively, his vision was never narrowed by language so simple and cutting as Clarke's. But he was schooled in the language of his day and however much he distanced himself from that language, we can still detect its influence in his own struggles to achieve maturity. He would never directly oppose coeducation. In fact, he was a relatively casual observer of the process by which it came into being. But the terms and the arguments of opponents of coeducation found their way into his personal fight against weakness and possible failure.

His student and near contemporary G. Stanley Hall was explicitly reliant on the work of Edward Clarke. Thirty years after the publication of *Sex in Education,* Hall quoted Clarke approvingly in his own monumental and influential study, *Adolescence: Its Psychology and Its Relation to Physiology, Anthropology, Sociology, Sex, Crime, Religion and Education.* In his eighty-six-page chapter titled "Adolescent Girls and Their Education," Hall said that "even though he may have 'played his sex symphony too harshly,' E. H. Clarke was right. Periodicity, perhaps the deepest law of the cosmos, celebrates its highest triumphs in woman's life," and he too argued that women's education ought to be organized accordingly. Beard and Mitchell are also among the authorities he cited, all of them agreeing, as Hall crisply put it, that it was a pity "to spoil a good mother to make a grammarian." Hall subscribed to the physiological argument (women are "weaker in body and mind," they are "by nature more prone than man to domesticity and parenthood," and so "their education should not aim to cultivate the thinking powers alone or chiefly"), and to racial and sexual ones as well (birthrates are dropping among the educated, "old families are being plowed under and leaders [being] recruited from the class below," soon we will have "a female sex without a female character").[23] When he paused to contemplate womanhood, however, he spoke in his own unusual voice, and exemplified how taxing it was for the men of James' generation to have to worry about where they stood as men.

Contradictions abound in their discussions of the other sex. Women are virgins and whores, pale and dark, sickly and Amazonian, just different but implicitly inferior—or is it superior? Hall's attitudes are not only contradictory, but—if one allows—touching. His conception of the education and destiny of women is, to begin with, highly conventional: "In an ideal society," he writes, "with ideal men in it, women's education should focus on motherhood and wifehood, and then seek in every way to magnify these functions and to invest them with honor." Women are fated by their "physical constitution"—their weakness, which is also their ability to sustain the race—and by characterological traits that are somehow connected: they want what they do not have; they are "spoiled by idleness and vacuity of mind"; they are "lazy, phlegmatic, and unambitious, or else restless." The recapitulationists of Hall's day had it that women were like "savages" and children, "phyletically [or in their lineage] older and more primitive" than man, "a more generic creature than man, nearer to the race."[24] But what in other writers is just misogyny or racism under a thin coating of bad science is in Hall's a kind of longing.[25]

Women were to him not just attractive embodiments of the Life Principle; they were better human beings—"more humanistic than man, more sympathetic and appreciative."[26] In *Adolescence,* Hall approvingly cited Havelock Ellis' observation that women were becoming more womanly because they were drowning themselves more frequently,[27] and a few years later he wrote a strange piece called "The Budding Girl," which he began by comparing a girl favorably to fresh fish ("her real nature is wild with a charming, gamy flavor"), but in it she is credited with more depth and insight than man, and with a double consciousness, one that was at once more social and esoteric than man's: "Woman, who was once thought soulless, now comes nearer to having two souls than does man."[28] Hall imagined woman there at our beginnings, but rather than have her merely represent earlier stages of man's evolution, he sees her as having taken on more inspiring form than man.

Accordingly, when he comes to consider her education, he thinks she is in fact more suited to it, she excels in it, and she enjoys it more. Whereas men are relatively insensitive to "the physical and psychic environment," and seek higher education only "because their careers depend upon it," she deserves "an education that is essentially liberal and humanistic." But as for coeducation, although Hall acknowledged that adolescent males benefited from the presence of women—adolescence was their "humanistic stage," the stage at which they developed a range of secondary sex qualities—he was firmly opposed. Women were, like adolescence itself, a stage that young males had to go through on their way to manhood.[29] Young men had their specialties without which their individualities would be incomplete, they had careers to consider, and, as he said in an article with the resounding title "Feminization in School and Home: The Undue Influence of Women Teachers—the Need of Different Training for the Sexes," "too much association with girls diverts the youth from developing his full manhood." Young men had to get on with the business of becoming men.[30]

What Hall unwittingly demonstrates is the sadness of the situation of young males coming of age around the turn of the century. Under the pressure of the culture—what with the home that had to be supported, the struggles that had to be won in the marketplace, the diversity of peoples with whom they had to compete, and the worlds that could be conquered—they had to learn to concentrate their energies. They had to learn to be men. They had to grow down to be men. "And yet this very singleness of vision and thorough oneness with his age is a mark of the successful man," W. E. B. Du Bois wrote in 1903. "Nature must needs make men narrow in order to give them force."[31] Gertrude Stein made the point more poignantly: there was little use being born a boy, she said, if you were going to grow up to be a man.[32] But the men had to and they persevered. Individually and institutionally, resisting womanliness and humanistic education or coeducation, they continued on their way to what passed for maturity.

From time to time, Hall did allow himself a few extraordinary, fanciful flights in the form of short stories. When he gathered them together, he called them *Recreations of a Psychologist*. The most fun, it seems, is imagining a reversal of sex roles, a prospect so enticing that in *Adolescence* he claimed that "in these days of intense new interest in feelings, emotions, and sentiments . . . many a psychologist now envies and, like Schleiermacher, devoutly wishes he could become a woman."[33] In one "recreation," "Adventure in Domestic Industries," Hall has an academic friend who is interested in industrial education for girls indulge in a bit of housekeeping in order to see what cause women might have for their growing complaints. He loves housework: "He is able to find, experienced as he is in athletics and in varied industries and handicrafts, nothing quite so wholesome for body and soul as doing precisely what woman is now turning her back upon," and he hopes that by the example of men like himself, and given the proper schooling, "woman" will no longer consider "abandoning her glorious kingdom." The story is, Hall said in the preface to his collection, "an illustration of one the various forms of midsummer madness which the author has experienced and observed." But it is not the sort of thing a man can own up to, and so at the end of his story he has a woman refer to his friend—by what can't be pure chance—as "a queer Dick."[34]

His strategy in many of his other stories is to tamp down his desires completely. In the most substantial of them, "A Leap-Year Romance: A True Tale of Western Life," his hero quotes Schleiermacher on "dependence, not independence [as] the true measure of human progress," but in it, and in several others in which otherwise brittle men manage to come to life through marriage, it is, as would be expected, the woman who exemplifies that ideal. Having won a Miss Newell away from her newfangled ideas about women's education, this professor says to her, "You completely fill woman's sphere for me"—which is to say, *you* are dependent, you represent that ideal for me.[35] There was to be no blurring of the lines. A man had to erase all traces of dependency and domesticity in himself if he was to be a man. Accordingly, in his autobiography, the *Life and Confessions of a Psychologist*, Hall said nothing about his two wives—nor anything about William James, to whom he was also deeply indebted.[36]

Equally ardent—and equally suspect—in their praise of women were two more famous Harvard men: Henry Adams and Frank Norris. Adams' adoration of women and, simultaneously, his use of them as a means of dismissing contemporary civilization echo throughout his life and works much more loudly than they do through Hall's. In 1876, in a lecture called "Primitive Rights of Women," delivered at the Lowell Institute, he went far back before colonial times in order to find cultures capable of doing justice to women's life-giving force. He cast his imaginings back to a golden age when marriage was unknown and the family was made up of women in their relationships to each other: "Mothers there were, but fathers were unknown." He began with a utopia in which women were not enslaved, not property, a time when the products of the earth were shared and men were "not devoured by the thirst for gold." And then, faithful to his proposition that "the social position of women [was] highest in the ages most distant," he traced a line of women who thrived, then struggled, then merely endured in marriage and the family, that went from Isis, the coequal of Osiris, to Penelope, who outwitted her suitors, to Hallgerda, the heroine of the Njalsaga, who murdered three husbands, to patient Griselda.[37]

In his lecture, Adams had said that though the church had "dethroned the woman from her place" in adopting the Trinity, "the irresistible spread of Maryolatry, the worship of the Virgin Mother, proved how strongly human nature revolted against the change."[38] (Hall ended his chapter on girls' education with the "tender declaration" that he was "more and more passionately in love with woman as I conceive she came from the hand of God," and he confessed to "keenly" envying his "Catholic friends their Maryolatry.")[39] In the writings for which Adams is best known, *Mont-Saint-Michel and Chartres* and *The Education,* Female Force survives as the Virgin of the thirteenth century, who puts men's petty mercantile and political schemings and theological reasonings to shame, and as iconic Woman, who is "reproduction—the greatest and most mysterious of all energies." But he imagined her being dragged down by the man out there washing the car, the Modern Man who "had turned his mind and hand to mechanics . . . his hand on a lever and his eye on a curve in his road."[40] For Adams, she was also the Oriental Kwannon deity, who inspired the great statue by St. Gaudens that marks his wife's grave, and the queens of Tahiti; she was Madeline Lee and Esther Dudley, the heroines of his two novels, *Democracy* and *Esther;* and she was all those women to whom he gestured in his letters and in *The Education* who, unlike men, had never let him down—"strong women and unyielding," as they have been described, "dominating the men who surround them and posing a contemptuous challenge to masculine institutions."[41]

The extent to which she is Marion (or Clover) Hooper, the woman whom Adams married in 1872, and who took her own life thirteen years later, and the extent to which he resented the challenge she presented are not finally to be gauged. Adams' incessant self-creatings, his self-reflections and refractions as a writer and a person, or what William James kindly called (in reference to *Mont-Saint-Michel and Chartres*) his "frolic quality of power,"[42] make that impossible. But Adams was well aware of what was likely to happen to women who were so adored. As he said of his Esther and her eager suitor, when she felt herself "really loved, she met her fate as women will when the shock is once over":

By the time he left her house this Saturday evening, he felt that he had found a soul stronger and warmer than his own, and was already a little afraid of it. Every man who has at last succeeded, after long effort, in calling up the divinity which lies hidden in a woman's heart, is startled to find that he must obey the God he summoned.[43]

Adams himself was not one to obey. From all that is known about the Adamses as a couple, one can at least understand how Henry James—who thought of Clover as "the incarnation of my native land," a model of "intellectual grace," and "a perfect Voltaire in petticoats"—might have found her "toned down and bedimmed from her ancient brilliancy" in her married state. James found Clover's "wit clipped a little." Others have imagined worse.

Given Adams' adulation of women, he could not and did not endorse the idea of their being confined, as mothers or as ornaments, to the home, nor was he happy with the way they were allowed to exhaust themselves going the social rounds, but his support for their being educated was hedged. When he reviewed Clarke's *Sex in Education* for the *North American Review,* he denounced idleness. Better the company of books, he said—as long as they were the right books—not "French novels, for instance"—and as long as there weren't too many of them. His reading of Clarke was judicious—what Clarke said of "excessive brain-work" was true for men as well as for women, he pointed out—but he inclined towards Clarke's views on women's education. Clarke's descriptions were "perhaps overdrawn," but Adams said of his book as a whole that "the tone is excellent," and it "can not fail to do good." He had to concede that "to resist the demand that women are making for education is a hopeless task." The "good" of the work of Clarke and of all those who opposed coeducation lay in controlling that demand, in their "defining, modifying, and improving the claims that continually present themselves with renewed force."[44] On other occasions, whether it was hopeless or not, Adams resisted with a vengeance: it was "worse than useless for women to study philosophy"; women were "utterly unconscious of the pathetic impossibility of improving those poor, little hard, thin, wiry, one-stringed instruments which they call their minds," and so on. When someone speculated that Clover might have written *Democracy,* he countered by saying that she had never written for publication, in fact could not write if she had tried.[45]

The dynamics in the writings of Frank Norris are clearer. Like Josiah Royce twenty years before, at Berkeley, Norris was drawn to the way the geologist Joseph LeConte put Darwinian science to spiritual use. Like Royce, he was inspired by the idea of the evolutionary process leading man out of his animal condition, by stages, into purer states of being. But unlike Royce, he assigned women pivotal parts in the drama of men's lives.

Wanting to be a writer, he came to Harvard as a special student for the academic year 1894–95. He took composition (English 22) under Lewis Gates—took it the same year Gertrude Stein did (though being a woman she had to take it at another time and in another place)—and received one of the five A's distributed among the 248 students in the course. For it he wrote more than twenty-five themes that would end up in his first novel, *Vandover and the Brute,* eleven that he included in the more famous *McTeague,* and seven that were relevant to *Blix,* a novel that he published (along with *McTeague*) in 1899. Among his other themes was this (in its entirety), which he titled "Good and Bad Woman":

> A woman is always the same with the men she meets. If she is a good woman she will still be good in the company of bad men. If she is bad she will be bad with good men. But with a man it is quite the other way, a good woman will bring out in him all that is best, a bad woman all that is worst.[46]

His were simple propositions, "awkwardly put," his reader said: women are either good or bad; more complexly human though they may be, men are saved or not according to the women they encounter; it is never the other way around. In his novels, Norris would vary and complicate this theme, and in fact never settle the issue of just how fated were men's lives, but women— masculine women especially—would in varying measures always determine whether or not men rose or fell.

Vandover and the Brute is essentially a product of Norris' one year at Harvard. While its hero is in residence, he is exposed to "chippies" and, much to his chagrin, is once so "moved by an unreasoned instinct" as to stay out all night with one. But otherwise he develops "a profound respect and an instinctive regard for women [that stands] him in good stead throughout all his four years of Harvard life." Norris says that, "in general, he kept himself pretty straight." He enjoys what President Eliot would later call, in the title of a speech, "The Solid Satisfactions of Life." "It is a very safe protective rule to live to-day as if you were going to marry a pure woman within a month," he told the incoming freshmen in 1905. "That rule you will find a safeguard for worthy living."[47] Upon Vandover's graduation, "for a second time the animal in him, the perverse evil brute, awoke and stirred." He is drawn into the accelerated life of the city, but again, though "the brute had grown larger in him . . . he knew that he had the creature in hand." He meets bad women like Flossie, who will mortally infect one of his friends; later he falls in love with the good Turner Ravis, who brings out the best in him, as does the painting he has taken up, as does music.

Similar figures sit on the shoulders of the hero of another novel, written two years later by Reginald Wright Kauffman, who also drew heavily on the themes that he wrote for English 22. In his *Jarvis of Harvard,* Kauffman was interested, he later said, in "the terrible woman that seduced innocent youths." Faced with her, he was willing to have his hero call on "the eternal masculine!" "Jarvis' tumultuous despair had to find some vent, and the man in him demanded that the woman should suffer."[48] She does, and Jarvis goes on to be saved by a woman of purity.

Though working with the same stereotypical women, Norris does not so simply project his hero's viciousness onto the seductive kind, but rather focuses more on the forces that contend *within* his Harvard man. "The eternal struggle between good and evil" rages in Vandover, and eventually "inexorably exacting" Nature drags him down into a life of brutish indulgence. One night, returning home from the opera, he looks "inward and downward into the depths of his own character" and sees one of those darker anti-selves that emerged in fictions at the end of the nineteenth century, one that may remind us, more specifically, of the ones that visited William James and his father in their worst moments of self-loathing and despair:

Far down there in the darkest, lowest places he had seen the brute, squat, deformed, hideous; he had seen it crawling to and fro dimly, through a dark shadow he had heard it growling, chafing at the least restraint, restless to be free. For now at last it was huge, strong, insatiable, swollen and distorted out of all size, grown to be a monster, glutted yet still ravenous, some fearful bestial satyr, grovelling, perverse, horrible beyond words.

Vandover descends into a wolf-like state (diagnosed as a disease of the nerves called *Lycanthropy-Mathesis*) and ends up—literally—on all fours, cleaning the grime and filth behind bathroom sinks in order to survive financially. "My God! to think I was a Harvard man once," Norris has him exclaim. It is all seemingly absurd, but there is also something powerfully eerie about this record of the young Norris' vision of the possible fate of someone who was like himself—a Harvard man.[49]

Before Norris' most powerful hero, the dentist McTeague, can advance beyond the sluggish, animal-like existence in which we first meet him, he is introduced to Trina, and, "obstinately cherishing that intuitive suspicion of all things feminine," he is troubled. Initially he sees her as being "without sex . . . almost like a boy," and "the keenness of his dislike of her as a woman began to be blunted," but seeing, smelling, touching her as she lies unconscious in his "operating chair" (her appointments falling, like Gates' classes, on Tuesdays, Thursdays, and Saturdays), what Norris calls "the old battle, old as the world, wide as the world," begins:

the sudden panther leap of the animal, lips drawn, fangs aflash, hideous, monstrous, not to be resisted, and the simultaneous arousing of the other man, the better self that cries "Down, down," without knowing why; that grips the monster; that fights to strangle it, to thrust it down and back.

He kisses her, "grossly, full on the mouth," and for a moment, like Vandover in his young manhood, McTeague has himself "once more in hand," but he had "awakened the Woman [and] their undoing had already begun." Three hundred and fifty pages later, it ends in a futile search for gold in Death Valley, the trek powerfully affecting if for no other reason than that the young writer is so committed to trying to understand what is to him the life-and-death issue of men's sexuality, the power of women, and the relation of both to America's frenzied quest for riches.[50]

In the far slighter and more nearly autobiographical *Blix,* a good woman succeeds in breaking the hero's (Condy's) fall. He is led away from the social whirl, and from the gambling that might otherwise ruin him, by Blix, a woman whom he describes as "a *man's* woman" (a phrase that Norris used as a title for yet another novel). He is taken, symbolically, for a walk on the shores of the Pacific, where

the simple things of the world, the great, broad, primal emotions of the race stirred in them. As they swung along, going toward the ocean, their brains were almost as empty of thought or of reflection as those of two fine, clean animals. They were all for the immediate sensation; they did not think—they *felt.*

As a result of Blix's influence, Condy is inspired to pursue his writing career and to take on the responsibilities of marriage. It is as if, in James' terms, he had been cured of "a certain blindness"; in Hall's, as if he had entered that amorphous, generic stage known as Woman and emerged a man—"all the fine, virile, masculine energy of him . . . aroused and rampant."[51]

In what is perhaps his best novel, *The Pit,* Norris has the appropriately named Laura Dearborn choose between "two existences . . . that of the business man [and] that of the artist," the one all martial and phallic, hardened by "the Battle of the Street," the other "who kept himself far from the fighting," living life "gently, in the calm, still atmosphere of art," a friend to women, but clearly inferior:

the figure that held her imagination and her sympathy was not the artist, soft of hand and of speech, elaborating graces of sound and colour and form, refined, sensitive, and temperamental; but the fighter, unknown and unknowable to women as he was; hard, rigorous, panoplied in the harness of the warrior, who strove among the trumpets, and who, in the brunt of conflict, conspicuous, formidable, set the battle in a rage around him, and exulted like a champion in the shoutings of the captains.

The latter, in the person of Curtis Jadwin, is explicitly and by no means "a *woman's* man," but for that very reason, "unknown and unknowable" captain of industry that he is, he is "the kind of man that makes the best husband."[52]

If it be asked how it was that Norris reconciled himself to his own life as an artist, the answer is that he presented himself not as an artistic type but as a man who was confronting reality directly in his writing. He did think that given the leisurely quality of women's lives, and given their temperaments (they are "impressionable, emotional and communicative"), they should excel as novelists—that writing *was* essentially a womanly activity—but he dismissed women novelists' efforts on the basis of their lack of "actual experience." He had learned from Gates (and dedicated *McTeague* to him in gratitude) that "life is more important than literature," that "experience is the best teacher," and armed with these banalities, he justified his being a writer: *his* writing was not art but life.

If it be asked what Norris' writing has to do with the question of the woman's movement and higher education, the answer is almost nothing. In his typology too, the ideal Woman required only so much education. In his essay "Why Women Should Write the Best Novels," he draws the familiar contrast: young women receive compulsory literary training in schools; young men "almost from the very first [study] with an eye to business or to a profession."[53] His wife-to-be immediately impressed him "as being a very normal girl. You did not expect to find her introspective."[54] He has Curtis Jadwin take the argument for women's being just healthy helpmates to its limits. "I believe in women as I believe in Christ," he tells Miss Dearborn:

But I don't believe they were made—any more than Christ was—to cultivate—beyond a certain point—their own souls, and refine their own minds, and live in a sort of warmed-over, dilettante, stained-glass world of seclusion and *ex*clusion. No, sir, that won't do for the United Sates and the men who are making them the greatest nation of the world. The men have got all the get-up-and-get they want, but they need the women to point them straight, and to show them how to lead that other kind of life that isn't all grind.[55]

Adams conceded that education was "absolutely indispensable, if women are at all anxious to adapt themselves for what is demanded of them by men who seek to make companions of their wives, and . . . to be able to understand what is going on about them."[56] Those who served—wives, Christ—needed some education. But they belonged out in the world, which also meant out of classrooms at "a certain point."

If even Christ was going to be a suspect candidate for college admission, it would seem that those who wanted to make a case for the higher education of women would have to do so with the utmost care. By 1903, however, when *The Pit* was published, resistance against it had weakened considerably. Radcliffe College had been in existence for a decade, and more and more Miss Dearborns were thinking of applying. But establishing Radcliffe had been far from easy, and even as it stood in 1903, it was a separate and clearly unequal institution.

In his inaugural address, President Eliot acknowledged that Harvard's attitude towards "the prevailing discussions touching the education and fit employments of women" required "brief explanation," and he devoted a paragraph to it. He said that Harvard would move cautiously, but under no circumstances would the Corporation "receive women as students into the College proper, nor into any school whose discipline requires residence near the school."[57] As he and Harvard wrestled with these questions over the next thirty-five or forty years, their tolerance of women's intellectual and professional existence increased, but they assumed all along that women were in some not quite definable way absolutely different and that the business of educating young men into manhood could not take place in their presence. Or as the *Graduates' Magazine* assured its readership upon the occasion of Radcliffe's incorporation in 1894, "The fact that the great majority of teachers in the country were women . . . made it the business of any institution of learning to consider their education, even if the male sex [was] the only object of ultimate interest."[58]

In 1869, Eliot was less sure than Clarke about "the innate capacities of women," but quite sure that it was not the University's business to have an opinion on the matter, or "upon the fitness or unfitness of women for professional pursuits." What the University would do was conduct a "safe, promising, and instructive experiment" in the form of allowing women to attend the recently established "University Courses of Instruction." Like modern-day extension courses, the University Courses of Instruction were explicitly of "no direct professional value," but, Eliot said, those that Harvard offered would "enrich and enlarge both intellect and character." Given that teaching was the one profession in which women had begun to prove themselves, they would indirectly benefit women. After the University Course experiment failed, Eliot paid more attention to women's education in fields other than education. He tolerated their presence at Divinity School lectures, and he tried (unsuccessfully) to get the Corporation to accept a gift of $10,000 offered to the Medical School on the condition that women be admitted on an equal footing. Beginning in 1874, Harvard was willing to administer examinations and award certificates for work done elsewhere, and at the turn of the century Eliot argued that Radcliffe itself should grant the Ph.D.

But while he welcomed women's participation in the fight against "the intellectual inertia of the human race" generally, he either left open the question of how they might best be educated, or he tipped his hand in conventional ways. In addressing the issue of women's education, his tone was uncharacteristically hesitant, even confusing.[59] At the dedication of the gymnasium that Mrs. Hemenway had given to Radcliffe—twenty years after her husband's gift to Harvard—he said, "I do not believe that we have yet discovered what is the wholesome and altogether desirable training for civilized women. We have it all to learn; and what prospect could be more delightful than that?"[60] He sounded receptive to new ideas about women's education, but he had already made up his mind about their character and the purposes of their lives. At the Radcliffe commencement the year before, he had risen to comparable heights, this time asking, "Can any greater gift be made to human society than to make it possible, generation after generation, for men and women to live together in this quick intellectual and spiritual sympathy?" But then he had quickly added: this gift could be bestowed "without fearing that, in developing this higher side of the life of woman, the beauty and charm of the feminine character may be impaired."[61] In his remarks on the same occasion four years later, he was more matter-of-fact. Men and women had different "mental destinations," he said. Nine-tenths of women became "builders of homes and rearers of families," so the most serious concerns of educated women ought to be "the care and training of children."[62] In other words, Eliot would be party to America's unprecedented and unrivaled willingness to educate women, but like most men, he would continue to set limits.

As colleges and universities, public and private, came into existence west of the Hudson, they almost invariably opened their doors to men and women alike. Only in the East, and in privileged male institutions especially, did administrations and faculties phobically insist that the sexes ought to be kept at a distance from each other. There were, therefore, coeducational institutions springing up in the West, and institutions holding on to their single-sexed identity in the East. Between the two there hung a third kind, of which the "Radcliffe Annex" (or, later, Radcliffe College) was the prime example: a woman's college that was and was not a part of a larger, male institution nearby. "The annex swings in the middle air," the president of Wellesley said in "A Review of the Higher Education of Women," in 1891. For years, its founders and leaders twisted and turned in response to Harvard's need to protect and elevate its own.[63]

The plan for the separate collegiate institution that would become Radcliffe College originated in 1879, but the history of women's education in Cambridge goes back at least to 1855, when the Agassiz family set up a school for young women on the third floor of their house on Quincy Street.[64] Louis

Agassiz himself lectured on physical geography, natural history, and botany (while his wife took notes); their son Alexander taught mathematics, as did (upon occasion) Peirce's distinguished father, Benjamin. There were language classes that were also conducted by Harvard professors, including those in Greek, given by Ephraim Whitman Gurney, who would go on to be dean of the University. James Russell Lowell and Francis Child taught English. Music and dancing and theatrical performances were of course encouraged, and (at least as Elizabeth Agassiz later recalled) Charles William Eliot lectured to the young women about manners. The students would elect courses, Louis Agassiz said, "as far as may be consistent with the order of a school, to individual character," a position not all that different from the one on which rests much of his etiquette teacher's claim to fame. Among the students were Emerson's daughter Ellen, Zina Peirce, Ellen Hooper, who would marry Whitman Gurney and become instrumental in the founding of Radcliffe, and her sister Clover, who would send money in support of Ellen's efforts.

It was a small and powerful group, just how small and powerful—and just how powerful were the tensions within it—being brought out by the facts that Ellen and Clover's brother Edward was treasurer of Harvard during the years that Radcliffe was coming into being, and that as treasurer, he was more loyal to his alma mater than to his sisters' cause. "I have no prejudice in the matter of education of women and am quite willing to see Yale or Columbia take any risks they like," he wrote Elizabeth Agassiz in 1893, "but I feel bound to protect Harvard College from what seems to me to be a risky experiment."[65] On the other hand, Ellen was married to Whitman Gurney, and it was in their parlor that the "Annex" held its first commencement.

During the Civil War the Agassiz School closed, and in 1865 the Agassizes went off to collect specimens in Brazil—on the expedition that forced William James to confront the question of what he wanted to do with his life. Then, in the fall of 1878, a Mr. Arthur Gilman, a former bank clerk with no connection with Harvard, but with a strong desire to provide for his daughter's education, approached Professor Greenough of the Classics Department (who was known to have had great success tutoring a young woman from Brockton) and President Eliot himself, with the idea of Harvard professors being enlisted to educate young women.* In January of the next year, Eliot

---

*That woman—Abby Leach—went on to be the head of the Greek Department at Vassar College. In 1908, at the twenty-fifth Radcliffe commencement, Leach gave the address. The moral she drew is a familiar one: "For it takes much courage in this world of ours to be one's self, to live according to one's own standards, to act according to one's beliefs." She asked the graduates to think of classics rather than social work, for example, which, as she pointed out, was all the rage for women. ("The age affects social service," she said sardonically.) One imagines Leach speaking from experience—as well as from Emerson—when she said that it took courage to be oneself. See *HGM*, XVII (September 1908), 105–8.

approved the formation of a committee composed of seven ladies who were all, Gilman assured him, opposed to coeducation. This association, or planning committee for the "Private Collegiate Instruction of Women," included Mrs. Greenough and Mrs. Gurney. Its chair was Elizabeth Agassiz.

A widow nearing sixty, hard at work on her husband's biography, ever cheerful and supportive, Elizabeth Cabot Cary Agassiz was the perfect choice. Traveling with her and her husband in South America, James had found her roseate view of the world annoying. An "excellent but infatuated woman," forever looking "at every thing in such an unnatural romantic light that she don't seem to walk upon the solid earth," he wrote in the Diary that he kept. But on the occasion of her eightieth birthday, he recalled instead the more substantial image that she had presented to Cambridge all her life—the perfect image of a well-educated lady. "I remember your freshness of interest, and readiness to take hold of everything," he wrote her, "what a blessing to me it was to have one civilized lady in sight, to keep the memory of cultivated conversation from growing extinct."[66]

In 1879, twenty-seven students signed up for "private instruction," three of them for what was considered a full course load. Three years later, the group, now expanded to include an academic board and a corporation, was chartered by the state of Massachusetts as "The Society for the Collegiate Instruction of Women"—more familiarly known as the Annex—with Agassiz as its president. The following year, 1883, the first graduates were awarded certificates. No one spoke of degrees.[67]

Most of the students—a large number of whom had already graduated from Smith or Wellesley, Cornell or the University of Michigan—commuted to lectures that were given in rented rooms on Appian Way by members of the Harvard faculty. Others boarded in town. They were all intent upon learning, in spite of (or perhaps spurred on by) the fact that Harvard refused to let them use the library—books had to be carted over from the Cambridge Public Library—or to attend graduate classes. Needing more resources for advanced study, and knowing they deserved more recognition from Harvard for work that was, after all, the equivalent of work done at Harvard, the corporation of the Annex set about raising $100,000 as a kind of dowry. By 1884, the corporation had only $93,000—and Harvard refused it. In 1885, it used the money to buy the institution's first home and, soon after, its own physics and chemistry laboratories. By 1890, the Annex's assets were worth over $150,000, which the corporation again was willing to turn over to Harvard in return for Harvard degrees. And again Harvard refused. As Clover and Ellen Hooper's brother said, the whole experiment was just too risky.

But the Annex could not be denied. Controversy and outside pressure mounted. Not to speak of the number of coeducational institutions in the West, Cornell granted equal access to women in 1872; Vasser began in the 1860s and Smith and Wellesley in 1875. The female seminary that Mary Lyon had started in South Hadley, Massachusetts, in 1836 became a college in 1888. Harvard might have been an incomparable educational institution for men in the eyes of many, but increasingly it looked like just a holdout when it came to the question of women's education.

By 1893, the Annex's enrollment was up to 263; Harvard teachers were never in short supply, if only because they welcomed the supplementary income. Citing precedent that would impress Anglophilic Harvard, the precedent of the relationships between Cambridge and Oxford and their women's colleges, John Gray, the Royall Professor at Harvard Law School, proposed that Harvard agree to serve as the Annex's "visitor." Harvard was to make sure that its own standards were maintained, and being satisfied, it would then countersign degrees, thereby attesting to the equivalency of work done at the two institutions. In 1894, President Eliot joined Agassiz in presenting the case to the Massachusetts legislature, which granted a new charter to what then became Radcliffe College. No monies changed hands, but the name was that of the first woman to contribute funds to Harvard College.

If anything compared to the women's desire to learn during these early years of their schooling in Cambridge it was their desire not to offend. Agassiz was especially intent upon doing everything she could to give that impression. In all her years of service, she found ways to allay everyone's fears about the threat her students presented to Harvard's all-male traditions. In the early days, to ensure that the "Private Collegiate Instruction of Women" was indeed private, she personally made and hung curtains in the Carrett house on Appian Way lest the students be seen in attendance at their lectures. When the Radcliffe graduates of 1894 wanted to celebrate their new relationship to Harvard by wearing caps and gowns, Agassiz asked that they not, saying that she thought they would look too masculine and "attract unfavorable attention." Gilman noted that "she never pressed herself into the foreground"; she asked that her students not do so either.[68]

"Our students themselves manifest no desire for co-education," she said in one of her earlier commencement talks. "The element of competition with men does not enter into their aims." By 1899, she was ready to acknowledge that teaching was no longer the only career a woman could imagine entering— in fact, the *Radcliffe Magazine,* which was founded that year, was publishing a series of articles on professions other than teaching—but in her commencement address, she was reluctant to comment, saying only,

I am confident of one thing, however, which is that the largest liberty of instruction cannot in itself impair true womanhood. If understood and used aright, it can only be a help and not a hinderance in the life-work natural to women. It can never impair, but rather will enlarge and ennoble, the life of the home.

She then went on to cite a sweet and wise and cultured woman with whom a friend had commiserated because she had been forced to do her own house-work. The woman responded, Agassiz said, "in the spirit of old [George] Herbert's poem, 'No one can prevent me from talking with the angels while I sweep the room.' "[69]

It was a far cry from women's call for public recognition—for the vote or other equal rights. Like so much of the rhetoric that characterized debate over women's education—at least around Boston—it was an extension of the demeaning marital and domestic arrangements that had inspired women to agitate in the first place. When Agassiz retired in 1903, her successor, Dean LeBaron Briggs, carried right on where she left off. In his commencement remarks in 1905, he told the graduates that what they did might be "outwardly a little thing," but that once they recognized it as their work, "the little things has become great, the doing of it may become heroic."[70] In a piece titled "To the Girl Who Would Cultivate Herself," he spoke again of women's "drudgery," this time calling it "her discipline, her part in the ceaseless renewal of that great and multifarious life which we call the world." It was the work she could do, he said, "for she has tasted the joy of 'the unconquerable soul.' "[71] In his 1906 address, he said,

The supreme claim of Radcliffe College is in the refined and sensitive rather than boisterous strength which characterizes the best Harvard men. I have little sympathy with the higher education of women if it battles against those distinctions between men and women which are radical and eternal.[72]

For their part, he thought most women were born with a love of poetry. At their best, he said, they *were* "a kind of poetry."[73]

During the years that Briggs and Agassiz were sending Radcliffe gradu-ates out into the world, fewer and fewer of them would go out to marry. The direst predictions of Clarke and Hall and others proved accurate: the more education a woman had, the less likely she was to raise a family. But in the minds of those in authority at Harvard and Radcliffe, the women who were graduating were still angelic, whether they were on their way to becoming wives or not. Accordingly, everyone who needed to could rest assured that the boisterous men of Harvard were still men.

In an article on the new relationship that had been established between the two institutions, in an unusual twist, the *Graduates' Magazine* reported with pride that Harvard was no leader in the field. "On the contrary," they said, she was "behind most of the great colleges in the world in taking public and official action." Some action had been taken, but the article characterized the new relationships between the young men and women in unthreatening terms. Speaking of the negotiations that had led up to the creation of Radcliffe, it said that "in the first place, of course, no one wanted to incorporate the Annex bodily into the University, and mingle its students with the young men." As for the tremors we might register as we read "incorporate," "bodily," "mingle," it is presumably only the modern reader who would choose to pick them up. According to the article, there were no such moves to record, nor had there ever been any:

There has never been an occasion of discipline, or complaint of improper deportment, since the enterprise was started. The attitude of the students of Harvard College toward the Annex students, and of the latter toward the former, appears to be that of un-concern.

Radcliffe had "avoided advertisement and publicity, shunned competition with other colleges for women"; the students who went there were unnoticed and unnoticing. The same held true for the men, whose education into man-hood, therefore, was proceeding without interruption.[74]

It was no doubt true that a student body that was approaching 2,000 around the turn of the century paid relatively little attention to one that had just passed 300. Moreover, there were so many more women in Boston who were likely to be socially interesting and acceptable in the eyes of Harvard men. When Harvard men did take notice, some paternalistically said that the women at the Annex deserved better accommodations, or even the right to cross-register for Harvard courses, but most of them resisted the idea of coedu-cation. Using a variety of rhetorical ploys, they fended off the challenge these women represented. The *Advocate* was open about its attempts to type, run-ning articles on "girls," and then on "feminology," which produced the *puella masculina* (who were "susceptible of scientific analysis" because they were so "pertinacious in thrusting themselves upon the public gaze"), the preferable *puella quieta,* and of course the *femina nova.* What with the humor worn threadbare by now, it is easy to see through it to the Harvard undergraduates' nervous concern, especially about "the new woman." Her numbers had in-creased, they said, as had her desire to emancipate her mind and to exhibit her legs; the *Advocate* could

only hope that the less insane specimens of *femina nova* will soon realize the futility of the objects for which they have striven, will renounce the barren privilege which they have attained, and will again envelop their minds and their bodies in that veil of modesty which has hitherto become them so well.[75]

The *Lampoon*'s expression of concern was more blatant. In 1898, for example, it ran a two-page drawing of a young man looking up at a woman seated in John Harvard's chair in the statue of him in Harvard Yard—with the caption reading, "The Usurper."[76]

The Radcliffe student could also be cast as a Gibson girl, a bit frigid, a bit flirtatious. Most obviously and most often, she was the forbidding figure of the bluestocking, unattractive (or as the term originally suggested, informally or drably dressed), unsociable, humorless, and—above all—frighteningly smart. She was not to be integrated into the Medical School, for example, because she would always come up with long and correct diagnoses. As one contribution had it:

> She walks with step and mien sedate,
> Her spectacles upon her nose,
> And wisdom from her ruby lips
> In pure Hellenic accent flows.
>
> She finds a charm in Arabic,
> And calculus is easy—quite;
> She writes in Hebrew, thinks in Greek,
> And dreams in Sanskrit every night.[77]

When "a member of the Annex" spoke up in the pages of the *Advocate* in 1889, she played complicitously with this prevailing stereotype. Calling her piece "The Slow Set at the Harvard Annex," she said that "the excessive moderation of certain members" had given her institution "a reputation which, to say the least, is grotesque," that there were such "monstrosities" as the bluestocking, but that in fact the typical Annex student had a proper sense of proportion: she had a high scholastic average, but she also played tennis. The Annex student was no angel, and she was no dullard. She was just a normal human being. "So, when you grow weary of contemplating the celestial giants of whom this paper treats," she concluded, "perhaps you will accept as a human reality the larger sisterhood of girls whose heaven is on earth."[78]

Even Gertrude Stein had to contend with this image of her sisters at Radcliffe. In a theme for English 22 that she titled "An Annex Girl," she portrayed a bluestocking who wishes she weren't a bluestocking:

> There she stood a little body with a very large head. She was loaded down with books and was evidently very dismal. Suddenly there broke forth a torment, "I don't want to be superior" she wailed despairingly, "I am tired to death of standing with my head craned constantly looking upward. I am just longing to meet one simple soul that don't want to know everything, one weak happy naive consciousness that thinks higher education is *(either rot or has never heard)* of it." She gave a long-drawn Oh! and *(then collapsed the books)* on top of the miserable little heap.[79]

Whether for social or psychological reasons, the anonymous contributor to the *Advocate* and Gertrude Stein were eager not to be seen up there at the head of the class. Many decades later, Matina Horner would document the same phenomenon among women at the University of Michigan—and then go on to be president of Radcliffe. Women's "fear of success" she would call it—

more specifically, a fear that if they spoke up in class, they would frighten men away.[80]

Most Radcliffe students seemed to go on about their business, seemingly unconcerned about what Harvard men were thinking, as the *Graduates' Magazine* had said. (There is little mention of what was going on at Harvard in the pages of the *Radcliffe Magazine*.) But of course they could not ignore their professors. When they considered and described them, they did indeed, as Gertrude Stein put it, look up. (The fullest contemporary account of the early days of Radcliffe is appropriately titled "The Gods Serve Hebe.")[81] And, in turn, those men continued to look down on them—beautiful, poetic, angelic, elevating presences that they were.

Whether or not they actually knew or read what the medical "experts" were saying, the men we have been considering categorized and characterized women the way Clarke and Hall and Mitchell did. They also shared their reservations about educating women. In 1896, S. Weir Mitchell brought the message in person. In a talk he gave at Radcliffe, he told the students that women were less able than men to endure the strain of higher education and that though they could choose whatever vocation they wanted, so far as he was concerned they could make right choices or they could make wrong choices: "I no more want them to be preachers, lawyers, or platform orators," he said, "than I want men to be seamstresses or nurses of children."[82] James' colleague in charge of the psychological laboratory, Hugo Münsterberg, was even more inflexible. He told Gertrude Stein that she was his idea of "the ideal student," but nothing followed from that remark. Genius, he said in his book *American Traits* (1901), was *"sui generis."* In that volume, and then again in *The Americans* (1904), he recited "scientific" arguments about Woman and her role that were news to no one by then, though his recitation was louder than that of most men. Woman had tact and aesthetic feeling, "instinctive insight," enthusiasm, sympathy, "natural wisdom and morality," but she lacked "clearness and logical consistency," she tended towards "hasty generalization . . . mixing of principles . . . undervaluation of the abstract and of the absent," and she was ever ready to "follow her feelings." Her "defects" could "beautify the private life," and "soften and complete the strenuous, earnest, and consistent public activity of the man"—the man possessing "harder logic"—but if allowed to influence the educational system or public life generally, she would render America impotent. His metaphors evoke the prospect of the nation's emasculation: "American intellectual work [would] be kept down by the women," births in New England would decline, and America would "never become a world power."[83]

George Herbert Palmer's version of these arguments, as he presented them to his Radcliffe students, went, "Concentration is power, but power in one direction. A man, with his fixed purpose, may exclude everything but his chosen field." A woman's work, on the other hand, was "diversified," the work of "daughter, wife, mother, housewife, hostess, neighbor." To Grace Hollingsworth Tucker, the author of "The Gods Serve Hebe," that meant reducing the angel of the house not to a sweeper in the kitchen (Agassiz's inspiration), but to "small potatoes." Looking back thirty years to the course Palmer had given on ethics ("the study of right and wrong"), and imagining how it would apply in the age of "the career women of today," Tucker quoted an adage as her consoling answer: "The big potatoes are always on top of the pile; but if it were not for the little potatoes, there wouldn't be any pile."[84]

In the classes that he gave at Radcliffe, Charles T. Copeland tried to toughen up his students a little, commending them for their "understanding, sense of humor and masculine mentality" when they smiled in the face of his criticisms of their work, but he also did what he could to keep them feminine. He refused to teach them "Argument," explaining in his jocular way, "How deplorable for women to become apt in argument. We can't obliterate a natural tendency, but why cultivate it?"[85] In the athletic arena, Dudley Sargent pioneered for women's physical education, teaching it at Radcliffe as well as at Harvard, admitting women to his summer programs, and opposing corsets in favor of bloomers—even trousers. But he too wanted to keep women pure. As it did in Copeland's teaching, that meant refining away impurities that might eventually corrupt men. To Copeland the problem was her potentially sharp tongue; to Sargent it was her sexuality. Thus, in a revaluation of the usual stereotypes, he defended women's participation in sports because it masculinized them and thus stifled their sexual curiosity. "There is a time in the life of a girl," he wrote, "when it is better for her and for the community to be something of a boy rather than too much of a girl."[86] Taking the idea to an extreme, the Psychology Department had a woman on its staff for nine years, beginning in 1899, but never listed her in the catalog, lest (as it was reported a few years later) doing so "create a dangerous precedent."[87]

Most professors were content simply to dwell on young women's goodness and purity. Nathaniel Shaler thought they were meant to save men's souls—and do no more. In his *Autobiography,* he expressed his indebtedness to women for keeping him from "the pit whereto I have seen so many go." On his own, Shaler said, "the male human is a mere fragment of his kind; he attains to his humanity through the shaping influence of its better half." But she was not to do that in public. He was present when Arthur Gilman explained how women might be educated in Cambridge, but like everyone else who attended that meeting, he entertained no thought of coeducation—"or of anything, indeed, which might take away from the poetic side of social life."[88] In his address to the graduates in 1901, Charles Eliot Norton described women in the same terms. They were "the living representatives of ideals of beauty in character and in conduct." That was "the justification of your power," he said, and it was the justification of their education as well. They were to go out into the world as "the fair image of true womanhood," which is to say, they were to join him in his struggle against "our vulgar, semi-civilized America."[89]

James taught several courses at Radcliffe, much to the delight of Stein and of at least one class that sent him flowers, but he never engaged in any debate over the issue of coeducation. However intensely he contemplated the role of women in his own life over the years, he was more than usually relaxed in the presence of his female students. At Radcliffe, he could repeat the courses he gave at Harvard without thinking much about the implications for men's lives. In 1896, when he was fifty, in banter to his brother he described teaching Radcliffe students as "a sweet consolation to one's declining years."[90] The next year, he gave his last course there—a course that recalls "On a Certain Blindness in Human Beings" and his relationship with Pauline Goldmark—"Philosophy 3: Philosophy of Nature." When his sister's friend Katharine Loring and others deplored Harvard's refusal to absorb the Annex, he objected to what he thought was their belligerence and foolishness, "since," he pointed out, "the Women who have always run the Annex, are best satisfied to have things, for the present, separate."[91] And so, presumably, was he.

His most famous Radcliffe student was Gertrude Stein, who, as we saw at the outset, worshiped him. "The really lasting impression of her Radcliffe life came through William James," she wrote in *The Autobiography of Alice B. Toklas*. "His personality and his teaching and his way of amusing himself with himself and his students all pleased her." When she wrote in an examination book that she was "so sorry," but that she really did "not feel a bit like an examination paper in philosophy to-day," she knew he would understand. His response—"I understand perfectly how you feel I often feel like that myself"—and his award of the highest grade in the class, are usually taken as proof that, like Münsterberg, he recognized her genius. But they can also be read as his indulgence. Would he have let a man quit like that?[92]

What Harvard agreed to in 1894 satisfied these men. It seemed that if Harvard would just "visit" Radcliffe and co-sign its students' degrees, Harvard's vision would not be blurred—at least "for now," as James put it. With hindsight, we can say that the momentum built up over the fifteen years since the Gilman meeting would inevitably lead to coeducation—even if it would take another seventy years—but at the time only one voice rose to make that point: Barrett Wendell's. It had to be Wendell. The most specific and sustained warning about what might be in store for Harvard had to be made by the man who defended all things masculine because, as he said, "muscularity" eluded him. With Wendell, the argument for the kind of manhood that depends upon the absence of all things womanly reaches its simple conclusion.

Having finished his work as chairman of the "Committee on the Relations between Harvard University and Radcliffe College" in 1898, he published the next year an article in the *Monthly* that spelled out the position he had taken.[93] His work on the committee, he said, "was perhaps the most far-reaching [he] ever did" at Harvard; Briggs' biographer reports that Wendell went further and repeatedly boasted that his opposition to coeducation at Harvard was "his most important service to education in America."[94] It was the "most contentious event" of the year in which it came out, Royce wrote James. Three years later, Royce wrote Münsterberg, saying that there were signs of "the deluge of feminism" that Münsterberg had predicted and that Wendell, "our Noah," was still preaching against it and building his ark. His protestations may have been something of a joke by then, but the laughter was that of old boys: Royce admitted that he was thinking of getting on board himself.[95]

In Wendell the contradictions are raw. In his article "The Social Life at Harvard," he spoke of his students' need for young girls. As G. Stanley Hall and Eliot and others would argue, they were an essential influence on their students, whose society, without them, would be unhealthy: "Nothing is so good for the moral tone of a growing man as knowing—and knowing well—young girls. Nothing so surely keeps him out of mischief; nothing better helps him out if he have once fallen in."[96] In the same spirit, Wendell thought that "the nature of our women"—as against that of French women—was "too high and pure easily to be lowered, or corrupted, or even injured" by anything that they read, so they ought to be allowed to read whatever they wanted. "I think we can trust them with anything with which they are willing to trust themselves," he told a correspondent who had raised the issue. In his personal life, he was among the many men we have encountered who was entirely dependent on his wife. "He was so obviously lost without her," his daughter wrote. "He depended upon her for everything. . . . For forty years together she shielded him from the petty irritations of daily existence."[97]

But She/Woman was to go nowhere near Harvard. For their moral uplift, the Harvard students were to go out—like Henry James' Mr. Burrage and Mr. Gracie in *The Bostonians*—into the homes of local residents. Whatever reading she did she would do at home. And there she would stay when Barrett Wendell lectured at the Sorbonne in 1904–5. When he was asked if Mrs. Wendell would be going to Paris with him, he reportedly replied, "Young man, would you take a ham sandwich to a banquet?"[98]

So Wendell would be the man to insist that Harvard remain an all-male institution, and argue for a strengthened Radcliffe, one with its own faculty, as a protective shield against coeducation—even to suggest that it might not be too late to reconsider the new arrangement with that institution. Amid all the changes since 1636, he said, "there has never before been a deviation from the principle that the influences amid which education should be obtained here must remain virile," and "virile" they should remain. It went without saying what havoc women would cause if allowed to share "common residence" with Harvard undergraduates. Wendell's argument was directed primarily at what was happening to his colleagues. To be at their best, they required "manly opposition," and "vigorous contest with men of [their] own size," he said. Not only would they not get it from women—for women suffered from "a comparative lack of mental resistance"—but in the presence of female students they were in danger of losing their *own* powers of resistance. "In brief, a man who likes to teach women is in real danger of infatuation." That all this shrinking and softening might lead to better teaching and learning was unimaginable.

Wendell's other main objection to his colleagues' teaching women was that it took time away from their research; it diminished their "scholarly vigor"—which is to say, it diminished them as men. But it was not research—or even learning—that Wendell cared most about. Of the countless witnesses to the fact that Harvard was educating men for other purposes as well, or for even more important purposes, Wendell is the star witness. "To me," he confessed, "Harvard seems, even more profoundly than it seems an institution of learning, a traditional school of manly character."

We must not overestimate how much the influence of the men of Wendell's generation was fading as the century turned. He and Copeland in English, Norton in fine arts, Shaler in Geology, Sargent in physical education, James, Münsterberg, Palmer, and Royce in philosophy, and President Eliot himself would not retire for quite a few years, and as the elders—as the Olympians that they were reputed to be—their influence would be felt right up to the end. Of course they were radically different in character and temperament, in intellect and achievement, but they were united in an effort not just to develop minds or encourage learning but to educate young men into a certain kind of manhood, and their attitudes toward women and toward their emergence at Radcliffe were remarkably similar. The two—their expectations of their students at Harvard and their characterizations of women—went hand in hand. Their figurings of women in their pronouncements and in their asides were essential to their confirmations of themselves as men.

"All the New Races"

In his inaugural address, President Eliot vowed that Harvard would produce an aristocracy of men of "capacity and character," rather than one that catered to "a stupid and pretentious caste," and as we saw in chapter 2, Harvard worked consciously to achieve that goal during the years of his presidency. In 1891, Edwin Arlington Robinson compared Harvard to other institutions in terms that looked forward to James' definition of "the true Harvard." At Harvard, he told a friend, "there is less of the real college spirit, but there is more equality. I have been treated first rate by everyone I have seen and have tried to do the same myself."[1] Looking back on *his* "true Harvard," John Reed remembered that there were "all sorts of strange characters, of every race and mind, poets, philosophers, cranks of every twist," and that "no matter what you were or what you did . . . you could find your kind." You were free to discover and develop your own talents and interests; you were not dragged down by "masses of mediocrely educated young men equipped with 'business' psychology."[2] By the time Reed graduated, in 1910, there were a multiplicity of "kinds" at Harvard, and between them there seemed to be, if not mutual respect, enough tolerance—or lack of caring—to allow each to go its own way. Harvard sought to become what Eliot had promised it would be when he began forty years before—"intensely democratic in temper."[3]

It goes without saying that keeping Harvard open and hospitable to all men presented continuous and difficult challenges. Eliot was still *proposing* to welcome "all the new races and to do its best for them" in 1902, still using the present tense after thirty-three years as president. Nor should we be surprised that not even Eliot meant "all" equally, or that not all students felt welcome at Harvard. Harvard was democratic in "temper," but as Eliot went on to say, it would be "American in affection." Some would feel—or be made to feel—the warmth of that affection more than others. The massive influx of immigrants was bound to create a difference between, say, young men of Irish descent who went to Harvard and Harvard men—just as it did between Irish-Americans and Americans.

During this period, in the name of scientific inquiry, and—whether they intended it or not—as a means of securing their own privileged positions, many men spent incalculable amounts of intellectual energy typing their fellow men, and thus slowing down efforts to realize the democratic ideal. Anti-evolutionists, Social Darwinists, and then—as they came into being—anthropologists and economists, psychologists and sociologists, categorized and compared what they loosely called the "races" that inhabited the globe. They grounded their typologies in different physical traits that they observed, which in turn they assumed were based on different biological essences. Building from that ground up, they then explained the supposed facts of differing psychological and social behavior among various "races."

In the main, they extolled the virtues of the so-called Anglo-Saxon race, a nonexistent pure breed of English—or sometimes British (but never Irish)—

people who had featured in political pronouncements well before our period. Growing out of the belief that the Puritan colonists were "chosen people," working its way through the establishment of the Republic during the Revolution, and gathering strength as the wilderness was thinned out and the country prospered materially, this idea of the "Anglo-Saxon" was integral to the idea of America's "manifest destiny."[4]

The cry itself was first raised in the 1840s to justify America's war against Mexico and the annexation of territories in the Southwest. Alaska was acquired in 1867; American influence prevailed in Latin America by the end of the 1880s; in 1898, President McKinley defended annexing the Sandwich Islands (Hawaii) by saying that we needed them as much as—or even more than—we needed California. "It is manifest destiny," he said. American expansion was not just a matter of acquisition, in other words. It was "our"—the Anglo-Saxons'—duty, "the White Man's burden," as Rudyard Kipling indelibly phrased it the next year. It was as clear by this reading of America's future—and of future relations to "lesser breeds without the law"—that the Anglo-Saxon way of life should be the model of a new world order as that the trusts headed by Armour or Carnegie or Rockefeller should determine how meat or steel or oil was produced and distributed.[5]

Compared to the ideal civilization that "we" were creating, the ways of life of all other peoples were found more or less wanting. With the Anglo-Saxons at the top, all the others were ranked on a scale that moved next to the races of western Europe, then over and down to eastern Europe, after which it descended precipitously to the east and to the south, to Africa or to China—to wherever skins were darker. As these "authorities" witnessed thousands of peoples of other races landing in America, many—especially those who were determined to trace their ancestry back to what Bernard Berenson (a Latvian immigrant Jew, class of 1887) called the "Angry Saxons"—feared being overwhelmed.[6] As we have often noted, whether counting the numbers of immigrants, or measuring body types, or realizing that their own women might put education before child rearing, many feared—as the titles of the most infamous books on the subject had it—*The Passing of the Great Race in America* (1916) and *The Rising Tide of Color against White World-Supremacy* (1920).[7]

Thus at Harvard, Louis Agassiz mapped out "zoological provinces" and climate zones, and then determined which were suitable for white habitation and dominance. The presence of large numbers of Negroes in the South was appropriate on those grounds, but he did not think they were of the same species as whites, and he feared that too many of them in the South would pose a threat to the Republic. Those in the North, he predicted, would in time weaken and die out.[8] Though he never taught at Harvard, Hall's word was influential nationally. He had it worked it out scientifically that Negroes were like women, "essentially children and adolescents in soul," existing at an evolutionary stage lower than that of the Caucasian male. He thought of Frederick Douglass and Booker T. Washington and Du Bois the way Münsterberg thought of Gertrude Stein: they didn't count; they were "not typical Negroes."[9] One of the seminars that Henry Adams offered at Harvard was on Teutonic and Anglo-Saxon institutions, and he himself studied the Anglo-Saxon language in his attempt to discover the source of modern political and legal institutions.[10] In his countless expressions of dismay over the present state of those institutions, it is the Jew who is most often the scapegoat.

There is a great deal of anti-Semitism in Frank Norris' writings too and, by contrast, a great deal of swooning over men he found in Icelandic sagas or in the *Song of Roland*. But unlike Adams, Norris was inspired when he contemplated America's expanding economy and the men who commanded it. "Had the Lion-Hearted Richard lived today, he would have become a 'leading representative of the Amalgamated Steel Companies,'" Norris wrote in "The Frontier Gone at Last." In his reading of history, "we Anglo-Saxons" began our push westward in a "little historic reach of ground in the midst of the Friesland swamps" centuries ago. Onward we pressed to England, then to the West Indies, to the Pacific, to Manila Bay, and finally to China, after which there was no longer any West, and thus "the problem of the centuries for the Anglo-Saxon was solved."[11]

Even Gertrude Stein was drawn to the "wonderful vitality . . . in those old Norse legends"—exclaiming in one of the themes she wrote for English 22, "What a pleasure in this psychological nineteenth century to live again the simple thoughts and the down-right strokes of the race of the Volsung."[12] For simple thoughts in the present, she turned to the Negroes she saw in the community around the Johns Hopkins Medical School (where she went after graduating from Radcliffe), who then appeared as the stereotypical unevolved sexual animal and the happy plantation worker in *Three Lives* (1909). In that otherwise great book, she blithely went on about "the simple, promiscuous unmorality of the black people" and of "the wide abandoned laughter that gives the broad glow to negro sunshine."[13]

As for James' immediate colleagues, some thought Cambridge might be spared. To them, Brattle Street was as safe as the close of an English cathedral, Bliss Perry wrote, "an island in the stream of new and alien races swarming into Greater Boston."[14] Many spoke disparagingly of the Irish and the Chinese, the blacks and the Jews—of blacks and Jews most often—in an attempt to defend what they considered truly "American." Thus Charles Eliot Norton wanted to restrict suffrage, to limit immigration to those who could already read and write English, and somehow to prevent New England's being overrun by the Irish and the Jews.[15] Thus Wendell declared that American literature had been polluted in the nineteenth century. "The floodgates are opened," he said. "Europe is emptying itself into our Eastern seaports; Asia overflowing the barriers we have tried to erect on our Western coast; Africa sapping our life to the southward." What remained pure was "emasculate," or "of little lasting potence"—what Santayana would call "genteel."[16] Imagining the end of the world as he had known it, Wendell eschewed the fictions of science and seemed to look forward to the science fictions of Edgar Rice Burroughs: "The racial agony in which we are being strangled by invading aliens, who shall inherit the spirit of us," he wrote a friend in 1904, "grows heavier with me, as the end of me—and of ours—comes nearer."[17] And as we might expect, after years of observing and measuring the "stock" in the Hemenway Gymnasium, Dudley Sargent edged away from his numerical tabulations to shaky propositions about origins and social class, concluding in his *Physical Education* that the original settlers and later immigrants from higher social strata (the Dutch, the Germans, and French especially) provided the "best inheritance of pure stock" and so "maintained their supremacy." Others, including "the driftwood and riffraff thrown up by the revolutionary contests and internecine wars" of recent years, were of lesser and of damaging quality. "This large infusion of foreign blood of an inferior quality," he said, "has undoubtedly impaired the physical status of our people as a whole."[18]

In his book *The Southern South,* the historian Albert Bushnell Hart said that he would not go so far as to agree with Hall. "The theory that the negro mind ceases to develop after adolescence perhaps has something in it," he conceded, but there were too many exceptions "to permit the problem to be settled by the phrase, 'The Negro is a child.' " He was, after all, Du Bois' thesis adviser. And agreeing with what Du Bois said in *The Souls of Black Folk* about the need for whites to help Negroes in their efforts to reconstitute their lives after the Civil War, he had to admit that many whites "do not set them in this respect a convincing example." But at the end of his chapter titled "Negro Character," he placed the Negro below the white man "in mental and moral status" and predicted that—"race measured by race"—the Negro would "remain inferior in race stamina and race achievement." As for "Race Association," it followed that "the union of the two races means a decline in the rate of civilization."[19]

Nathaniel Shaler, who had become the dean of the Lawrence Scientific School in 1891, faced the race issue head-on. He was not the only faculty member to join the Immigration Restriction League when it was formed in Boston in 1894. Ten years later, in *The Neighbor: The Natural History of Human Contacts,* he singled out and analyzed "The Hebrew Problem" and "The Problem of the African" at great length and in great detail. He found, for example, that "the Israelitic spirit makes a much swifter response to the greeting the stranger gives them than the Aryan, and that the acquaintance is forced in such an irritating manner as to breed dislike," and that Jews are "incapable of subjection, being in this regard even more obdurate than the American Indian or the Chinese." In Negroes, on the other hand, Shaler discovered "capacities for affection and good faith," "an ability to toil which is of a high order," "certain musical powers which may have high value, and are sure to be serviceable," and, above all, "a curious disposition to come near to, and to profit largely from, close contact with our own people." This last made them— in spite of their "simple human nature" and their inability to maintain a civilization on their own—"hopeful material for use in our society." But as if recalling James' criticism of man's tendency to rely on substantives in his renderings of his thoughts, Shaler recognized the baseness of what he called "the categoric motive." He said that "in all man's dealing with men of other races or tribes or classes," his classifications had been "the cloak of ignorance," and he called for "the extension of the sympathies and understandings to the point where we shall look upon all men as individuals." He looked forward to the day when race hatred would atrophy because it was no longer necessary for survival, but then he blocked what he called "the way out" with the tenor of his recommendations to his reader. First experiment by making contact with "a common laborer," he said, and then "having extended his conceptions of what constitutes a man, by satisfying himself that the most out-lying members of his own stock are essentially like himself, the inquirer should then apply the same method of closely sympathetic yet observant contact to some distinctly alien race." Jews are a good test, because though judged by "the *modulus of alienity*" they are more foreign than American Indians or Chinese, they are "our" intellectual equals, and if we are "true observers," we will overcome our initial exasperation and "surely fall in love with the instructive specimen." Negroes, no. They are "ineradicably alien," and "the blood of the races must be kept entirely apart."[20]

Student attitudes as they were represented in the pages of the *Lampoon* were unremittingly and dispassionately racist. Usually it was enough to criticize the ineptitude of the Negroes who waited on tables in the dining commons in Memorial Hall, or to make jokes about Negroes stealing chickens, but in 1879 they were enlisted in the debunking of the incorporation of the Annex. On one cover, young Mr. Holworthy is approached by his black servant, asking that he might borrow his algebra book because his wife's "fitting for de Annex." The Irish were depicted as barroom brawlers and then—again on a cover—made to join Ikey to answer his question: "Ven ve die, vere do you t'ink ve shall go?" What with the nose of one hooked and the other's vibrant from drink, the answer is: "we'll aich foller our noses."[21]

As they had done in response to the woman's movement, the editors of the *Advocate* had some of these "others" speak for themselves. In 1903, they reprinted "Religion in the Education of the Negro," the commencement speech of the future poet and educator Leslie Pinckney Hill. Echoing Du Bois—and like him, shifting the idea of race off its biological base and placing it on a broader historical and social one—Hill said that it was the Negro's "deep innate sense of religion," and not "his material advancement," that would contribute to the realization of the ideals of democracy. Four years later, in "The Jew in America," A. L. Mayer (who would have a distinguished career in film) wrote that the Jew was also "an integral part of this nation," and that *his* services were not "solely materialistic" either. "Neither age or suffering has made the stock degenerate," he said, and so he asked, "Grant us your patience, your forbearance, and we promise that the bread ye cast upon the waters will return to you a hundred fold."[22]

There was little or no social activism in those days. Examples of students protesting discrimination against Negroes—boycotting the barber who refused to give the all-American football star William Henry Lewis a haircut in one instance, refusing to play the University of Virginia because it insisted on Harvard's benching the black third baseman in another—tell us at least as much about the desire to win games that was heating up during these years as about young men's allegiance to democratic principles. There was no protest when a barber refused the business of Harvard's first black member of Phi Beta Kappa, Monroe Trotter.

Such was the scientific and social environment into which most men have since faded. The exceptional ones retained a sense of men's worth, or defined manhood, in terms that were not conventionally or cruelly limited by the unthinking majority's ideas of race and class.

First, there was Eliot himself, of whom it can be said that at the very least he maintained a standard that was higher than that of most of his faculty. Surrounded by talk that pitted one ill-defined race against another, he opposed or transcended it in his own speeches, and he enabled students to refute it with their records at Harvard. In his theorizing about race, he pointed out that those who prided themselves on their English ancestry were, like everyone else in America, more than likely to be of mixed heritage—"a veritable ethnological conglomerate very much like that which is now forming on a larger scale in the United States," he said in 1892. He even thought he detected a "Jewish strain" in many old New England families—his own, he hoped, included.[23] He thought what the Immigration Restriction League was trying to do was "vicious," and affirmed his faith in America's ability to absorb immigrants, in statements that supported the work of another organization, the National Liberal Immigration League. He frequently asserted that Harvard could do no less. "Among its officers and students," he said, it would recognize "neither class, caste, race, sect nor political party."

But as we have seen, Eliot did nothing to blur social distinctions between and among the undergraduates, nor did he do much to erase them in his thinking about American society. In fact, he did less and less as the numbers of different peoples arriving in America increased. He opposed organized labor's attempts to protect its own from the competition of the newly arrived, saying that the men who already had jobs ought to have confidence in their ability to retain them, but at the same time he was inclined to blame "the large number of foreigners" who were arriving "year after year" for strikes and other labor troubles.[24] He was uneasy about the growing influence of the Irish in Boston politics. Similarly, though he honored the intelligence and achievement of individual black—or Chinese, or Japanese—men, in 1907 he defended the state of Kentucky when it made Berea College establish a separate branch for its Negro students. There were a number of Negro students at Harvard, he said, but they were "hidden in the great mass and . . . not noticeable. If they were in equal numbers or in a majority, we might deem a separation necessary."[25] Eliot was always far more concerned with a man's individual intelligence and fulfillment than with his existence as a representative social force.

The distinction was not so clear in William James' mind: he insisted on the sanctity of the individual, but did so while engaging with the social and political world. That he was a man of his class is sometimes painfully obvious. "Most of the American nation (and probably all nations) is white-trash," he wrote a cousin in 1896. Ten years before that, in the same letter in which he congratulated his brother for his handling of Basil Ransom in *The Bostonians,* he described America's labor troubles the same way he would describe them in "What Makes a Life Significant"—as "a healthy phase of evolution"—and then went on to point out that he was not talking about "the senseless 'anarchist' riot in Chicago"—the Haymarket Riot on May 4, 1886. On May Day, police had opened fire on a combined meeting of supporters of the eight-hour workday and strikers at the McCormick reaper company; at a protest meeting four days later in Haymarket Square, a bomb exploded, killing seven or eight policemen. That was not "normal" labor trouble; that, James said, "was the work of a lot of pathological Germans and Poles."[26]

But James possessed what by his seemingly humble definition was "genius"—genius which was, he wrote in his *Psychology,* "little more than the faculty of perceiving in an unhabitual way." His genius was to question the thoughts of others and, at the same time, to acknowledge that none of us finally knows what is going on in anyone else's mind. That was true of his own individual thinking and of his thinking about individuals. It also held true of his social views. In them too he resisted received ideas, arguing that individuals were oppressed by such thinking; it stifled both themselves and others. In his famous essay "Habit," he said that habit was "the enormous fly-wheel of society, its most precious conservative agent"; and wisely, sadly, sympathetically, he went on to say that habit "alone prevents the hardest and most repulsive walks of life from being deserted by those brought up to tread therein."[27] He knew how to categorize and affix labels, and occasionally he did only that, but habitual thinking that kept people in their places did not suit his temperament.

We have seen many testaments to his openness to the thoughts of every Harvard undergraduate. To them we can add that of Berenson, whom James once singled out, saying, "Come let us gossip about the universe." Not surprisingly, Berenson later singled him out in return, placing him on a list of personal influences—as distinguished from the more impersonal, educational forces in his life—along with Arnold and Pater as writers, and Burckhardt and Morelli as attributer and critic.[28] Du Bois' reminiscences about his years at Harvard often include references to James' advice and hospitality as well as to his teaching.[29]

By the same token, James had little tolerance for the intolerant. Responding to newspaper clippings that Du Bois sent him from Atlanta, he wrote in 1903 "A Strong Note of Warning Regarding the Lynching Epidemic" to the *Springfield Daily Republican*.[30] Closer to home, he objected to Wendell's snobbery,[31] and when his wife balked at his inviting a Jewish colleague to their house, he called her a "Jew-baiter."[32] The most impressive display of his public indignation occurs in the long Ingersoll Lecture on Human Immortality—subtitled "Two Supposed Objections to the Doctrine"—which he delivered in 1897. One objection was a literal one: there just wasn't enough room in heaven now that Darwin had redefined who was and who was not human, and now that hordes of newcomers were landing on American shores. He knew how his audience felt about immigrants:

We have, as the phrase goes, *no use for them*, and it oppresses us to think of their survival. Take, for instance, all the Chinamen. Which of you here, my friends, sees any fitness in their eternal perpetuation unreduced in numbers?

To the obvious answer, none, he responded with astonishing vehemence:

But is not such an attitude due to the veriest lack and dearth of your imagination? You take these swarms of alien kinsmen as they are *for you:* an external picture painted on your retina, representing a crowd oppressive by its vastness and confusion. As they are for you, so you think they positively and absolutely are. *I* feel no call for them, you say; therefore there *is* no call for them. But all the while, beyond this externality which is your way of realizing them, they realize themselves with the acutest internality, with the most violent thrills of life. 'Tis you who are dead, stone-dead and blind and senseless, in your way of looking on.

Moving behind their retinas, he told the members of his audience that "each of these grotesque or even repulsive aliens is animated by an inner joy as hot or hotter than that which you feel beating in your private breast," and this being a version of his more famous essay "On a Certain Blindness in Human Beings," he concluded by saying, "To miss the inner joy of him . . . is to miss the whole of him."[33]

James was open to the potential of every individual student, and in the same spirit, he spoke out in defense of the human right of groups or classes or "races" to define their own lives for themselves. Whether his subject was a person's weltanschauung, or his religious experience, or his ethnic identity, James' attitude was pluralistic—responsive to what was to each man his own truth. In some measure, he developed this "philosophy" because of his own ethnic background—though one has immediately to add that he made very little of it, because for him to name it would be to invite the kind of arrested and arresting thought that he deplored. Nevertheless, it is there, and it informs his sense of the belittling power of prejudice. Many have quoted James's remark about "pathological Germans and Poles," but few have gone on to his gloss. The English papers were distorting news of the Haymarket Riot in order to discredit Gladstone, he tells his brother. He knew for facts that "all the Irish names are among the killed and wounded policemen. Almost every anarchist name is Continental." As their sister, Alice, said of her older brother in her Diary, "he seems sound eno' on Home Rule, but how could a child of Father's be anything else!!"[34] It went without saying—and William did not want to say—but he empathized with the outsiders, the "undisciplinables," at Harvard because he was not an alumnus, but also because he was—in a manner of speaking—Irish.*

More apparently, he was the less blind to other human beings because of his sense of the workings of language. He was eloquent about the damage bad usages could cause, especially in passages in *The Pluralistic Universe* that pick up where his thoughts about language and experience left off in "The Stream of Thought." To his observations about the reductive effects of substantives generally, he added a sense of the drama of misunderstanding and resentment created by people's lazy, inconsiderate typing of each others' way of thinking. It all began with Socrates and Plato, James said. They taught us that "reality

*Anti-Irish sentiment at Harvard is well represented by one Casey—from Mudville—whose failure is known to all Americans. He is the creation (in 1888) of Ernest Lawrence Thayer—an editor of the *Lampoon*, a magna cum laude graduate, and a student of William James'. See Donald Hall, *Principal Products of Portugal* (Boston: Beacon Press, 1995), pp. 1–2.

consists of essences, not of appearances, and that the essences of things are known whenever we know their definitions."

It is but the old story, of a useful practice first becoming a method, then a habit, and finally a tyranny that defeats the end it was used for. Concepts, first employed to make things intelligible, are clung to even when they make them unintelligible.

Thus in philosophical debate, or in one group's or one man's dealings with another, names are treated as if they legitimately excluded from something "what the name's definition fails positively to include." He called such habits of mind "vicious intellectualism," and neatly described the limits of social discourse: "Individuality outruns all classification, yet we insist on classifying every one we meet under some general head." These heads "usually suggest prejudicial associations to some hearer or other," after which battle lines are drawn. "The life of philosophy," James said, "largely consists of resentments at the classing, and complaints of being misunderstood."[35]

James himself seemed instinctively to watch his own language. Coming upon large numbers of blacks for the first time on his trip to Brazil with the Agassizes, for example, he reported the experience to his parents in a way that called Americans' wearied understandings into question. (The year was 1865.) "The town 'realizes' my idea of an African town in its architecture and its effect," he said. There was a visual fit, but (his syntax faltering) "almost everyone is a negro or a negress, which words I perceive we don't know the meaning of with us." Twenty years later, he was just as hesitant to make pronouncements about what all of his contemporaries were calling "race." Touring an industrial school in Florida, he was struck all but speechless by the singing. He later said that what was foremost on his mind as he addressed the students was "that great human fact with nothing but an interrogation Point—?—ahead of it. *That* is the most *real* impression I've got from this trip so far."[36] He knew the names, and knew how easy it would be to dwell on what Shaler called "certain musical powers," but he knew too how much the names and the stereotype failed to include—so a "?" would have to do.*

The only one of James' colleagues whose thinking about "race" matched James' was Josiah Royce. Temperamentally, Royce was much more of an outsider. Being from California—the first man born in that state, according to student legend—[37] where he witnessed rampant prejudice against the Chinese, he was the more sympathetic to those who dwelt on the periphery. In the ideal society that he argued for in his writings, there would be no place for one group's feeling of superiority over another. Such feelings ran counter to his

* Or he might turn a stereotype on its head, speaking of a black servant Alice had brought up from South Carolina as "superior in intelligence industry ability and conscience to all the yankees of the region put together," and concluding, " 'Shiftlessness' seems now a days to be the great New Hampshire characteristic." *Correspondence*, II, 89.

idea of "loyalty to loyalty," a point he made clear in the speech "Race Questions and Prejudices," which he delivered before the Chicago Ethical Society in 1905. Running through his lecture are warnings about how little we know about "the true psychological and moral meaning of race-differences," and about how much prevents our learning more. Something was wrong, he pointed out, when all our theories supported our thinking that "we ourselves are the salt of the earth." Modern civilization had brought benefits (especially as administered by the English, Royce thought), but it had also brought "new mental burdens, such as our increasing percentage of insanity in recent times." One thing was certain: "Our so-called race-problems are merely the problems caused by our antipathies," and, as James had pointed out, those problems arise in the process of our naming. Royce's speech predates *The Pluralistic Universe* by a few years, but rather than raising any question of influence, it is a clear example of the closeness of the thinking of these two friends. Either could have summed up the insidious workings of prejudice the way Royce did: "Hence the antipathy, once by chance aroused, but then named, imitated, insisted upon, becomes to its victims a sort of sacred revelation of truth . . . merely because it has won a name and a social standing."[38]

But Royce ended there, admitting he had been speaking mostly about "human illusions," little about "human justice." By sharp contrast, on such occasions, James often went on to protest against men's brutish behavior towards other peoples—behavior sanctioned by their loose talk. His efforts as vice-president of the Anti-Imperialist League are the best known, but he opposed not only the Spanish-American War and America's invasion of the Philippines but its intrusion into the border dispute between Britain and Venezuela in 1895 as well. He also criticized England for its treatment of the Boers in South Africa, and although inclined toward pacificism, he yielded "before the presence of deeper animal instincts" during the Russo-Japanese War and allowed himself to be decidedly "pro-Jap." The issue, he wrote Pauline Goldmark, was "unquestionably 'Shall all races succumb to the white race?' "; the answer was no, not just yet anyway.[39] Watching nations jostle and maneuver for position in the world during this period, James said that "the biggest indictment 'of our boasted civilization' " was England's "Russophobia." He astutely traced "the Armenian massacres" to it, pointing out to his brother Henry, "It *requires* England I say nothing of the other powers to maintain the Turks at that business."[40]

James could not share Santayana's jaundiced view that America's invasion of Cuba, or the presence of its fleet in Manila Bay, were just inspiring proof that she was showing signs of growing up. ("William James had not lost his country," Santayana later wrote, "his country was in good health and just reaching the age of puberty.")[41] On the other hand, as has often been suggested, James might have noted comparable moves that his own country had taken against peoples in its efforts to expand its borders.[42] But he was surveying world politics, and though he may have been relatively shortsighted, and his protests relatively weak, compared to those who prevailed he still seems heroic.

Given his thinking on language and experience, it would follow that in order to prepare people for war, you must first abstract them from their observable, individual existence. (In a similar vein, thinking of the damage done to individuality by names, Stein would ask if they were good for anything but cashing checks or calling roll.)[43] Having succeeded in categorizing people, you then contrasted or opposed them to other types, your type obviously having been defined as superior to theirs. In the mid-1890s, the Cubans were what have been subsequently and often called "freedom fighters," and American public opinion supported them. The Spanish were their oppressors. Gradually, and then—with the sinking of the *Maine* in Havana harbor in February of 1898—irrevocably, Spain became America's enemy. In that theater, but more explicitly in the Venezuelan border dispute, the programming was facilitated and made to seem the more authoritative by America's having declared in the Monroe Doctrine that it was its right to define and protect its own interests in the Western Hemisphere. The hemispheric leap to the Philippines a few months later was not covered by the doctrine. Nor, when President McKinley ordered it, was American public opinion inclined to defend the rights of the Filipinos to govern themselves. Quite the contrary. Having commandeered Manila Bay, we refused to recognize the claims of the government of Emilio Aguinaldo—who then became "Little Brown Brother" and the like in the press—and when he and his forces rebelled, we put them down by force. "Hostile Natives Whipped," the headline of the *New York Times* read on February 6, 1899.

These imperialistic moves showed manhood at its worst. Over the years, James had spoken on behalf of those Harvard men who would go out into the practical world and, given their intelligence and their hardiness, take the lead. We may recall his characterization (in 1891) of those "excellent fellows" who would benefit from the "three-year course," those men who "need contact with the fighting side of life, with the world in which men and women earn their bread." All through these years, James acknowledged and, in his own way, experienced the thrill and virtues of the sporting life. At the beginning of the Spanish-American War, in a letter to his friend Theodore Flournoy, he extended his appreciation to include what "great generals and rulers and aristocracies" had wrought. Hadn't the spirit of such men's lives, he asked, "always been the spirit of sport carried to its supreme expression?" Though he admitted that civilization might be defined as the ability to "resist the mere excitement of sport," he lunged forward anyway: "But *excitement!*" he exclaimed. "Shall we not worship excitement? And after all, what is life for, except for opportunities of excitement?!"[44]

But six months later, after he had sorted out what he called "the Philippine Tangle," James realized that the breadwinning and the fighting had gone too far. For all the talk of "raising and educating inferior races," there was nothing honorable about America's motives; we were in the Philippines for the adventure of it, "the uplift of mere *excitement*" only. What we were after, he said, was "mastery and mere success." James has been faulted for adhering so closely to a nineteenth-century ideal of individuality as to fail to take sufficient account of the economic forces that were at work, but he knew well enough that material fortunes were at stake in the Philippines. He knew that the growth of the "great Yankee business concern" was not to be impeded, and he likened the treatment of Aguinaldo to "the infernal adroitness of the great department store, which has reached perfect expertness in the art of killing silently and with no public squealing or commotion the neighboring small concern." He realized too that men who stood for "reflection" were in a rather odd position "when they fan the flames of such excitements by lending . . . high sounding words to decorate the business withal."[45] Having none of such business himself, and disheartened by the jingoistic atmosphere that prevailed even around Harvard, he gave this succinct and magisterial command to his students: "Don't yelp with the pack!"[46]

There may have been some relief mixed with the dismay we hear in his observation that American imperialism showed "that there is no danger of mankind, however civilized, ever growing emasculated with senility,"[47] but he knew that too much of the tonic was poisonous. As he had almost laconically observed at the unveiling of the Robert Gould Shaw memorial two years before, "War has been much praised and celebrated among us of late as a school of manly virtue; but it is easy to exaggerate upon this point."[48] He watched "nascent dogma" turn into the "hardened theory like [Cleveland's secretary of state] Olney's unspeakable rot" during the Venezuelan affair.[49] In America's Philippine policy, he saw the opposite of everything he believed in. Abstraction had replaced concreteness, the general the individual. Men had willfully narrowed and hardened themselves and crushed others in their thinking and in their language.

In response, his own words took on the more individual life. Fueled by righteous indignation, in one of the several letters that he wrote the *Boston Evening Transcript* protesting America's involvement in the Philippines, he spoke of "the cold pot-grease of President McKinley's cant" that he found in a speech McKinley delivered in Boston—"surely as shamefully evasive a speech, considering the right of the public to know definite facts, as can often have fallen even from a professional politician's lips"—and he went on to say of politicians in general:

The worst of our imperialists is that they do not themselves know where sincerity ends and insincerity begins. Their state of consciousness is so new, so mixed of primitively human passions and in political circles, of calculations that are anything but primitively human; so at variance, moreover, with their former mental habits; and so empty of definite data and contents; that they face various ways at once, and their portraits should be taken with a squint. One reads the President's speech with a strange feeling— as if the very words were squinting on the page.

In another he spoke of "our delicious phraseology" about making the Filipinos " 'fit,' " whereas we were in fact killing them in what he called a "stark-naked abstract" operation.[50]

The worst was the "newspeak" of the press. "Our yellow journals have abundant time in which to raise new monuments of capitals to the victories of Old Glory," he wrote the *Transcript*—a proposition that was true of none more than those journals that were under the control of another of his former students, William Randolph Hearst. Hearst was as much proof as he needed of the point that he made in "The True Harvard" that "there is not a public abuse for which some Harvard advocate may not be found." Hearst's time at Harvard had been cut short by his expulsion for having sent chamber pots to his professors (including James) with their photographs inside,[51] but he was still a Harvard man and he must have been among those whom James had in mind when he spoke bitterly in that speech of "Harvard men [who] defend our treatment of our Filipino allies as a masterpiece of policy and morals." (The more reason to honor the lonely thinkers, "our undisciplinables," on that occasion.) Distraught over his organization's failure to affect policy, that same year (1903) he recommended that the Anti-Imperialist League itself resort to phrase-mongering. "We must individually do all we can to circulate two phrases, so that the public ear becomes inured—'Independence for the Philippine Islands,' and 'Treat the Filipinos like the Cubans,' " he recommended. "Constant dropping wears the marble. Phrases repeated have a way of turning into facts."[52]

But his own anti-imperialism remained forceful and distinctive, nowhere more obviously so than in his exchanges with another student whom he surely had in mind when he spoke of apologists for our treatment of the Filipinos— Theodore Roosevelt. Their first encounter occurred after Roosevelt (then president of the Board of New York Police Commissioners) wrote a letter to the *Harvard Crimson* in which he called those who opposed the Cleveland administration's Venezuelan policy "traitors" and argued that it was their "stock-jobbing timidity," their "colonial dependence on England," and not the administration's readiness to intervene that was likely to lead to war. James responded in the same pages with a dignified plea that Harvard continue to foster clear and active thinking:

May I express a hope that in this University, if no where else on the continent, we shall be patriotic enough *not* to remain passive whilst the destinies of our country are being settled by surprise. . . . Let us refuse to be bound over night by proclamation, or hypnotized by sacramental phrases through the day.

The true citizen would be like the philosopher—careful with his language. "Let us consult our reason as to what is best," he concluded, "and then exert ourselves as citizens with all our might."[53]

Roosevelt's complaints about what he perceived to be a cult of "non-virility" in Cambridge became more vociferous and offensive after his return from Cuba and his election to the governorship of New York. And once again James made sure that he was not "allowed to crow all over our national barnyard and hear no equally shrill voice lifted in reply."[54] On April 10, 1899, at the Hamilton Club in Chicago, Roosevelt delivered what is perhaps his most famous speech: "The Strenuous Life." From his long, one-sentence opening paragraph, in which he announced his subject ("I wish to preach, not the doctrine of ignoble ease, but the doctrine of the strenuous life, the life of toil and effort, of labor and strife . . ."), to his final peroration ("Let us therefore boldly face the life of strife, resolute to do our duty well and manfully . . . "), Roosevelt led his auditors in rhetorical calisthenics that were intended to condition them for world leadership. It was either the strenuous life, he said, or the shameful example of China, a nation that had "trained itself to a career of unwarlike and isolated ease" and was therefore "bound, in the end, to go down before other nations which have not lost the manly and adventurous qualities." More specifically, and at some length, Roosevelt trumpeted the virtues of war with Spain, the necessity of meeting "the responsibilities that confront us in Hawaii, Cuba, Porto Rico, and the Philippines," and the wisdom of strengthening America's armed forces. He blamed the anti-imperialists for the bloodshed that had already occurred. It was they who had "deliberately invited a savage people to plunge into a war fraught with sure disaster for them," they for whom "our brave men who follow the flag must pay with their blood" (4,200 dead and 2,800 wounded in the Philippines). The "they" that Roosevelt had in mind might well have been the eighty-six members of the Harvard faculty who had just the week before declared their opposition to the war, but for this occasion Roosevelt's "they" were, more sweepingly, just babbling, spoiled children whom he could deride. "Prattlers who sit at home in peace" with their "silly, mock humanitarianism," he called them.[55]

In his response, published five days later in the *Boston Evening Transcript,* James was not shrill at all. Having had Roosevelt in his comparative anatomy and physiology class over twenty years before, and having already learned that there was nothing to be gained by entering into an argument with him at his level—James "settling back in his chair, in a broad grin . . . and waiting for T. R. to finish," is how a classmate described James' response to him[56]—James dressed Roosevelt down for the mediocre student that he was, and had been in his course. There was no purchase on reality in his language: "Of all the naked abstractions that ever applied to human affairs, the outpourings of Governor Roosevelt's soul in this speech would seem the very nakedest." There was no reason in his talk: "Not a word of the cause,—one foe is as good as another, for aught he tells us. . . . He swamps everything together in one flood of abstract bellicose emotion." In fact, his days as a student had not even begun: "Although in middle life," James wrote, "and in a situation of responsibility concrete enough, he is still mentally in the *Sturm und Drang* period of early adolescence."

James' was itself a stirring performance, fueled perhaps by memories of having already missed one war, but more obviously inspired by the challenge to his own manhood. Even the prattlers with their "silly mock humanitarianism," he said, "must feel that it would be ignominious to leave him in uncontradicted possession of the field." He would do battle with the man; he would turn Roosevelt's position on its head. Roosevelt had spoken about human affairs

from the sole point of view of the organic excitement and difficulty they may bring, gushes over war as the ideal condition of human society, for the manly strenuousness which it involves, and treats peace as a condition of blubberlike and swollen ignobility, fit only for huckstering weaklings, dwelling in gray twilight and heedless of the higher life.

But from James' point of view, it took more strength and courage to stand up for peace:

To enslave a weak but heroic people, or to brazen out a blunder, is a good enough cause, it appears, for Colonel Roosevelt. To us Massachusetts anti-imperialists, who have fought in better causes, it is not quite good enough.

The wars went on, of course, but in the very elevation and sternness of his tone, James took the argument to another level, and there he clearly won.

Behind James' ardor also lay the fact that he himself had taken stances like Roosevelt's many times. He would not allow himself to gush over the strenuous life, but in scores of ways and on scores of occasions, he had himself represented it. He himself had spoken of a good fight, of war, of shipwreck, and the like, as antidotes to a life of sybaritic ease. In his climactic essay "The Moral Equivalent of War," he even enlisted Roosevelt in his defense of militarism. "Militarism is the great preserver of our ideals of hardihood, and human life with no use for hardihood would be contemptible," he wrote.

There was "a type of military character which every one feels that the race should never cease to breed." Such characters ought to be kept "in stock," James said, if not for use then as "pure pieces of perfection." James had an *equivalent* to war in mind, of course, but the character, the temperament, that he was describing was a lot like Roosevelt's; and the man he set up for the sake of contrast was in fact the type of man Roosevelt had often scorned. We keep these characters in stock, James said, "so that Roosevelt's weaklings and mollycoddles may not end by making everything else disappear from the face of nature."[57]

James was a man of his class—a gentleman—and, like the typical gentleman of his day, he made manhood a goal in life. For decades, Harvard had nurtured and encouraged its students to work toward that goal, and in Harvard's eyes, James had as nearly approached it as any other man. But there were differences—and they made all the difference. Roosevelt's "moral fibre" was just "too irredeemably coarse," James wrote Norton in 1902.[58] What was more to the point, in displaying his own manliness, Roosevelt blinded himself to the lives of other human beings. He was like all the imperialists, James said in his letter to the *Transcript,* talking about "manly strenuousness" and mouthing abstract phrases about the Filipinos' being "unfit to govern themselves"—and all the while not even acknowledging their existence, not seeing them "face to face as a concrete reality." As he strives toward manhood, a man's vision is bound to be limited, but no one could ever have said that James' vision was as limited as that.

"After All Who Are Men?": W. E. B. Du Bois

Many of the men who represented Harvard's dominant culture at the end of the nineteenth century sought to exclude "the new races"; many others cautiously welcomed them. A few tried sympathetically to understand groups and individuals from backgrounds that differed from theirs. No one better represented what such an "outsider" might be thinking than W. E. B. Du Bois, of the class of 1890.

Du Bois often addressed questions about manhood—and questions about manhood at Harvard, in particular—and he addressed them from a perspective different from that of any of the men we have so far considered in this study. His perspective was necessarily different, for he was a man of African-American descent or, as he put it on his application to the Slater Fund for the Education of Negroes, "about one half or more Negro, and the rest French and Dutch."[1] And it was inevitable that he would ask such questions. Either he would ask them, or he would have to countenance some version of the idea that a Negro was three-fifths of a man, and one or another racial theory that placed the likes of him at the bottom of one of those lists of races that were headed by the Anglo-Saxons—which is unimaginable.

Du Bois worked with the materials of contemporary debates about race and transformed them for his own purposes. He also knew what his contemporaries were thinking about manhood, but knew too that he could not do justice to himself or others with African ancestry if he accepted the meanings that they attached to it. "I Am Resolved," he titled a manifesto that he wrote for the *Crisis* in January 1912. He started by declaring, "I am resolved *in this New Year to play the man—to stand straight, look the world squarely in the eye, and walk to my work with no shuffle or slouch,*" and went on, "I am resolved *to be satisfied with no treatment which ignores my manhood and my right to be counted as one among men.*"[2] It was, and it would continue to be, a common theme among African-Americans. In the words of Richard T. Greener, the first man of African descent to graduate from Harvard (in 1870), the Negro "had early learned the value of his own manhood [and] was willing to fight for it."[3] Over the years, in what Du Bois forced his readers to see, he retained about half of what James and others had meant by the idea of manhood.

Manhood was the goal toward which Du Bois strove in much of his writing. For example, in the section of his conclusion to *The Philadelphia Negro* (1899) that he titled "The Meaning of All This," he added to the educational, economic, and social problems that he addressed what he called "that question of questions: after all who are Men?"[4] In his article "Strivings of the Negro People," which appeared in the *Atlantic* in 1897 and then (as "Of Our Spiritual Strivings") became the first chapter of *The Souls of Black Folk* five years later, he characterized the Negro's struggles as a "longing to attain self-conscious manhood." The Negro's was, as he famously put it, a "double-consciousness." He was blessed and cursed with the gift of "second-sight," seeing himself through the eyes of the "American world," considering himself to be a man who was both part of that world and a Negro too:

two souls, two thoughts, two unreconciled strivings; two warring ideals in one dark body, whose dogged strength alone keeps it from being torn asunder.

The history of the American Negro is the history of this strife—this longing to attain self-conscious manhood, to merge his double self into a better and truer self.[5]

But it would be foolhardy to try at this juncture to rehearse the many steps Du Bois took in order to arrive at definitions of that self and its relations to its environment—especially foolhardy given the way he worked through biological to broader historical and social definitions of race. Moreover, upon arrival we would have a definition of manhood that would be so all-encompassing as to be meaningless.

Relevant here (and in fact helpful to an understanding of these later theories and later texts) are his first speculations and pronouncements as a student at Harvard about American men. Gifted with "second sight," Du Bois was even then aware of how he was viewed and also of what most of his classmates were learning insofar as they were being educated into manhood.

Although he had wanted to go straight to Harvard from the high school in Great Barrington in 1884, Du Bois did not arrive until four years later—after he had graduated from Fisk University. Admitted as a junior, he earned his B.A. from Harvard in 1890, took an M.A. the next year, and then, after two years' study abroad, returned to Harvard for his Ph.D. He received it in 1895. He was the first black man to earn a doctorate from Harvard.

Du Bois' assessments of his Harvard years shifted as he repositioned himself in later life—moving from "the Grateful Outsider" to "the Imperial Self," as David Levering Lewis puts it. At no time did he feel at home there. He was probably the sixth African-American to attend Harvard College since Greener. (The first to graduate from Radcliffe would do so in 1898.) He lived in a rented room in the house of a black woman in Cambridge, took his meals first in the commons in Memorial Hall and later in the nonexclusive Foxcroft Club. The Glee Club rejected him his first year, and though he would have liked to write for the *Monthly,* he assumed that its staff too would turn down his efforts. Socially, he occasionally saw a few men who would later make their mark in the world of letters—Hutchins and Norman Hapgood, Robert Herrick, Robert Morss Lovett—but given his economic and social situation—not to speak of his temperament—he was not one to fraternize. He could not follow the advice or the example of the gregarious and popular Monroe Trotter, who had warned him, "Colored students must not herd together, just because they were colored." The center of such social life as he had was the small, elite African-American community of Boston that gathered in the Charles Street home of Mrs. Josephine St. Pierre Ruffin, a founder of the National Association of Negro Women, and her husband, Judge George Lewis Ruffin, the first black graduate of the Harvard Law School. As a student, Du Bois was—in his Byronic summation—"in Harvard but not of it."[6]

Du Bois' promise was recognized by many of the men we have focused on, and yet even as he appreciated their attention and their tutelage, he was at the same time aware of the racial prejudices of many of them. It was Albert Bushnell Hart, he said, who drew him away "from the lovely but sterile land of philosophic speculation to the social sciences," where he could gather and interpret facts that would give authority to his "program for the Negro."[7] Hart guided his research, supported his work in Germany, and helped usher his doctoral thesis, titled *The Suppression of the African Slave-Trade to the United States of America, 1638–1870,* into print as the first volume of the Harvard Historical Monograph series in 1896. While Du Bois understandably thought of himself as one of Hart's favorite pupils, at some point his growing pride in his racial identity and Hart's racism had to cross. By 1905, in response to a note in which Hart told Du Bois he deplored what he took to be widely held misconceptions regarding a rift between Du Bois and Booker T. Washington, Du Bois made his differences with Hart clear: those people were right, he wrote back; "the people who think that I am one of those who oppose many of his ideas are perfectly correct. . . . [H]is platform has done the race infinite harm and I'm working against it with all my might."[8] Recording the fact that Nathaniel Shaler expelled from his geology class a Southerner who refused to sit next to him, he said nothing about Shaler's assessment in "The Problem of the African," versions of which had already appeared in the *Atlantic* before Du Bois's arrival at Harvard. Of his instructors in English 12 (Barrett Wendell's course), he said that they did not understand "the Negro problem," and concentrated only on his technical improvement. It being inconceivable to him that they had the slightest understanding of "the problem of the color line," he was simply and extremely pleased when Wendell read his theme "Something about Me" aloud in class. In it, Du Bois spoke guardedly of "a great bitterness" that he experienced in his youth, one that "kindled a great ambition" (presumably a reference to the exchange of visiting cards that he would tell about in the second paragraph of *The Souls of Black Folk*), but it was probably only Du Bois' determination to take full advantage of his course that caught Wendell's attention. "I believe, foolishly perhaps but sincerely, that I have something to say to the world and I have taken English twelve in order to say it well," is how "Something about Me" ended.[9]

It is tempting to try to establish a strong Jamesian influence on Du Bois. The two might seem conjoined in their use of the idea of the "double-consciousness," a phrase that had already made its appearance in the psychological literature and in James' *Psychology,* before Du Bois used it. Going back still further, however, we find it in Emerson, but nowhere does it take anything like the form given it in Du Bois' writing.[10] Even in the "pragmatic" approach to social problems that Du Bois can be said to have learned from James, there are significant differences. Du Bois was not so willing as his teacher to live tentatively "under the sword of the future," as Du Bois' notes quoted James as saying in a lecture. The pull towards the idealistic philosophies of Kant and Hegel, as represented by Santayana and Royce, was finally stronger, as he was more intent than James upon discovering immutable truth.[11] James gave Du Bois an A minus in the version of Philosophy 4 (Palmer's course in ethics) that he taught while Palmer was on leave, and a B plus in "Psychology and Logic"; and then he implicitly led him away from philosophy altogether by warning him about the near impossibility of earning a living in the field. Whether or not he was thinking of Du Bois' ancestry as well as his record when he warned Du Bois, we cannot say, but it is not hard to imagine that for all of James'

kindnesses, Du Bois was more at ease reading Kant's *Critique of Pure Reason* with Santayana in Santayana's quarters—with another, more obvious outsider—than he was studying under the older and more august William James.*
He knew Royce and Royce's interpretations of Hegel mostly through his reading, his only experience of him as a teacher being in English C, a required course in forensics.[12]

Du Bois never refers to James in the process of interpreting the relations of men and women at Harvard, and, in his concomitant construction of the ideal Harvard man, he was much more flexible than James, or almost anyone else at Harvard in the nineties. In the themes he wrote for English 12, he is downright playful. For example, as would be expected of an up-and-coming man at Harvard, Du Bois attended to his physical education, assuring Rutherford B. Hayes, then chairman of the Slater Fund, that he was "in good physical condition as may be ascertained by the records of the Harvard gymnasium."[13] But he kept Harvard's enthusiasm over the health and activities of men's bodies in perspective. The month before he wrote Hayes, he submitted a paper to Wendell in which he described his reaction to the many unhealthy people he saw around him. "I frequent the 'Gym' more often," he said, "eat like a confirmed dyspeptic, walk untold distances every time I get a chance, and go through an Indian war-dance before going to bed and upon arising."[14] If that seems a little heavy-handed, in another (untitled) theme on what he found estimable in a man, he is astonishingly agile. He tells of being struck by someone who seemed exceptionally dignified, someone in whose face he read an air of self-respect, a consciousness of self-worth, and of being even more impressed by this person's unaffected manner in the company of others. But as it turns out, he is not a "he" at all. "I am really quite interest [*sic*] in him," Du Bois concluded. "He is a girl."

The one English 12 theme that has attracted attention is ostensibly (and without trickery) about "the American girl." It is usually taken to be an angry diatribe against her, "its harshness,—even cruelty," Du Bois' editor remarks, being "most unusual in his writings."[15] Angry it is. "When I wish to meet the American Hog in its native simplicity," DuBois begins,

when I wish to realize the world-pervading presence of the Fool; when I wish to be reminded that whatever rights some have I have none; when I wish, by a course of systematic vulgarity, to be made to forget whatever little courtesy I have, when I wish to be doubly sure that the man lied who asserted that men's dead selves would furnish steps enough for a rise in the world: when I wish any of these things I seek the company of the American girl.

---

*Rollo Walter Brown suggests the connection in a causal remark about people's response to Santayana's *Persons and Places:* "Beneath the exquisiteness of detail in Santayana's technique they felt a lack of whiteness that they could not believe was in accord with greatness of spirit." *Harvard Yard in the Golden Age,* p. 66.

Discourteous it is. Even as he picks up on contemporary debates over whether blacks or women or both deserve the vote ("whatever rights some have I have none"), and even as he speaks of man's doubleness of being (his soul rising from its earthly bonds), Du Bois' attack on this hog seems vicious. In fact, in a kind of reversal of his admiration for the man who proved to be a girl, Du Bois is here attacking this girl for being only a girl—which is to say, for not being manly enough. "The American Girl" points us not to Du Bois' misogyny but to his feminism.

His fury is directed not at women but rather at a culture that infantilizes them by insisting that they act out a role deemed to be feminine. In the lengthy portrait of the American girl that follows, Du Bois describes her as "more shrewd than intelligent, arrogant than dignified, silly than pleasant, and pretty than beautiful." What he reveals as he moves further behind her appearance is her resentment, her bitterness, over other women's efforts to fight for what she has allowed herself to lose: "Finally she has a more or less definite idea of certain rights which she has lost and with her usual consistency taboos her sisters who have taken the rational method of demanding them, because they are 'mannish, you know.'" That is the worst: mannishness . "At the very pinnacle of this girl's character," Du Bois goes on to say, "stands a horror of being "mannish,' which generally means a constitutional aversion to the use of commonsense." What Du Bois is finally protesting against is the extreme genderization of men and women—the simple understanding of what it is to be a man or a woman—that made it shocking for a woman to be wholly self-possessed or sensible enough to insist on her rights. If that made her mannish, so be it. As for a man's girlishness, Du Bois might countenance that idea too. He was no admirer of men who were only men.

What he recommended in the conclusion of "The American Girl" was that women too become citizens of the world:"When my lady wishes to cultivate her brains instead of her nose, first: Emancipate herself from the rule of the Ribbon. Secondly, get an education on something else beside the piano; and lastly, go to work." There is a direct line connecting this theme for English 12 to Du Bois' resounding defense in "Woman Suffrage" in 1915 and then to his lament in "The Damnation of Women" in *Darkwater* in 1920. "The soul longest in slavery and still in the most disgusting and indefensible slavery is the soul of womanhood," he wrote in 1915 essay, and in 1920 he added that if women were to remain enslaved, if they were to continue to be only American girls, men would suffer too. They would remain beasts: "The present mincing horror at free womanhood must pass if we are ever to be rid of the bestiality of free manhood," he said.[16] For decades, the argument had been that men's brutishness would be curbed or tamed by the eternal feminine. Du Bois knew better.

Commenting on "The American Girl," Wendell's assistant Jefferson B. Fletcher wrote, "The taste of this is questionable," and advised that "rudeness rarely pays." The paper was, he added, "rudely truculent." Wendell concurred. He had admired the verve of "Something about Me," but now, six months later, he recoiled from the uses to which Du Bois had put that verve in "The American Girl." "Well criticized," he said of his assistant's work. "Such truculence as yours is thoroughly injudicious. Nothing could more certainly induce an average reader to disagree." He was right, of course. The average reader, certainly the average reader Wendell and Fletcher had in mind, would not have countenanced this assault on what was supposedly American womanhood. Too much was at stake, not the least of which was their conception of American manhood.

When he addressed *that* subject directly, Du Bois did so on a more momentous occasion and did so more diplomatically. The occasion was commencement day, June 25, 1890. The fact that Du Bois gave one of the six orations that day—one recounted how the elective system had caused an increase in admissions applications from the West, another was on what Harvard owed the country, and yet another was a scientific paper—suggests that though he himself knew few men at Harvard, many of them recognized his merit and felt his presence. He had won two prizes for oratory. When he ascended the platform of Sanders Theater in Memorial Hall and bowed to the seated dignitaries, "the applause burst out heartily," the *Nation* reported, "as if in recognition of the strange significance of his appearance there." He chose as his subject the idea of manhood, the idea as it was represented by a most unlikely figure and also, implicitly, the idea as he saw it being nurtured at Harvard. He confronted the issue head-on—head-on, but at the same time with what the *Nation* nicely described as "absolute good taste, great moderation, and almost contemptuous fairness."[17]

The title of his speech was "Jefferson Davis as a Representative of Civilization."[18] For what the *Nation* called "a slender, intellectual-looking mulatto" to be talking on the president of the Confederacy in the hall that had been built less than twenty years before in honor of Harvard graduates who had died to preserve the Union was good theater indeed. There had to be irony somewhere, but Du Bois would not muster it in any simple way. He would keep his audience in doubt as to whether or not there was contempt in what he said. Ever preparing himself to be the Moses of his people, he admired great men; he had already spoken in praise of Bismarck at his Fisk commencement. As he began his speech, he seemed to elevate the members of his audience above the terrible strife just past and have them honor a worthy foe. For a minute or so—the whole speech would take about seven—he built Davis up as "a typical Teutonic hero," the embodiment of "the Strong Man," an "Anglo-

Saxon" whose life would have "graced a medieval romance." But it could not last. "A soldier and a lover, a statesman and a ruler; passionate, ambitious and indomitable; bold reckless guardian of a people's All—judged by the whole standard of Teutonic civilization," Du Bois said, "there is something noble in the figure of Jefferson Davis." "Something"—only "something"? This alone might have prepared some in the audience for the deflation of Davis in the final clause of his introductory paragraph. If, by the standard of Teutonic civilization, Davis was somewhat noble, then, "judged by every canon of human justice, there is something fundamentally incomplete about that standard."

Du Bois' talk was not about Jefferson Davis (it tells us almost nothing about him) but about what he stood for: the Teutonic Hero, the Strong Man, the Strong Nation, Civilization as Du Bois' audience conceived of it. Davis' was the Rod of Empire too. The "Spanish war interludes and Philippine matinees" (as he called them in *The Souls of Black Folk*)[19] were still to come, but "the logic of even modern history" as represented by Davis, or what Du Bois called "individualism coupled with the rule of might," already held sway in 1890. Though "a naturally brave and generous man," Jefferson Davis was, in Du Bois' words,

now advancing civilization by murdering Indians, now hero of a national disgrace called by courtesy [a favorite word with Du Bois], the Mexican War, and finally, as the crowning absurdity, the peculiar champion of a people fighting to be free in order that another people should not be free.

Davis was all this—from the Strong Man to the Rod of Empire—and then, daringly, Du Bois asked his audience to imagine that he was also inextricably connected to social life at Harvard. He did so by moving from one to the other, from "the logic even of modern history" in one clause to "the cool logic of the Club" in the next. While others spoke of Harvard athletics as preparation for world conquest and leadership, Du Bois pointed to the ethos created by the clubs at Harvard. He was closer to the truth: Harvard men were much more likely to recognize the rights of blacks on their teams and on playing fields than in clubs; they were much better prepared by their social bonding to assume their superiority over others than they were by athletic contests in which the best men—whoever they were—usually won.

Summing up "the type of civilization which Jefferson Davis represented," Du Bois said it was "a field for stalwart manhood and heroic character," only once again to whip out the supports, adding that it was a field "at the same time for moral obtuseness and refined brutality." What Du Bois was leading up to, and what prevented his audience from taking umbrage at what he had suggested about them so far, was a seemingly humble offer: what their hero lacked, he promised them, the Negro would provide. There was another kind of man, representing another kind of civilization, who would be "the check and complement of the Teutonic Strong Man." Echoing something he might have heard from James, he asserted, " 'To no one type of mind is it given to discern the totality of Truth.' " In a theme titled "Unrepresentative Men," which he wrote for English 12, Du Bois called this figure the Forgotten Man. (It was also, ironically, the title of a famous essay by America's strongest apologist for Social Darwinism, William Graham Sumner.) This man was not one of those "jolly devil-may-care boys who are engaged in getting rid of their fathers' surplus cash and cutting recitations," he wrote. In fact, his kind outnumbered theirs, but it was his kind that was "forgotten," theirs that set the tone at Harvard. In his speech, this "Forgotten Man" could not have been less threateningly introduced: "Not as the muscular warrior came the Negro," Du Bois said, "but as the cringing slave." It also helped that Du Bois introduced this new, or forgotten, man as the Submissive Man, and that he characterized the civilization he represented as "an effete civilization."

There were hints in all this of a more militant Du Bois to come. He spoke, for example, of "the race which by its very presence must play a part in the world of tomorrow," but there would be no outright dismissal of the Teutonic Man. Nor would he ever entirely abandon this seemingly feminine man. In "The Conservation of the Races," Du Bois would say he was "destined to soften the whiteness of the Teutonic"; and in a more prominent example, the conclusion of the first chapter of *The Souls of Black Folk,* he is made integral to the fulfillment of "the greater ideals of the American Republic."[20] Facing the men of Harvard and their parents, Du Bois presented an accommodating and an inclusive figure of a man, a more complexly and interestingly constructed being than the manly idol that had been routinely held up before them during their years as undergraduates.

Three years later, on his twenty-fifth birthday, Du Bois looked back at this commencement when, he said that "the Harvard applause awoke echoes in the world."[21] The *Nation* told a different story. It reported that Du Bois had "dwelt largely upon Davis' intellectual strength, personal courage, and private integrity," and then contrasted his type to the "patient, trustful, submissive African" type that "the world would some day honor." Having thereby thoroughly domesticated Du Bois' speech, the reporter concluded, "For the moment the audience showed itself ready to honor this type as displayed in the orator." Nothing beyond the moment, nothing upsetting about his performance, nothing for the world to hear.

While Harvard could honor a "patient, trustful, submissive African" type and assume that he was not really contemptuous of Teutonic men, Harvard could nonetheless be much more confident and enthusiastic when it honored Booker T. Washington. He was their obvious choice from among men of his

race. Of course he was older, more established, "certainly the most distinguished Southerner since Jefferson Davis," Du Bois would say in *The Souls of
Black Folk,* an irony that perhaps not everyone detected. He was "the one with
the largest personal following."[22] But all knew what Washington stood for—
or thought they knew—and he knew Harvard. He had taken a five-week
course on physical fitness at Harvard under Dudley Sargent in the summer of
1887. ("I think I would now be a more useful man if I had had time for
sports," he would later say.)[23] In 1896, he received an honorary M.A., the first
black man to receive any honorary degree from any New England university.
In his recounting of the occasion in *Up from Slavery* (1901), he said that the
letter from President Eliot informing him of Harvard's intentions was "the
greatest surprise that ever came to me."[24] At the Memorial Hall dinner afterwards, he charmed those who were assembled in his honor when he said at the
beginning of his acceptance speech that he felt like "a huckleberry in a bowl of
milk."[25] The next year, he and William James gave the principal orations at the
unveiling of St. Gaudens' monument to Robert Gould Shaw. When *Up from
Slavery* came out, Barrett Wendell was unambivalent in his praise of its "simple,
manly distinctiveness."[26] During this period, it was Harvard's applause for
Washington that echoed around the world.

After graduating from Harvard, Du Bois also courted Washington. He
applied to him for a job at Tuskegee Institute in 1894; he wrote to congratulate
him on his Atlanta Exposition speech the next year, and soon thereafter gave
him the idea for his National Negro Business League. But with the publication
of "Of Booker T. Washington and Others" as the third chapter of *The Souls of
Black Folk,* their differences were unmistakable. So too were changes that Du
Bois had undergone since he had delivered the commencement speech in
1890. Washington had given "submission" a terrible name. Du Bois repeated
the word again and again, indicating each time that in Washington's use of it,
the word, the quality of being, was no longer compatible with strength: "Mr.
Washington's counsels of submission overlooked certain elements of true
manhood"; "Mr. Washington represents in Negro thought the old attitude
of adjustment and submission. . . . Mr. Washington's programme practically
accepts the alleged inferiority of the Negro races," and he "counsels a silent
submission to civic inferiority such as is bound to sap the manhood of any race
in the long run."[27]

Although he had appreciated Harvard's faculty and its "broader atmosphere for approaching truth," Du Bois went there, he later grandly said, "to
enlarge [his] grasp of the meaning of the universe."[28] He was more directly
engaged than that at the time, but he knew from the start that he was not
wholly accepted. In 1899, writing about Philadelphia's attitude toward the
Negro, he shrewdly noted, "the same contradictions so often apparent in social

phenomena; prejudice and apparent dislike conjoined with widespread and deep sympathy."[29] He had to have sensed "the same contradictions" at Harvard. But he never despaired of men's ability to overlook or transcend the "color line."

At Harvard, he nurtured and strengthened that ability by criticizing the forms of manhood (and womanhood) taking shape all around him. If nothing else, he revealed the Harvard man's certain blindness.

5

Smile When You Carry a Big Stick

Teddy Roosevelt '80 and Dan Wister '82

THE LOUDEST AND MOST INFLUENTIAL VOICE ever to come out of Harvard crowing "manhood" was unquestionably that of Theodore Roosevelt, Class of 1880. His voice was raised and coached at Harvard; afterwards, as it carried all over what William James called "the national barnyard," it echoed and resounded back at Harvard again and again. What Roosevelt had to say about manhood is almost painfully familiar. For our purposes, it is enough to appreciate the fit between it and Harvard, to see how much Roosevelt's talk about manliness meshed with the rhetoric about education and athletics, about class and race and sex, that prevailed at Harvard during these years.[1]

Roosevelt's prodigious energy was already on display when he was an undergraduate. What people remember is his activity—his racing across the Yard to class, his interruptions during lectures, the number of clubs and organizations that he joined—rather than anything distinctive that he actually did. He was an editor of the *Advocate,* for example, but the editor in chief could not remember his ever having attended a meeting, and his three contributions to its pages (all in one issue) were short editorial appeals—one on behalf of the Athletic Association, another proposing a track meet against Yale, and a third exhorting the members of the football team to exercise daily. William Roscoe Thayer, who was a class behind him (and who went on to edit the *Harvard Graduates' Magazine* for over twenty years), thought of him as "a joke . . . active and enthusiastic and that was all."

Roosevelt performed well academically, graduating Phi Beta Kappa, and ranking 21st in a class of 171, but in a thorough review of Roosevelt's academic career, one of his former professors still concluded, "It is obvious that

Roosevelt showed no marked intellectual power nor scholarship in college."[2] Roosevelt had nothing memorable to say about anything that he learned, or about any of the men who taught him. He found James' anatomy course "extremely interesting" at the time, but later confessed to his son that he had coasted after midterm, trusting to "natural smartness to give a specious appearance of familiarity with the subject," and ending up doing badly because of "shortcomings in my finals."[3] His English teacher, A. S. Hill, was the only professor for whom he had a kind word in his *Autobiography,* but when he was an undergraduate he singled Hill out as the one teacher he disliked. His love of nature and of the great outdoors was reflected in the strange and repellent forms of animal life that he (supposedly) kept in his rooms, in the hours spent working at Agassiz's Museum of Comparative Zoology, and in his serving as undergraduate vice-president of the Natural History Society, but he later criticized Harvard for murdering his dreams of a career in science with its emphasis on laboratory work. (Legend had it that—inadvertently or in protest—he once got off a streetcar leaving behind lobsters that were intended for dissection.) It has been suggested that Nathaniel Shaler was the one teacher who really influenced him—"some strong and vital emanation of [his] spirit may have passed into the character of Theodore Roosevelt," as one classmate put it—and indeed, the spirit of that robust outdoor naturalist probably added to his impatience with the classroom. For his teachers' part, James waited him out, Hill embarrassed him by having him read a romantic composition out loud and then criticize it for the class (thus presumably inspiring his dislike), and Shaler confronted him, exclaiming, "Now look here, Roosevelt, let me talk. I'm running this course."

Roosevelt was determined to learn. "No man ever came to Harvard more serious in his purpose to secure there first of all an education," Massachusetts Governor Curtis Guild wrote in 1901, but Roosevelt came with an eye that was always on learning for the sake of something other than learning. In his *Autobiography* he said that he enjoyed Harvard and that Harvard did him good—"but only in general effect, for there was very little in my actual studies which helped me in after life."[4] Guild added that Roosevelt's "personal influence did much to encourage the wholesome notion that a manly man might be serious in purpose in his college days without becoming a prig."[5] Betraying no sign of being a bookworm or a "grind," he was proof to all that you could be a learner and a "manly man." After he graduated, he would take Eliot's and Harvard's ideas about the practical purpose of education to their extremes. He reduced Emerson's American Scholar to a doer. Knowledge had to be put to use, he would argue; the student had to serve.

His ardent pursuit of physical education was further proof of his being "a manly man." His nearsightedness kept him from participating in competitive team sports, but he sparred and rowed (single scull), hunted and climbed mountains, as if he were in constant competition with others. What he remembered from a climb in Maine, for example, was the weight of his pack and the fact that his companions gave up before reaching the top. "An attacker always," Guild said of his fighting style, he "sought to offset his fatally weak point by leading swiftly and heavily himself without waiting for attack."[6] It is the way he protected any kind of weakness. Physically, he felt he had to overcompensate not only for his eyesight but also for the asthma that had afflicted him since he was three or four. One of his best biographers speaks of his mother as a major cause, of asthma as the " 'suppressed cry for the mother'—a cry of rage as well as for help." Thus, as he points out, absence from her, time alone with his father, time devoted to horseback riding and other outdoor activities, was a remedy. But Roosevelt also tried to defeat his asthma with strenuous exercise, first at the gymnasium of Mr. John Wood and then, with Wood's guidance, in one that was set up on the Roosevelts' own premises at Oyster Bay. When he was twelve, a doctor told him that if he did not set about *making* his body, his mind would be held back—"It is hard drudgery to make one's body," he told him, "but I know you will do it." Thereupon Teddy immediately vowed, "I'll make my body."[7]

Harvard itself offered an escape from his mother and thus a relief from his asthma, but once there, Roosevelt continued to drive himself. His workouts at the Hemenway Gymnasium were so strenuous that, just before he graduated, Dudley Sargent warned him of the danger to his heart. After a physical examination, he told Roosevelt that he would have to lead a sedentary life lest he die young, to which Roosevelt of course replied that he would do just the opposite: "If I've got to live the sort of life you have described," he told Sargent, "I don't care how short it is."[8]

It goes without saying, too, that Roosevelt's cultivation of manly strength was accompanied by unquestioned and uncompromised devotion to ideals of physical purity. He deeply regretted the one or two times he drank too much. He never smoked or swore. He taught Sunday school. When his cousin married a French actress, he noted in his diary, "He is a disgrace to the family— the vulgar brute." His father had sent him off to Harvard with instructions that he was to take care of his morals first, his health next, and finally his studies. At Harvard he followed those instructions religiously.

He was an exemplary manly presence at Harvard, and, like the exemplary man whom Eliot and James and others had in mind, he was most assuredly a gentleman. He was a snob, in fact. He was a member of the Art Club, the Rifle Club, the Finance Club (which he helped found), the Glee Club, the Hasty Pudding Club, the O.K., the A.D., the Dickey, the Institute of 1770—and crowning them all—the Porcellian Club. The night he reached that height was one of those rare occasions on which he drank too much. From the best clubs, he moved effortlessly between and among the homes of the Saltonstalls and Shaws and Welds in and around Boston. He knew that social success was to be found among them, not in company with the few New Yorkers who were at Harvard. "On this very account," he said, "I have avoided being very intimate with the New York fellows." He even calculated his academic success in social terms. After the fall term of his senior year, he reported to his sister that he stood nineteenth in his class, and assured her, "Only one gentleman stands ahead of me."

At Harvard, his life was dizzyingly strenuous, but strenuous within the rarefied circles in which he traveled. He lived very well indeed. He had his own suite of rooms in a boarding house on Winthrop Street. The average American family lived for six years on what he spent on clothes and club fees in two. That same family could live for two on what his horse cost him in one. In his senior year, wearing the silk hat that he had his family send up from New York—*"at once"*—wrapped in a lap robe, whip in hand, he drove a small tillbury, or "dog cart," about town. The figure that he cut made its way into a song that a sophomore, Owen (or "Dan") Wister, wrote for a theatrical performance that the Dickey put on:

> The cove who drove
> His doggy Tillbury cart . . .
> Awful tart,
> And awful smart,
> With waxed mustache and hair in curls:
> Brand-new hat,
> Likewise cravat,
> To call upon the dear little girls!

Roosevelt was said to be angry at Wister at the time, but the two soon struck up a friendship that would last a lifetime. It was not the portrait that offended Roosevelt so much as the suggestion that he was still courting girls, for he was in fact engaged to be married to Alice Lee. (But how was he to know? Wister asked. Roosevelt hadn't announced it to the Dickey.)[9] Even in the political world he entered after graduation, he continued to carry himself in such a way as to earn him titles like "his Lordship," "Jane-Dandy," and "Oscar Wilde" in the Democratic press. It was not until his discovery of the West, and the deaths of Alice and of his mother—both occurring, incredibly, on February 14, 1884—that he would begin to shed the elegance and re-present himself in a form that was more easily recognizable as manly.[10]

Dan Wister was right behind Roosevelt, both as an elegant undergraduate and then as a seeker after a Western manner that would help him recover from sufferings *he* endured. He was, like Roosevelt, from a distinguished family—but, like Roosevelt's, his was not a distinguished Boston family. He was from Philadelphia. At Harvard, he was one of two students from Pennsylvania, over half of his class of 218 being from Massachusetts. He prepared for Harvard at St. Paul's School (where he befriended John Jay Chapman); once at Harvard he joined the right clubs, ending up, like Roosevelt, a member of the Porcellian Club. He was, if anything, more inward with Boston society than Roosevelt was. In one weekend, he told his mother, he passed a day and a night with the Cabots, had tea with the Lowells, and spent time with a Miss Bacon and the Saltonstalls. In another letter, he told of turning down a dinner with Henry James and Charles Eliot Norton. By the eve of his return home for Christmas his senior year, his tracks were covered: he knew "nothing and therefore care[d] nothing about Philadelphia society," he warned his mother.[11]

In 1901, he published a novelette—or as its subtitle has it, "A Story of Harvard University"—called *Philosophy 4*. It was widely praised for its rendering of college life. A few years after it came out, the *Monthly* said it marked "pretty well the *desideratum* for a college story."[12] Even as late as 1958, a chronicler of Harvard fiction called it "a joyous tale," and said, "Within its brief limits the story reflects undergraduate spirit so faithfully that no Harvard man even to this day can read it without being transported back to those earlier days with complete nostalgia."[13] His friend Roosevelt read more into it: "Have just been re-reading Philosophy 4," he wrote Wister in 1916. "*You* may think it a skit. *I* regard it as containing a deep and subtle moral."[14]

Philosophy 4 is the story of two sophomores with the "colonial names" Rogers and Schuyler who hire an impecunious classmate to tutor them for the final examination in that course. *His* name—Oscar Maironi—serves to set up both dandies and recent immigrants at once. With Maironi's help they cram, they get down a few phrases about "the Greek bucks" and "Hobbes and his gang" and the like, and then go off carousing. They barely get back in time to take the exam, but they do very well on it—better, in fact, than Maironi, who does little more than parrot back the professor's lectures. That tells us something about the virtues of an active pursuit of knowledge, and perhaps William James had that in mind—that as well as a gentleman's obligation to be courteous—when he wrote what Wister said was a "delightful" letter about the story. "William James took neither himself nor Harvard too solemnly," he added.[15] But there is more to be learned from the contrasting backgrounds and manners of these three students. We can see racial and immigration policy in the making; we can see simple manliness in the making as well. Whereas Rogers and Schuyler are drawn to the champagne and port and fine food provided at the Bird-in-Hand tavern, Maironi enjoys reading translations of Armenian folk songs in salons on Newberry Street. Whereas Rogers and

Schuyler end up at the New Amsterdam Trust Company and the New York and Chicago Air Line after graduation, Maironi goes on to publish "a careful work entitled 'The Minor Poets of the Cinquecento' " and to write book reviews for the *Evening Post*.[16]

There is really nothing deep or subtle about the story. Another admirer of Wister's, a man whose concern about manliness rivaled Roosevelt's—Ernest Hemingway—couldn't understand why Wister even allowed *Philosophy 4* to be published. Mincing no words—in man talk—he wrote Maxwell Perkins in 1929, "We all write shit but something should prevent you from publishing it or at least re-publishing it."[17]

Wister himself was a more focused and committed student than Roosevelt. At Harvard, he developed an interest in music that can be traced at least as far back as a trip to Europe, when at the age of ten he met Franz Liszt—a friend of his grandmother, the redoubtable English actress Fanny Kemble—and heard him extol the virtues of Wagner. At Harvard, he received highest honors in music, composed and conducted burlesques and comic opera for the Dickey and the Hasty Pudding Club, and published a poem in the *Atlantic* on Beethoven. He was more focused; but he was also more playful. He ultimately had to scoff at Maironi, but not before he had taken a look around his world. While at St. Paul's, he and John Jay Chapman mapped out a novel about an Italian who fled the country disguised as a woman and then fell in love with a woman dressed as a man. At Harvard, he and another man went with a friend, disguised as a girl, to a play in Boston. He donned periwigs for Harvard theatricals, and obviously experienced the erotic side of club life—the "natural wholesome" quality of it, he would insist in retrospect. "Bless the old merry brutal ribald orgiastic natural wholesome Dickey!" he wrote in a book on his friendship with Roosevelt. "Bless the handful of wild oats we sowed there together so joyously!"[18]

As Wister seemed determined to pursue a career in music, his parents took him back to Europe in order to get Liszt's opinion. When in spite of Liszt's encouragement his father objected to his devoting his life to music, Wister agreed to go to work for the investment firm of H. L. Higginson in Boston. When his father changed his mind and offered to support his son's musical ambitions, he vengefully *insisted* on going to work for Higginson.

Whatever tension built up between the claims of Rogers and Schuyler and Maironi—to put it in terms as crude as those of *Philosophy 4*—apparently weakened a constitution that had already shown many signs of collapsing. He is another in the long list of neurasthenics of his class and times. His mother was so cold that even *her* mother—Fanny Kemble—commented on how little Owen was likely to get from her.[19] Headaches, eyestrain, mysterious ailments began to appear while he was at St. Paul's, and they intensified at Harvard, as his parents visited their own tension upon him and created more with stern letters to him about doing well—and *relaxing*. He was never so militant as Roosevelt in his efforts to fight his body's weakness, but he tried the usual antidotes—cricket, rowing, riding, tennis, boxing—and they did not work. In 1885, anxious over family and career—and perhaps sexual—issues, he suffered a collapse that was severe enough to draw him back to Philadelphia to consult an old family friend, the doctor who had delivered him—S. Weir Mitchell.

Mitchell's "cure" for women was rest in a locked room; for men it was travel, or the great outdoors. He prescribed something that Wister had never even given a thought to: a trip to the West. He told him to take riding clothes and light reading—but no French novels—and added this advice:

See more new people. Learn to sympathize with your fellow man a little more than you're inclined to. . . . You don't feel kindly to your race, you know. There are lots of humble folks in the fields you'd be the better for knowing.[20]

It is fair to assume that as well as being another neurasthenic, Wister was also another man whose attentiveness to keeping himself intact made him less than open to the lives of others, especially those who were not of his own class. And so at the end of June 1885—soon after Roosevelt went out West again in his effort to forget his wife's and his mother's deaths—Dan Wister boarded a train in Philadelphia, along with two maiden friends of his mother (who were delegated to watch over him), in order to reconstitute his life in the West.

The West had already proven useful to Harvard men in search of manhood. The historian Francis Parkman was the first to take advantage of it.[21] Having combatted various forms of psychosomatic or actual sickliness with exercise in the old Harvard gymnasium and vacation hikes and climbs, Parkman subjected himself to the more grueling test of a trip along the Oregon Trail after his graduation in 1846. Though he never did get his body to perform with the energy and strength that his rhetoric prescribed, his famous account of his trip (dictated from notes while he convalesced at the Brattleboro Retreat) provided hope and inspiration for generations of young men to come. In 1875, Roosevelt's younger brother, Elliott, left St. Paul's School—and the homesickness and night fears and mysterious seizures that haunted him there—to find a "cure" at a military outpost in central Texas.

Roosevelt's first trip West was one he took with Elliott just after his graduation from Harvard. In 1883, he went again, seeking relief from his recurring asthma and—what Harvard men were beginning to look for in the West—good financial investments.[22] In his first speculative venture, he became part owner of a Wyoming cattle ranch run by a classmate. During the next several years, he shuttled back and forth between the Bad Lands of Dakota and New York. He never stayed for long, nor did he ultimately make money, but he found solace for his grief over the losses of his mother and Alice, the solace of the wilderness and, more specifically, of hunting. One biographer has marveled at "just how much blood was needed to blot out 'thought,' " noting that the diaries that he kept after Alice's death became "a monotonous record of things slain."[23] He found what has been called "regeneration through violence," or "regeneration through regression," to a more primitive existence.[24] He also gathered a seemingly inexhaustible amount of material out of which he created the mythic man whom he was later determined to establish as a world power.

Implicitly, he wrote about him in *Hunting Trips of a Ranchman* (1885), which he dedicated to his brother Elliott, in *Ranch Life and the Hunting Trail* (1888), and in the immensely popular, multivolume *The Winning of the West* (1889–96), which he dedicated to Francis Parkman. In the course of his voluminous writings, these writings especially, Roosevelt traced the evolution of this manly figure through historical stages that began in Roman times, through the usual array of races that culminated with the Anglo-Saxon, and through various classes that he neatly separated out of the mix of men he encountered in the West. To take the last first, out of all the newcomers to the West—cowboys, hunters, settlers, trappers—he focused on the cowboys and, in doing so, erased all ethnic differences between them. "Although there are among them wild spirits from every land, yet [they] soon become undistinguishable from their American companions," he wrote in *Hunting Trips of a Ranchman*. They were all "sinewy, hardy, self-reliant . . . daring and adventurous." At the same time, he transformed earlier images of them as uncouth and sometimes brutal "herders" into that of "the grim pioneer of our race." He moved from acknowledgments (in the same book) that there was "much boisterous, often foul-mouthed, mirth" in their gatherings, and that they were "prone to drink, and when drunk, to shoot," to a characterization of them as "rather silent, self-contained men when with strangers, and . . . frank and hospitable to a degree."[25] Three years later, in *Ranch Life and the Hunting Trail,* he had them ideally suited for invidious comparisons to farmers and union members, philanthropists and pacifists:

They are much better fellows and pleasanter companions than small farmers and agricultural laborers; nor are the mechanics and workmen of a great city to be mentioned in the same breath. . . . A cowboy will not submit tamely to an insult and is ever ready to avenge his own wrongs; nor has he an overwrought fear of shedding blood. He possesses, in fact, few of the emasculated, milk-and-water moralities admired by the pseudo-philanthropists; but he does possess, to a very high degree, the stern, manly qualities that are invaluable to a nation.[26]

Ten years after that, this figure would turn into Roosevelt himself, pitted against those "prattlers who sit at home" questioning the wisdom of American policy in the Philippines.

But this "grim pioneer" only "prepares the way for the civilization before whose face he must himself disappear."[27] He is easily replaced. His successor is the cattle rancher, who himself first appears as an independent rider on the range and then evolves into a proprietor, a manager, or—again like Roosevelt—an absentee landlord.

Because Roosevelt could not neglect what was Dutch in his own makeup, this man is not an exact replica of the Anglo-Saxon hero whom we have already met, but he is still very easily recognizable. Roosevelt read Cooper avidly as a youth, then Longfellow's *The Saga of King Olaf* and *The Song of Roland,* and (repeatedly) the *Nibelungenlied.* He was inspired, consumed, we might say, by Parkman's history of the colonial powers' struggle for domination over the New World, the seven-volume *France and England in North America.* When he came to write *The Winning of the West,* which carries on from where Parkman left off, he used it as a guide. In those volumes, he first went back to the triumph of the Teutons over Rome, and from there he followed the purest strain of the Teutonic, or Germanic, "blood line" to the British Isles—skirting the Celtic, the French, the Latin, as much as possible. He then recounted the triumph of the special American breed of Anglo-Saxons over all other races, over German and Irish immigrants, over Mexicans in the Far West, and over Indians everywhere. Later imperialistic moves off America's eastern and western shores would be made under the cover of the same language. Only the "stay-at-homes" would be so "selfish and indolent," so "lacking in imagination," he said, as to fail "to understand the race-importance of the work which is done by their pioneer brethren in wild and distant lands."[28] Wars against the Indians blended easily into wars against the Spaniards.

His attitudes towards immigrants, towards Indians, towards peoples of color, are well known. He was hardly one to hide them. It is worth pointing out, however, that with his blindness, with all his contempt, went a readiness to welcome any immigrant, any black or Indian or Japanese man, so long as he became an American—"nothing but an American."[29] The hyphen was anathema to him. In an article called "True Americanism," he asked his reader to remember "that the one being abhorrent to the powers above the earth and under them is the hyphenated American—the 'German-American,' the 'Irish-American,' or the 'native-American.' "[30] He was capable of saying that in nine cases out of ten a good Indian was a dead Indian—adding, "And I shouldn't like to inquire too closely into the case of the tenth." He had no tolerance for "sentimental nonsense . . . about our taking the Indians' land," but he was prepared to treat the individual Indian—not the tribe member—as an individual:

Give each his little claim; if, as would generally happen, he declined this, why, then let him share the fate of the thousands of white hunters and trappers who have lived on the game that the settlement of the country has exterminated, and let him, like these whites, who will not work, perish from the face of the earth which he cumbers.

Applying the same principles of Social Darwinism to immigrants (and taking to their extremes opinions that he surely heard expressed by Nathaniel Shaler), he advocated a policy that would "keep out races which do not assimilate readily with our own, and unworthy individuals of all races."[31]

Wister's experience of the West was not quite so extensive as Roosevelt's, but the figure of the man whom he brought back East was in its way every bit as compelling and influential as the man Roosevelt represented. Wister's first trip—to the ranch of a family friend near Laramie—transformed him. Not only did it restore him to health, but it provided him with a clear and salutary vision of his country's future as well—all in a matter of weeks. It was there, in the West, that Wister saw the American man of the future evolving. The well-bred man everyone was looking for was now emerging in the West, by natural selection, he thought, but of course only because that is what he chose to see. He turned his back on the men who were already there—his daughter said that in all his time in the West he met only two men who "won his heartfelt admiration"[32]—and focused instead on his own kind. "Every man, woman, and cowboy I see comes from the East—and generally from New England, thank goodness," he sighed in his journal. "No matter how completely the East may be the headwaters from which the West has flown [sic] and is flowing, it won't be a century before the West is simply the true America, with thought, type, and life of its own kind."[33]

A few years before, in *The American,* Henry James had told quite another story of a young man's exploration of what was—for the American—a new world. His name is Christopher Newman, and his too is "an intensely Western story," a parable really, of a determined, enterprising, adventurous, indefatigable young man—a veteran of the Civil War—who goes west for the sole purpose of making money and who, after doing so ("Successful in copper . . . only so-so in railroads, and a hopeless fizzle in oil," as Newman puts it), goes east to Europe for cultivation.[34] Wister reversed the situation. Easterners were "too clogged with Europe to have any real national marrow," he wrote Chapman. It was only in the West that you could now find "an entirely original American gentleman."[35] James registered the historical fact about the West, made light of it in his fiction, and eventually repaired to Europe, in flight from what he had observed. Wister came up with a fantasy about the West, took it very seriously, and returned to the East to write about it, thereby bolstering the social and economic position of upper-class eastern men like himself.

In the fall of 1885, Wister went back to Harvard to enter the Law School. He lived with several other law students, including Chapman, and together they established an eating club, to which they invited both current members of A.D. and Porcellian and distinguished elders like Oliver Wendell Holmes Jr., William James, and Charles Eliot Norton. It was in their second year that

Chapman plunged his offending hand into a fire. Wister told his parents that it was a gesture so wild as to convince him that his friend was "utterly and irretrievably warped," but he loyally went to visit Chapman in the hospital and read *Treasure Island* to him in its entirety.[36] He himself suffered relatively undramatic relapses of his own at the end of that year, and again after graduation, and yet again after he reluctantly took up the practice of law in Philadelphia. Each time he sought, and found, rejuvenation in the West. He had tried to live up to his word to his father, but he had as little of the makings of a Philadelphia lawyer as he did of a Boston businessman. All the while, he resumed his work on comic operas, one on Charlemagne, in collaboration with Thomas Wharton, a friend who had abandoned the law for journalism and novel writing, and another on Montezuma. He began to write more, encouraged by being asked to join a literary circle that met at the home of S. Weir Mitchell "Saturdays after nine."

The man Wister was looking for—the man of sound mind and body, the heroic gentleman—was not to be found either in a Philadelphia office or in foreign epics. Wister had already found him in the "entirely original American gentleman" he imagined he had met after a few weeks in the West. All that was needed now was for him to get him down in writing. The final push came in a conversation with his friend Walter Furness (son of a great Shakespearean editor) over dinner at the Philadelphia Club in the fall of 1891. They agreed: it was a pity that the American West had yet to find its Kipling. Roosevelt had brought back stirring firsthand reports, and Frederic Remington's illustrations were by then well known, but no man had immortalized the West in fiction. As he later reported it, Wister declared right then and there that he would try his hand. He went upstairs to the club library, and around midnight reappeared with a substantial portion of his first story, "Hank's Woman." Soon after, he wrote another, "How Lin McLean Went East," and then he sent both of them to Harper & Brothers (with a cover letter from Mitchell), which agreed to publish them in its magazine. In several successive years, Wister went back out West to gather more materials; in 1892, his law office became primarily a place to write.

Wister continued his music, writing a romantic opera with Wharton that had François Villon and Louis XI as its central characters, and performing publicly in a piano quartet, but he concentrated more and more on his writing, regularly turning out stories, and then collections of stories: *Red Men and White* in 1895, *Lin McLean* in 1897, and *The Jimmyjohn Boss and Other Stories* in 1900. Roosevelt heaped praise on Wister's work and, at the same time, more scorn on the writings of the ninety-eight-pound weaklings who had emigrated. "To read his writings is like walking on a windy upland in fall, when the hard weather braces body and mind," Roosevelt said,

There is a certain school of American writers that loves to deal, not with the great problems of American existence and with the infinite picturesqueness of our life as it has been and is being led here on our own continent . . . but with the life of those Americans who cannot swim in troubled waters, and go to live as idlers in Europe. What pale, anaemic figures they are, these creations of the emigré novelists, when put side by side with the men, the grim stalwart men, who stride through Mr. Wister's pages!

It is this note of manliness which is dominant through the writings of Mr. Wister.[37]

In 1900, Wister published a short biography of Ulysses S. Grant that William James thought was "really colossal" (he didn't know Wister was "so great a man!" he told Sarah Whitman) and that Roosevelt thought was "the very best biography which has ever been written of any prominent American."[38]

Together the two former Harvard and Porcellian men erased all traces of their frailer selves—Roosevelt in his persona, Wister in his fictions. They also did so as members of the Boone and Crockett Club, a group of men dedicated to big-game hunting and to conservation. In 1893, Wister joined Roosevelt in Chicago to help him set up the club's exhibit at the Columbian Exposition— a rustic cabin on a wooded island—and to dine with him there on fish and steak, washed down, at Wister's insistence, not with whiskey and beer, as Roosevelt had wanted, but with champagne. ("We dined well and simply, camp fashion," he said, with what one assumes is haughty irony.)[39] At the same time, another member of the Boone and Crockett Club, Frederic Remington, had been commissioned by Harper's to illustrate Wister's stories of the West. He had already done illustrations of Roosevelt's work. Wister's and Furness' wishes were coming true. Another that they didn't even make almost came true too: in 1895, Roosevelt—then civil service commissioner—invited Wister to his home in Washington to meet Kipling. But the circle did not complete itself. Though Remington was also invited, he declined, citing ill health as his reason but actually backing off because he realized that Wister had set a limit to their friendship: he had not told Remington that his nickname was Dan.[40] (Nor was Roosevelt totally sure about Wister. Just after he became president, a publisher suggested that Wister—seemingly the obvious choice—write his biography, but Roosevelt said no. "I have a kind of feeling that the man who is to write about me ought if possible to be a man who has lived near the rough side of things," he said, "and knows what it is actually to accomplish something—not just to talk about accomplishing it.")[41]

In 1895, Wister published an essay in *Harper's Monthly* titled "The Evolution of the Cow-Puncher"—and Remington illustrated it—which re-struck with especial clarity what Roosevelt called the dominant note of manliness.[42] Wister begins with a bit of a narrative. An Englishman and an American meet on a train, the one a peer (good rugs, good umbrella, and a monogrammed leather traveling bag from which emerge cut glass and brandy), the other a rough of "the trans-Missouri variety." Though they growl at each other with "the Anglo-Saxon's note of eternal contempt for whatever lies outside the beat of his personal experience," they *are* both Anglo-Saxons—both, in essence, Wister's "entirely original American gentleman"—and so they are inevitably drawn to each other. The Englishman sniffs out and is attracted to what turns out to be his dark and elemental Other:

Directly the English nobleman smelt Texas, the slumbering untamed Saxon awoke in him, and mindful of the tournament, mindful of the hunting-field, galloped howling after wild cattle, a born horseman, a perfect athlete, and spite of the peerage and gules and argent, fundamentally kin with the drifting vagabonds who swore and galloped by his side.

"Naturally" he becomes a cowboy. "The man's outcome typifies the way of his race from the beginning," Wister says. One with the medieval knight, the fox hunter, and the perfect specimen trotting off Soldier's Field, "The Last Cavalier," as depicted in a Remington illustration that Wister said almost brought tears to his eyes, the Englishman ends up on the Texas range, his brethren having lit out across the empire, to Canada, Australia, India, or some place "further into the wilderness."

Wister's "Anglo-Saxon is forever homesick for out-of-doors." By the same token, he is forever (and unshamefacedly) fleeing an urban civilization that Wister says is being debased by "encroaching alien vermin . . . who degrade our commonwealth from a nation into something half pawn-shop, half broker's office," from "Poles or Huns or Russian Jews," and so on. The "evolution" of the cowpuncher is his discovery of his true being, his survival as the fittest and racially purest American, but the moral of Wister's depiction of him in his natural habitat also points in the opposite direction: "his modern guise fell away and showed once again the mediaeval man. It was no new type, no product of the frontier, but just the original kernel of the nut with the shell broken." "The Evolution of the Cow-Puncher" is not so much about his forward movement as about the American man's deep and, according to Wister, fortunate regression.

The cowpuncher is the last in a line that goes back at least as far as the Middle Ages—and his days are numbered. Remington's final illustration, titled "The Fall of the Cowboy," shows two of them, one having dismounted in order to open up the dreaded, archetypal fence that will confine them and their horses at the end of the day. "Three things swept him away," Wister says of the cowpuncher, "the exhausting of the virgin pastures, the coming of the wire fence, and Mr. Armour of Chicago, who set the price of beef to suit himself." Two years before, at the Columbian Exposition, the historian Frederick Jackson Turner had presented his famous interpretation of the closing of the frontier. He had talked about the fencing everywhere, and thus about the vanishing of an environment that had nurtured the most "striking characteristics" of "the American intellect," which he defined as "coarseness and strength combined with acuteness and inquisitiveness; that practical, inventive turn of mind . . . a mind lacking in the artistic," but one able to "effect great ends." The characterization of this practical, masculine individual is familiar, even though Turner's man was more of a husbandman, a farmer, a small entrepreneur than a warrior or a hunter or a conqueror.[43]

Of course the cowpuncher did not really have to retreat after all. He only had to relocate and change costumes. He has survived, he has thrived, in fact, in hard-boiled detectives, gangsters, superannuated cold warriors and new frontiersmen, in fictive space probers, rogue stock manipulators, or purchasers of second homes "in the country." He has taken up permanent residence at the heart of American culture. We need only concentrate on this man's send-off into the world of the Western, where he has prospered best. His beginnings occurred—just after the frontier closed, just after the cowboy had supposedly fallen and his horses were fenced in—in the form of the novel that Wister wrote in Charleston, South Carolina—about Wyoming—called *The Virginian* (1902). Its hero is an all-purpose model of manhood. The book is dedicated to Theodore Roosevelt—and then was re-dedicated to him in 1911.

The Virginian cannot be said to call Harvard specifically to mind, but it is a conscious construction of American manhood, and it touches on all of the themes that we have seen Harvard attend to in its educational efforts—the Anglo-Saxon presence, class consciousness, sexual identities, and the challenge of women, to name the most prominent. Although many readers are still stirred by its depiction of love and valor, and by its occasionally rich evocations of the Western landscape, the novel does not have much to do with cowboys' lives. What little it does offer it offers at second hand—a report of what happened when cattle were driven up North, for example—one reason being that the Virginian is destined to become a foreman on the Judge's ranch and the promotion, or evolution, as Roosevelt had made clear, leaves the cowboy behind. The novel does contain a fair amount of the violence and death that we expect of the genre, but we need that in order to appreciate what is most significant about *The Virginian*—namely, the stylishness with which an exemplary man faces violence and death, faces women, faces others, faces any threat to his manhood.

He does so, as we well know, with as few words as possible. It is not easy to imagine the loud and verbose Roosevelt going softly while he went forward with his big stick—"the mere monstrous embodiment of unprecedented and resounding noise," Henry James called him[44]—but his response to his ailments and to the tragedies in his life was in fact to say very little about them and to press on. Another of his most famous sayings was "Black care rarely sits behind a rider whose pace is fast enough."[45] As a writer, Wister was the more conscious of the power of a few, well-chosen words to deflect attention away from one's own anguish or to ward off another's blow. One of the most distinctive qualities of the evolved "cow-puncher" was what Wister called "his craft of wordmaking," especially "his unpremeditated art of brevity." The Virginian's use of the word "smile"—"Smile when you call me that"—after the villainous Trampas calls him a son of a bitch, is the perfect example. As Wister said in his essay, "The cow-puncher's talent for making a useful verb out of anything shows his individuality." (And then Wister went on, in a pugnacious image, to associate that talent with the race's control over language: "Any young strong race will always lay firm hands on language and squeeze juice from it.") In the course of the novel, the Virginian wins out in altercations with Trampas that are all verbal—challenges to lies and insults to women, the telling of taller tales—until the final, requisite shoot-out. Even that is made to seem like repartee, what with Wister saying that the Virginian's fatal bullet "replied" to Trampas' initial firing.[46] He himself is so terse, so self-contained, so much the individual who wisely keeps much in reserve, that he doesn't even have a name.

The Virginian is a tight-lipped man who is at home on the range; on the other hand, Wister devotes a surprising number of pages to his talk about books. Though most of his successors keep going west after the fade-out or the last page, Wister ultimately wants to draw this vital force back into civilization, where it can be put to patriotic use in the fight against compromise and corruption—so he needs to be educated. His teacher is a familiar schoolteacher, Molly Stark Wood, from Bennington, Vermont. Her name suggests a toughness that not only qualifies her for Western life but also makes her a candidate for manhood—and indeed she tells the Virginian, "I've always wanted to be a man." But he and Wister have other plans for her. Her greataunt in Vermont knows Molly—"She is like us all. She wants a man who is a man."[47] She puts up an amount of resistance that would disqualify her for domestic life in the East, but her kind of womanliness is what is needed in the West, and it serves ultimately to make his manliness the more impressive.

The Virginian's preferences among the books he is assigned fall neatly along gender lines: he doesn't like Jane Austen, *Emma* in particular, because the writing isn't *about* anything, but he does like an unnamed Russian for his ability to tell the truth; he likes Scott; he likes the fighting in *Henry IV;* he doesn't like Romeo ("Romeo is no man"), but he likes Mercutio (Mercutio "gets killed," he says. "He is a man"). He likes George Eliot for drowning Maggie Tulliver and her brother (they talk too much), until he finds out George Eliot is a woman, at which point he says that *she* talks too much. We learn that the Virginian also knows another kind of literature, knows all seventy-nine verses of a song the cowpunchers sing, but seventy-eight of them are unprintable, so we who are reading *The Virginian* are not to hear them: some things "should not be put down in fine language for the public," the Virginian says.[48]

What is at stake is nothing less than the American family as it was defined by most of the men in this study during this period. The cowpunchers' songs are part of an oral tradition that is passed down and altered by men on the move. As we know from other sources, the omitted verses are about a woman's smashing one child's head in with a rolling pin while another gets away. *The Virginian* is ultimately a cagey strengthening of the family and the position of the man at the head of it, and the last thing Wister is going to include in its pages is infanticide. The Virginian may be a man of few words, but the "fine language" in which he appears makes it clear that the race has to continue under his manly guidance.[49]

In order for that to be the case, Wister must cope not only with the relatively subtle issue of oral versus print culture but also with the larger issues of the vote and education. Setting *The Virginian* in Wyoming was experientially right, but it was also true that when Wyoming applied for statehood in 1890, it proposed a constitution that granted women the vote—the first of its kind. Wyoming needed women—only one of its eight thousand residents was a woman at the time—and its being the "Equality State" made it attractive to them. But if *The Virginian* had anything to say about it, women would come out to circumstances that were essentially like those they had left back in the East.[50] Molly smooths off the rougher edges of the Virginian, but *he* prevails. Brushing her objections aside, brushing aside symbolic representatives of religion and the law, like many a Western man, he takes the law into his own hands, seeing to it that his best friend turned cattle rustler is hung, and then, at the end, gunning down Trampas on the main street in town. Women might get the vote, but men would continue to call the shots.

Wister's response to the question of education is equally blunt. He does not actually mention Radcliffe, but in a long tale about a hen named Emily he ridicules women's aspirations to education generally. Emily's "manly-lookin'," and her legs are "blue, long, and remarkably stout." The Virginian says, "She ought to wear knickerbockers. She'd look a heap better'n some o' them college students." And it follows that, as a "bluestocking," she can't reproduce, or is not allowed to, because she spends so much time with other barnyard creatures. The Virginian and the narrator play cruel tricks on her, switching stones and eggs, that drive her to distraction and death. In a letter to Molly many chapters later, the Virginian makes the point: "She had poor judgment and would make no family ties," he writes. "She would keep trying to get interest in the ties of others taking charge of little chicks and bantams and turkeys and puppies one time. . . . She died without family ties one day while I was building a house for her to teach school in." That is one of his courting moves, the kind that Molly ultimately finds irresistible, but the Virginian means it. He makes it very clear to Molly's mother that "she shall teach school no more when she is mine."[51] It is something that Wister wished he could have said to his own wife, whom he also called Molly. She too was civic minded, being, among other things, the youngest member of the Philadelphia Board of Education. "I have at times a rush of blind feudal hatred at seeing my girl on her feet in public, talking to men—and such men," Wister confessed to his mother. But there were limits to what a modern knight could do in real life.[52]

Instead of teaching, Molly Stark Wood has "many children." (Mary Channing "Molly" Wister died in 1913, at the age of forty-four, giving birth to her sixth child.) For his part, the Virginian is "able to give his wife all and more than she asked or desired." He becomes the Judge's partner and then, as the cattle industry begins to slow down, builds a ranch "where the coal was." We learn that the railroad has built a branch to his land, so presumably he will try to do for coal what Armour did for beef. Molly worries that "his work would kill him," but we are assured in the last sentence that he will hold on: "Their eldest boy rides his horse Monte; and strictly between ourselves," Wister writes, "I think his father is going to live a long time."[53] Harboring his energies, developing his own little trust, the Virginian will be immune to neurasthenia and to thoughts of suicide.

In the very first pages, Wister had dismissed Jews and "a Dutchman with jew'lry" and all other "drummers," or traveling salesmen. His hero has assured Molly's mother that he is of old Virginia stock, and now he is reproducing his kind. Having selected out the right kind of texts, he is sufficiently, but not too, educated, and after eyeing the Judge's eastern visitors, he has even had a tailor spiffy up his wardrobe. It is 1902, and the Virginian has become a gentleman, the incarnation of what many thought of as ideal manhood. Along with an advance copy of *The Virginian,* Wister sent a note to Oliver Wendell Holmes Jr. saying that he had tried to "draw a man of something like genius—the American genius."[54] Now he just seems like a lot of other men.

But what about other men? The Virginian is, of course, glorious to behold. We first see him through the eyes of the narrator, who has come out from the East. He is "a slim young giant, more beautiful than pictures," his thumb hooked in the cartridge belt that falls across his hips, his complexion glowing the way "ripe peaches look upon their trees in a dry season." Whatever Wister's contemporaries might have thought, we need not be surprised at the narrator's ardent responses. Early on, he imagines what it would be like to be married to him ("Had I been the bride, I should have taken the giant, dust and all"); when he later sees him smile at the woman he will marry, he switches roles ("had I been a woman, it would have made me his to do what he pleased with on the spot").[55] Active, passive, he cannot get enough of him, but then again, the Virginian is, like the rough in "The Evolution of the Cow-Puncher," already a part of him. He is—as countless descriptions of him in the text have it—the dark, wild man who gives life to the Englishman. He is the "cure" for the neurasthenic Easterner. In a letter to Wister, after having graciously complimented him on his novel, Henry James let himself "loose among [his] reserves" and lost himself in just this sort of rejuvenating fantasy. How much better would it have been if the reader could have had the Virginian all to himself! "Nothing would have induced me to unite him to the little Vermont person, or to dedicate him in fact to achieved parentage, prosperity, maturity, at all," he wrote. All that was "mere *prosaic* justice, and rather grim at that. I thirst for his blood. I wouldn't have let him live and be happy; I should have made him perish in his flower and in some splendid noble way."[56]

Wister could no more do that than he could let Molly continue teaching. Gender justice as he and his friends defined it—prosaic though it might have been—precluded it. No more undergraduate high jinks, Maironi must pay, the narrator seems to fade from the text as Wister concentrates on the courtship and union of the Virginian and Molly Stark Wood. As for the poetry, as for what is in reserve, there is Steve, the Virginian's best friend, the man who must hang. We learn little about him or about his friendship with the Virginian, nor do any words pass between them as Steve's death approaches. That is how it would have to be, as a note from Steve explains: "I could not have spoke to you without playing the baby." But for a moment the Virginian allows himself that luxury. "I expect in many growed-up men you'd call sensible there's a little boy sleepin'," he tells the narrator,

the little kid they onced was—that still keeps his fear of the dark. You mentioned the dark yourself yesterday. Well, this experience has woke up that kid in me, and blamed if I can coax the little cuss to go to sleep again! I keep a-telling him daylight will sure come, but he keeps a-crying and holding on to me.[57]

It is an extraordinary confession, not one that any of the Virginian's countless descendants in the twentieth century would allow himself to make. But the little kid will let go soon enough. He will have to. He will have "parentage, prosperity, maturity" to think about.

The Virginian was first printed in April, and had to be reprinted fifteen times by the end of the year. It is one of the most popular books ever written; it is also the basis for three films and a television series. The *Graduates' Magazine* was right in imagining that it would be read "as long as anybody is interested in that curious half-barbaric, half-romantic creature, the cowboy," but wrong in adding "as he existed on the American plains a decade or two

ago." If actual cowboys had been Wister's subject, Wister would indeed have
"exhausted the cowboy as a subject for fiction," as they claimed.[58] But *The
Virginian* is not about cowboys so much as about a particular kind of manhood, the kind that Harvard had had in mind for years.

Theodore Roosevelt was a simple version of it, the most popular version
of it, the one that everyone could understand. He was a voluminous writer,
but he was first and foremost an active citizen of the world. He was physically
fit, his energies fueled by contact with various forms of wildness and unruliness, but always the more powerful for being under his control. He was a
gentleman, but there seemed to be nothing of the leisurely or privileged aristo-
crat about him. He is probably most famous for opposing those of his own
class who created exclusive trusts, and for creating a massive conservation and
park system where—this was his intention—men could be reinvigorated by
reimmersion in the state of nature. He made it seem as if every man could will
or work himself into health and prosperity, no matter what his background or
his condition. In him, American individualism left the courageously creative
mind (where Emerson best represented it), left the more social confines of the
academy (where James and others manifested it), and confidently strode out
into the world.

Both he and Wister were loyal and honored sons of Harvard. Wister was
active in alumni affairs, and he became a member of the Board of Overseers.
In 1899, he delivered the Phi Beta Kappa poem, called "My Country: 1899,"
the burden of which was, generally, that America had abandoned its originat-
ing purpose and ideals in its pursuit of material wealth. In applying this familiar theme, he expressed a brand of anti-imperialism very different from that of
James and his fellow "mugwumps." Hands off the Philippines, he argued,
because our intentions there *were* only materialistic, and, moreover, contact
with the "natives" would inevitably muddy the gene pool. President Eliot's
anti-imperialism was James' anti-imperialism, but he thought Wister's success
as a writer "would be a good thing for the College," so in 1904 he invited him
to become a member of the English Department. Wister was greatly flattered,
but he declined.[59] A few years later, he addressed an academic award ceremony
held in Sanders Theater, which, as was duly noted, demanded "courage, if not
temerity—especially from the author of 'Philosophy 4.' "[60]

Roosevelt's presence at Harvard was much more pronounced. On numer-
ous occasions he came back to proclaim what he meant by manhood and—in
the same loud voice—to explain what he thought was the purpose of a Harvard
education. As he loomed ever larger in the public eye, his alma mater followed
him and paid him homage. The *Graduates' Magazine* reviewed his books, ran
pictures of him as a Rough Rider and as a leader in Washington, and recorded
activities that ranged from his becoming president in 1901 and his reelection

in 1905 to his return to Cambridge to celebrate his son's entrance into Porcellian in 1907. The Harvard Union made him an honorary member, he was elected president of the Alumni Association, and, in 1902, he was awarded an LL.D. On that occasion, Wister was a deputy marshal and Roosevelt's special escort. Rather than acknowledge all the attention and move on, Roosevelt kept close watch over Harvard and often tried to influence its handling of its students.

He was most vocal in addressing athletic issues. He monitored various committees' attempts to encourage, yet contain, the growth of intercollegiate athletics, and he served on at least one. We know of his summoning President Eliot and Coach Reid to Washington in 1905 in order to make sure that Harvard did not do "the baby thing" and abolish football. He also stepped in three years later—in the month of Eliot's last commencement—when two crew members were suspended for taking books out of the library illegally and under false names. One rowed number two for the varsity, and the race against Yale was approaching. Roosevelt and his assistant secretary of state (and classmate) Robert Bacon telegraphed Eliot, saying there had to be another way to punish the lads. Eliot countered by saying that dishonorable conduct had to be condemned and—picking just the right metaphor—that "the College should also teach that one must never do scurvy things in the supposed interest or for the pleasure of others."[61] Eliot won on principle, and he won rhetorically—and, as it turned out, the Harvard crew won as well.

Roosevelt returned to Harvard for athletic rallies and celebrations. In 1898, for example, he came over from the Lowell Institute, where he was lecturing, to join 450 others (200 applied too late to get tickets) to attend a Graduate Athletic Association dinner held in honor of the football team's victory over Yale. (The next weekend, 700 gathered at Delmonico's in New York for the same purpose.)[62] But he was anything but a mindless booster. Being Roosevelt, he obviously found little good to say about the spectator's role; he had nothing good to say about it when the former athlete filled it. "The amateur athlete who thinks of nothing but athletics, and makes it the serious business of his life, becomes a bore, if nothing worse," he wrote in the *North American Review*. A man who played a sport in college might be worthy of some respect, "but if, when middle-aged, he has still done nothing more in the world, he forfeits even this claim which he originally had."[63] Athletic competition was vital, but vital because of its moral potential, because it built character. Morals first, then health, then studies, his father had told him. When his son Kermit was fourteen he passed the lesson on:

I would rather have a boy of mine stand high in his studies than high in his athletics, but I would a great deal rather have him show true manliness of character than show either intellectual or physical prowess.[64]

Kermit must have known that his father could not imagine manliness *without* "physical prowess." A few years before, to take a particularly blunt example, the last words of his "The American Boy" were:

> In short, in life, as in a football game, the principle to follow is:
> Hit the line hard; don't foul and don't shirk; but hit the line hard![65]

But however prominent a part Roosevelt imagined physical activity playing in the life of a boy who aspired to manhood, he knew it played only a part.

"If the boy really amounts to anything and has got the right stuff in him," Roosevelt told an audience at Georgetown University, "this means that he is going to keep his nerve and courage in more important things in after life."[66] He told the nation—and on many occasions he told Harvard—what those were. In 1888, he published an article in the *Monthly* titled "The Immigration Problem," in which he spoke of the many "unhealthy elements" entering America, and of the need that they be "genuinely Americanized." Either that or immigration would have to be forbidden altogether.[67] When he became president of the Alumni Association, he gave an address that was unambiguously titled "Americans Should Be Educated at Home."[68] In 1902, he gave a talk in which he celebrated Elihu Root, William Howard Taft, and Leonard Wood—"Three College-Bred Americans." When William James addressed a similar topic, in "The Social Value of the College-Bred," a few years later, he spoke of the dangers of priggishness and the obligation of an institution like Harvard to "catch the robuster tone." He too was speaking in the name of manliness, but he concluded his remarks with his warning that what was at stake here was "tone"—"a terribly vague word to use, but there is no other."[69] Characteristically, there was nothing tentative about Roosevelt's performance. He forged ahead. A college education imposed a heavy burden on a man; the men whom he singled out had assumed it. Root had been governor of Cuba for four years, Taft was head of the Philippine Commission, and Wood was secretary of the islands and secretary for the colonies, as well as secretary of war. They had put their education to use, they were manliness in action, they had extended the reach of empire.

In 1905, Roosevelt gave the commencement address. It was called "The Harvard Spirit," but again, what he wanted to convey was a sense of that spirit in action.[70] A great college like Harvard produced a small number of scholars, he said, scholars who would do "productive work of the first class," but most of its graduates would go forth "with the balanced development of body, of mind, and above all, of character, which shall fit them to do work both honorable and efficient." He wanted even the scholars to be "strong and virile youths," but his focus was on the kind of man who would do the institution proud "by doing useful service for the nation." The "normal function of the

College" was to produce such men, and in order to fulfill it, Harvard had to combat "the growing tendency to luxury" and to keep athletics in its place. As for the alumni, especially "the men of vast fortune," they had to set an example by obeying the law and meeting "a high standard of applied morality." There was little or no room for easefulness or play or genuine disinterestedness, but, as we know, such qualities of mind or temperament did not ordinarily figure in contemporary definitions of "the Harvard spirit."

It is not surprising that in the prevailing atmosphere William James was sympathetic to the idea of Roosevelt's succeeding Eliot as the president of Harvard. A month after hearing the commencement address, he wrote H. L. Higginson—donor of Soldier's Field and the Harvard Union, a most prominent member of the Corporation, and the manager of James' financial affairs—praising Roosevelt's "mighty good-will," his "power as a preacher," and his "increased courage." Forgetting his own antipathy to "bigness," James thought it would be a shame for Harvard not to take advantage of Roosevelt's "significance . . . in the popular mind"—what he called "a great national asset"—before it went to waste. So caught up was he by Roosevelt's mighty power that he cited as one of his qualifications something that is otherwise hard to discover: "the safety of his second thoughts."[71]

But two years later, Roosevelt gave a speech at the Union called "The College Man," which as James said, "quenched" his enthusiasm entirely.[72] In it Roosevelt restated his views on the proper place of athletics—adding, for the students' benefit, a defense of roughness as a way of producing vigorous men rather than "mollycoddles"—and restated his views on the need for educating men for citizenship and on the proper apportioning of athletics, study, and the development of character. But then he went on to make fun of what James ultimately stood for. In phrase after phrase, he mocked the critical mind: "too fastidious, too sensitive to take part in the rough hurly-burly of the actual work of the world," "overcultivated, so over-refined," "the weakling and the coward," "intellectual conceit," "impotent spirit of fancied superiority." One of his formulations—"In popular government results worth having can only be achieved by men who combine worthy ideals with practical good sense"— might have been lifted from James' own essay "What Makes a Life Significant." But it was clear where he was headed with his remarks. He was still out after James and his fellow anti-imperialists; and they appeared near the end of his talk as "those who merely indulged in the personal luxury of advocating for the islands a doctrinaire liberty." More generally, he was defending the simplest— almost mindless—form of education: "In short," he concluded, "you college men, be doers rather than critics of the deeds that others do."

Many of the students loved Roosevelt's talk, of course, but there were those who did not. One of them referred, nicely, to Roosevelt's "violent commonplaces." We know that, and we know that student was not alone, because the following June, at the Radcliffe commencement, LeBaron Briggs used Roosevelt's detractors as a means of warning his own audience about the way the devil attacked "the better men and women through their depressed nervous systems." He called it "the temptation of the scholarly and the sensitive," and he made it clear that he, for one, was grateful for Roosevelt's remarks. Roosevelt "stirred those boys as no other man in the world could stir them," he said. "He pleaded for an affirmative life, and no one whose blood was young could think a lazy thought.[73]

Almost ten years before, with enthusiasm for war with Spain at a fever pitch, Colonel T. W. Higginson had asserted that Harvard should be as proud of the anti-imperialists in their midst as of Theodore Roosevelt. Defending their right to speak out, he said that it "might often require more courage than the winning of battles; and it was the glory of a great university to produce alike leaders in action and in thought."[74] When Roosevelt's collection of essays featuring "The Strenuous Life" was published in 1900, the *Graduates' Magazine* pointed out that "strenuousness can be practiced in silence as well as by shouting," and it went on to say that Roosevelt had unfortunately "lost the power of discerning how very important a part reformers play in a free government."[75] The *Lampoon* ran two-page cartoons featuring Roosevelt as captain of the good ship Harvard, and John Harvard welcoming him back from Cuba—"Well done, Roosevelt," the caption read. "May Harvard Men always be to the fore." But a few years later the magazine depicted him firing his pistol at a tea he hosted in honor of the football team. The month after his speech at the Harvard Union, it ran a large cartoon that showed him ranting, "Football! Foot-ball! That's the game for me," while a faculty group—with what looks like James prominently in its midst—at the rear of the hall sat frowning.[76]

Though Harvard was not of one mind about Roosevelt, it was Harvard that had loosed him upon the country. The man who reviewed *The Strenuous Life* in the *Graduates' Magazine* did not overstate the case when he wrote, "These essays, we may be sure, will not be overlooked fifty years hence by the historian who wishes to understand the temper of a large part of the American people at the end of the 19th century."[77] The manhood that Theodore Roosevelt stood for dominated the country's thinking about men's and women's lives in the last quarter of the nineteenth century and the first decade of the twentieth. Subtler versions of it are still commonplace.

But around 1910 Harvard stopped talking about it.

After 1909

As Eliot's retirement from the presidency of Harvard approached, it was clear to everyone that his successor would be Abbott Lawrence Lowell. On the list of possible candidates that was nevertheless and necessarily drawn up by the Corporation, Roosevelt's name did not even appear—though Owen Wister's did.[1] As a distinguished professor and scholar, as a man who had been making his opposition to Eliot and to the excesses of his elective system known for at least a decade—and as a Lowell—he was the obvious choice.

The baton was passed at the 1909 commencement. In his inaugural address the following October, Lowell made it clear that Harvard would thenceforth move along a new track. He began by citing Aristotle:

> Among his other wise sayings, Aristotle remarked that man is by nature a social animal; and it is in order to develop his powers as a social being that American colleges exist. The object of the undergraduate department is not to produce hermits, each imprisoned in the cell of his own intellectual pursuits, but men fitted to take their place in the community and live in contact with their fellow men.[2]

It went without saying: under Eliot, students had been allowed too much freedom; the institution was no more than an aggregate of individual men. Lowell's Harvard would educate young men to assume their *social* responsibilities. Harvard had grown (although the undergraduate body still numbered only about 2,150 in 1909); had it not been for intercollegiate athletic contests, students would have had little sense of themselves as fellow students; there was nothing that was "really systematic" about the elective system. Under the circumstances, it was now important to think of man as a "social animal," to invoke the idea of his "community," and to prize—repeatedly in Lowell's address—"solidarity."

The world that the graduate would be entering was a social world. Preparing him for it, Harvard would itself become a model of such a world. The freshmen would all live together in the Yard; the elective system would be altered so that students would no longer be allowed to pursue only their own special interests—or follow the path of least resistance, as had too often been the case—and the quality of their work would improve because they would be competing against each other, competing on more common ground and in a newly devised honors system. It was on that note that Lowell ended his address; it was that "most painful defect" in American college life that he touched on last. "High scholarship" was undervalued at Harvard and by the culture as a whole, he said; "a greater solidarity in college, more earnestness of purpose and intellectual enthusiasm, would mean much for our nation."[3]

After the speech, James wrote Lowell (who had been his student) to congratulate him on his performance, telling him that if he ever had the urge to be lyrical, not to resist it ("that is what gives the most exquisite delight," he said), and wishing him well in his attempt to make "intellectual prowess a distinction in the undergraduate world of opinion." But he said he did not share Lowell's faith in the "artificial expedients," the honors and the prizes, that Lowell had proposed as a means of bringing about such a change of attitude. For his part, it was the power of example, "the unconscious pressure throughout the years of personal examples," that was "the normal force to apply."[4] But Lowell was interested in social cohesion and the competition that would (paradoxically) create it—not in individual examples.

Eliot, on the other hand, had tempered his individualistic belief. As the century turned, he became more and more of a progressive, emphasizing the social service that the College graduate should be prepared to perform. But whereas Lowell spoke of generic man and of his social being, Eliot had continued to define the Harvard undergraduate in the way that he had been defined at Harvard for decades. In 1905, for example, he talked about "the expert" as "a highly individualistic product," and then went right on to make him responsive to "an intelligent collectivism [that] calls for, regulates, and supports" him. But this expert, this product of a Harvard education, was still manly. "Nowadays," Eliot said in 1905,

a scholar is not a recluse, or a weakling incapable of the strenuous pursuits. He is not a book worm, although he masters some books. He studies something thoroughly, learns all there is to know about it, and then pushes beyond. . . . He must use strenuously a tough and alert body, and possess a large vitality and a sober courage.[5]

For Eliot he was still manifestly masculine.

Lowell's use of hermits in his inaugural address indicates how little he would be interested in Harvard men as men. Unlike weak, reclusive, bookish types, hermits were not enough to shame a man into leading a more strenuous life. Their opposite, in Lowell's formulation, would not be a strong and vital man, master of his mind and body, but rather a man who had been showing up in academic discourse for some time—"the well rounded man." Eliot had discouraged his appearance at Harvard from the very outset. In 1869, in his article "The New Education," he said that "to reason about the average human mind as if it were a globe" was to be "betrayed by a metaphor." In its place, he offered one that he considered trustworthy: "A cutting-tool, a drill, or augur would be a juster symbol of the mind."[6] But at other educational institutions he was a familiar figure. During this period, according to the historian of the institution, Yale "offered no narrow experience but an education of soul, mind, heart, and body: all at once and in a sort of balance. The emphasis was on the whole man among his fellows."[7]

Lowell introduced "the well rounded man" at commencement. "There is a wide difference between a body of men many of whom are remarkable for some one thing, so that collectively they represent interests of every kind," he said,

and a body of men each one of whom is well developed in all directions. Do we want the college today to turn out men one of whom is only an athlete, another only a club man, another only a linguist, another only a mathematician, and so forth? Is that our ideal of a college? Or is our ideal that it shall turn out well rounded men, developed so far as possible in every direction?[8]

That afternoon he told the alumni the same thing: "The object of a college is to produce well rounded manhood, men each as perfect as may be in body, mind and soul."[9] In his inaugural address it went this way:

The individual student ought clearly to be developed so far as possible, both in his strong and in his weak points, for the college ought to produce, not defective specialists, but men intellectually well rounded, of wide sympathies and unfettered judgment.[10]

A new figure had emerged at Harvard, a man whose strengths were various, with none likely to diminish any other, or those of any fellow "well rounded man."

In the rhetoric that Lowell was implicitly jettisoning, individual men— clubmen or athletes, scientists or (even) poets, average amenable souls or "undisciplinables"—all went about their business with an ideal of Harvard manhood in mind, even as they might parody or reject it. The man whom Lowell was introducing in his place would be especially proficient in one field, but he would be "liberally" educated once again. He would not be presented with a required curriculum, but he would have to be exposed to various subjects and ways of learning. He would be studious; he would also be athletic *and* be sociable *and* be a good soul. If too ardent in his pursuit of one kind of knowledge, or too committed to one undergraduate activity, he would be—in a word that suggested both a physical grotesque and a faulty social mechanism—"defective." As a "well rounded man," he would run smoothly. His manhood or his manliness would never be an issue—nor, by the same token, would Lowell mention women and their education as he took over.

At the end of Lowell's freshman year at Harvard (1873–74), he had just barely ranked in the top third of his class of about two hundred. Four years later, upon graduation, he was second in his class. James and Henry Adams had been among his teachers. As a member of the Boston elite, he was all but automatically made a member of the Hasty Pudding Club and the Institute of 1770, but he was elected to no other club—though in 1904 he accepted an honorary membership to the Fly. Subsequently he mentioned Harvard clubs only to deplore the social barriers that they threw up. "Clubs are useless," he would say, "unless you can keep somebody out."[11] He was the fastest long-distance runner at the Harvard of his day, but he ran only in intra-College meets. After graduating from the Law School and practicing for a few years, he accepted Eliot's offer to join the Government Department as a lecturer in 1897. He was soon a distinguished professor; his writings, especially *The Government of England,* gained him a national reputation. He was ideally suited to the task of administering a twentieth-century university dedicated to the production of a meritocracy: a man with an ever-improving intellect, a member of the community but not a joiner, a crack runner who never starred.

The new elite would ideally be one that came into being without benefit of invidious social comparisons, but in fact, Lowell continued to privilege the social aristocracy from which both he and Eliot came. As his colleague and biographer said, Lowell was "absolutely convinced . . . that the College and the nation were on the road to disaster if the descendants of old, well-to-do American families lost intellectual capacity and vigor."[12] In the minds of his predecessors, such an outcome could be avoided by encouraging and rewarding manhood in one's course elections, on the athletic field, in one's social relations, and in one's energetic efforts to make life significant. Lowell looked instead to curricular and social engineering to keep everyone in the running. At the same time, he kept a close watch over American immigration policy generally, and at Harvard he implemented policies that limited the number of Jewish students and barred Negro students from freshman dorms.

That is another chapter in the history of Harvard College. With a new emphasis on man as a social being came a new concern for men's social problems. The men who would figure largely in that next chapter, many of them undergraduates during the last of the Eliot years, addressed them. "Why not organize our intellectual enthusiasms?" a writer for the *Advocate* asked the year before Eliot stepped down. He spoke of the need for more serious drama; "more or less trivial operettas" and revivals would no longer do. "What we need also," he went on, "is a reform club where we can hear from the constructive social theorists, socialists, communists, and even the exponents of the single tax."[13]

Such clubs were coming into being, even as he wrote. In 1908, Walter Lippmann founded the Socialist Club at Harvard. Heywood Broun was among the charter members; John Reed, still concerned about joining one of Harvard's more traditional clubs, only attended meetings. In two years, the Socialist Club would be influential enough to get three hundred signatures on a petition that asked the administration for a course on socialism—a request that was granted. The next year, according to a report of the Intercollegiate Socialist Society, Harvard's club was the strongest of its kind in the nation, its membership approaching a hundred.[14] In 1909, a group of faculty and students founded the Social Politics Club; soon after, there would be the Harvard

Men's League for Women's Suffrage, the Single Tax Club, and even an anarchist group. In the same spirit, the future leader of the Chicago school of sociology, Robert Park, left Harvard in 1903 to learn more about "the race problem," and, in Van Wyck Brooks' words, Conrad Aiken '11, e. e. cummings'15, and John Dos Passos '16 "turned towards whatever was 'salt in the mouth' and 'rough to the hand' " and evoked "the slums, the gutter and the 'sore of morning' " in their writings.[15]

Not that such interests had suddenly attracted attention overnight. There had been many staunch abolitionists, most notably T. W. Higginson and James Russell Lowell, in the Harvard community. There were those—Du Bois is the obvious example—who never lost sight of issues of national concern for a minute. Nor did Du Bois have to maintain his focus all alone. He had the example of Francis Peabody, professor of Christian morals, who taught him in social ethics, a course in which Peabody tried to instill some social consciousness in his students. (Measuring his success, one must take into account their name for his course—"Drains, Drink, and Divorce"—which suggests there was a limit to what was meant by "social.")[16] But it is understandable why Oswald Garrison Villard observed that "practically nobody in the class [of 1893] was interested in world events." Harvard was "entirely satisfied with itself," he said—to which he added, "It had reason to be."[17]

One understands what John Jay Chapman was up against, shouting at Josiah Royce at a party sometime in the 1890s, in an attempt to convince him of "the duty of the philosopher toward practical politics." Chapman later wrote that he cried,

"There's no philosophy in the world anyway. It's a question of power,—whether I can get your attention to my ideas, or you mine to yours. Now I *won't* think about your ideas, and you *shall* think about mine!"

but he said it took the German invasion of Belgium for Royce to hear him.[18] This is the Chapman who tried to establish a social center for juveniles on Tenth Avenue and Forty-ninth Street in "Hell's Kitchen," who published an impassioned biography of William Lloyd Garrison in 1913, and who the year before, on the anniversary of a lynching there, hired a hall in Coatesville, Pennsylvania, and gave what is still a stirring speech—to an audience of three—in which he tried to awaken the nation to its involvement in the deadly event.

But whenever these later concerns for the nation's well-being were voiced, and whatever their scope or aim, the rhetoric in which they found expression did not characteristically depend on the idea of manhood for its strength. The Progressives did not have to think of themselves as masculine in order to mobilize. There was not the posturing, not the need to contrast what a woman would do under the same circumstances. As Brooks had noted in 1907, the life had gone out of such talk. He found it merely morbid.[19] It was time to stop.

It was time to stop for the simple reason that there were more important things to talk about. And in talking about them, the rhetoric of manhood was not of much use. For a long time, men had spoken and written about manhood in the faith that it drew to it or created understandings about how they should carry themselves in the world. The language of manhood guided men in their attempts to take proper care of their bodies, to control their sexual behavior and the potentially enervating activities of their minds; it helped them in their encounters with women and other people unlike themselves; it evoked an image of the male figure that could successfully make his way in an ever more complicated and accelerated life; it could also help him tap into (or even supplement) supernatural forces that he could believe were working towards the same ends as he was. If a man had achieved manhood, it was assumed that he was at least surviving—and probably succeeding—physically, domestically, socially, and spiritually.

But after 1909 being a man was not enough. It could always have its individual and temporary uses. A man might call up the image of himself as manly in an effort to assure himself that he could make it through his days, but if he had the nation's physical and social and moral well-being in mind, he was not likely to consider advice about manhood sufficient guidance. Power would continue to be gendered, but it would have become increasingly obvious that there was more to power than masculinity. The value of "the fighting spirit" became questionable as James' life and the Eliot years came to a close. Nor did the Great War revivify that ideal. Whereas the Civil War had compelled a generation of men to honor and strive after manhood, World War I could not do that. The images of No Man's Land—of trenches, of mustard gas, of carnage—were too strong.

And finally—though in the first place—what men understood by manhood was undergoing radical change. Manhood as it had been understood at Harvard was of severely limited use to men when they addressed social problems on a national scale; it was proving to be of little psychological use to them as well. In this realm, too, another baton was symbolically passed in 1909— this one from James to Freud.

More than any of his philosophical colleagues, James was attracted to the idea—and the possible experience—of ineffable selves and states of consciousness. Initially, in *The Principles of Psychology,* for example, he described them in terms derived from the Transcendentalists, in terms of the "double-consciousness," of material and spiritual, of lower and higher selves. For years, he worked with psychical researchers in an attempt to verify and record others' experiences of higher—but (he ruefully admitted) to him unknown—realms of being. In *The Varieties of Religious Experience* he tried, as a scientist, to find words for such psychological phenomena. "Since one of the duties of the science of religions is to keep religion in connection with the rest of science," he said, "we shall do well to seek first of all a way of describing the 'more,' which psychologists may also recognize as real." The way, he thought, lay through the subconscious:

The *subconscious self* is nowadays a well-accredited psychological entity; and I believe that in it we have exactly the mediating term required. Apart from all religious considerations, there is actually and literally more life in our total soul than we are at any time aware of.

And he went on:

whatever it may be on its *farther* side, the "more" with which in religious experience we feel ourselves connected is on its *hither* side the subconscious continuation of our conscious life. . . . *[T]he conscious person is continuous with a wider self through which saving experiences come.*

In our subconscious selves, James would assure his readers, lay the source of ever richer life. The unknown was what we were striving for, the possibility of "an ideal order that shall be permanently preserved"; from the *"hither"* side, it was the support and inspiration that resided within ourselves.[20] Not so, of course, to Freud, who posited that there was far more conflict in the drama of consciousness, and who never imagined that it could be so easily resolved.

After his one-day meeting with Freud at Clark University in September 1909, James wrote his friend Flournoy that Freud and his pupils couldn't "fail to throw light on human nature."[21] At the conference itself, he was "very friendly" to Freud and his pupils. Ernest Jones remembers his putting his arm around him and saying, "The future of psychology belongs to your work."[22] For his part, Freud has left us with this moving image of James:

I shall never forget one little scene that occurred as we were on a walk together. He stopped suddenly, handed me a bag he was carrying and asked me to walk on, saying that he would catch me up as soon as he had gone through an attack of angina pectoris which was just coming on. He died of that disease a year later; and I have always wished that I might be as fearless as he was in the face of approaching death.[23]

The man whom Stein had described lecturing on the theme "Is Life Worth Living?"—"He stands firmly, nobly for the dignity of man"—stood firmly to the end.

After his death, George Herbert Palmer had this to say about James: "Whenever that alert figure comes to my mind—he of the handsome face, upright bearing, energetic movement, swift step, and tempered voice—there always comes with it the adjective 'manly.' "[24]

During his lifetime, James had been instrumental in establishing the standard by which men measured themselves in post–Civil War America. He represented energy, virility, perseverance, and even—if properly deflected—militarism. But he was also different—inspiring in his awareness of the limitations of the very standard he so impressively met.

Around 1909–10, talk of manhood died down. But for all the unbridgeable differences, the idea of manhood is like Freudian psychology itself: it lives on whether people talk about it, accept it or reject it, or not. We cannot stop noticing, encouraging, and privileging it—even as we seek ways to diminish its influence. By now it is systemic in our culture. *Manhood at Harvard: William James and Others* is an account of how it got into our system.

Notes

Introduction

1. This assumes that Harvard held a commencement every year, after its first in 1642. The proceedings of the 1908 commencement are reported in *Harvard Graduates' Magazine*, XVII (September 1908), 55–78 (hereafter cited as *HGM*).
2. Robert D. Richardson Jr., *Emerson: The Mind on Fire* (Berkeley: University of California Press, 1995), p. 534.
3. Gail Bederman, *Manliness & Civilization: A Cultural History of Gender and Race in the United States* (Chicago: University of Chicago Press, 1995), pp. 18–19; Michael Kimmel, *Manhood in America: A Cultural History* (New York: Free Press, 1996), pp. 119–20.
4. Nell Irvin Painter, *Standing at Armageddon: The United States, 1877–1919* (New York: W. W. Norton, 1987), pp. 162–63.
5. Howard Mumford Jones, *The Age of Energy: Varieties of American Experience, 1865–1915* (New York: Viking Press, 1971), pp. 157–58; Irving S. and Nell M. Kull, *A Short Chronology of American History, 1492–1950* (New Brunswick: Rutgers University Press, 1952).
6. Alan Trachtenberg, *The Incorporation of America: Culture and Society in the Gilded Age* (New York: Hill and Wang, 1982), pp. 84–85.
7. Kull and Kull; Painter, p. xx; Thomas J. Schlereth, *Victorian America: Transformations in Everyday Life, 1876–1915* (New York: Harper Collins, 1991), pp. 33–34.
8. *Educational Reform: Essays and Addresses* (New York: Century, 1898), p. 34.
9. (New York: G. P. Putnam's Sons, 1881), pp. vi–vii.
10. *Harvard Memorial Biographies*, 2 vols. (Cambridge: Sever and Francis, 1866), I, iv–v.
11. *The Frontier in American History* (New York: Henry Holt, 1920), p. 37.
12. *HGM*, XVII (September 1908), 34.
13. (New York: E. P. Dutton, 1952), pp. 19–20.
14. *The Selected Writings of John Jay Chapman*, ed. Jacques Barzun (New York: Minerva Press, 1957), p. 217.
15. Charles H. Compton, *William James: Philosopher and Man* (New York: Scarecrow Press, 1957), p. 111.
16. *Writings, vol. 1, 1878–1899* (New York: Library of America, 1992), 618–46 (hereafter cited as *Writings*). All references to James' writings are to this volume and to *Writings*, vol. 2, *1902–1910* (New York: Library of America, 1987), unless otherwise noted.
17. Ibid., I, 648.
18. Ibid., II, 639.
19. *The Letters of William James*, ed. Henry James, 2 vols. (Boston: Atlantic Monthly Press, 1920), II, 355 (hereafter cited as *Letters*).
20. James Hoopes, *Van Wyck Brooks: In Search of American Culture* (Amherst: University of Massachusetts Press, 1977), p. 39; *Harvard Advocate*, LXXXIII (April 12, 1907), 35–37.
21. *Sketches in Criticism* (New York: E. P. Dutton, 1932), p. 40.
22. *Harvard Advocate*, LXXXIII (April 26, 1907), 50.
23. *Writings*, I, 651.
24. George Wilson Pierson, *Yale College: An Educational History, 1871–1921*, 2 vols. (New Haven: Yale University Press, 1952), I, 48.

1. *William James*

"Is Life Worth Living?"

1. Rosalind S. Miller, *Gertrude Stein: Form and Intelligibility* (New York: Exposition Press, 1949), pp. 146–47.
2. James B. Gilbert, *Work without Salvation* (Baltimore: Johns Hopkins University Press, 1977), pp. 9–10.
3. *Letters,* II, 15.
4. Ibid., p. 39.
5. *HGM,* IX (June 1901), 511.
6. M. A. DeWolfe Howe, *Barrett Wendell and His Letters* (Boston: Atlantic Monthly Press, 1924), p. 47.
7. *Letters,* I, 313.
8. Ralph Barton Perry, *The Thought and Character of William James,* 2 vols. (Boston: Little, Brown, 1935), I, 802 (hereafter cited as *TCWJ*).
9. R. W. B. Lewis, *The Jameses: A Family Narrative* (New York: Doubleday, 1991), pp. 320–21.
10. *The Diary of Alice James,* ed. Leon Edel (New York: Penguin, 1982), p. 52.
11. Lewis, p. 415.
12. *Writings,* I, 480–503.
13. Ibid., II, 141–46, 171–73.
14. Ibid., p. 463.
15. *Letters of Sarah Wyman Whitman* (Cambridge: Riverside Press, 1907), p. 117.
16. LXII (November 1896), 64.
17. "Harvard in the Nineties," *New England Quarterly,* IX (1936), 66–67.
18. *Letters,* II, 11, 14.
19. *Persons and Places* (New York: Charles Scribner's Sons, 1963), II, 159; I, 242; II, 166; *The Genteel Tradition* (Cambridge: Harvard University Press, 1967), p. 55.
20. Van Wyck Brooks, *Scenes and Portraits: Memories of Childhood and Youth* (New York: E. P. Dutton, 1954), p. 99.
21. *TCWJ,* I, 24–26; *College in a Yard: Minutes by Thirty-nine Harvard Men,* ed. Brooks Atkinson (Cambridge: Harvard University Press, 1957), p. 119.
22. M. A. DeWolfe Howe, "A Packet of Wendell-James Letters," *Scribner's Magazine,* LXXXIV (December 1928), 678.
23. *The Correspondence of William James: William and Henry,* ed. Ignas K. Skrupskelis and Elizabeth M. Berkeley, 3 vols. (Charlottesville: University of Virginia Press, 1992–94), III, 233 (hereafter cited as *Correspondence*).
24. *Writings,* I, 146.
25. Letter of May 26, 1895, by permission of the Houghton Library, Harvard University (shelf mark bMS Am 1092.9, 3922).
26. *Letters,* I, 214–15.
27. *Writings,* II, 1237.
28. We learn most about the difficulties James had in settling upon a career from Howard M. Feinstein, *Becoming William James* (Ithaca: Cornell University Press, 1984).
29. *TCWJ,* I, 145.
30. *Writings,* I, 587.
31. "William James," *Atlantic Monthly,* CVI (December 1910), 848.
32. *TCWJ,* I, 258.
33. *Letters,* II, 260.
34. Ibid., I, 43–44.
35. "William James," p. 837.
36. *Writings,* I, 872, 874.
37. Ibid., II, 333.
38. Gay Wilson Allen, *William James* (New York: Viking Press, 1967), p. 196.
39. *Selected Writings,* p. 205.
40. *Character and Opinion in the United States* (New York: Charles Scribner's Sons, 1920), pp. 77–82.
41. *The Diary,* pp. 51, 57, 68.
42. *Writings,* II, 1129.
43. "A Reminiscence of William James," *HGM,* XX (March 1912), 581–82, reprinted from the November 1911 issue of *American Magazine.*
44. Elizabeth Glendower Evans, "William James and His Wife," *Atlantic Monthly,* CXLIV (September 1929), 385.
45. Dickinson S. Miller, "William James, Man and Philosopher," in *William James: The Man and the Thinker* (Madison: University of Wisconsin Press, 1942), p. 52.
46. *Selected Writings,* p. 206.
47. *Letters,* II, 255.

Chained to a Dead Man

1. *Letters,* I, 129.
2. *TCWJ,* I, 216.
3. *Writings,* II, 149.
4. *Correspondence,* III, 153–54.
5. *Letters,* II, 214.
6. Ibid., I, 75.
7. Ibid., pp. 127–33.
8. *Writings,* I, 148.
9. *HGM,* V (June 1897), 536.
10. *The Letters of William James and Theodore Flournoy,* ed. R. C. LeClair (Madison: University of Wisconsin Press, 1966), p. 200.

11. Excerpts from James' Diary of 1868–73 are reprinted by permission of the Houghton Library, Harvard University (shelf mark bMS 1092.9, 4550).
12. *Writings*, I, 149.
13. Gerald E. Myers, *William James: His Life and Thought* (New Haven: Yale University Press, 1986), p. 34.
14. (Cambridge: Harvard University Press, 1983), p. 144.
15. *TCWJ*, I, 339–40.
16. Ibid., p. 323.
17. December 30, 1876, by permission of the Houghton Library, Harvard University (shelf mark bMS Am 1092.9, 3874).
18. See Feinstein, pp. 307–11, for a fuller account of this supposedly climactic moment.
19. *Writings*, I, 522.
20. Joseph Brent, *Charles Sanders Peirce* (Bloomington: Indiana University Press, 1993), p. 49.
21. *TCWJ*, I, 240.
22. Ibid., p. 276. See also James William Anderson, " 'The Worst Kind of Melancholy': William James in 1869," *Harvard Library Bulletin*, XXX (October 1982), 379–80.
23. *The Selected Letters of William James*, ed. Elizabeth Hardwick (New York: Farrar, Straus and Cudahy, 1960), p. 51.
24. May 27, 1868.
25. February 1, 1870.
26. *Writings*, II, 149–51.
27. John S. Haller Jr. and Robin M. Haller, *The Physician and Sexuality in Victorian America* (Urbana: University of Illinois Press, 1974), p. 203.
28. M. A. DeWolfe Howe, *John Jay Chapman and His Letters* (Boston: Houghton Mifflin, 1937), p. 200.
29. Alfred Habegger, *The Father: A Life of Henry James, Sr.* (New York: Farrar, Straus and Giroux, 1994), p. 415n.
30. *Letters*, I, 219–20.
31. John Owen King III, *The Iron of Melancholy: The Structure of Spiritual Conversion in America from the Puritan Conscience to Victorian Neurosis* (Middletown: Wesleyan University Press, 1983), pp. 90–94, compares the James' visions.
32. *TCWJ*, I, 165.
33. F. O. Matthiessen, *The James Family* (New York: Alfred A. Knopf, 1947), p. 136.
34. *Correspondence*, II, 68.
35. *TCWJ*, I, 165.
36. *The Death and Letters of Alice James*, ed. Ruth Bernard Yeazell (Berkeley: University of California Press, 1981), p. 180.
37. *The Literary Remains of the Late Henry James*, ed. William James (Boston: James R. Osgood, 1884), pp. 347–48, 355–56, 359.
38. *Selections from Ralph Waldo Emerson*, ed. Stephen E. Whicher (Boston: Houghton Mifflin, 1957), p. 219.
39. *The Literary Remains*, p. 297.
40. "Woman in Revelation and History," by permission of the Houghton Library, Harvard University (shelf mark bMS Am 1094.8, 74).
41. *Literary Remains*, p. 262.
42. Habegger, *Henry James and the "Woman Business"* (New York: Cambridge University Press, 1989), pp. 27–62, and *The Father*, pp. 329–42, 464–72, have helped me learn what he calls in the former "The Lessons of the Father."
43. (New York: Dewitt & Davenport, 1849), p. vi.
44. "The Logic of Marriage and Murder," *Atlantic Monthly*, XXV (June 1870), 744.
45. (Weston: M & S Press, 1975), pp. 92–95.
46. *The Diary*, p. 79.
47. James William Anderson, "In Search of Mary James," *Psychohistory Review*, VII–IX (1978–80), 67.
48. *TCWJ*, I, 112–13.

The Man—and Wife
1. *Writings*, II, 333.
2. Myers, p. 490, n. 31.
3. Bruce Kuklick, *The Rise of American Philosophy: Cambridge, Massachusetts, 1860–1930* (New Haven: Yale University Press, 1977), p. 48.
4. *TCWJ*, I, 509.
5. Liva Baker, *The Justice from Beacon Hill: The Life and Times of Oliver Wendell Holmes* (New York: HarperCollins, 1991), p. 154.
6. *TCWJ*, I, 514–15.
7. *Correspondence*, I, 102.
8. Ibid., p. 269.
9. Baker, p. 159.
10. *Correspondence*, III, 110.
11. *The Diary*, p. 35.
12. *TCWJ*, I, 518.
13. Lewis, p. 252.
14. *Letters*, I, 239–40.
15. Ibid., pp. 210–11.
16. "The Woman Thou Gavest with Me," *Atlantic Monthly*, XXV (January 1870), 66–72; *North American Review*, CIX (October 1869), 556–65.
17. *Putnam's Monthly Magazine*, I (March 1853), 279–88.

18. *Correspondence,* I, 141.
19. pp. 1053–55, 34–35.
20. Howe, *Chapman,* p. 199.
21. *A Victorian in the Modern World* (Seattle: University of Washington Press, 1972), p. 77.
22. *Psychological Review,* I (1894), 199; Eugene Taylor, *William James on Exceptional Mental States* (New York: Charles Scribner's Sons, 1982), pp. 70–71.
23. Dorothy Ross, *G. Stanley Hall: The Psychologist as Prophet* (Chicago: University of Chicago Press, 1972), p. 393.
24. *Sketches and Reminiscences of the Radical Club,* ed. Mrs. John T. Sargent (Boston: James R. Osgood, 1880), p. 210.
25. Typescript of a Memoir of Alice Gibbens James by their son Henry James III, p. 34, by permission of the Houghton Library, Harvard University (shelf mark MS Am 1095.1).
26. Ibid., p. 35.
27. Unless otherwise noted, citations of James' letters to his wife are to those in the Houghton Library, by permission of the Houghton Library, Harvard University (shelf mark bMS Am 1092.9, 1160–2487). I have made occasional silent corrections.
28. Jean Strouse, *Alice James* (Boston: Houghton Mifflin, 1980), p. 180.
29. p. 1150.
30. November 12, 1876.
31. June 7, 1877.
32. August 24, 1877.
33. Dated only 1877.
34. *Letters,* I, 199–200.
35. March 15, 1877.
36. May 30, 1877.
37. March 10, 1888, and September 3, 1890.
38. Habegger, *Henry James and the "Woman Business",* p. 244, n. 12.
39. December, 16, 1882. All citations to Alice's letters to her husband are by permission of the Houghton Library, Harvard University (shelf mark bMS Am 1092.9, 270–345). There are seventy-six of them, the rest having been destroyed by James or, later, by their son Henry.
40. December 31, 1882.
41. January 6, 1883.
42. Letter of September 4, 1891, by permission of the Houghton Library, Harvard University (shelf mark bMS Am 1854, 877).
43. January 11, 1883.
44. December 24, 1893.
45. May 28, 1905.
46. *Letters,* II, 135.

47. Ibid., I, 250–52.
48. *The Complete Notebooks of Henry James,* ed. Leon Edel and Lyall H. Powers (New York: Oxford University Press, 1987), p. 20.
49. *TCWJ,* I, 786.
50. *The Inner Civil War: Northern Intellectuals and the Crisis of the Union* (New York: Harper & Row, 1965).
51. *Correspondence,* I, 303.
52. Strouse, p. 25.
53. p. 1054.
54. *Correspondence,* I, 193.
55. Ibid., II, 220.
56. *Letters,* I, 346–47.
57. *Writings,* II, 242–43.
58. Memoir of Alice Gibbens James, p. 3.
59. *Atlantic Monthly,* CXLIV (September 1929), pp. 380–81.
60. Memoir, pp. 36, 74.
61. Myers, p. 38.
62. Ibid., p. 39.
63. *The Complete Notebooks,* p. 198.
64. Included in the correspondence between James and Mrs. Whitman, by permission of the Houghton Library, Harvard University (shelf mark bMS Am 1092.9).
65. *William James: Selected Unpublished Correspondence, 1885–1910,* ed. Frederick J. Down Scott (Columbus: Ohio State University Press, 1986), pp. 231, 257, 198, 187 (hereafter cited as *Selected Unpublished Correspondence*).
66. *Correspondence,* III, 65.
67. September 5, 1895.
68. August 8, 1908, September 5, 1909. Citations of James' letters to Pauline Goldmark are by permission of the Houghton Library, Harvard University (shelf mark bMS Am 1092.1).
69. *Letters,* II, 75–78.
70. Saul Rosenzweig, *Freud, Jung, and Hall the King-Maker* (St. Louis: Hogrefe & Huber, 1992), pp. 186.
71. Josephine Goldmark, "An Adirondack Friendship: Letters of William James," *Atlantic Monthly,* CLIV (October 1934), 270.
72. Strouse, pp. 52–55. Cushing Strout pursues the question of Alice's hysteria and its possible relation to her sexual fantasies in his review of Strouse's book in the *Henry James Review* (Fall 1981), 59–63.
73. *The Death and Letters,* p. 152.
74. p. 96.
75. *The Death and Letters,* pp. 116–17.
76. *The Diary,* p. 208; *The Death and Letters,* pp. 192, 45. See also Kristin Boudreau, " 'A Barnum Monstrosity': Alice James and

the Spectacle of Sympathy," *American Literature,* LXV (March 1993), 53–67.
77. Allen, p. 170.
78. Letter of April 18, 1899.
79. H. V. Kaltenborn, *Fifty Fabulous Years* (New York: G. P. Putnam's Sons, 1950), p. 49.

80. Richard B. Hovey, *John Jay Chapman: An American Mind* (New York: Columbia University Press, 1959), p. 169.
81. Henry James III, *Charles W. Eliot: President of Harvard University, 1869–1909,* 2 vols. (Boston: Houghton Mifflin, 1930), II, 86–87.

2. Teaching Men Manhood at Harvard

1. XI (September 1902), 68–69.
2. The number of students in the undergraduate body is from Charles F. Dunbar, "President Eliot's Administration," *HGM,* II (June 1894), 466. Eliot's inaugural address is in Charles William Eliot, *Educational Reform,* pp. 1–38.
3. *Four American Universities: Harvard, Yale, Princeton, Columbia* (New York: Harper & Brothers, 1895), pp. 32, 35.
4. On Norton, see Rollo Walter Brown, *Harvard Yard in the Golden Age* (New York: A. A. Wyn, 1948), pp. 141–58; John Jay Chapman, *Memories and Milestones* (New York: Moffat, Yard, 1915), pp. 129–45; Richard Norton Smith, *The Harvard Century: The Making of a University to a Nation* (New York: Simon and Schuster, 1986), pp. 47–48.
5. *Untriangulated Stars: Letters of Edwin Arlington Robinson to Harry DeForest Smith, 1890–1905* (Cambridge: Harvard University Press, 1947), p. 76.
6. *Correspondence,* III, 376–77.
7. *Letters,* II, 187.

6. Charles Hopkinson, in *College in a Yard,* p. 99.
7. James, *Eliot,* II, 87.
8. *Fighting Years: Memoirs of a Liberal Editor* (New York: Harcourt, Brace, 1939), p. 84.
9. *HGM,* V (March 1897), 382.
10. *Letters of James Russell Lowell,* ed. Charles Eliot Norton, 2 vols. (New York: Harper & Brothers, 1894), II, 51.
11. Hawkins, pp. 60–61.
12. XXIII (February and March 1869), 216.
13. *Letters,* I, 216–17.
14. *Writings,* II, 11–12.
15. James, *Eliot,* I, 236–38.
16. Allen, pp. 76–77.
17. Hawkins, p. 67.
18. *TCWJ,* I, 440–41.
19. Allen, p. 158.
20. Hawkins, p. 73.
21. XII (June 1904), 581.
22. Gilbert, p. 133.
23. Sudhir Kakar, *Frederick Taylor: A Study in Personality and Innovation* (Cambridge: MIT Press, 1970), pp. 10–11.
24. See Ronald Story, *The Forging of an Aristocracy: Harvard & the Boston Upper Class, 1800–1870* (Middletown: Wesleyan University Press, 1980).
25. Hawkins, p. 216.
26. *Selected Writings,* pp. 208–20.
27. "The Spirit and Ideals of Harvard University," *Educational Review,* VII (April 1894), 321.

"First Citizen of the Republic"

1. On Eliot, see Samuel Eliot Morison, *Three Centuries of Harvard, 1636–1936* (Cambridge: Harvard University Press, 1937), pp. 323–99; Laurence R. Veysey, *The Emergence of the American University* (Chicago: University of Chicago Press, 1965); Donald Fleming, "Eliot's New Broom" in *Glimpses of Harvard Past* (Cambridge: Harvard University Press, 1986), pp. 63–76; Henry James III, *Charles W. Eliot: President of Harvard University, 1869–1909;* and, esp., Hugh Hawkins, *Between Harvard and America: The Educational Leadership of Charles W. Eliot* (New York: Oxford University Press, 1972).
2. Richard Norton Smith, pp. 27–28.
3. *College in a Yard: Minutes by Thirty-nine Harvard Men,* p. 83.
4. *Selected Writings,* p. 218.
5. James, *Eliot,* I, 12–14, 310.

The Harvard Aristocracy

1. See Oscar Handlin, "Making Men of the Boys," *Glimpses of Harvard Past,* pp. 45–62.
2. *HGM,* X (June 1902), 506–7.
3. David McCullough, *Mornings on Horseback* (New York: Simon and Schuster, 1981), pp. 198–99.
4. *HGM,* XI, (March 1903), 434.
5. Marcia Graham Synnott, *The Half-Opened Door: Discrimination and Admissions at Harvard, Yale, and Princeton, 1900–1970* (Westport: Greenwood Press, 1979), pp.

37–57; Veysey, pp. 271, 285–88.
6. I (October–December 1892), 58–59.
7. Veysey, p. 289.
8. McCullough, pp. 205–6.
9. "Harvard University in 1890," *Harper's Magazine*, LIII (September 1890), 587.
10. Morison, pp. 422–28.
11. CXLVII (November 1888), 542–53, and (December 1888), 645–53.
12. Story, pp. 92, 95, 176–77.
13. March 5, 1907.
14. Hawkins, p. 33.
15. Ibid., p. 12.
16. p. 406.

"Manly Sports"
1. *HGM*, II (September 1893), 1–18.
2. See V. L. Parrington, *The Beginnings of Critical Realism in America: 1860–1920* (New York: Harcourt, Brace, 1930), pp. 111–17.
3. *Proceedings of the American Antiquarian Society*, n.s., XIV (1900–1901), 116–17.
4. XII (March 1904), 372.
5. For Sargent, see Bruce L. Bennett, "Dudley A. Sargent—A Man for All Seasons," *Quest*, XXIX (Winter 1978), 33–45, and "Dudley Allen Sargent: The Man and His Philosophy," *Journal of Physical Education and Recreational Dance*, LV (November–December 1984), 61–64.
6. "Physical Education in College," *North American Review*, CCCXIV (February 1883), 177.
7. *Health, Strength, and Power* (New York: H. M. Caldwell, 1904), p. 56.
8. "Physical Characteristics of the Athlete," in D. A. Sargent et al., *The Out of Door Library: Athletic Sports* (New York: Charles Scribner's Sons, 1897), p. 104.
9. "Physical Education in College," p. 177.
10. *Physical Education* (Boston: Ginn, 1906), p. 23.
11. *HGM*, III (December 1894), 172.
12. Bennett, "Dudley A. Sargent—A Man for All Seasons," p. 38.
13. *Physical Education*, pp. 39–40.
14. Bennett, "Dudley A. Sargent—A Man for All Seasons," p. 38; *HGM*, XVI (June 1908), 616.
15. Ronald A. Smith, *Sports and Freedom: The Rise of Big-Time College Athletics* (New York: Oxford University Press, 1988), pp. 127–31.
16. Ira N. Hollis, "Football," *HGM*, XI (March 1903), 351.
17. Ibid., IV (December 1895), 181, 184.
18. Ibid., V (September 1896), 67.

19. Ibid., III (March 1895), 369.
20. Donald J. Mrozek, *Sport and American Mentality, 1880–1910* (Knoxville: University of Tennessee Press, 1983), p. 244, n. 41; Frederick Rudolph, *The American College and University* (New York: Vintage Books, 1962), p. 375.
21. (New York: G. P. Putnam's Sons, 1893), p. 293.
22. Morison, p. 412.
23. V (March 1897), 342.
24. *HGM*, XI (March 1903), 350–55.
25. Ibid., V (March 1897), 341–43, and 397.
26. p. 407.
27. *The Letters of Henry Adams*, ed. J. C. Levinson, Ernest Samuels, et al., 6 vols. (Cambridge: Harvard University Press, 1982–88), IV, 220.
28. *HGM*, XIII (June 1905), 630–31. For Reid, see Ronald A. Smith, *Sports and Freedom*, pp. 154–62, 195–98, and *Big-Time Football at Harvard, 1905: The Diary of Coach Bill Reid* (Urbana: University of Illinois Press, 1994).
29. *HGM*, XIII (June 1905), 602–3.
30. Smith, *Big-Time Football*, p. 327.
31. *HGM*, XIV (September 1905), 5.
32. Smith, *Sports and Freedom*, p. 95.
33. Rudolph, pp. 375–77.
34. Smith, *Sports and Freedom*, p. 195.
35. Ibid., p. 97.
36. VI (April 1888), 51.
37. Morison, p. 409.
38. *HGM*, XIII (March 1905), 384, 387.
39. Ibid., VII (March 1899), 384.
40. Ibid., p. 417.
41. *Selected Unpublished Correspondence*, p. 410.
42. *The Autobiography of Nathaniel Southgate Shaler, with a Supplementary Memoir by His Wife* (Boston: Houghton Mifflin, 1909), pp. 98–99.
43. Ibid., pp. 336–37.
44. Santayana, *Persons and Places*, I, 196.
45. *Letters*, II, 325.
46. p. 30.
47. *HGM*, VII (December 1898), 199.
48. Ibid., XII (September 1903), 64.
49. *Letters*, II, 325.
50. *Writings*, I, 825–40.
51. *Letters*, II, 159.
52. *Correspondence*, III, 207–8.
53. XII (December 1903), 228–29.
54. *Correspondence*, III, 250–51.
55. p. 216.
56. *Race Questions, Provincialism, and Other American Problems* (New York: Macmillan, 1908), pp. 229–87.
57. XVIII (July 1894), 181–90.

58. *HGM,* VI (December 1897), 196.
59. Smith, *Sports and Freedom,* p. 144.

"Scholarly Manliness"
1. *The Letters of Josiah Royce,* ed. John Clendenning (Chicago: University of Chicago Press, 1970), p. 237.
2. CIL (July 1889), 10–15.
3. *The Autobiography of a Philosopher* (Boston: Houghton Mifflin, 1930), pp. 109–10.
4. Morison, p. 341.
5. Ibid., pp. 344–45.
6. Albert R. Kitzhaber, *Rhetoric in American Colleges, 1850–1900* (Dallas: Southern Methodist University Press, 1990), pp. 1–6.
7. Rudolph, pp. 303–4; Veysey, pp. 50–52.
8. *Educational Reform,* pp. 132–33.
9. Morison, p. 343.
10. *The Triple Thinkers* (New York: Oxford University Press, 1948), p. 150.
11. *HGM,* II (June 1894), 601.
12. VIII (March 1889), 4.
13. *Persons and Places,* I, 240; Fleming, "A Small Community," pp. 92–93.
14. Veysey, p. 272.
15. Henry A. Yeomans, *Abbott Lawrence Lowell, 1856–1943* (Cambridge: Harvard University Press, 1948), p. 70.
16. p. 14.
17. "Liberty in Education," *Educational Reform,* pp. 148, 140.
18. *A Victorian in the Modern World,* pp. 66–67.
19. *The Changing Years* (New York: Farrar & Rinehart, 1930), p. 46.
20. *All Our Years* (New York: Viking Press, 1948), pp. 32–34.
21. Stephen R. Fox, *The Guardian of Boston: William Monroe Trotter* (New York: Atheneum, 1970), p. 19.
22. LXXXVI (1900), 463–70.
23. *Literature and the American College: Essays in Defense of the Humanities* (Boston: Houghton Mifflin, 1908), p. 47.
24. Ibid., pp. 76–78.
25. *HGM,* XI (March 1903), 356.
26. *Literature and the American College,* p. 79.
27. Ibid., pp. 118–19.
28. Ibid., pp. 100–01.
29. *Letters of Wallace Stevens,* ed. Holly Stevens (New York: Alfred A. Knopf, 1966), p. 26.
30. Ibid., p. 180.
31. See Frank Lentricchia, "Patriarchy against Itself—The Young Manhood of Wallace Stevens," in *Ariel and the Police* (Madison:

University of Wisconsin Press, 1988), esp. pp. 136–39 and 158–63.
32. LXXXIII (April 12, 1907), 35.
33. (New York: E. P. Dutton, 1965), p. 122.
34. Hoopes, *Van Wyck Brooks,* p. 39.
35. Hawkins, p. 220.
36. *Scenes and Portraits,* pp. 120–21.
37. Ibid., pp. 105–6.
38. "Discipline in American Colleges," p. 14.
39. Hall, pp. 99, 105; Santayana, "The Spirit and Ideals of Harvard University," p. 315.
40. *Letters,* II, 90.
41. *Living Age,* CCLIX (1908), 647–48, reprinted from *Contemporary Review* for December 12, 1908; *Scenes and Portraits,* p. 116.

"Man to Man"
1. *Educational Reform,* pp. 16–17.
2. *Trades and Professions* (Boston: Houghton Mifflin, 1914), pp. 33–34.
3. XXII (1897), 513.
4. *HGM,* I (April 1893), 344–47.
5. "Failure," *The Education of Henry Adams* (Boston: Houghton Mifflin, 1973), pp. 299–313. For Adams' teaching years at Harvard, see also Ernest Samuels, *The Young Henry Adams* (Cambridge: Harvard University Press, 1948), pp. 203–18.
6. For example, Clive Bush, *Halfway to Revolution: Investigation and Crisis in the Work of Henry Adams, William James and Gertrude Stein* (New Haven: Yale University Press, 1991), p. 38.
7. *The Selected Letters of Henry Adams,* ed. Newton Arvin (New York: Farrar, Straus and Cudahy, 1951), p. 65.
8. Brown, *Harvard Yard,* p. 195; Morison, p. 403; Smith, *The Harvard Century,* p. 90; Aiken, *The Clerk's Journal* (New York: Eakins Press, 1971), pp. 2–3.
9. *Men, Women, and College* (Boston: Houghton Mifflin, 1925), p. 144.
10. "Some Old-Fashioned Doubts about New-Fashioned Education," pp. 57–59.
11. *HGM,* XVI (September 1907), 113.
12. *Men, Women, and College,* p. 18.
13. Rollo Walter Brown, *Dean Briggs* (New York: Harper & Brothers, 1926), p. 60; Veysey, pp. 222–23.
14. Howe, *Wendell,* pp. 11–12, 50–51, 121.
15. Morison, p. 408.
16. Howe, *Wendell,* p. 327.
17. *Persons and Places,* II, 170–72.
18. Howe, "A Packet of Wendell-James Letters," p. 677.
19. (New York: Charles Scribner's Sons, 1908), pp. 21–24.

20. Ronald Steel, *Walter Lippmann and the American Century* (Boston: Little, Brown, 1980), p. 17.
21. Brooks, *Scenes and Portraits,* p. 110; Wendell, *Stelligeri and Other Essays* (New York: Charles Scribner's Sons, 1893), p. 144.
22. Howe, *Wendell,* p. 68; "The Harvard Undergraduate," *Harvard Monthly,* VIII (March 1889), 6, 8.
23. Howe, *Wendell,* p. 109.
24. (Boston: James R. Osgood, 1885), pp. 17, 100–01.
25. *Educational Review,* VII (April 1894), 313–25.
26. *Official Guide to the World's Columbian Exposition* (Chicago: Columbian Guide Company, 1893), p. 85.
27. pp. 35, 42–43, 49.
28. Steel, p. 21.
29. (Boston: Gorham Press, 1902), pp. 7, 65, 77.
30. XXXIV (December 11, 1897), 107.
31. VI (March 1898), 335.
32. XXV (January 1898), 159–60.
33. XXXIII (December 1901), 127.
34. *HGM,* XVI (September 1907), 114.
35. *Persons and Places,* I, 183; III, 8.
36. *Sonnets and Other Verses* (New York: Duffield, 1906), p. 63.
37. II (June 1894), 596.
38. Daniel Cory, *Santayana: The Later Years* (New York: G. Braziller, 1963), pp. 40–41.
39. See, for example, William Dana Orcutt, "Clubs and Club Life at Harvard," *New England Magazine,* XII (1892), 81–98.
40. p. 92.
41. *Character and Opinion,* p. 186; *Persons and Places,* II, 156.
42. Veysey, p. 97; John McCormick, *George Santayana* (New York: Alfred A. Knopf, 1987), p. 97.
43. Cory, p. 42.
44. *Selected Unpublished Correspondence,* pp. 57, 140, 169.
45. pp. 1053–54.
46. *Persons and Places,* II, 166–67.
47. Ibid., p. 39.
48. *The Portrait of a Lady* (New York: Penguin, 1963), pp. 168–71, 208, 92.
49. Edmund Morris, *The Rise of Theodore Roosevelt* (New York: Coward, McCann & Geoghegan, 1979), pp. 467–68.

John Jay Chapman on the Spirit of the Age
1. Howe, *Chapman,* pp. 67, 106.
2. Ibid., pp. 17, 25, 63, 39; Hovey, p. 48.
3. Hovey, pp. 10–12.
4. M. A. DeWolfe Howe, ed., "John Jay Chapman to William James: A Packet of Letters," *Harper's Magazine,* CLXXIV (December 1936), 54.
5. Howe, *Chapman,* p. 207.
6. Ibid., pp. 26, 28.
7. Ibid., pp. 43, 56–60.
8. Chapman's and Minna Timmins' letters are in Hovey, pp. 51–55, with the exception of Chapman's letter about Holmes, which is cited by permission of the Houghton Library, Harvard University (shelf mark bMS Am 1854).
9. Hovey, p. 63.
10. *The Collected Works of John Jay Chapman,* 12 vols. (Weston: M & S Press, 1970), X, 120, 133, 135–36.
11. *Selected Writings,* pp. 163, 169, 151.
12. *Collected Works,* II, 59, 65, 71.
13. Howe, *Chapman,* p. 213, 197, 76.
14. *Selected Writings,* pp. 208–20.
15. "John Jay Chapman to William James," pp. 49–50.
16. Hovey, p. 306.
17. Howe, *Chapman,* p. 97.
18. *HGM,* XXI (September 1912), 20–21.
19. Howe, *Chapman,* p. 168.
20. Van Wyck Brooks, *The Confident Years: 1885–1915* (New York: E. P. Dutton, 1952), p. 404.
21. Hovey, p. 253.
22. "John Jay Chapman to William James," p. 50.
23. *Collected Works,* II, 75.
24. Hovey, p. 75.
25. *Vanity Fair,* XII (May 1919), 30, 84.

3. *William James' Teaching*

The "Undisciplinables" and the "Pass Men"
1. *Character and Opinion,* p. 92.
2. *TCWJ,* I, 476.
3. XXIX (May 1880), 75.
4. XLIV (March 1907), 57.
5. *Letters of Charles Eliot Norton,* ed. Sara Norton and M. A. DeWolfe Howe, 2 vols. (Boston: Houghton Mifflin, 1913), II, 412.
6. *Ludwig Wittgenstein: Personal Recollections,* ed. Rush Rhees (Totowa: Rowman and Littlefield, 1981), p. 121.
7. *TCWJ,* I, 435–36.
8. *HGM,* XVIII (December 1909), 361, and XVII (June 1909), 748.
9. Ibid., XVI (September 1907), 21, 23, 25.
10. XXIV (May 1897), 132.

11. Veysey, p. 420.
12. *Writings,* II, 639.
13. Ibid., pp. 13, 21, 26.
14. Ibid., p. 502.
15. Ibid., p. 1159.
16. Ibid., I, 837.
17. Santayana, *Character and Opinion,* p. 96.
18. *All Our Years,* p. 38.
19. "William James and the Philosophy of Life," *William James and Other Essays* (New York: Macmillan, 1911), p. 7.
20. Lewis, p. 442; Lawrence Thompson, *Robert Frost: The Early Years, 1874–1915* (New York: Holt, Rinehart and Winston, 1966), p. 536.
21. Rudolph, p. 395.
22. *Writings,* II, 1111–18.
23. I am thinking of "Whoever You Are Holding Me Now in Hand" from *Calamus.* Other references are to his "Song of Myself."
24. *A Victorian in the Modern World,* pp. 67, 77.
25. "An Open Mind: William James," *Everybody's Magazine,* XXIII (December 1910), 801.
26. *College in a Yard,* p. 84.
27. XXVIII (January 21, 1895), 67.
28. *Writings,* II, 1126–29.
29. *Persons and Places,* I, 241.
30. *HGM,* XVIII (June 1910), 631.
31. *Letters,* II, 100–01.
32. *HGM,* XII (September 1903), 64.
33. *Writings,* II, 1242–49.
34. Letter dated 1902.
35. "The Proposed Shortening of the College Course," *Harvard Monthly,* XI (January 1891), 127–37.
36. *Writings,* I, 614–17.
37. *TCWJ,* I, 435–36.
38. "William James and the Philosophy of Life," pp. 17, 31, 45.
39. Miller, *Stein,* p. 147.
40. *Writings,* I, 834.
41. Ibid., p. 829.
42. Ibid., II, 1224–28.
43. Ibid., pp. 330–33.
44. Ibid., pp. 1281–93.
45. Ibid., p. 79.
46. p. 1181.

"The Fullness of Living Itself"
1. *Writings,* II, 109–31.
2. ed. Richard Ashley Rice (New York: Charles Scribner's Sons, 1915).
3. *Race Questions, Provincialism, and Other American Problems,* pp. 149–50, 157.
4. *The Principles of Psychology,* pp. 219–40.

5. *Writings,* II, 603.
6. Ibid., pp. 1236–37.
7. Ibid., I, 466.
8. Ibid., II, 729, 740.
9. Pierson, p. 11n.
10. *Letters,* II, 279.
11. *Writings,* II, 487–89.
12. Kuklick, p. 159.
13. *Writings,* II, 490–92, 500–501.
14. (Oxford, 1907), I, 179.
15. *Writings,* II, 505, 518–19.
16. Wendy Lesser, *His Other Half* (Cambridge: Harvard University Press, 1990), pp. 119–20.
17. *Writings,* I, 511, 522, 960, 523.
18. Ibid., II, 30–31.
19. Ibid., I. 508–9.
20. Schlereth, pp. 253–55.
21. *Writings,* I, 863–64, 876.
22. Ibid., II, 533.
23. Ibid., p. 463.
24. Ibid., p. 510.
25. Ibid., p. 599.
26. Ibid., I, 533.
27. *Character and Opinion,* p. 92.
28. Ibid., p. 96.
29. *Letters,* 11, 76.
30. *Writings,* II, 1215–22.
31. *Correspondence,* III, 313n.
32. *Writings,* II, 941.
33. Ibid., pp. 614–15, 619.

Differences with Others
1. *TCWJ,* II, 575.
2. *Sketches in Criticism* (New York: E. P. Dutton, 1932), pp. 39, 42–43.
3. Brent, p. 1.
4. Ibid., p. 317; *TCWJ,* I, 536, 539–41. For Peirce, see also Kuklick, pp. 104–26, 264–69.
5. *TCWJ,* II, 432–33.
6. Ibid., pp. 430, 432.
7. John Clendenning, *The Life and Thought of Josiah Royce* (Madison: University of Wisconsin Press, 1985), pp. 63–64.
8. *TCWJ,* I, 779.
9. Clendenning, pp. 131–32.
10. Ibid., pp. 244–46.
11. Robert V. Hine, *Josiah Royce: From Grass Valley to Harvard* (Norman: University of Oklahoma Press, 1992), p. 117.
12. *TCWJ,* I, 780.
13. *Letters,* II, 136.
14. Clendenning, p. 313.
15. *Writings,* I, 904.
16. *TCWJ,* I, 812.
17. *The Letters of Josiah Royce,* pp. 511–12.
18. *TCWJ,* I, 402–5.

19. Letter of August 7, 1888, by permission of the Houghton Library, Harvard University (shelf mark bMS Am 1092.9, 600).
20. *Letters,* II, 229.
21. Ibid., pp. 122–24.
22. McCormick, pp. 88–90.
23. *Character and Opinion,* p. 73.
24. pp. 43, 47, 59, 84–85.

25. (New York: Charles Scribner's Sons, 1936), p. 187.
26. *Persons and Places,* II 166.
27. June 7, 1877.
28. Henry Samuel Levinson, *Santayana, Pragmatism, and the Spiritual Life* (Chapel Hill: University of North Carolina Press, 1992), pp. 181–83.

4. On a Certain Blindness

1. p. 353.
2. *Writings,* I, 841–60.
3. *The Letters of William James and Theodore Flournoy,* p. 79; Elizabeth Evans, "William James and His Wife," p. 377.
4. VIII (September 1899), 135.
5. Rosenzweig, pp. 182–95.
6. Josephine Goldmark, "An Adirondack Friendship," pp. 266, 447, 265.
7. *Writings,* I, 877–80.
8. *The Education,* p. 72.
9. Sydney Kaplan, "Taussig, James and Peabody: A 'Harvard School' in 1900?" *American Quarterly,* VII (Winter 1955), 315–31.
10. *Fighting Years,* p. 105.
11. On the limitations of James' cure for blindness—and for an insightful comparison of the James brothers generally—see Ross Posnock, "Henry and William James and the Trial of Curiosity," in *The Trial of Curiosity: Henry James, William James, and the Challenge of Modernity* (New York: Oxford University Press, 1991), pp. 27–53.
12. Helen Keller, *Midstream* (New York: Doubleday, Doran, 1929), pp. 316–17; *TCWJ,* II, 455.
13. *Writings by W. E. B. Du Bois in Non-Periodical Literature Edited by Others,* ed. Herbert Aptheker (Millwood: Kraus-Thomson, 1982), p. 164.

bridge: MIT Press, 1981), pp. 67–89.
7. Strouse, p. 115.
8. XXIII (January 1869), 29–30, 39.
9. *The Autobiography of Nathaniel Southgate Shaler,* p. 420.
10. *Letters,* II, 244.
11. Letter to William, December 3, 1882.
12. Hayden, p. 82.
13. Strouse, pp. 136, 170–75.
14. *A Room of One's Own* (New York: Harcourt, Brace & World, 1957), p. 57.
15. "Present Tendencies in Women's Colleges and University Education," *Educational Review,* XXV (1908), 68.
16. (Boston: James R. Osgood, 1873), pp. 41, 45, 69, 111. For Mitchell's "rest cure," see Suzanne Poirier, "The Weir Mitchell Rest Cure: Doctor and Patients," *Women's Studies,* X (1983), 15–40.
17. *American Nervousness,* p. 96.
18. *Sex in Education,* pp. 120–21, 19, 62–63, 139–40, 97.
19. Christopher Jencks and David Riesman, *The Academic Revolution* (New York: Doubleday, 1969), p. 294.
20. *American Nervousness,* p. 93.
21. p. 1054.
22. *The Development of Harvard University since the Inauguration of President Eliot, 1869–1929* ed. Samuel Eliot Morison (Cambridge: Harvard University Press, 1930), p. 561.
23. 2 vols. (New York: D. Appleton, 1904), II, 639, 573, 579, 622, 578, 605–6, 619.
24. Ibid., 610–11, 578, 194, 616.
25. The best book on the bad science is Stephen Jay Gould, *The Mismeasure of Man* (New York: W. W. Norton, 1981).
26. *Adolescence,* II, 624.
27. Ibid., 194.
28. *Appleton's Magazine,* XIII (January 1909), 47, 49.
29. *Adolescence,* II, 614–17, 625.
30. *World's Work,* XVI (1908), 10241–42.
31. *The Souls of Black Folk,* in *W. E. B. Du Bois: Writings* (New York: Library of America, 1986), p. 393. Unless otherwise noted, all

"As the Men Saw Her"

1. *The Complete Notebooks,* pp. 18–20.
2. (New York: Penguin, 1984), pp. 327, 315, 377.
3. Ibid., pp. 145–46.
4. pp. 105, 199.
5. *HGM,* IV (December 1895), 321; Robert A. Rosenstone, *Romantic Revolutionary: A Biography of John Reed* (New York: Alfred A. Knopf, 1975), p. 45.
6. For Melusina Fay Peirce, see Dolores Hayden, *The General Domestic Revolution: A History of Feminist Designs for American Homes, Neighborhoods, and Cities* (Cam-

citations of Du Bois are to this edition.

32. See William Gass, *The World within the Word* (New York: Alfred A. Knopf, 1978), p. 120.
33. II, 634.
34. (New York: D. Appleton, 1920), pp. vi, 219–20.
35. Ibid., pp. 232, 296.
36. (New York: D. Appleton, 1923).
37. *Historical Essays* (New York: Charles Scribner's Sons, 1891), pp. 3, 5, 13.
38. Ibid., p. 15.
39. *Adolescence*, II, 646.
40. *The Education*, pp. 384, 445.
41. Edward N. Saveth, "The Heroines of Henry Adams," *American Quarterly*, VIII (1956), 232.
42. Allen, p. 477.
43. *Esther* (New York: Scholars' Facsimiles & Reprints, 1938), p. 168.
44. CXVIII (January 1874), 140–52.
45. Eugenia Kaledin, *The Education of Mrs. Henry Adams* (Philadelphia: Temple University Press, 1981), pp. 13, 77, 166. Kaledin makes a strong case for seeing the worst in the Adams's marriage. See also William Dusinberre, *The Myth of Failure* (Charlottesville: University of Virginia Press, 1980), pp. 55–56.
46. *A Novelist in the Making*, ed. James D. Hart (Cambridge: Harvard University Press, 1970), p. 74.
47. *HGM*, XIV (December 1905), 215.
48. Quoted in Hamilton Vaughan Bail, "Harvard Fiction," *Proceedings of the American Antiquarian Society*, LXVIII (1958), 274; (Boston: L. C. Page, 1901), p. 35.
49. *The Argonaut Manuscript Limited Edition of Frank Norris's Works*, 10 vols. (New York: Doubleday, Doran, 1928), V, 20–21, 24–25, 188, 293. All references to Norris's writings are to this complete edition.
50. VIII, 20, 26, 27, 77–78.
51. III, 123, 171.
52. IX, 60, 67.
53. VII, 177–81.
54. Franklin Walker, *Frank Norris* (New York: Doubleday, 1932), p. 151.
55. IX, 118.
56. "Dr. Clarke's 'Sex in Education,' " p. 142.
57. *Educational Reform*, pp. 22–24.
58. II (March 1894), 330.
59. As Hawkins puts it, "Eliot could firmly deny both that Harvard deprived women of their intellectual rights and that it had embarked on so perilous a course 'what is called co-education.' " P. 196.
60. *HGM*, VII (March 1899), 416.
61. Ibid., pp. 83.

62. Ibid., XI (September 1902), 77.
63. *Forum*, XII (September 1891), 39.
64. For the Agassiz School and the founding of Radcliffe, see Kaledin, pp. 37–50.
65. Ibid., p. 50.
66. Brazil Diary, p. 7, by permission of the Houghton Library, Harvard University (shelf mark MS Am 1092.9, 4498); *Letters*, II, 181.
67. For the history of Radcliffe see Paul Buck, "Harvard Attitudes toward Radcliffe in the Early Years," *Proceedings of the Massachusetts Historical Society*, LXXIV (1962), 33–50; Dorothy Elia Howells, *A Century to Celebrate: Radcliffe College, 1879–1979* (Cambridge: Radcliffe College, 1978), pp. 1–19; Elaine Kendall, *"Peculiar Institutions": An Informal History of the Seven Sisters Colleges* (New York: G. P. Putnam's Sons, 1976), pp. 62–70.
68. *HGM*, XVI (September 1907), 43.
69. Ibid., VIII (September 1899), 68.
70. Ibid., XIV (September 1905), 111.
71. *Girls and Education* (Boston: Houghton Mifflin, 1911), p. 28.
72. *HGM*, XV (September 1906), 98.
73. *Girls and Education*, pp. 22, 92.
74. II (March 1894), 343, 338–39.
75. LVI (March 1894), 148–49, 68–69; LX (October 1895), 35–37.
76. XXXV (June 24, 1898), 170–71.
77. *Lampoon*, XXX (January 21, 1896), 131.
78. XLVII (April 1889), 40–41.
79. Miller, *Stein*, p. 120.
80. "Toward an Understanding of Achievement-Related Conflicts in Women," *Journal of Social Issues*, XXVIII (1972), 157–75.
81. Grace Hollingsworth Tucker, "The Gods Serve Hebe," *Radcliffe Quarterly*, XVII (October 1933), 192–204.
82. Ernest Earnest, *S. Weir Mitchell* (Philadelphia: University of Pennsylvania Press, 1950), pp. 150–51.
83. Donald Gallup, ed., *The Flowers of Friendship: Letters Written to Gertrude Stein* (New York: Alfred A. Knopf, 1953), p. 4; *American Traits* (Boston: Houghton Mifflin, 1901), pp. 160–63.
84. Tucker, pp. 200–202.
85. Ibid., p. 197.
86. Bennett, "Dudley A. Sargent—A Man for All Seasons," pp. 40–41; Mrozek, pp. 147–48.
87. Hayden, p. 268.
88. pp. 210, 373.
89. *HGM*, X (September 1901), 45.
90. *Correspondence*, II, 388.
91. Ibid., p. 300.

92. (New York: Modern Library, 1933), pp. 78–79.
93. "The Relations of Radcliffe College with Harvard," *Harvard Monthly*, XXIX (October 1899), 1–10.
94. Howe, *Wendell*, p. 87; Brown, *Dean Briggs*, p. 211n.
95. *The Letters of Josiah Royce*, pp. 395, 439.
96. p. 162.
97. Howe, *Wendell*, pp. 50, 333–34.
98. Fleming, "A Small Community," p. 88.

"All the New Races"

1. *Untriangulated Stars*, p. 47.
2. "Almost Thirty," *New Republic*, LXXXVI (April 29, 1936), 332–33.
3. *Educational Reform*, p. 22.
4. Reginald Horsman, *Race and Manifest Destiny: The Origins of American Racial Anglo-Saxonism* (Cambridge: Harvard University Press, 1981), pp. 1–6.
5. Painter, pp. 142–53.
6. Ernest Samuels, *Bernard Berenson: The Making of a Connoisseur* (Cambridge: Harvard University Press, 1979), p. 34.
7. Madison Grant, *The Passing of the Great Race in America* (New York: Charles Scribner's Sons, 1916); Lothrop Stoddard, *The Rising Tide of Color against White World-Supremacy* (New York: Charles Scribner's Sons, 1920).
8. George M. Fredrickson, *The Black Image in the White Mind: The Debate on African-American Character and Destiny* (New York: Harper & Row, 1971), p. 161; Thomas F. Gossett, *Race: The History of an Idea in America* (New York: Schocken, 1963), pp. 59–60.
9. "Civilization and Savagery," *Proceedings of the Massachusetts Historical Society*, 2nd ser., XVII (1903), 11; "The Negro in Africa and America," *Pedagogical Seminary*, XII (1905), 361.
10. Gossett, pp. 103–5.
11. VII, 53–56.
12. Miller, *Stein*, p. 130.
13. (New York: Modern Library, 1936), pp. 86, 92.
14. *And Gladly Teach* (Boston: Houghton Mifflin, 1935), p. 227.
15. Robert L. Beisner, *Twelve against Empire: The Anti-Imperialists, 1898–1900* (New York: McGraw-Hill, 1968), p. 65.
16. *Stelligeri and Other Essays*, p. 16, 144; Van Wyck Brooks, *Scenes and Portraits*, p. 110.
17. Howe, *Wendell*, p. 162.
18. pp. 21–23.

19. (New York: D. Appleton, 1910), pp. 104–5, 158.
20. (Boston: Houghton Mifflin, 1904), pp. 111, 120, 156–57, 199–200, 317, 330.
21. VIII (October 24, 1879), 37; XXXVIII (January 11, 1900), 105.
22. LXXV (June 24, 1903), 128–30; LXXXIII (June 26, 1907), 149–50.
23. For Eliot's admissions policies and attitudes toward the diversity of Harvard students, see Hawkins, pp. 168–72, 180–93.
24. Gossett, p. 295; Hawkins, p. 183.
25. Hawkins, p. 192.
26. *Letters*, II, 44; I, 252.
27. pp. 754, 125.
28. Samuels, *The Making of a Connoisseur*, p. 31; Bernard Berenson, *Sunset and Twilight: From the Diaries of 1947–1958* (New York: Harcourt, Brace & World, 1963), p. 348.
29. For example, *Dusk of Dawn*, in *W. E. B. Du Bois: Writings*, pp. 581–82.
30. July 23, 1903, p. 11.
31. Steel, p. 17.
32. Henry James III, Memoir, p. 63.
33. *Writings*, I, 1122–25.
34. p. 54.
35. *Writings*, II, 728–29, 657, 631.
36. *Letters*, I, 58; Lewis, p. 541.
37. John Jay Chapman, "Portrait of Josiah Royce the Philosopher," p. 3, by permission of the Houghton Library, Harvard University (shelf mark bMS Am 1854, 6657).
38. *Race Questions, Provincialisms, and Other Essays*, pp. 8, 9, 38, 47, 52–53.
39. Letter of February 24, 1904.
40. *Correspondence*, II, 403.
41. *Persons and Places*, II, 170.
42. Beisner, p. 52.
43. *Writings and Lectures, 1909–1945* (Baltimore: Penguin, 1967), p. 126.
44. *TCWJ*, II, 307–8.
45. *Boston Evening Transcript*, March 1, 1899; *TCWJ*, II, 309–10.
46. Morison, p. 413.
47. *TCWJ*, II, 310.
48. *The Monument to Robert Gould Shaw* (Boston: Houghton Mifflin, 1897), p. 84.
49. *TCWJ*, II, 306.
50. March 1 and April 15, 1899.
51. *Correspondence*, III, 27–28n.
52. *Writings*, II, 1134.
53. January 7 and 9, 1896.
54. *Boston Evening Transcript*, April 15, 1899.
55. Seymour Martin Lipset and David Riesman, *Education and Politics at Harvard* (New York: McGraw-Hill, 1975), pp. 115–16; *The Works of Theodore Roosevelt*,

28 vols. (New York: Charles Scribner's Sons, 1902–16), XX, 3–22. References to Roosevelt are to this edition unless otherwise noted.
56. *TCWJ*, II, 313.
57. *Writings*, II, 1285.
58. *TCWJ*, II, 314.

"After All Who Are Men?"
1. *The Correspondence of W. E. B. Du Bois, 1877–1934*, ed. Herbert Aptheker (Amherst: University of Massachusetts Press, 1973), I, 13.
2. In *W. E. B. Du Bois: Writings*, p. 1137.
3. *Blacks at Harvard*, ed. Werner Sollors, Caldwell Titcomb, and Thomas A. Underwood (New York: New York University Press, 1993), p. 45.
4. (New York: Schocken, 1967), p. 385.
5. *W. E. B. Du Bois: Writings*, pp. 364–65.
6. Ibid., p. 581. For Du Bois at Harvard, see "A Negro Student at Harvard at the End of the 19th Century," *Massachusetts Review*, I (Spring 1960), 439–58; David Levering Lewis, *W. E. B. Du Bois: Biography of a Race, 1868–1919* (New York: Henry Holt, 1993), pp. 79–116.
7. "A Negro Student," p. 453.
8. Letter of April 24, 1905, W. E. B. Du Bois Papers at the University of Massachusetts, Amherst (Reel 2).
9. "A Negro Student," pp. 450–51; *Against Racism: Unpublished Essays, Papers, Addresses, 1887–1961*, ed. Herbert Aptheker (Amherst: University of Massachusetts Press, 1985), p. 17.
10. See Dickinson D. Bruce Jr., "W. E. B. Du Bois and the Idea of Double-Consciousness," *American Literature*, LXIV (June 1992), 299–309; Adolph Reed Jr., "Du Bois's 'Double-Consciousness': Race

and Gender in Progressive Era American Thought," *Studies in American Political Development*, VI (Spring 1992), 93–139.
11. See David Levering Lewis' reading of "The Renaissance of Ethics: A Critical Comparison of Scholastic and Modern Ethics," the fifty-two-page essay that Du Bois wrote for James, pp. 93–96.
12. For Du Bois and Royce, see Robert Gooding-Williams, "Philosophy of History and Social Critique in *The Souls of Black Folk*," *Social Science Information*, XXVI (1987), 99–114.
13. *The Correspondence of W. E. B. Du Bois*, p. 13.
14. Du Bois' themes are in the W. E. B. Du Bois Papers at the University of Massachusetts, Amherst (Reel 87). Eight of them are in *Against Racism*, pp. 16–20.
15. *Against Racism*, p. 16.
16. *W. E. B. Du Bois: Writings*, pp. 1170, 953.
17. LI (July 1890), 14–15.
18. *W. E. B. Du Bois: Writings*, pp. 811–14.
19. Ibid., p. 466.
20. Ibid., pp. 822, 370.
21. *Against Racism*, p. 29.
22. *W. E. B. Du Bois: Writings*, p. 393.
23. (New York: Penguin, 1986), p. 5.
24. Ibid., pp. 295–96.
25. Louis R. Harlan, *Booker T. Washington: The Making of a Black Leader, 1856–1901* (New York: Oxford University Press, 1972), p. 236.
26. *Booker T. Washington Papers*, ed. Louis R. Harlan and Raymond W. Smock, 13 vols. (Urbana: University of Illinois Press, 1972–84), VI, 87.
27. *W. E. B. Du Bois: Writings*, pp. 394, 398, 399.
28. "A Negro Student," pp. 439–40.
29. *The Philadelphia Negro*, p. 355.

5. Smile When You Carry a Big Stick

Teddy Roosevelt '80 and Dan Wister '82
1. For Roosevelt at Harvard, see Curtis Guild Jr., "Theodore Roosevelt at Harvard," *HGM*, X (December 1901), 177–83; J. Laurence Laughlin, "Roosevelt at Harvard," *American Review of Reviews*, LXX (1924), 391–98; McCullough, pp. 195–217; Morris, pp. 81–133; Donald Wilhelm, *Theodore Roosevelt as an Undergraduate* (Boston: J. W. Luce, 1910).
2. Laughlin, p. 395.
3. *The Letters of Theodore Roosevelt*, ed. Elting E. Morison, 8 vols. (Cambridge: Harvard

University Press, 1951–54), I, 29, and VI, 944.
4. (New York: Charles Scribner's Sons, 1929), p. 22.
5. pp. 182–83.
6. Ibid., p. 180.
7. McCullough, pp. 98–106; Morris, p. 60.
8. Morris, p. 129.
9. Owen Wister, *Roosevelt: The Story of a Friendship* (New York: Macmillan, 1930), p. 15.
10. Gore Vidal renders the transformation incisively in "Theodore Roosevelt: An Amer-

ican Sissy," *United States: Essays, 1952–1993* (New York: Random House, 1993), pp. 723–37.

11. Darwin Payne, *Owen Wister* (Dallas: Southern Methodist University Press, 1985), p. 37.
12. XXXVII (January 1904), 147.
13. Bail, pp. 281–82.
14. *Roosevelt: The Story of a Friendship,* p. 358.
15. Owen Wister, *Safe in the Arms of Croesus* (New York: Macmillan, 1928), pp. x–xi.
16. (New York: Lippincott, 1901), pp. 94–95.
17. *Selected Letters,* ed. Carlos Baker (New York: Charles Scribner's Sons, 1981), p. 316.
18. Payne, pp. 21, 31; *Roosevelt: The Story of a Friendship,* p. 12.
19. Payne, p. 15.
20. Ibid., p. 76.
21. Kim Townsend, "Francis Parkman and the Male Tradition," *American Quarterly,* XXXVIII (1986), 97–113.
22. See Richard M. Allen, "Harvard Men in the Range Cattle Business," *HGM,* II (December 1893), 183–92.
23. Morris, p. 285.
24. Richard Slotkin, *Regeneration through Violence: The Mythology of the American Frontier, 1600–1869* (Middletown: Wesleyan University Press, 1973); *Gunfighter Nation: The Myth of the Frontier in Twentieth-Century America* (New York: HarperCollins, 1992). In the latter, see esp. "The Winning of the West: Theodore Roosevelt's Frontier Thesis, 1880–1900," pp. 29–62.
25. III, 7–8.
26. Ibid., VII, 16, 86.
27. Ibid., pp. 153–54.
28. *Theodore Roosevelt Cyclopedia* (New York: Roosevelt Memorial Association, 1941), p. 245.
29. Ibid., p. 243.
30. Thomas G. Dyer, *Theodore Roosevelt and the Idea of Race* (Baton Rouge: Louisiana State University Press, 1980), p. 133.
31. *Cyclopedia,* pp. 251, 249, 244.
32. *Owen Wister Out West: His Journals and Letters,* ed. Fanny Kemble Wister (Chicago: University of Chicago Press, 1958), p. 255.
33. Ibid., pp. 32–33.
34. (New York: Penguin, 1981), pp. 52, 67.
35. Payne, p. 85.
36. Ibid., pp. 95–96.
37. *Harper's Weekly,* XXXIX (December 21, 1895), 1216.
38. Payne, pp. 189–90.

39. *Owen Wister Out West,* p. 164.
40. Peggy Samuels and Harold Samuels, *Frederic Remington* (New York: Doubleday, 1982), pp. 230–31. G. Edward White, *The Eastern Establishment and the Western Experience: The West of Frederic Remington, Theodore Roosevelt, and Owen Wister* (New Haven: Yale University Press, 1968), neatly presents the parallels of these men's lives.
41. Payne, p. 191.
42. XCI (September 1895), 602–17.
43. *The Frontier in American History,* p. 37. See Slotkin, *Frontier Nation,* pp. 29–36.
44. Leon Edel, *Henry James: The Master, 1901–1916* (Philadelphia: Lippincott, 1972), p. 267.
45. Morris, p. 273.
46. (New York: Penguin, 1988), p. 375. See Lee Clark Mitchell, " 'When You Call Me That . . . ': Tall Talk and Male Hegemony in *The Virginian,*" *Publications of the Modern Language Association,* CII (January 1987), 66–77.
47. pp. 103, 203.
48. p. 217.
49. See Blake Allmendinger, *The Cowboy: Representations of Labor in an American Work Culture* (New York: Oxford University Press, 1992), pp. 131, 136–37.
50. Mitchell, " 'When You Call Me That . . . ,' " p. 73.
51. pp. 56, 218, 290.
52. Payne, pp. 171–72.
53. p. 392.
54. Payne, p. 198.
55. pp. 3, 195.
56. *Henry James Letters,* ed. Leon Edel, 4 vols. (Cambridge: Harvard University Press, 1974–84), IV, 232–34.
57. pp. 329, 326. See Jane Tompkins, *West of Everything: The Inner Life of Westerns* (New York: Oxford University Press, 1992), esp. pp. 152–55.
58. XI (September 1902), 159–60.
59. Payne, p. 232.
60. *HGM,* XVI (March 1908), 445.
61. *HGM,* XVII (September 1908), 127.
62. *HGM,* VII (March 1899), 406–7.
63. CLI (August 1890), p. 190.
64. *Cyclopedia,* p. 54.
65. XX, 158.
66. *Cyclopedia,* p. 31.
67. VII (December 1888), 90.
68. *HGM,* XIX (September 1910), 14–17.
69. *Writings,* II, 1248.
70. *HGM,* XIV (September 1905), 1–9.
71. *Letters,* II, 232.
72. The speech is in Wilhelm, pp. 78–90.
73. *HGM,* XVI (September 1907), 113.

74. Ibid., VII (September 1898), 57.
75. Ibid., IX (March 1901), 436–37.
76. XXXV (May 28, 1898), 110–11; LIII (March 7, 1907), 13.
77. IX (March 1901), 437.

After 1909
1. Yeomans, p. 90.
2. *HGM,* XVIII (December 1909), 211–23.
3. Ibid., pp. 221–22.
4. Yeomans, p. 106.
5. Hawkins, pp. 148–49, 166.
6. Ibid., p. 90.
7. Pierson, p. 37.
8. *HGM,* XVIII (September 1909), 68.
9. Yeomans, p. 109.

10. *HGM,* XVIII (December 1909), 214.
11. Yeomans, p. 38.
12. Ibid., p. 68.
13. LXXXIV (January 1908), 99–101.
14. Lipset and Riesman, pp. 119–21.
15. *Scenes and Portraits,* p. 116.
16. Morison, p. 377.
17. *Fighting Years,* pp. 88, 80.
18. "Portrait of Josiah Royce the Philosopher," pp. 7–8.
19. LXXXIII (April 12, 1907), 36.
20. *Writings,* II, 457–62.
21. *Letters,* II, 327–28.
22. Rosenzweig, pp. 176–77.
23. *An Autobiographical Study* (New York: W. W. Norton, 1963), p. 99.
24. *HGM,* XXIX (September 1920), 29.

Select Bibliography

Adams, Henry. "The Primitive Rights of Women." In *Historical Essays*. New York: Charles Scribner's Sons, 1891.

———. *The Education of Henry Adams*. Ed. Ernest Samuels. Boston: Houghton Mifflin, 1973.

Adams, J. D. *Copey of Harvard*. Boston: Houghton Mifflin, 1960.

Allen, Gay Wilson. *William James*. New York: Viking Press, 1967.

Babbitt, Irving. *Literature and the American College*. Boston: Houghton Mifflin, 1908.

Bail, Hamilton Vaughan. "Harvard Fiction," *Proceedings of the American Antiquarian Society*, LXVIII (1957–58), 211–347.

Bailyn, Bernard, Donald Fleming, Oscar Handlin, and Stephan Thernstrom. *Glimpses of Harvard Past*. Cambridge: Harvard University Press, 1986.

Baker, Liva. *The Justice from Beacon Hill: The Life and Times of Oliver Wendell Holmes*. New York: HarperCollins, 1991.

Barker-Banfield, G. J. *The Horrors of the Half-Known Life: Male Attitudes toward Women and Sexuality in Nineteenth-Century America*. New York: Harper & Row, 1976.

Bederman, Gail. *Manliness & Civilization: A Cultural History of Gender and Race in the United States*. Chicago: University of Chicago Press, 1995.

Beisner, Robert L. *Twelve against Empire: The Anti-Imperialists, 1898–1900*. New York: McGraw-Hill, 1968.

Bennett, Bruce. "Dudley A. Sargent—A Man for All Seasons," *Quest*, XXIX (Winter 1978), 33–45.

———. "Dudley Allen Sargent: The Man and His Philosophy," *Journal of Physical Education and Recreational Dance*, LV (November–December 1984), 61–64.

Bjork, Daniel. *William James: The Center of His Vision*. New York: Columbia University Press, 1988.

Brent, Joseph. *Charles Sanders Peirce*. Bloomington: Indiana University Press, 1993.

Briggs, LeBaron Russell. *Routine and Ideals*. Boston: Houghton Mifflin, 1904.

———. *Men, Women, and Colleges*. Boston: Houghton Mifflin, 1925.

Brooks, Van Wyck. "Varied Outlooks," *Harvard Advocate*, LXXXIII (April 1907), 35–37.

———. "Harvard and American Life," *Contemporary Review*, XCIV (December 1908), 613–17.

———. *Sketches in Criticism*. New York: E. P. Dutton, 1932.

———. *Scenes and Portraits: Memories of Childhood and Youth*. New York: E. P. Dutton, 1954.

Brown, Rollo Walter. *Harvard Yard in the Golden Age*. New York: A. A. Wyn, 1948.

Buck, Paul. "Harvard Attitudes toward Radcliffe in the Early Years." *Proceedings of the Massachusetts Historical Society*, LXXIV (1962), 33–50.

Chapman, John Jay. *Memories and Milestones*. New York: Moffat, Yard, 1915.

———. "John Jay Chapman to William James: A Packet of Letters." Ed. M. A. DeWolfe Howe. *Harper's Monthly Magazine*, CLXXIV (December 1936), 46–54.

———. *The Selected Writings of John Jay Chapman*. Ed. Jacques Barzun. New York: Minerva Press, 1957.

Clendenning, John. *The Life and Thought of Josiah Royce*. Madison: University of Wisconsin Press, 1985.

Cotkin, George. *William James: Public Philosopher*. Baltimore: Johns Hopkins University Press, 1990.

Diggins, John. *The Promise of Pragmatism*. Chicago: University of Chicago Press, 1994.

Dubbert, Joe. *A Man's Place: Masculinity in Transition*. Englewood Cliffs: Prentice-Hall, 1979.

Du Bois, W. E. B. *Against Racism: Unpublished Essays, Papers, Addresses, 1887–1961*. Ed. Herbert Aptheker. Amherst: University of Massachusetts Press, 1985.

————. *Writings*. New York: Library of America, 1986.

Eliot, Charles W. *Educational Reform*. New York: Century, 1898.

Emerson, Ralph Waldo. *Selections*. Ed. Stephen E. Whicher. Boston: Houghton Mifflin, 1957.

Feinstein, Howard M. *Becoming William James*. Ithaca: Cornell University Press, 1984.

Flandrau, Charles Macomb. *Harvard Episodes*. Boston: Copeland and Day, 1897.

Foner, Eric, and Garraty, John A., eds. *The Reader's Companion to American History*. Boston: Houghton Mifflin, 1991.

Fredrickson, George M. *The Inner Civil War: Northern Intellectuals and the Crisis of the Union*. New York: Harper & Row, 1965.

Gilbert, James B. *Work without Salvation: America's Intellectuals and Industrial Alienation, 1880–1910*. Baltimore: Johns Hopkins University Press, 1977.

Gossett, Thomas F. *Race: The History of an Idea in America*. New York: Schocken, 1965.

Habegger, Alfred. *Henry James and the "Woman Business."* New York: Cambridge University Press, 1989.

————. *The Father: A Life of Henry James, Sr*. New York: Farrar, Straus and Giroux, 1994.

Hall, G. Stanley. "Student Customs." *Proceedings of the American Antiquarian Society*, n.s., XIV (October 1900), 83–124.

————. *Adolescence: Its Psychology and Its Relations to Physiology, Anthropology, Sociology, Sex, Crime, Religion, and Education*. 2 vols. New York: D. Appleton, 1905.

————. *Recreations of a Psychologist*. New York: D. Appleton, 1920.

Haller, John S., Jr., and Robin M. Haller. *The Physician and Sexuality in Victorian America*. Urbana: University of Illinois Press, 1974.

Hapgood, Hutchins. *A Victorian in the Modern World*. Seattle: University of Washington Press, 1972.

Hart, Albert Bushnell. *The Southern South*. New York: D. Appleton, 1910.

Hawkins, Hugh. *Between Harvard and America: The Educational Leadership of Charles W. Eliot*. New York: Oxford University Press, 1972.

Hingham, John. "The Recreation of American Culture in the 1890s." In *Writing American History*. Bloomington: Indiana University Press, 1970.

Hoopes, James. *Van Wyck Brooks: In Search of American Culture*. Amherst: University of Massachusetts Press, 1977.

Hovey, Richard B. *John Jay Chapman: An American Mind*. New York: Columbia University Press, 1959.

Howe, M. A. DeWolfe. *Barrett Wendell and His Letters*. Boston: Atlantic Monthly Press, 1924.

————. *John Jay Chapman and His Letters*. Boston: Houghton Mifflin, 1937.

————. "A Packet of Wendell-James Letters." *Scribner's Magazine*, LXXXIV (December 1928), 675–87.

James, Alice. *The Diary of Alice James*. Ed. Leon Edel. New York: Penguin, 1982.

————. *The Death and Letters of Alice James*. Ed. Ruth Bernard Yeazell. Berkeley: University of California Press, 1981.

James, Henry, Sr. *The Literary Remains*. Ed. William James. Boston: James R. Osgood, 1885.

James, Henry. *The American*. New York: Penguin, 1981.

————. *The Portrait of a Lady*. New York: Penguin, 1984.

————. *The Bostonians*. New York: Penguin, 1984.

————. *The Complete Notebooks*. Ed. Leon Edel and Lyall H. Powers. New York: Oxford University Press, 1987.

James, Henry, III. *Charles W. Eliot: President of Harvard University, 1869–1909*. 2 vols. Boston: Houghton Mifflin, 1930.

James, William. "H. Bushnell's *Women's Suffrage* and J. S. Mill's *Subjection of Women*." *North American Review*, CIX (October 1869), 556–65.

————. "The Proposed Shortening of the College Course." *Harvard Monthly*, XI (January 1891), 127–37.

————. *The Principles of Psychology*. Cambridge: Harvard University Press, 1983.

――――. *Writings.* 2 vols. New York: Library of America, 1987, 1992.
――――. *The Letters of William James.* Ed. Henry James III. 2 vols. Boston: Atlantic Monthly Press, 1920.
――――. *The Correspondence of William James: William and Henry.* Ed. Ignas K. Skrupskelis and Elizabeth M. Berkeley. 3 vols. Charlottesville: University of Virginia Press, 1992–94.
James, William, Jr. "Sport or Business?" *Harvard Graduates' Magazine,* XII (December 1903), 225–29.
Jones, Howard Mumford. *The Age of Energy: Varieties of American Experience, 1865–1915.* New York: Viking Press, 1971.
Kaledin, Eugenia. *The Education of Mrs. Henry Adams.* Philadelphia: Temple University Press, 1981.
Kendall, Elaine. *"Peculiar Institutions": An Informal History of the Seven Sisters Colleges.* New York: G. P. Putnam's Sons, 1976.
Kimmel, Michael. *Manhood in America: A Cultural History.* New York: Free Press, 1996.
King, John Owen, III. *The Iron of Melancholy: The Structure of Spiritual Conversion in America from the Puritan Conscience to Victorian Neurosis.* Middletown: Wesleyan University Press, 1983.
Kuklick, Bruce. *The Rise of American Philosophy: Cambridge, Massachusetts, 1860–1930.* New Haven: Yale University Press, 1977.
Kull, Irving S., and Nell M. Kull. *A Short Chronology of American History, 1492–1950.* New Brunswick: Rutgers University Press, 1952.
Lasch, Christopher. "The Moral and Intellectual Rehabilitation of the Ruling Class." In *The World of Nations: Reflections on American History, Politics and Culture.* New York: Alfred A. Knopf, 1973.
Lears, Jackson. *No Place for Grace: Antimodernism and the Transformation of American Culture, 1880–1920.* New York: Pantheon, 1981.
Lewis, David Levering. *W. E. B. Du Bois: Biography of a Race, 1868–1919.* New York: Henry Holt, 1993.
Lewis, R. W. B. *The Jameses: A Family Narrative.* New York: Doubleday, 1991.
Lipset, Seymour M., and David Riesman. *Education and Politics at Harvard.* New York: McGraw-Hill, 1975.
McCormick, John. *George Santayana.* New York: Alfred A. Knopf, 1987.
McCullough, David. *Mornings on Horseback.* New York: Simon and Schuster, 1981.
Miller, Rosalind S. *Gertrude Stein: Form and Intelligibility.* New York: Exposition Press, 1949.
Morison, Samuel Eliot. *Three Centuries of Harvard, 1636–1936,* Cambridge: Harvard University Press, 1937.
Morris, Edmund. *The Rise of Theodore Roosevelt.* New York: Coward, McCann & Geoghegan, 1979.
Mrozek, Donald J. *Sport and American Mentality, 1880–1910.* Knoxville: University of Tennessee Press, 1983.
Münsterberg, Hugo. *American Traits.* Boston: Houghton Mifflin, 1902.
Myers, Gerald E. *William James: His Life and Thought.* New Haven: Yale University Press, 1986.
Norris, Frank. *The Argonaut Manuscript Limited Edition of Frank Norris's Works.* 10 vols. New York: Doubleday, Doran, 1928.
Painter, Nell Irvin. *Standing at Armageddon: The United States, 1877–1919.* New York: W. W. Norton, 1987.
Payne, Darwin. *Owen Wister.* Dallas: Southern Methodist University Press, 1985.
Pierson, George Wilson. *Yale College: An Educational History, 1871–1921.* 2 vols. New Haven: Yale University Press, 1952.
Perry, Ralph Barton. *The Thought and Character of William James.* 2 vols. Boston: Little, Brown, 1935.
Poirier, Richard. *Poetry and Pragmatism.* Cambridge: Harvard University Press, 1992.
Posnock, Ross. *The Trial of Curiosity: Henry James, William James, and the Challenge of Modernity.* New York: Oxford University Press, 1991.
Post, Waldron Kintzing. *Harvard Stories: Sketches of the Undergraduate.* New York: G. P. Putnam's Sons, 1893.
Roosevelt, Theodore. *The Works of Theodore Roosevelt.* 28 vols. New York: Charles Scribner's Sons, 1902–16.
――――. *Theodore Roosevelt Cyclopedia.* Ed. Albert Bushnell Hart and Herbert Ronald Ferleger. New York: Roosevelt Memorial Association, 1941.
Rosenzweig, Saul. *Freud, Jung, and Hall the King-Maker.* St. Louis: Hogrefe & Huber, 1992.

Ross, Dorothy G. *G. Stanley Hall: The Psychologist as Prophet.* Chicago: University of Chicago Press, 1972.

Royce, Josiah. *The Philosophy of Loyalty.* New York: Macmillan, 1908.

———. *Race Questions, Provincialism, and Other American Problems.* New York: Macmillan, 1908.

———. *William James and Other Essays on the Philosophy of Life.* New York: Macmillan, 1911.

———. *The Letters of Josiah Royce.* Ed. John Clendenning. Chicago: University of Chicago Press, 1970.

Rudolph, Frederick. *The American College and University.* New York: Vintage Books, 1962.

Santayana, George. "The Spirit and Ideals of Harvard University." *Educational Review,* VII (April 1894), 313–25.

———. "Philosophy on the Bleachers." *Harvard Monthly,* XVIII (July 1894), 181–90.

———. *Character and Opinion in the United States: With Reminiscences of William James and Josiah Royce and Academic Life in America.* New York: Charles Scribner's Sons, 1920.

———. *Persons and Places.* 3 vols. in 1. New York: Charles Scribner's Sons, 1963.

Sargent, Dudley A. *Physical Education.* Boston: Ginn, 1906.

Schlereth, Thomas J. *Victorian America: Transformations in Everyday Life, 1876–1915.* New York: HarperCollins, 1991.

Shaler, Nathaniel S. *The Neighbor.* Boston: Houghton Mifflin, 1904.

———. *The Autobiography of Nathaniel Southgate Shaler, with a Supplementary Memoir by His Wife.* Boston: Houghton Mifflin, 1909.

Slotkin, Richard. *Gunfighter Nation: The Myth of the Frontier in Twentieth-Century America.* New York: HarperCollins, 1992.

Smith, Richard Norton. *The Harvard Century: The Making of a University to a Nation.* New York: Simon and Schuster, 1986.

Smith, Ronald A. *Sports and Freedom: The Rise of Big-Time College Athletics.* New York: Oxford University Press, 1988.

———, ed. *Big-Time Football at Harvard, 1905: The Diary of Coach Bill Reid.* Urbana: University of Illinois Press, 1994.

Sollors, Werner, Caldwell Titcomb, and Thomas A. Underwood. *Blacks at Harvard.* New York: New York University Press, 1993.

Steel, Ronald. *Walter Lippmann and the American Century.* Boston: Little, Brown, 1980.

Story, Ronald. *The Forging of an Aristocracy: Harvard & the Boston Upper Class, 1800–1870.* Middletown: Wesleyan University Press, 1980.

Strouse, Jean. *Alice James.* Boston: Houghton Mifflin, 1980.

Synnott, Marcia Graham. *The Half-Opened Door: Discrimination and Admissions at Harvard, Yale, and Princeton, 1900–1970.* Westport: Greenwood Press, 1979.

Trachtenberg, Alan. *The Incorporation of America: Culture and Society in the Gilded Age.* New York: Hill and Wang, 1982.

Tucker, Grace Hollingsworth. "The Gods Serve Hebe." *Radcliffe Quarterly,* XVII (October 1933), 192–204.

Veysey, Laurence R. *The Emergence of the American University.* Chicago: University of Chicago Press, 1965.

Villard, Oswald Garrison. *Fighting Years: Memoirs of a Liberal Editor.* New York: Harcourt, Brace, 1939.

Wendell, Barrett. "Social Life at Harvard." *Lippincott's Magazine,* XXIX (January 1887), 152–63.

———. "The Relations of Radcliffe College with Harvard." *Harvard Monthly,* XXIX (October 1899), 1–10.

White, G. Edward. *The Eastern Establishment and the Western Experience: The West of Frederic Remington, Theodore Roosevelt, and Owen Wister.* New Haven: Yale University Press, 1968.

Wiebe, Robert H. *The Search for Order, 1877–1920.* New York: Hill and Wang, 1967.

Wister, Owen. "The Evolution of the Cow-Puncher." *Harper's Monthly,* XCI (September 1895), 602–17.

———. *Philosophy 4.* New York: Lippincott, 1901.

———. *The Virginian.* New York: Penguin, 1988.

———. *Roosevelt: The Story of a Friendship.* New York: Macmillan, 1930.

———. *Owen Wister Out West: His Journals and Letters.* Ed. Fanny Kemble Wister. Chicago: University of Chicago Press, 1958.

Yeomans, Henry A. *Abbott Lawrence Lowell, 1856–1943.* Cambridge: Harvard University Press, 1948.

Index